Nicho...
GUID...
ENGL...
CHURCHES

*Foreword by the
Archbishop of Canterbury*

English
Tourist Board

ROBERT NICHOLSON PUBLICATIONS

First published by **Robert Nicholson Publications Limited**
17 Conway Street, London W1P 6JD and the **English Tourist Board**
4 Grosvenor Gardens, London SW1W 0DU

Text by **Stella Vayne**

Regional introductions by **Ian Dunlop**, author of *Cathedrals' Crusade* and
Collins *Companion Guide to the Ile de France*. The Reverend Canon Ian
Dunlop is Chancellor of Salisbury Cathedral
Drawings by **Towler Cox**
Architectural Survey and drawings by **Richard Reid**
Design by **Bob Vickers**

Robert Nicholson Publications Limited
17–21 Conway Street
London W1P 6JD

In a book of this size and scope the selection of individual parish churches
poses a difficult problem. Whilst the publishers have made every effort to
provide a balanced and interesting range of churches which are open to
visitors, they would welcome a response from readers which might be
helpful for future editions of the guide. Great care has been taken throughout this book to be accurate, but the publishers cannot accept responsibility
for any errors which appear.

Phototypeset in England by Input Typesetting Limited
Durnsford Road, London SW19 8DR

Printed and bound in Great Britain by
Blantyre Printing and Binding Limited, London and Glasgow

ISBN 0 905522 87 7

FOREWORD

by the Archbishop of Canterbury

It has been my great good fortune to spend much of my life in beautiful surroundings, and I am proud of the contribution which England's inheritance of fine churches – of all periods, from Saxon times to those of architectural distinction of the present day – makes to the landscape of our country, and to our towns and villages. Churches are an enduring symbol of our Christian faith, and of its continuity, and they are centres of their communities in all kinds of ways.

Our churches are also, as is well known, virtually the only places where certain categories of English art and architecture can be seen and studied – medieval sculpture, for example, or wall paintings, or stained glass. Because all of us who have responsibility for these churches want to share them with others, I particularly welcome the initiative of the English Tourist Board and its co-publishers, Robert Nicholson Publications, in producing this Guide. It does not claim to be comprehensive – if it did, it would be hundreds of pages longer! This splendid selection will, however, whet the appetite and ensure that many of the visitors whom we welcome from abroad, and those who like visiting churches and a sense of being on pilgrimage in their own country, will turn off on to a B-road and explore some of those which are less well known but so well worth a visit. They are ours both to enjoy and to use.

Robert Cantuar.

Acknowledgements

The publishers would like to thank the incumbents and churchwardens of every church included in the guide, for their cooperation in responding to the author's requests for information; the Council for the Care of Churches for invaluable advice and assistance at every stage; Max Hanna at the English Tourist Board for his help in supplying church opening times from his own research; Lena Joffe for her overall view of the book; the National Monuments Record for providing the photographs, and many others who helped.

CONTENTS

INTRODUCTION

Enter an English parish church and the history of a community unfolds before you. Each church tells an individual social, economic and religious story, which is still in the process of evolution. It would be a mistake to regard churches solely as ancient monuments or museums; they are also living organisms drawing strength and inspiration from the communities which they serve. Often, the rector is in the church, ready to share his love of the place and act as guide; or parishioners are preparing the church for a wedding, recital, or festival, and are delighted to share with others their joy in and knowledge of their church. If no-one is there, signs of care and activity are apparent in current notices about parish affairs, in flowers and a children's corner furnished with diminutive chairs and well-thumbed books. The atmosphere is that of a cherished home.

The early history of the church in England can be seen in a striking Saxon tower or sculpted preaching cross – witness of the days when Christianity was taught in the open. Vestiges of the first church buildings include small, round-headed windows, once in the outer walls, but now appearing above the nave arcades constructed by the Normans, and the private entrance used by the local Saxon lord. Vigour swept in with the Normans, frequently expressed in a doorway scintillating with zigzag and beak-head carving. Many towers form sturdy fortresses, with extra thick walls, tiny slits for windows and no doors on the outside – a reminder of the times when the church offered refuge when a village was under attack.

In the Middle Ages, the nave served not only as a place of worship but also as a village hall, where plays were performed. 'Church ales' were held on holidays, that is, Holy Days, when attendance at mass was obligatory. Celebrations included excessive consumption of ale, which led to unbridled behaviour and eventually to the cessation of the ales. Many transactions were conducted in the porch, marriages among them. Indeed, Chaucer's *Wife of Bath* was 'married four times at chirche door'.

Brilliantly coloured wall paintings, stained glass and sculpture preached lessons, full of miracle and mystery, to the illiterate peasant congregation. Great eloquence was achieved by the Doom, or Last Judgement, confronting the people from above the chancel arch. Its impact may be imagined from surviving examples, forcefully depicting the ascent of the blessed to the heavenly Jerusalem and the descent of the damned to everlasting torment in hell, with much devilish prodding along the way. Tithes were willingly contributed as an insurance against hellfire. An additional insurance by the wealthy against its flames lay in the foundation and endowment of chantries, where priests were employed to pray for the souls of the departed for a number of years, sometimes in perpetuity.

The Black Death in 1348 abruptly halted the lavish programme of church building, which had flourished during the early Middle Ages, as the ranks of skilled craftsmen were decimated by the plague. A socio-economic consequence of the sudden reduction in the population was a lack of manpower to plough the land; big landholders seized the opportunity and bought off their peasants, merging their strips into fields given over to wheat or sheep. The resulting wealth of the landowners and wool merchants – expanded through export trade with Flanders – was invested in fine houses and opulent Perpendicular churches, particularly in East Anglia and Gloucestershire. Skilled guilds also played their part, either by creating new churches, or by taking over existing chapels and modifying them to suit their spiritual requirements.

The 16thC was a time of turbulence and upheaval for the Church throughout Western Europe. In England, it was the Crown which spearheaded the movement towards reform and the establishment of a national church independent of Papal jurisdiction. The personal and sovereign ambitions of Henry VIII instigated the break with Rome; the ruthless destruction of the monasteries and the confiscation of church wealth and privilege followed.

It must have been heart-rending for churchwardens to hand over the treasures, or to see them smashed by Protestant and later, Puritan reformers, who believed the English Reformation had not gone far enough. The rood or crucifix, above the carved rood screen, symbolising Christ's Passion, survived until Edward VI ordained its destruction and that of statues and images, by then considered idolatrous. As the Reformation gathered momentum, the Royal Arms took the place of the rood and Doom, the communion table replaced the altar and the pulpit became the focus of the church.

Many churches bear the marks of axes or bullets, scars of their occupation during the Civil War by Roundheads or Cavaliers. Under the Commonwealth, numerous choirs of glorious angels in wooden hammerbeam roofs were peppered with Cromwellian shot, while more accessible statues were mutilated or decapitated, and stained glass was smashed to smithereens. It is a great wonder and tribute to the devotion of communities that so much medieval beauty yet survives.

Adversity has often cleared the path for new waves of church building. It was, after all, the Great Fire of London in 1666 which gave the supreme English architect Christopher Wren the unique opportunity to adorn the capital with more than 50 magnificent churches and his work remains today an outstanding feature of London's skyline. The fully-fledged 18thC Protestant church expressed different values from the medieval church, of equal life and beauty. Bareness and spareness of decoration characterised it – clear glass, plain white walls, box pews; the pulpit, of paramount importance, was a three-decker to emphasise the preaching of the Word.

The 19thC Gothic Revival sought to recover the pre-Reformation ordering and furnishing of churches, and again much destruction took place in the name of religious zeal. Delightful Georgian fittings were demolished, walls were scraped of plaster and furnishings were introduced which often lacked the inspiration of medieval Gothic. However, the Victorians deserve praise for much commendable and essential restoration, as well as for building many marvellous churches in the revived Gothic idiom.

From the vast number of parish churches which stud the English landscape, the selection in this guide spans the history of Christianity in this country and illustrates its development in buildings great and small. The unique features of the churches included, whether they be historical, architectural, decorative, or scenic, have been clearly pinpointed in the entries. Descriptions of monuments commemorating crusader knights, lords, ladies, merchants, statesmen and bishops vividly demonstrate how each individual church is a source book for the social history of our country. And wherever possible, anecdotes of both a secular and religious nature are told to bring the story of the church to life.

HOW TO USE THIS GUIDE

England is divided into 10 regions, each with its own introduction. Every region is made up of a number of counties, and each place name in the guide is listed alphabetically within its county section, followed by the name of the church. Each entry is map referenced to the two-colour touring maps at the back of the book. This enables you to see at a glance how many churches in the guide are to be found in the area you are visiting. Once you decide where to go, look for the map reference on the right-hand side of the entry for the location on the map. In the case of villages, more specific directions are given in italics at the beginning of the entry. When the location is a large town, the church address has been given wherever possible. Parking facilities are indicated towards the end of the church entry by the symbol **P**. Opening times of the individual churches follow in italics. Please note, these were accurate at the time of going to press, but they should be used as guidelines only, since unforeseen circumstances may prevent their observance.

When reading the descriptions, you may come across unfamiliar architectural terms or periods of history. Accordingly, for easy reference, we have included an illustrated architectural survey and a glossary.

For the purpose of this guide, Sussex has been treated as one county. It would be helpful to obtain detailed street plans for locating churches in the major cities and conurbations.

The scale of the touring maps starting on page 213 is approximately 12 miles:1 inch, or 1:750,000.

GLOSSARY

Albigenses: Heretics of 12thC–14thC in South of France.

Ambulatory: (lit a place for walking) Continuous aisle enclosing an apse.

Anchorite: Hermit.

Anglo-Saxon: Period from early 5thC to the Norman Conquest in 1066. Characteristics: simple masonry – long-and-short work and pilaster strips.

Apse: Semi-circular or polygonal recess, arched or dome-roofed.

Apsidal: In the form of an apse.

Arcade: Series of arches supporting a wall or roof.

Ashlar: Square hewn stone.

Aumbry: Closed recess or cupboard in wall.

Bailey: Fortified enclosure; open area within a castle.

Ballflower: Globular flower of three petals enclosing a ball.

Baluster: Small pillar or column, pear-shaped at base, slender above.

Balustrade: Row of balusters supporting a rail or coping – forming ornamental parapet to terrace, balcony, etc.

Baroque: 17thC Italian style; lavishly ornamented, dynamic spatial effects.

Barrel-vault: See vault.

Bastion: Projecting part of fortification.

Beak-head: Norman decoration made up of a series of bird or beast heads, usually with beaks biting into a roll moulding.

Bede house: (archaic form of bead house): The inmates prayed for the founder's soul.

Bedesman (archaic form of Beadsman): One who prays for the soul of another; one who is paid to pray for his benefactor's soul.

Bellcote: Housing on roof for bell.

Belvedere: A turret or lantern built on a house to provide a view.

Benefaction boards: Wooden boards recording charitable bequests.

Boss: Ornamental projection at intersecting points of vault ribs or panelled ceiling.

Broach-spire: A broach was the device used to make the transition from a square or rectangular tower top to an octagonal spire.

Capital: Head or cornice of pillar or column.

Carolean: Style popular in the reigns of Charles I 1625–49 and Charles II 1660–85.

Carolingian (Carlovingian): Of the 2nd French Dynasty founded by Charlemagne (d814).

Cartouche: Tablet framed by ornate scroll, often bearing an inscription.

Caryatid: Female figure used as a pillar.

Ceil: To line a roof with some form of covering.

Censing: Worshipping with burning incense.

Ciborium: Canopy over an altar supported on columns.

Chalybeate: Impregnated with iron.

Chancel: East end of church where altar is placed.

Chantry: Endowment within a church for priest to say Mass for the soul of the founder.

Classical: Style inspired by that of Ancient Rome and Greece.

Clerestory: Upper storey of the nave walls, pierced by a series of windows.

Cloister: Covered walk attached to a monastery, often around an open space with a wall on one side and columns or windows on the other.

Clunch: Soft white limestone used for internal carving.

Coffer: Box; sunk panel in ceiling.

Colonnade: Series of columns.

Colonnette: Small column.

Commonwealth: Republican government of England 1649–53; Oliver Cromwell's Protectorate was established 1653–58 and collapsed after the succession of his son. See Restoration and Interregnum.

Corbel: Bracket of stone or timber projecting from a wall, intended to support something.

Corbel table: Row of corbels, usually decoratively carved.

Corinthian: Column style with fluted shaft and bell-shaped capital.

Corona: Circular chandelier hung from roof.

Cove, coving: Concave arch, curved hollow surface or moulding at join between wall and ceiling.

Crenellated: With battlements.

Crocket: Small ornament, usually a curled leaf or bud, decorating the edge of pinnacles, gables, etc.

Crossing: Space at intersection of nave, chancel and transepts, sometimes supporting a central tower.

Crossing tower: Tower over crossing.

Cross-vault: See vault.

Crown-post: The middle post of a trussed roof which supports the crown of the roof.

Crozier: Bearer of a cross before an archbishop; a bishop's crook or pastoral staff.

Cruciform: Cross-shaped.

Crypt: Underground vaulted chamber in a church.

Culvert: Channel for carrying water under a road, canal, etc.

Cupola: A small domed roof or turret on a roof.

Cusp: Projecting point between small arcs in Gothic tracery.

Dark Ages: Saxon and Celtic periods from 5thC to 11thC AD.

Decorated: Second stage of English Gothic, 14thC.

Diaper: Ornamental design of squares or diamonds.

Diptych: Painting, particularly altarpiece, of two leaves, closing like a book.

Dissolution (of the Monasteries): Commenced in 1536 as part of the Reformation under Henry VIII.

Dogtooth: Small, pyramidally raised ornament (Early English) consisting of four leaves meeting in a central point; used in series within moulding.

Doric: Column style with inclined projections at the base of the cornice.

Early English: First stage of English Gothic, 13thC. Characteristics: lancet windows with little or no tracery.

Easter Sepulchre: Tomb-chest in wall recess which received Christ's effigy at Easter.

Entablature: The group of three mouldings above a column or wall, comprising architrave, frieze and cornice.

Fan-vault: See vault.

Finial: Ornamental finishing off.

Floriate: Ornament with flower designs.

Flushwork: Flint and dressed stone used to make patterns on a flat surface.

Foliate: Decorate with leaves.

Font: Bowl for baptismal or holy water.

Frontal: Covering for front of altar.

Fuller: One who cleans and thickens cloth.

Georgian: Style of the period covering the reigns of the four Georges 1714–1830; neo-Palladian.

Golgotha: Graveyard.

Gothic: Style including Early English, Decorated and Perpendicular. Characteristics: pointed arch and vault.

Gothic Revival: Revival of Gothic style in 18thC and 19thC; 18thC version called Gothick.

Green men: Heads or faces with foliage appendages, relics from pagan fertility rites.

Grisaille: Grey monochrome painting on wall or glass, representing objects in relief.

Half-timbering: See timber-framing.

Hammerbeam: A timber bracket that supports a trussed roof, eliminating the need for a tie-beam.

Hammer-pond: A pond that stores water to drive a hammer-mill which activates a hammer in a small forge.

Hatchment: Dead person's arms inscribed on a large tablet, often shaped like a diamond.

Heptagonal: Seven-sided.

Hipped: Sloped instead of vertical ends to a roof.

Hood-mould: Moulding which juts out in outline above a door, arch or window.

Interregnum: 1649–1660. A term used to cover the period between the execution of Charles I (1649) and the Restoration (1660), when the various governments of the Commonwealth and the Protectorate held sway.

Ionic: Column style with a spiral scroll on the capital and basal moulding.

Jacobean: Style predominating in the reign of James I 1603–25. Characteristic: blend of Gothic and classical forms.

Lancet: Tall, narrow, pointed window.

Lantern: Windows all round the small circular or polygonal turret topping off a roof.

Laudian rails: Used to rail-off communion table at east end.

Lierne ribs: See vault.

Light: An opening to admit light, or the vertical section of a mullioned window.

Linenfold: Wooden panel patterned to look like a piece of linen arranged in vertical folds.

Long-and-short work: Saxon stonework alternating tall quoins with flat slabs.

Lozenge: Diamond-shaped.

Lucarne: Small aperture to let in light.

Lychgate: (lit corpse gate) Covered gateway at entrance of churchyard where coffin awaits clergy's arrival.

Middle Ages: Period from c1000–1400, or more broadly c600–1500.

Misericord: Bracket on the underside of a hinged choir stall seat, often elaborately carved; serving when seat is turned up to give support during periods of standing.

Motte: Steep mound forming the site of a castle, surrounded by a deep ditch and usually surmounted by the keep.

Nail-head: Ornamentation consisting of four-sided raised pyramids, repeated in series.

Nave: Main body or central aisle of church, excluding transepts and chancel.

Neo-classical: Revival of classical style in 18thC and 19thC.

Norman: The period following the Norman Conquest in 1066; architectural style which continued through the 12thC until the start of the Gothic.

Obelisk: Tapering, monolithic pillar of stone, square or rectangular at the base, pyramidal at the apex.

Ogee: Double continuously curved moulding, convex above, concave below.

Order: Term in classical architecture – columns with base, shaft, capital and entablature; main types are Greek, Doric, Roman Doric, Tuscan Doric, Ionic, Corinthian and Composite.

Oriel: Bay window supported by corbels or brackets, projecting from an upper floor.

Oxford Movement: c1833, worked towards revival of Catholic doctrine and observance in Church of England. Tractarianism.

Pantocrator (Pantokrator): Representation of Christ enthroned.

Palimpsest: (lit scraped again) reuse of a surface; brass which has been turned over and engraved on the reverse; wall painting which overlaps an earlier one.

Parclose screen: Separates chapel from main body of the church; screen (or railing) enclosing a tomb or altar.

Pediment: Low pitched gable in classical architecture; also used over doorways, windows, etc.

Pendant: Decorative boss hanging down from ceiling or vault.

Perpendicular: Third stage of English Gothic, 1377-mid 16thC. Characteristics: strong vertical tracery, large windows.

Pew: Fixed wooden seat, partially enclosed to aisles with bench ends.

Pilaster: Shallow, rectangular pillar, set in relief against a wall.

Pilaster strips: Like pilasters but without base or capital.

Piscina: Shallow basin with drain in which Communion or Mass vessels are washed.

Portcullis: Sliding door used as part of a defensive fortification; figure used in heraldry.

Portico: Covered colonnade supported by columns, forming a porch.

Pre-Raphaelite: Brotherhood of artists formed in 1848 with the aim of producing paintings 'true to nature'. Original members were Holman Hunt, Millais and Rossetti; later adherents included Ford Madox Brown, William Morris and Edward Burne-Jones.

Prie-dieu: Kneeling-chair used for prayer.

Protectorate: See Commonwealth.

Pulpit: Raised, enclosed platform from which sermons are preached.

Three-decker pulpit: Pulpit with reading desk below and clerk's stall below reading desk.

Two-decker pulpit: Pulpit with reading desk below.

Pulpitum: A device, generally a stone screen, which divides the monastic choir from the parochial nave.

Purbeck: Hard limestone from Purbeck in Dorset; also Purbeck marble.

Putto (pl putti): Cherub, a small naked boy, often with wings.

Quarter boy: A Quarter Jack in the form of a boy.

Quarter Jack: Figure (on clock) that strikes the quarter hour.

Quatrefoil: Four-lobed opening in tracery, resembling a leaf or flower.

Queen Anne: Style of the reign of Queen Anne, 1702–14, a time when Wren, Vanbrugh, Hawksmoor, etc. were building.

Quoins: The angles of a building or the dressed stone forming the angle; corner-stone.

Ragstone: Large coarse slab or stone used for roofing.

Reformation: 16thC movement for reform of doctrine and practices of the Roman Catholic Church ending in the establishment of Reformed or Protestant churches. In England it was Henry VIII's need for the annulment of his first marriage that led to the Act of Supremacy, 1534, which destroyed papal supremacy over the English church and transferred it to the crown.

Regency: Early 19thC style fostered by the Prince Regent, later Georve IV. Characteristics: elegant details typified in secular architecture by the bow-fronted terraces of Brighton.

Reliquary: Receptacle for relics.

Renaissance: (lit the great revival of arts and letters in the 14thC–16thC under the influence of Classical models). Styles in art and architecture characteristic of this period. In England especially from late 16thC–18thC, including Classical and Baroque features.

Reredos: Ornamental screen of wood or stone covering the wall at the back of the altar.

Restoration: Restoration of the monarchy (in the person of Charles II) in 1660.

Rib-vaulted: See vault.

Rococo: Fanciful interior decorative style. Characteristic: plant motifs.

Rood: Cross or crucifix.

Rood screen: Wooden or stone screen, once supporting cross, at W end of chancel, separating nave and choir.

Roundel (or Patera): Round or oval ornament in shallow relief.

Sanctuary: Part of the chancel between altar rails and E window or screen, containing high altar.

Sanctus: Music for the hymn closing the Eucharistic preface.

Sanctus bell: Bell in turret at junction of nave and chancel: handbell rung at the sanctus.

Sedilia: Series of seats (usually three) for the clergy on S wall of the chancel.

Sepulchre: Tomb.

Soffit: Lower surface of architrave, arch, balcony, etc.

Sounding board: Horizontal board or canopy over a pulpit.

Spandrel: Triangular space between arch and surrounding rectangular moulding or framework; or between two arches.

Spirelet (or flèche): Slender wooden spire on the centre of a roof.

Splay: Oblique-angled surface, usually the jamb (vertical side) of a window, door, etc.

Squint (or Hagioscope): A hole through a wall or pillar to enable the altar to be seen clearly.

Stalls: Fixed seats in choir or chancel, for use of clergy or choir; often canopied and elaborately carved with misericords.

Stations of the Cross: 14 pictures representing Christ's passion.

Stellar-vault: See vault.

Stoup: A basin for holy water.

Strapwork: Ornamentation imitating plaited straps – usually late 16thC–early 17thC.

String course: Horizontal moulding or band projecting from a wall.

Surcoat: Outer coat worn by people of rank; often worn over armour displaying heraldic arms.

Table tomb: A memorial slab raised on free-standing legs, or on chest.

Taper: Thin candle or wick covered with wax.

Tester: See sounding board.

Three-decker pulpit: See pulpit.

Tie-beam: Main horizontal transverse beam connecting the two slopes of a roof at its base.

Timber-framed: A form of building in which walls and partitions are made of wood and filled in with lath, plaster, wattle and daub, or brickwork.

Tracery: Ornamental carving forming open pattern in stonework in the head of Gothic windows, etc.

Tractarianism: High church reaction against rationalism, expressed by Newman among others, in a series of tracts published 1833–4; movement towards primitive Catholicism.

Transepts: The transverse area of a cruciform church.

Transitional: Change from Norman to Early English architecture.

Trefoil: Three-lobed ornamentation in tracery.

Triptych: Set of three panels with pictures or carvings.

Tudor: Period extending from 1485–1603 but often used to mean the first half of the 16th.

Two-decker pulpit: See pulpit.

Tympanum: The space between a lintel and the arch above it.

Undercroft: Crypt, usually used for secular buildings.

Vault: Stone ceiling, sometimes copied in timber or plaster.

Cross-vault: Vault made up of two tunnel-vaults of identical shape intersecting at right angles.

Fan-vault: All ribs spring from one point and are of the same length, same distance from the next, and the same curvature; decorated with tracery and producing a fan-like pattern.

Lierne ribs: Subsidiary ribs which do not spring from the vaulting compartment.

Rib-vault: The arch supporting the vault. Main types of ribs include transverse ribs, wall ribs, diagonal ribs and ridge ribs; also lierne – see above.

Stellar-vault: Lierne ribs arranged in a star formation.

Tunnel – or barrel-vault: Simple continuous arch.

Vestibule: Entrance hall, lobby or porch.

Vestry: Room in which vestments are kept.

Victorian: Styles popular during reign of Queen Victoria 1837–1901; Gothic Revival and Neo-classical.

Wagon roof: Roof formed by closely set rafters with curved braces, resembling the inside roof of a covered wagon.

Wimple: Headcovering that falls in folds round cheeks, chin and neck, like nuns wear.

Zigzag: Norman moulding forming a zigzag pattern.

ARCHITECTURAL SURVEY

ANGLO SAXON (5thC–11thC)
Simple, masonry buildings, often
emulating timber prototypes as in the
characteristic long-and-short work, seen
at the wall angles at Earl's Barton church,
Northamptonshire. Towers were
generally austere, and rather crude,

Earls Barton church.
c 1000 Normans

occasionally relieved by light pilaster
strips. The Saxon helm, a tower
terminating in a short-hipped spire,
shows the influence of the Carolingian
architecture of the Rhineland; a rare
example can be seen at Sompting,
Sussex. Buildings were generally
composed of fragments or rough copies
of Roman architectural details. Windows
are either round, as in the churches of
Worth and Bosham in Sussex; or
triangular-headed, as in the church at

Worth church, Sussex

Double belfry
window, Deerhurst
ch., 900.

Brixworth church,
Northamptonshire.

Deerhurst, Gloucester-
shire. Aisled church
plans of this period
are rare: typical plans
consist of a rect-
angular nave with
a small chancel at the
east end.

Saxon capital

NORMAN (1066–late 12thC)
The early decades were a period of great
military and church building following
the Conquest. The architecture was
bolder and more massive, characterised
by semi-circular arches, short and
ponderous cylindrical or polygonal piers,

Typical capital
details

Typical base
details

and flat buttresses. Towers were
generally short and sturdy, positioned
either centrally, in a cruciform church
plan, or centred over the chancel, or
placed at the western end. Rib- and
panel-vaulting were introduced.
Windows are small and deeply splayed,
often enriched by chevron (sometimes
known as zigzag), beak-head, star or
nail-head ornament. Characteristic
features include a bold soffit roll, a hood-
mould to internal arcading, simple blind

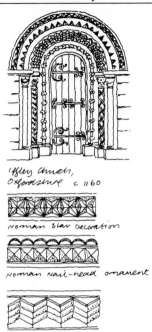

Iffley Church,
Oxfordshire c 1160

Norman Star Decoration

Norman Nail-head ornament

Norman Chevron ornament.
(also called 'zigzag')

arcading flanking single lights, and
lozenge, chevron and vertical channelling
on cylindrical piers. Portals were often
richly decorated, as at Iffley, while some
have carved tympana.

EARLY ENGLISH GOTHIC (late 12thC–early 14thC)

Walls retain the ponderous construction
of Norman churches, but the roof loads
are now carried on more elaborate

Clare Church, Suffolk.

Oundle Church,
Northamptonshire
five lancet windows.

buttressing. Wall surfaces are generally
plain. Increasing use was made of cut-
stone, while the potential of the pointed
arch resolved the difficulties created by
the intersection of irregular-sized semi-
circular vaults. Towers are richer in
decoration with a composition of tall,
lancet windows under a single hood and
contained by string courses. A
characteristic feature is the broach-spire.
Capitals have boldly moulded foliage
designs to give deep shadows, while the

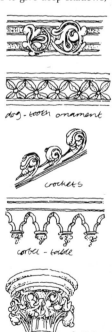

dog-tooth ornament

crockets

corbel - table

Galilee Porch
Ely, Cathedral

ponderous columns of the Norman period are replaced by compound columns of cylindrical or octagonal shafts or detached shafts. Mouldings are generally of dogtooth or leaf design while crocketing was used to enrich angles and window gables.

DECORATED GOTHIC (14thC)

Further developments in elaborate buttressing led to thinner walls and wider windows, characteristic of the period. Angle buttresses were set diagonally as at Bloxham, Oxfordshire. Vaulting was more elaborate with the adoption of both inter-mediate and ridge ribs as well as the use of lierne ribs – any rib, other than a ridge rib, which does not spring from the vaulting com-partment. The resulting pattern is called stellar-vaulting. Towers generally have battle-mented parapets, often pinnacled at the corners and occasionally with flying buttresses to the spire. Window tracery consists of geometric forms; later curvilinear or flowing lines were introduced. The circular or rose window is another characteristic feature. Carving was generally more naturalistic.

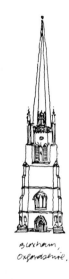

Bloxham, Oxfordshire.

carved capital

circular church window c 1320

characteristic window

PERPENDICULAR GOTHIC (late 14thC–mid 16thC)

Church towers are often extremely high, and elaborately decorated with panels and fretted stonework. Some, like St Botolph's, Boston, are crowned by octagonal lanterns of one or more stages. The stellar-vaulting of the previous period is gradually developed, with numerous ribs and panels, into hand-some fan-vaulting.

Thaxted church, Essex.

Typical windows

Windows grew larger with a vertical emphasis to both tracery and panelling. Buttressing was accentuated for decorative rather than structural effect, often crowned by tall pinnacles. Hammer-beam roofs are numerous; piers more slender, while carved figurework is of a more secular

church Kenton, Devon.

parapet details.

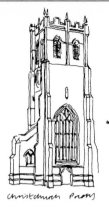

christchurch Priory

and often heraldic content. The Tudor rose, the portcullis and the fleur-de-lys are all characteristic ornaments.

The 16thC saw the building of greater timber-framed and stone mansions together with the expansion of the universities. The two great ecclesiastical projects of this period were the rebuilding of Bath Abbey (1501–39) and the completion of the Henry VII Chapel at Westminster Abbey in 1512. A number of chapels were built in the universities, most notably that of Trinity College, Cambridge, which epitomises the Perpendicular style. The major development in the parish churches was the inclusion of carved screens and tombs.

THE RENAISSANCE (late 16thC–18thC)
Most church building which took place during this period was comparatively simple in plan, and generally without

st. Mary's church, ingestre, Staffs. 1673-7

chancels. Typical is the church at Groombridge, Kent. The designs were generally a mix of styles, as in the chapel of Peterhouse, Cambridge, 1628, which is an amalgam of Perpendicular Gothic and Baroque. A number of churches had porches added, usually in an ornamental Baroque style as at St Mary the Virgin, Oxford.

wilen church, Buckinghamshire 1877-80

The major influences on church building in the early Renaissance were the numerous City of London churches designed by Sir Christopher Wren (1631–1723), such as St Mary-le-Bow, St Bride and St Martin of Tours. Characteristic features were an austere main block containing nave and flanking aisles and crowned by a bold cornice. Roofs were hipped and sometimes hidden by parapets. The large built-up windows were abandoned for small rectangular ones set in a large wall space. The tower was boldly articulated; either a tall, square block, divided in stages by string courses with quoins and pilasters highlighting the angles; or comprising a square pilastered tower, decorative

st. Mary-le-Bow by Wren.

merewoorth church, Kent
1744-6

parapet, central drum and encircling columns crowned by an obelisk. Later the tower often pierced the ridge of the principal roof, as at Mereworth, Kent, which was influenced by James Gibbs' design for St Martin-in-the-Fields.

THE 19th CENTURY

This century was characterised by the battle of the styles, fought between two camps, both looking backwards for inspiration: the handsome Greek Revival, as epitomised by W. Inwood and H. W. Inwood's design for All Saint's Church, Camden Town (1822–4), a two-storey drum with encircling Ionic columns and

crowned by a tall tower, based on the Tower of the Winds, Athens; and the Gothic Revival as exemplified by the magnificent country churches of A. W. N. Pugin (1812–1852), such as St Marie's, Derby (1838–9). In the end the rhetoric of

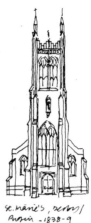

St. Marie's, Derby/
Pugin -1838-9

Pugin was both more persuasive and more appropriate for Victorian ecclesiastical sensibilities, and the battle was won for the medievalists, as illustrated by a series of magnificent late Victorian churches such as J. L. Pearson's design for St Augustine's, Kilburn (1870–80).

All Saints, Camden Town
1822-4 by W & H.W. Inwood.

St. Augustine, Kilburn
1870-80/ J.L. Pearson

THE 20TH CENTURY
The more memorable churches built in this century, such as St Wilfred's Brighton, designed by Goodhart-Rendel in 1933, show a return to a more austere, boldly articulated kind of architecture.

st. wilfred's, Brighton 1933
Goodhart - Rendel

St. Jude, 1910
Sir Edwin Lutyens
Hampstead Garden Suburb.

The best have something of the simplicity and utility of the Arts and Crafts Movement with its emphasis on traditional building and natural materials, combined with the toughness and straightforwardness of Carolingian architecture (an earlier influence on our island's church architecture). The underlying influence of these 20thC churches was still Gothic, however.

THE
—WEST COUNTRY—

Cornwall   Devon   Somerset   Avon

Cornwall has always had a strong tendency towards non-conformity: it showed in the widespread acceptance of John Wesley and in the armed resistance to Cranmer's Prayer Book, which was dismissed as a 'Christmas game'. Its origins lie in the fact that Cornwall was converted to Christianity not from Rome but from Ireland, and converted to a Celtic expression of that faith. Celtic memory lingers on in names of saints unknown to any calendar – St Just, St Eval, St Buryan, St Enodoc, and in the sites of churches, often remote from the village heart of a parish.

A county with its own language, where intruders from east of the Tamar were called 'foreigners', is likely to have a distinctive local style. In Cornwall this distinctiveness is greatly enhanced by a local stone that is wholly in keeping with the character of the county – granite.

Granite is exceptionally resistant to pollution and to penetration by water. It is much used for kerbstones, bridges and prisons. But for private building it is expensive and ill-suited for decorative enrichment. Launceston is one of the few churches on which such decoration was attempted and it has not really succeeded. Aesthetically, granite produces a monochrome effect to which absence of mouldings adds monotone. It can, however, be effective. The moorland churches lie low as befits a windswept region, but their sturdy towers could act as beacons, landmarks and lookout points as occasion required. In an age of greater prosperity many of the churches were enlarged by trebling the nave.

There was a considerable campaign of building in Devon during the 14thC, and many churches of that date reflect the simple, cruciform plan of Crediton, which was once the episcopal seat in this part of the world. The campaign owed much to Bishop Grandisson, who gave Exeter Cathedral its nave and built the fine church at Ottery St Mary.

An exceptional number of splendid rood screens have survived in Devon, often extending the whole width of the church and decorated by local craftsmen with an abundance of carving, mostly inspired by the seasonal round of agriculture. Local resistance to the tenets of the Reformation probably helped preserve them. These screens, together with the richly embossed ceilings, as at Cullompton, greatly enhance the architecture; and Devon is more renowned for its carving than its architectural distinction.

Part of the attraction of Somerset churches is in the contrast between the high professional skill of the masons, exemplified in a hundred magnificent towers, and the simple vernacular style of the wood carvers who provided the furnishings.

The towers of Somerset are justly famous. They owe their perfection to the easily worked oolitic limestone which attracted the most competent masons to the great centres of Glastonbury, Bristol and Wells, but particularly the last: Wells Cathedral led the way. The first of these towers, Shepton Mallet (begun 1375), was clearly meant to carry a spire. Later towers were not. They developed corner pinnacles to produce a comparable sky-piercing effect, and are further distinguished by delicate tracery, pierced parapets and pinnacled buttresses. Needless to say these towers were an invitation to bellringers, and many of the best peals in England are to be found in this part of the country.

Avon is a relatively new county, centred along the river Avon, and boasting the possession of both Bath, that supreme product of 18thC civilisation, and Bristol, whose rich church heritage shows the zenith of medieval architecture. Outside these centres, as one would expect, churches reflect the styles of the county's near neighbours, Gloucestershire and Somerset, and are often constructed of local Cotswold or Bath stone.

◀ CORNWALL ▶

Altarnun, St Nonna   **2 E3**
7m SW of Launceston off A30. In a picturesque village of stone cottages straggling down a slope to a bubbling stream, on the NE edge of Bodmin Moor. Over the medieval packhorse bridge rises the 15thC church, with one of the tallest towers in Cornwall, shielded by a hillside. The church's patroness was a 6thC Celtic missionary and mother of St David. A Celtic cross from St Nonna's time is by the gate. Distinctive Perpendicular windows light the interior with wide arches and pillars of single blocks of moorstone. There is a spectacular Norman font, bearded faces at its corners and large, round floral motifs between, a 17thC altar rail stretching across nave and aisles, as does the 19thC rood screen, and wagon roofs. Further enhancements are the 79 16thC bench ends, carved with subjects secular and sacred, including a flock of sheep and strolling musicians, signed by 'Robart Daye, Maker of this Work'. **P.** *Open approx 09.00–dusk daily.*

Bodmin, St Petroc   **1 D3**
In the county town, close to Bodmin Moor, it is Cornwall's largest parish church. St Guron's Well, outside the W end, is on a site which was probably sacred long before his arrival c500. The Welsh prince Petroc followed Guron later in the century and founded a monastery here. The present church was built 1469–72, and restored in the 19thC. Its spire was destroyed by lightning in 1699. The church's great treasure is the 12thC ivory casket, which once held relics of St Petroc: returned in 1177 at Henry II's behest, after having been stolen by a delinquent monk, it was lost again after the Dissolution. The casket eventually reappeared, without a single bone, and

St Petroc, St Guron's Well

was restored to the church in 1957. See too the beautiful 12thC font, ornamented with intertwined foliage and nasty beasts, serene angel faces and wings at the corners; the slate slab memorials to two 17thC men with two wives each and a multitude of children; the effigy of Thomas Vivian, d1533, penultimate prior of Bodmin, accompanied by charming cherubs with shields; and the roofless 14thC chapel of St Thomas a Becket at the E end for its Decorated E window, sedilia, piscina and crypt. **P** nearby. *Open summer 08.00–18.00 Mon–Sat, 07.30–19.30 Sun; winter to approx 15.30.* Lanhydrock, 2½m SE, a grand 17thC and 19thC house, has formal gardens and a magnificent plaster ceiling in its gallery.

Gunwalloe, St Winwalloe   **1** B1
3m S of Helston off A3083. Solitary in a combe on a magnificent coastline, haunted by seabirds, sheltered by a cliff: everything about it is redolent of romance. It is the site of the 'Church of the Storms', founded in the 6thC by Winwalloe, close to the site of a manor house whose lord, Roger de Carminowe, was a descendent of King Arthur, and beside sandbanks where treasure chests were buried by the buccaneer, Captain Avery. And a ship full of treasure, the St Anthony of Lisbon, sunk in 1526 in Church Cove. Rebuilt in the 14thC and 15thC and restored in the 19thC, the church has lovely wagon roofs in the S aisle and porch, a granite altar designed by Comper, and parts of the 16thC rood screen, with beautiful tracery and paintings of apostles, made from the wreckage of the St Anthony. The separate tower built into the rock, with pyramidal cap, belongs to an older church and there is an ancient cross in the churchyard. **P.** *Open daylight hours daily.* Gold might wash up at your feet in nearby Dollar Cove, site of a Spanish shipwreck of 1785. Unfortunately, cliff erosion threatens the church.

Helston, St Michael   **1** B1
Church Rd. In an agreeable market town, the church was built by the Earl of Godolphin in the 18thC in classical style, with a handsome granite tower crowned by obelisk pinnacles, and a galleried interior with iron columns. He donated the splendid brass chandelier. The church was restored in the 19thC and in this. Don't miss the delightful piece of local colour reflected in the top of the E window, where two small angels dance the famous Floral Dance, the music for

which is in a scroll under their feet. The branches they carry allude to the annual feast of St Michael, who (according to legend) saved the town from a shower of boulders hurled by the devil. See the brass to Thomas Bougins, d1602, and the churchyard memorial to Henry Trengrouse, inventor of the Rocket Life Saving Apparatus for use at sea. **P.** *Open summer 09.00–20.00 Mon–Sat, 08.00–20.00 Sun; winter to 16.30 Mon–Sat, 20.00 Sun.* Fanned by cypresses, 16thC–17thC castellated and colonnaded Godolphin Court is 5m NW.

Kilkhampton, St James the Great   **2** D4
4m NE of Bude on A39. The beautiful Norman S doorway is the oldest part of the church, rebuilt in the 16thC. John Granville, rector from 1524–80, built the S porch in 1567 and left his initials on it. The wagon roofs of different heights and lovely, soaring arches, on pillars carved from single pieces of stone, create a majestic interior. The granite, tapering tower has a fine internal arch. There is a rich feast of 16thC bench ends, carved with a great variety of subjects, among which are two of exceptional quality and earlier date, in the SW and NW corners. 18thC memorials to the Granvilles, among others, and the Royal Arms of George II, were carved by a local craftsman, Michael Chuke, 1679–1742. The church has a Father Smith organ. **P.** *Open daylight hours daily.*

Lanreath, St Marnarch   **1** D2
7m NW of Looe on B3359. There are Norman walls in the transept and nave, but the church is otherwise Perpendicular and was sensitively restored by Bodley in 1887. The Norman altar stone is preserved and so is the lavishly carved, cup-shaped font, with a Jacobean cover of distinction. The lovely 16thC rood screen, restored in 1905, has 13 of its original paintings of saints in the lower panels. Don't miss the Elizabethan pulpit, the chancel stalls with very impressive carved figures on them and the 17thC Grylls monument, fascinatingly imitating stone, yet carved entirely in wood. *Open daylight hours daily.* The inn and cottages opposite form a delightful group.

Lanteglos-by-Fowey, St Wyllow   **1** D2
8m E of St Austell. A lovely 14thC church in undulating countryside. Inside are numerous 16thC bench ends, coats of arms from Jacobean pews, a 13thC font with foliage decoration, a 15thC brass

and fine timber roofs; especially interesting is the 14thC roof in the N aisle. See the lantern cross in the churchyard. **P**. *Open 08.30–dusk daily.* Wonderful coastal scenery close by and historic Fowey harbour.

Launcells, St Swithin   **2 D4**
2m E of Bude off A3072. In bosky seclusion, with St Swithin's Well just over the bridge. There are tall pinnacles on the tower and a white and light interior, untouched by Victorian restorers. The Ten Commandments are pronounced from a polished marble reredos, the Royal Arms of Charles II hang over Georgian box pews in the N aisle and the Georgian pulpit has a delightful, hanging, sounding board. The Norman font has a pretty 17thC cover. There is a very fine series of medieval bench ends, ingeniously devised to illustrate the Passion without using human figures: for example, the Ascension is represented by dangling feet and the hem of a robe disappearing into a cloud above a pair of footprints. 15thC tiles from Barnstaple, of lions, griffins, pelicans and flowers, decorate the chancel. **P**. *Open daylight hours daily.*

Little Petherick, St Petroc Minor   **1 D3**
9m NW of Bodmin on A389. In a creekside village, fringed by a delightful wooded valley. In between founding monasteries at Padstow and Bodmin in the 6thC, St Petroc spent a great deal of time sitting up to his neck in the Little Petherick river praying, as was the wont of Celtic saints. He lived on 'bread and water, with porridge on Sundays' and kept a pet wolf to guard his sheepskin cloak. The 14thC church was rebuilt by William White in 1868 for a rector with Tractarian tastes. Comper added the high altar and reredos and the rood screen, impressive rood and loft in 1908. Great treasures were bestowed on the church early this century, including a 17thC Spanish painting of St Mary Magdalen, a 16thC Venetian processional cross, a 12thC Byzantine cross, and a number of rich medieval vestments. **P**. *Open summer 09.00–19.00 daily, winter to 16.00.*

Madron, St Maddernus   **1 B2**
1m NW of Penzance off A307. Once the parish church of Penzance, it is mainly medieval. The elaborate rood screen retains some 16thC panels in its base. There are interesting bench ends, 18thC altar rails and pulpit, and an exquisite panel of alabaster angels. Monuments include a brass of 1623 to a mayor of Penzance, Elizabethan slate tablets, and a classical mausoleum in the churchyard. Most fascinating of all is the Trafalgar Banner, commemorating Nelson's victory and death in 1805, news of which was brought to England by a Penzance fishing boat. **P**. *Open summer 09.00–dusk daily, winter to 19.00.* Through a field NW of the village are St Madron's ruined baptistry and well. Relics of prehistoric Britain are scattered over this part of Cornwall, consisting chiefly of massive monoliths.

Mawgan-in-Meneage, St Mawgan   **1 C3**
5m NE of Newquay off B3271. A very satisfying 15thC granite tower, with pronounced pinnacles on the castellated crown. The W doorway is carved with foliage and the coats of arms of noble families. The church is 13thC–15thC with a 19thC N transept. Discover the knightly effigy of Sir Roger de Carminow, d1308, a descendant of King Arthur, and that of his wimpled wife, the elaborate squint through to the chancel, the lovely E window in the 15thC N aisle, which has its original wagon roof with bosses, including a set of the Mystic Rose, a symbol of Mary. **P**. *Open daylight hours daily.* The inscribed Mawgan Cross in the village marks an early preaching place.

St Michael the Archangel, rood and screen

Newquay, St Michael the Archangel 1 C3
An Edwardian expression of medieval forms, in a large, gracious church by Sir Ninian Comper, 1909–11. The rood above the finely detailed screen is splendidly gilded and the flanking cherubim, with wings flying off in different directions, are glorious. A great host of angels has flown up above the choir in the chancel. There is a vivacious and interesting wall

hanging in the Galilee Chapel, made by the local comprehensive school. **P.** *Open 06.30–17.00 Mon, Tue & Thur–Sat, 10.00–16.00 Wed, 07.30–21.00 Sun.* There are miles of wonderful sandy beach in Newquay and nearby are Bedruthen Steps, vast black rocks said to be the stepping stones of the giant Bedruthen, who has no competition since humans can only admire and gasp from above.

Padstow, St Petroc 1 C3

The medieval church stands at the end of the ancient town and fishing port. The 6thC missionary, St Petroc, sailed here in a coracle from Ireland and founded his monastery in what is now the garden of the Elizabethan manor house beside the church, Prideaux Place. The beautiful 15thC octagonal font is carved with figures of the apostles and angels, a fox preaches to geese on a bench end and the Tudor pulpit has panels with symbols of the Passion. Impressive Prideaux monuments, a 15thC brass and, in the churchyard, an ancient cross shaft. **P.** *Open 08.00–19.00 daily.* See the pretty quayside houses and Raleigh's Court House.

Probus, St Probus 1 C2

3m NE of Truro on A390. The splendid 16thC tower is the highest in Cornwall and of the Somerset rather than Cornish type, with statue niches, profuse ornamentation at each stage, and pinnacles sprouting small versions of themselves. Inside are graceful nave arcades, a tall tower arch and noble E windows. See the monument to Thomas Hawkins, d1766, whose portrait is held by a seated, mourning female figure – one foot disconsolately dangling over the monument's edge – oblivious of the diving angel overhead. *Open 08.00–18.00 Mon–Thur & Sat, to 21.00 Fri, to 19.30 Sun.* 18thC Trewithen House and gardens are nearby.

St Cleer, St Cleer 1 D3

2m NW of Liskeard off A390. A beautiful granite tower, small pinnacles clambering up the buttresses and culminating in the magnificent large ones on top. A Norman door on the N side testifies to the church's early origin. The nave arcades are in interesting contrast to one another; the N has plain 14thC octagonal piers, and the S more complex 15thC arches and piers with decorated capitals. The chancel roof, reredos and rood screen are modern additions. Look at the 17thC painted text boards, flamboyant Royal Arms of Queen Anne, the Langford monument and adjacent Langford Creed, which recipients of his charity were obliged to recite, and the parish stocks of 1744 in the N aisle. The ravages of the plague may account for the fact that six vicars are named on the list of incumbents between 1400 and 1413. **P.** *Open 07.45–19.00 Mon–Sat, to 20.00 Sun.* The Holy Well, 200 yds E, is a delightful 15thC baptistry, square and simple like a tiny chapel. Beside it is a tall stone cross. 1m NW is an inscribed Celtic cross base, King Doniert's Stone, which may be associated with Durngarth, 9thC Cornish king. Outsize prehistoric tomb, Trethevy Quoit, is also nearby.

St Ia, medieval lantern cross

St Ives, St Ia 1 B2

St Andrew's St. A most imposing 15thC granite tower, with unusual projecting pinnacles, announces the church. Capitals carved with grapes and vine leaves are on the pillars leading through to the Lady Chapel, where Barbara Hepworth's fine *Madonna and Child* sculpture is displayed. The 15thC granite font has delightful but austerely carved angels holding shields, sharing a spareness of detail with the Hepworth sculpture. The wagon roofs are beautiful and the 15thC choir stalls finely carved. St Ia, who it is said, sailed here on a leaf in the Dark Ages, is represented in a reredos statue. See the tall medieval lantern cross in the churchyard. *Open Mar–Oct 09.00–18.00 daily (later in summer), Nov–Feb to 16.00.* As a port St Ives received draughts of pilchards, later drawing Victorian artists to its sparkling light and picturesque, steep cobbled streets round the harbour. Virginia Woolf's *To the Lighthouse* was partly inspired by childhood holidays here. A Nonconformist influence speaks through names like Teetotal St and Salubrious Pl. Barbara Hepworth's house is now a museum of her work. Beaches and coastal walks abound.

St Just

St Just in Roseland, St Just　　**1 C2**
2m N of St Mawes on A3078. The sort of churchyard one would be happy to be buried in. There is a glorious view from the lychgate of trees, palms and brilliantly coloured shrubs, tropical and temperate, cascading among the gravestones down to the church beside an exquisitely serene creek. On an ancient site, the present church is 13thC–15thC, much restored in the 19thC. The stair-turreted tower has weathered to a silvery grey and has pretty 14thC windows at the top. Examine the impressive brass of a priest, c1520. **P**. *Open daylight hours daily.* The nearby fishing and sailing village of St Mawes has an august Tudor fortress, built by Henry VIII in the 1540s, as part of a network of south coast castles, and St Mawes' Well, half way up the hill from the Victory Inn, with reputed healing powers.

St Newlyn East, St Newlina　　**1 C2**
3m S of Newquay off A3075. The church, with a Norman origin, was rededicated in 1259 and refashioned in the 14thC and 15thC. The Norman font is similar to that at Bodmin, with stylised floral decoration

and angel faces looking out from the corners. Look out for the bench ends and the Royal Arms made of plaster. Beware of the fig tree with a curse on it: anyone plucking a leaf will die within a year and scoffers have not always survived to pluck another. **P**. *Open 07.40–dusk or 18.30 Tue–Sun, from 09.00 Mon.* Nearby is Trerice, mullioned and curvy-gabled Elizabethan manor house.

St Winnow, St Winnow　　**1 D2**
5m NE of St Austell off A390. In rural retirement on the delightful brink of the Fowey river, alone but for farm, vicarage and trees. A Perpendicular church with carved wagon roofs, 16thC bench ends and glorious late medieval stained glass in the S aisle E window, of kneeling and standing figures and coats of arms. The lovely rood screen is one of the few remaining in Cornwall, and was restored by E. H. Sedding in 1907. Primitively carved angels hold hands on the granite font. The pulpit is 17thC. *Open daylight hours daily.*

St Winnow

Tintagel, St Materiana　　**2 D3**
12m N of Bodmin on B3263. A Norman church with Saxon elements and medieval additions, whose severity of outline matches its exposed, isolated position on a bare headland. Note the little slits of windows and ancient doorways, the 12thC hinges on the N door, the font with faces at its corners, the 15thC rood screen, and the Roman milestone. **P**. *Open 09.00–dusk daily, or end of evening service Sun.* Romance is inseparable from the island of black ruin-strewn cliffs, lashed by waves, site of a 6thC Celtic monastery and a Norman castle, and legendary scene of the court of King Arthur and his knights. In the village, see the Old Post Office, an

ancient stone cottage with undulating roofs, perhaps originally a small, medieval manor house.

Towednack, St Tewennicus 1 B2
1m S of St Ives on B3311. Deep in the country, the church has a plain granite tower and 13thC nave and chancel, with the distinctions of a chancel arch, unique in this part of Cornwall, and of a pre-Reformation stone altar. The S aisle was built in the 15thC and the font with faces at the corners is of 1720. **P**. *Open 09.00–dusk daily.*

Zennor, St Senara 1 B2
4m SW of St Ives on B3306. Two glorious legends are associated with the church. One is to do with the enchanting carving of a mermaid, whose prototype lured a chorister down to the stream running through the village, and out to sea, where they can be heard singing at Mermaid's Cove. The other revolves around the church's patron saint, depicted in a chancel window, a virtuous princess of Brittany condemned to be burnt through the machinations of her jealous stepmother. Because she was pregnant and her jailors didn't want to be guilty of murdering the unborn child, they nailed her into a barrel and threw it in the sea, where she was fed by an angel and where her son was born. She founded the church on her way back to Brittany. The present church, Norman in origin, is mostly later medieval, with a substantial tower and an interior of lovely simplicity. Inspect the Lord's Prayer in Cornish near the organ, the schooner commemorating W. A. Proctor and shipwrecked sailors, and the memorial outside the porch to John Davey, the last person to speak Cornish as his native tongue, who died in 1891, much later than Dolly Pentreath of Mousehole, who is usually given that distinction. *Open 09.00–dusk Mon–Sat, from 08.15 Sun.* Visit the Wayside Museum and the Tinners' Arms; also Zennor Head for a wonderful view, and inland moorland for granite tors and the megalithic thrill of Zennor Quoit.

◁ DEVON ▷

Ashburton, St Andrew 2 F3
The beautiful, wrought-iron entrance gate is by a local smith, c1700, beyond which the majestic 15thC castellated and stair-turreted tower soars in a tree-clad churchyard. Inside are 15thC nave arcades of local granite, the octagonal pillars with unusual, concave surfaces, a wonderful wagon roof stretching through nave and chancel, aisle roofs with bosses, and 18thC brass candelabra of great distinction. *Open 08.00–dusk Mon–Thur & Sat, from 07.00 Fri; 08.00–19.30 Sun.* A pleasing town of slate-hung and gabled buildings with projecting upper storeys, close to Dartmoor.

Ashton, St John the Baptist 2 F3
6m SW of Exeter off B3193. Up rocky steps to the church on a knoll, in the hilly, wooded farming country of the Teign valley; a beautiful and peaceful place with a few thatched cottages. Nice obelisk pinnacles crown the tower. Notice the Civil War bullet holes in the studded oak S door. Immediately striking is the richly carved rood screen, so much a feature of Devon churches, with birds pecking grapes in the cornice and 15thC painted figures below. The cross was erected on top in 1915. Behind the screen, in the chapel, and on the N side of the parclose screen, are marvellous half-length paintings of gesticulating prophets with curly scrolls, stylised yet eloquent. Fragments of 15thC glass in the chapel include a plump Gabriel from an Annunciation and a kneeling knight. On the wall beside them is a 15thC painting of Christ with the instruments of the Passion. There is a fine, Jacobean pulpit with sounding board and iron hour-glass stand. Limited **P**. *Open daylight hours daily.*

Babbacombe, All Saints 3 G3
District of Torquay on B3199. Cary Av. Built by William Butterfield, 1868–74, in distinctive, Gothic revival style. Wide, soaring arches and short, polished marble pillars form the nave arcades, decorated above by patterned tiles within diamond shapes. See the font and pulpit. **P**. *Open 09.00–18.00 or dusk daily.* Torquay is the Cannes of the English south-west, laid out with sub-tropical shrubs and grand terraces, such as Hesketh Cres. The remains of Tor Abbey include a 14thC gatehouse. Another notable Victorian church is St John, by G. E.

All Saints, 19thC Gothic chancel

Street, with glass and murals by Pre-Raphaelite Burne-Jones. Visit Kent's Cavern for the magnificent display of stalactites and stalagmites.

**Bovey Tracey, St Peter, St Paul   2 F3
and St Thomas of Canterbury**
3m NW of Newton Abbot on B3344. On a slight eminence at the end of the town, with a view over to Dartmoor. Tall, pinnacled tower and impressive embellishments of battlements and pinnacles on the S side. Four heads joined by the neck meet in the central roof boss inside the S porch, one with a crown and one with a mitre; other fascinating bosses include a face with foliage issuing from the mouth. Birds peck pomegranates, and leaves and stems intertwine in the sumptuous rood screen frieze. The restored coloured and gilded screen is painted with apostles and prophets and dates from the early 15thC. The pulpit too is lushly carved, with dense foliage and figures in panels. The parclose screens are 16thC. Exuberantly patterned organ pipes seem to burst out from the NE corner. There are two 17thC monuments in the chancel to Alice Bray's husbands, owners of nearby Parke House, and in the churchyard, Maria Forbes' tomb of 1655 with prominent obelisks on top, a mermaid on one. (See the jaunty angels on the tomb opposite.) James Forbes, her husband, was ejected from his incumbency during the Commonwealth and recalls 'the bloody Parliament 1642' and 'wicked Parliament' in memorials to Archbishop Laud and the Bishop of Exeter at the W end of the church. *Open daylight hours daily.*

Brentor, St Michael of the Rock   2 E3
5m N of Tavistock off A386. According to legend, built by a rich merchant who, in the midst of a great storm at sea, vowed he would build a church on the first land he saw if he survived. The site could not be more spectacular, on the summit of a volcanic cone, 1100ft above sea level and commanding views over moor and sea, breathtaking in expanse and, often, in windiness. It is a beautiful, simple 13thC church, built from the volcanic stone of the tor, with a 15thC tower fronting the precipice and it is one of the smallest complete parish churches in England. Restored in 1890, it has an ancient granite font and colourful glass of St Michael, 1971, in the E window. **P.** *Open daylight hours daily.*

Bridford, St Thomas a Becket   2 F3
9m SW of Exeter off B3193. In the Teign valley and close to the granite boulders of Dartmoor from which it is built. The 13thC chancel is the earliest part of the church, otherwise it is a Perpendicular building with beautiful windows either side of the S porch. In contrast to the painted saints characteristic of rood screen decoration in Devon, delightful eight-inch figures are carved on Bridford's 16thC screen, retaining some

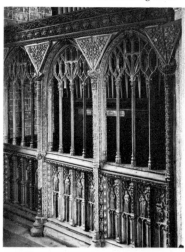

St Thomas a Becket, 16thC rood screen

original colouring and forming a lively gathering of ecclesiastics and laymen, including jesters, although the faces were vandalised by Puritan soldiers. Look for the boss in the nave roof, of three rabbits sharing three ears, symbol of the medieval tinners who mined the area. **P**. *Open daylight hours daily*. Not far off is Blackingstone Rock, from which a marvellous panoramic view can be had.

Chagford, St Michael 2 F3
12m SW of Exeter off B3212. In an ancient stannary town, where tin was stamped and weighed, above the Teign river on Dartmoor. The nave pillars are of single blocks of granite, traditional material for Dartmoor churches, and the church has been refloored in granite. Dedicated in 1261, the present building is largely 15thC, with a cool, dark interior, contrasting with the vividly coloured medieval parclose screens and the organ case. In the chancel is a lovely 15thC Italian painting of the madonna and child, and an ornately detailed monument to Sir John Whyddon, d1575, without its effigy, but with charming mermaids and mermen at the top, with such childish faces that they might be merbabies. Here too is the tombstone of Mary Whyddon, shot by a former lover as she left the church after her wedding in 1641, whose ghost appears whenever a girl is married from the house where she lived. Glance up at the chancel roof boss of three rabbits sharing three ears, the tinners symbol. *Open 08.00–dusk daily. Chancel closed except by prior request*. From the E end of the churchyard is a lovely view, taking in Castle Drogo, by Lutyens, 1911–30, one of the last stately homes to be built in England. Opposite the church tower is the thatched Three Crowns, haunted by the poet Godolphin, who was shot in its porch during the Civil War.

Chittlehampton, St Hieritha 2 F5
3m S of South Molton on B3227. Heathen villagers killed St Hieritha, or St Urith, with their scythes in the 6thC, and the well that sprang where she fell is at the E end of the village. The church faces a large square, the upper stages of its glorious tower resembling the Somerset type. The handsome church was rebuilt late in the 15thC and restored in the 19thC. The pulpit of c1500 has a figure of St Urith on it; her burial place and what is now called her shrine, are on the N side of the chancel. It was a place of pilgrimage until 1539, after which

vicarage revenues fell because of the 'takyn away of the Imagys of St Urithe & cessyng of offerynges used to be made there by pulgremes'. The 16thC and 17thC monuments in the Giffard Chapel include a recumbent effigy of Grace Giffard, who died in 1667 from pricking herself with a fern, which she holds. *Open 07.30–19.00 Mon–Sat, 08.00–19.30 Sun*.

Clovelly, All Saints 2 E4
9m W of Bideford off A39. A small tower, pleasing in its plainness, on a church whose S porch outer doorway testifies in its zigzag decoration to a Norman origin. A Perpendicular rebuilding added the arcade and aisle and lovely wagon roofs. The stained glass in the E and W windows is by Kempe, and there is also a window by Comper. Observe the imposing monument in the chancel to Sir Robert Cary, who died in 1586 as a result of attending Exeter Assizes where all present contracted jail fever. There are many other memorials to the Carys, lords of the adjacent manor until the 18thC, and to their successors, the Hamlyns. Note the delightful wrought-iron light pendants, and the 'bracket seats' on the ends of the three back pews on the N side of the nave, which were used by pauper apprentices, who were boarded out with farmers and not allowed to sit with the other children. **P**. *Open summer 09.00–21.00 daily, winter 09.00–dusk daily*. The church is some way above the charming, traffic-free, tourist-swarming village. Luxuriantly wooded slopes frame the enjoyable jostling of Georgian houses down the steep, cobbled street, with steps careering down to the fishing harbour at its foot.

Crediton, Holy Cross 2 F4
Preceded by a Saxon cathedral, the castellated sandstone church was collegiate until the Reformation. 12thC piers support the central tower, but the church is mainly 15thC. The two-storeyed S porch is vaulted and has foliage bosses and, most uncommon in Devon, there is a magnificent clerestory in nave and chancel. See the late 14thC monument to Sir John Sully and wife, she wearing the costume of the day, he armour; the standing effigy of 1605; and the appealing Tuckfield monument of 1630, from two medallions on which melancholy faces of father and son incline towards Elizabeth Tuckfield's seated figure, the whole in an impressive surround. Visit the Chapter House

museum. **P**. *Open 08.30–17.30 Tue–Thur, from 09.30 Mon, Fri & Sat, 08.30–19.30 Sun.*

Cullompton, St Andrew 3 G4
The red sandstone tower is the latest part of the church to be built, in 1545–9. Above its W window are sculptured figures in panels, and the tower is further embellished by gargoyles and pinnacles. On the S side is the Lane Aisle of 1526, the outpouring of a rich cloth merchant's wealth, with a commemorative inscription on its W wall to let everyone know. The buttresses have ships, sheep-shears and other emblems on them. Some are repeated on the pendants of the exceedingly beautiful and sumptuous fan-vault inside. Unusual buttressed pillars with statuary separate the Lane Aisle from the S aisle. The Golgotha of skulls, bones and rocks formed the base of the medieval rood. The rood screen is a glorious expanse of glowing colour, as is the cross-ribbed roof. The capitals of the slender nave pillars are decorated with leaves, heads and figures and the clerestory, uncommon in Devon, adds to the lightness of the interior. There are box pews and a squire's pew in the N chancel chapel and a Jacobean W gallery. **P**. *Open 09.00–17.00 Mon–Sat, 08.00–18.00 Sun.*

Dartington, St Mary the Virgin 2 F3
1m NW of Totnes off A385. Built 1878–80 by J. L. Pearson, architect of Truro Cathedral, the church replaced a medieval building, the tower of which stands near Dartington Hall. Incorporated from the old church are the Beer stone arcades, the beautiful star-vault in the porch, the altar and the pulpit, from which preached Tractarians John Keble and J. H. Newman, friends of Hurrell Froude, the famous historian's brother, whose father was rector from 1799–1859. Christ Pantocrator is the subject of stained glass by Clayton and Bell in the E window. The tower decorations are by Harry Hems. **P**. *Open 08.00–dusk daily.* In beautiful grounds, Dartington Hall is a combination of medieval splendour and modern social conscience, built in the late 14thC and bought in 1925 by two rich and idealistic Americans, to promote rural crafts and industries and the arts. It is flourishing and famous.

East Budleigh, All Saints 3 G3
9m SE of Exeter off A376. The church where the great Elizabethan statesman,

Sir Walter Raleigh, born at nearby Hayes Barton, worshipped as a boy. It was built in the 15thC by Bishop Lacy, whose arms are in stained glass in the N aisle. The Raleigh arms on a bench end dated 1537 designate the family pew. Examine the fascinating profusion of 16thC bench ends, including the head of an American Indian, possibly the first likeness of the kind. There is a fine wagon roof, the bosses on which were regilded in 1974. Look up at the memorial in the S aisle E window to a 19thC vicar, Ambrose Stapleton, who had fine oratorical qualities, but above all, an exceptional talent for organising the village's smuggling activities, at a time when smuggling was rife along this coastline. **P**. *Open daylight hours daily.* Lovely views from the churchyard and a pretty village.

Frithelstock, St Mary and St Gregory 2 E4
4m S of Bideford off A386. Beside the ruins of a 13thC Augustinian priory, whose tall lancets in a roofless wall are an impressive sight. The church has a high tower and an elegant frieze in the castellation of the S porch. Notice the canopied niches for statues and leaf decoration on the capitals in the beautiful S arcade. The early 14thC E window has fine tracery. There are bench ends and bench fronts with tracery. **P**. *Open daylight hours daily.*

Holbeton, All Saints 2 F2
7m SE of Plymouth off A379. An imposing steeple and church with a spacious interior and remarkably fine carved woodwork. The 16thC screens, and that renewed by Sedding in the 19thC, have intricate tracery with budding and blooming shapes, and a frieze of leaf-like faces and shallow urns, motifs with a Renaissance flavour. Scrutinise the excellent 19thC work in the bench ends carved with dense foliage, birds, berries and animals, the reredos and the impressive S and W doors. The Norman font decoration includes lions and trees. A 17thC monument commemorates 23 members of the Hele family, kneeling in tiers. **P**. *Open 09.00–17.00 daily.* Near a coastal area designated one of out-standing natural beauty.

Ilfracombe, Holy Trinity 2 E5
The church was enlarged in the 14thC and again in the 15thC and 19thC. The N tower is the oldest part. There are wonderful ceiled wagon roofs, that in the nave decorated with angels and gargoyles, and sumptuously adorned at

the E end, above the former rood screen. This richest part is aptly called a Glory. See the Norman font, Elizabethan pulpit with floral motif in the panels, and the knocker on the S door. *Open 08.00–dusk Mon–Sat, 07.30–20.00 Sun.* In a hilly, seaside resort which began to flourish in the Victorian era, reflected in its houses and terraces.

Lapford, St Thomas of Canterbury   **2 F4**
8m NW of Crediton on A377. The 16thC rood screen has delightfully ornate Renaissance motifs on the coving. Above it is a beautiful and elaborately decorated roof or Glory. The 16thC bench ends are carved with profile heads emerging from foliate forms, initials and Renaissance details. Norman S doorway. **P** nearby. *Open summer 07.30–21.00 daily, winter to 17.30 daily.* In the village is a mill and the 16thC Old Malt Scoop Inn.

St Petrock, Lydford

Lydford, St Petrock   **2 E3**
10m E of Launceston off A386. Lydford was an important Saxon town and the present medieval church stands on an ancient site. It has a short, granite ashlar W tower with prominent crocketed pinnacles. The N aisle was added in 1890. See the carved modern bench ends and the Watchmaker's tomb. **P** nearby. *Open 08.30–dusk daily.* Set in the enchantment of its wooded ravine on the edge of Dartmoor, the village was the tinners' headquarters in the Middle Ages, and Lydford Castle, built 1195, their prison. Lydford Gorge offers a spectacularly lovely walk through overhanging woods beside the river.

Manaton, St Winifred   **2 F3**
12m SW of Exeter on B3344. In a moorland village, the rock pillar, Bowerman's

Nose, in sight, tors and Iron Age hill-forts close by, and surrounded by the granite that helped build the 15thC church. The stair-turreted tower has obelisk pinnacles. An ancient cross stands near the W gate of the footpath through the churchyard. Faces of the saints on the bottom of the lovely, coloured rood screen of c1500 were probably removed in the 16thC purge of images in churches, instigated by Edward VI. The central doorway is unusually decorated with statuettes. A storm in 1779 damaged the church and probably destroyed the medieval glass, of which four figures remain, in the N aisle. **P**. *Open approx 09.00–dusk Mon–Sat, 09.30–dusk Sun.*

Molland, St Mary the Virgin   **2 F5**
5m NE of South Molton off A361. A pleasingly stark, whitewashed Georgian interior, untouched by Victorian gothicising fervour. Wide Perpendicular arches lead through to the N aisle, where the three-decker pulpit stands, an angel trumpeting from the sounding board. Box pews fill nave and aisle. The Royal Arms and the Ten Commandments loom large and authoritatively above the chancel screen. There are 17thC and 18thC mural monuments to the Courtneys, who lived at West Molland, 1m W. **P**. *Open daylight hours daily.*

Ottery St Mary, St Mary   **3 G4**
9m E of Exeter on B3174. Bishop Grandisson of Exeter rebuilt the church in the 14thC, although the towers over the transepts, in imitation of Exeter Cathedral, are 13thC, one with a lead spire. There is great grandeur in the diversity and complexity of vaulting throughout the church; most astonishing and daring are the curved patterns of the chancel vault, and most elaborate the

St Mary, Ottery St Mary

early 16thC Dorset Aisle with fan-vaulting and pendants. Don't miss the beautiful roof bosses in the Lady Chapel, the splendid reredos, the 14thC parclose screens, the gilded wooden eagle lectern, given by Grandisson, and the misericords. There is much 19thC stained glass, and wonderful 14thC canopied tombs on opposite sides of the nave to Otho de Grandisson, d1358, the bishop's brother, and his wife, d1374, burgeoning with decoration. Other interesting monuments; a fascinating 14thC clock in the S transept. **P.** *Open daylight hours daily.*

Paignton, St John the Baptist   **3** G2
A large medieval church of red sandstone, with a striking portal from a Norman predecessor, whose columns are striped red and white. The N door has a small door at the bottom for expelling unruly dogs. Bishop Lacy, Henry V's chaplain at the Battle of Agincourt, built the chancel windows and the top part of the tower. The 15thC Kirkham Chantry is of immense lavishness in its treatment. Sculptured saints, apostles and mourners, headless as a result of Tudor or puritan fervour, cluster round two tombs with effigies. Crowning the fan-vaulted, arched canopies with pendants are pinnacles and angels who have kept their heads. A rather noisome monument of a decomposing corpse is in the S aisle. Of further interest are the 15thC stone pulpit with figures and protuberant foliage, and the scratches round the outside of the N chancel door, made by sharpening arrows for archery practice in the churchyard. *Open 09.00–17.30 Mon, Tue & Fri, from 07.30 Wed, from 08.00 Thur & Sat, 07.30–19.00 Sun.* Part of Torbay, Paignton is a popular seaside resort.

South Tawton, St Andrew   **2** F4
3m E of Okehampton off A30. The thatched medieval Church House and the lychgate form a fine composition with the large Perpendicular granite church. The nave has white Beer stone arches, while angels and bosses decorate the beautiful wagon roof. In 1563, the 'Hedwarden was excommunicated because the rode lofte was not taken down', following Elizabeth I's edict of 1559 that they should be. See the delightful 18thC oak pulpit, inlaid with figures and foliage. **P.** *Open 08.00–dusk daily.* Stone crosses in the parish, at Oxenham, Ringhole Copse, Addiscott and Moon's Cross, may mark the spots where early Christian missionaries preached before churches were built.

Tavistock, St Eustachius   **2** E3
Enlarged and partly rebuilt in the 15thC, when the cloth trade flourished on the fleeces of Dartmoor sheep. The unusual second S aisle, the Clothworkers' Aisle, was added by the widow of a wealthy wool merchant. In the E window of the N aisle are vivacious figures in a stained glass window by William Morris, 1876, above a tomb chest with effigies of John Fitz, d1590, his wife and kneeling son. The Glanville monument in the Lady Chapel is a much more powerful composition because the faces convey a strong sense of character and personality; John Glanville, d1600, reclines in judge's robes and his wife kneels on the floor facing the altar. Their children have unfortunately mostly lost their heads. The font is the one in which it is believed Sir Francis Drake, Armada victor and circumnavigator of the world, was baptised. The arched doorways in the tower, whose base is part of a church dedicated in 1318, formed the entrance to a medieval abbey, of which scant remains are visible. **P.** *Open 09.00–19.00 Mon–Sat, 07.30–19.30 Sun.* Picturesque market town with a Victorian flavour in its municipal buildings.

Wembury, St Werburgh   **2** E2
1m S of Plymouth off A379. The church stands dramatically on the cliff edge, facing out to sea. The plainness of tower and church contributes to the drama of their position. The chief ornaments within are two 17thC monuments; that to Sir John Hele, d1608, shows him propped up on one elbow, his wife recumbent, and small daughter on a chair by her feet. Four lions support the great marble sarcophagus on which Lady Narborough, d1678, kneels at a prie-dieu. **P.** *Open summer 09.30–19.00 Mon–Sat, 07.30–19.45 Sun; Oct–Easter to 16.30.*

Widecombe-in-the-Moor, St Pancras   **2** F3
16m SW of Exeter off B3212. Poetically named place, inseparable from the song recording the visit of Uncle Tom Cobley and all to Widecombe Fair. In a glorious sequestered valley, enfolded by Dartmoor and creating a delightful picture with the village green and the square with Church House on its N side. The tall, majestic, early 16thC tower stands in prominent contrast to the modest church, and was probably built by prosperous tin miners, whose symbol of three rabbits with three ears forming a triangle appears on a boss above the communion rails. Inspect the early 16thC paintings of saints on what

remains of the rood screen and the quaint verses by the village school master, describing a great storm in 1638, when lightning struck and toppled a pinnacle during the service, killing some present. Limited **P**. *Open 09.00–18.00 daily.*

St Pancras, Widecombe-in-the-Moor

Woodbury, St Swithun   **3** G3
4m SE of Exeter on B3170. Gargoyles peer down from the tower, which was added to a 13thC church and consecrated in 1409. Note the four faces carved on the capital of the pillar opposite the S door, in the fine N aisle arcade. The Chantry Chapel has medieval stained glass in its E window and a hatchment with the arms of the Drake family on its W wall, commemorating a descendant of the famous Elizabethan seaman and navigator, Sir Francis Drake, whose family lived in the parish from the 18thC to 1938. Look out for the remarkable Jacobean altar rails and font rails of fluted columns, the substantial font with a delightful cover and the restored rood screen, regilded by Herbert Read in 1964. The angel trumpeting from the summit of the organ case once did so from the pulpit's sounding board. The churchwardens' accounts make a fascinating summation of the vicissitudes churches underwent in Tudor times, with Henry VIII's commissioners stealing everything removeable, the boy king Edward VI having the altars replaced by communion tables, and sisters Mary and Elizabeth putting up altars and images and taking them down again, respectively, until the great dynasty seems engaged in nothing but a family squabble. **P**. *Open approx 08.00–20.00 daily.* Woodbury Common and the seaside nearby.

◁ SOMERSET ▷

Axbridge, St John the Baptist   **4** H5
3m NW of Cheddar on A371. The church is in a prominent position in the small Mendips town and has a fine tower, beautifully fan-vaulted inside. The nave's azure and white plaster ceiling of 1636, with elaborate pendants, is a glorious expression of Jacobean decoration, with a hint of Gothic in the cusps. The local craftsman who made it was paid 10 guineas. Spot the gathering of angel busts under the lovely 15thC font. The monument to Anne Prowse, d1668, has interesting half-mermaid, half-angel figures either side. There are wood panelled roofs in the aisles, Victorian screens, a magnificent three-tiered candelabrum of 1729, and an altar frontal embroidered over seven years by the Bishop of Wells' daughter c1710. **P**. *Open 09.00–18.00 or dusk daily.* The link between the Elizabethan house in the town called King John's Hunting Lodge and that king is tenuous, but it seems that he hunted from here.

Bridgwater, St Mary the Virgin   **3** H5
The church has an early 14thC tower, climbed by the ill-fated Duke of Monmouth, Charles II's illegitimate son, who was proclaimed king in Bridgwater and routed at Sedgemoor. The exquisite stone spire is of the late 14thC, and the church mainly Decorated and Perpendicular, with much remarkable window tracery. Balconies open into the church from the upper storeys of the porches. The lovely chancel roof is Perpendicular and the nave roof Victorian. The S transept has a Jacobean screen of great character and benches of the same period behind. There is a beautiful 15thC pulpit and a 17thC painting forms the altarpiece. **P**. *Open 08.30–17.30 Mon–Fri, to 16.30 Sat; 07.30–20.00 Sun.*

Bruton, St Mary the Virgin 4 J5

7m SE of Shepton Mallet on B3081. An impressive two-towered church. The N tower is a modest, 14thC structure and the 15thC W tower soars in splendid contrast, with pinnacled buttresses and window shafts, and battlemented parapet with quatrefoils, shields and roses. There is a 14thC crypt below the 18thC classical-style chancel, a 15thC nave and a lavishly detailed 16thC Somerset king-post roof. Discover the recumbent effigies of a 16thC gent and his two wives in the chancel and the Royal Arms of Charles II over the N door. Both he and Charles I stayed in Bruton and worshipped here. **P** nearby. *Open 08.00–19.00 Mon–Wed, Fri & Sat, to 18.00 Thur & Sun.* A picturesque packhorse bridge crosses the river Brue opposite the W end of the churchyard, and there are remains of a medieval abbey wall and the abbey's grand dovecote close by.

Cheddar, St Andrew 4 J5

Roman bricks were used in the tall, graceful Perpendicular tower, embellished by Somerset-style pierced parapets and pinnacles, as is the N side of the church. The nave has a moulded oak roof and a beautiful 15thC painted stone pulpit, with canopied niches and angel busts underneath. In the chancel are brasses of Sir Thomas de Cheddre, d1442, and Lady Isabel, his wife, d1474. 15thC stained glass in the St Nectan Chapel includes the Annunciation and arms of local families, and the 17thC altar painting is by Jan Erasmus Quellinus. Look out for the pre-Reformation bench ends in the N aisle, illustrating the sin of gossiping by two interlaced tongues and that of deceit by three faces. **P**. *Open daylight hours daily.* Cheddar is famous for the spectacular, fossil-encrusted gorge, cut into the limestone of the Mendips.

Chewton Mendip, St Mary Magdalene 4 J5

12m S of Bristol on A39. A breathtaking tower, at 126ft one of the highest in the county and a century in the building, from 1440–c1541, when the antiquarian Leland commented on the 'goodly new high tourred steple'. It has features in common with the tower of St Andrew at Mells and with that of St John at Glastonbury. On its W face a statue of Christ is attended by censer-swinging angels and seraphim with feathered legs. The church is Norman and later medieval with Victorian improvements, not all of which are felicitous. Fascinatingly, some

of the medieval stained glass in the N window of the chancel was found by a pedlar in a ditch near Glastonbury earlier this century. See too the effigies of a 14thC knight and lady and the Jacobean lectern. **P**. *Open 07.45–dusk daily.* 4m away is spectacular, fossil-encrusted Cheddar Gorge.

Crewkerne, St Bartholomew 3 J4

The imposing, castellated W front has a remarkable doorway with an ogee gable and busts of unknown figures either side, illustrated by Thomas Rowlandson, c1800. In the SE angle of the S transept is a curious seat, older than the rest of the church, whose purpose is unknown. It is conjectured that it was a bishop's seat for the settlement of disputes, or a memorial to an anchorite. Anchorites are known to have lived in cells in the churchyard later, because in 1523 a curate left to the 'ancresse of Crookehorn 40d and a pair of sheets and to the Ermyt 3s.4d. and a pair of sheets'. Exceptionally large windows fill the aisles and N transept. The latter is lavishly decorated and has a rare stone oven, once used for baking bread for the Eucharist. Note the wonderful display of the Perpendicular style made by transept, aisle and nave. **P**. *Open 07.30–17.30 Mon, Thur & Fri, to 19.15 Wed & Sat; 08.45–17.30 Tue; 07.30–16.30 Sun, to 19.00 summer.*

St Bartholomew, Crewkerne

Croscombe, St Mary the Virgin 4 J5

2m E of Wells on A361. The stone steeple soars above the attractive river valley village of stone cottages. Rebuilt in the 15thC and 16thC under the aegis of the Lord of the Manor, Sir William Palton, whose arms of six roses are on two of the wagon roof bosses. Bosses reflecting the importance of the early weaving industry in the village include one of a clothier with a roll of cloth spread round him. The unusual barred treasury was used as a parish armoury and lock-up at different periods. The greatest splendour of the church is in the Jacobean woodwork: the ornately carved screen and pulpit are extremely beautiful; consonant with them are readers' desks, box pews, and later chancel roof. Handsome spidery chandeliers and brasses to the Bisse family, 16thC and 17thC clothiers. *Open 08.30–19.30 daily.*

Culbone, St Beuno 2 F5
7m E of Lynton off A39. In a still glade, beside a stream, and with a view of the sea, the church is claimed to be the smallest complete church in England. Its origins are 12thC, although tradition holds that Culbone was a spiritual centre before the time of Christ, and that Christ came here. It has an anchorite's cell, medieval rood screen and benches, quaint slate-covered spire, rubble walls, and perfect harmony with its rural seclusion. *Open daylight hours daily.*

Curry Rivel, St Andrew 4 H4
9m E of Taunton on A378. Sabina Revel, d1254, the last of the great family which gave the village its name, is thought to be buried in one of the unusual series of 13thC tomb recesses in the N chapel, whose building she probably financed. Slender 15thC arcades, tall screens to the chapels, 16thC carved bench ends and later pews, under some of whose seats are racks for top-hats, are other notable features. There are wonderfully traceried 15thC windows on the S side of the church and a fan-vaulted porch which has on the frieze outside the portcullis of Lady Margaret Beaufort, mother of Henry VII, and the Prince of Wales' feathers. The tower, rebuilt in 1860, is very handsome, with tall bell openings. Notice the grotesques round the church, including a fiddler and a piper, known locally by the colourful name 'hunky punks'. **P**. *Open 08.15–20.00 Mon–Sat, 07.45–20.00 Sun.*

East Coker, St Michael and All Angels 3 J4
3m S of Yeovil off A37. A path of yews and cedars leads past a row of 17thC gabled almshouses, up to the golden Ham Hill stone church and Coker Court. The church dates mostly from the 13thC and 15thC; the tower was refashioned early in the 19thC. 17thC navigator and pirate, William Dampier, was baptised at the Norman font and is commemorated in a brass memorial. There is also a memorial to poet T. S. Eliot, whose ashes

were buried here at his request. His ancestors emigrated to America from the village, which he made the subject of one of his *Four Quartets* in 1940. **P**. *Open daylight hours daily.* The entire village is delightful.

Glastonbury, St John Baptist 4 J5
The 134½ft-high 15thC tower is the second tallest of any parish church in the county. It becomes more remarkable at each stage, culminating in the dazzling display of the pierced, battlemented parapet, topped by outsize pinnacles. 'A fair lightsome church' was antiquarian Leland's description of it in 1534, and this is still the effect today, created by the tall nave arcades and clerestory, with shafts on angel corbels supporting the handsome timber roof. Vestments worn by Abbot Whiting, the last abbot of Glastonbury Abbey, executed on the Tor in 1539 for refusing to accept Henry VIII's Dissolution of the Monasteries, are on display. There is some beautiful 15thC stained glass in the chancel, a fine coat of arms of Charles II, and camels carved around the tomb chest of John Camell, d1487. A Glastonbury thorn, said to have sprung from Joseph of Arimathea's staff, flourishes in the churchyard. **P**. *Open summer 08.00–20.00 daily, winter to 18.00 daily.* The legend of the Holy Grail, the tradition that Arthur and Guinevere were reburied here, the abbey ruins and the great Tor, make Glastonbury a poignant and powerful place to visit.

Huish Episcopi, St Mary the Virgin 4 H4
10m NW of Yeovil on A372. A wonderful Perpendicular tower, niches and pinnacles complementing the delicate lacy-looking tracery and friezes, which hardly look like stone at all. The large S doorway is late Norman, decorated with zigzag, and the interior 14thC and 15thC. The stained glass in the E window of the S chapel is of 1899 by Morris & Co, designed by Burne-Jones, and shows the adoration of the magi, resplendent with attendant angels. **P**. *Open daylight hours daily.*

Ilminster, St Mary 4 H4
Silver St. A cathedral-type, cruciform Perpendicular church of great beauty, built in golden Ham Hill stone. The surface of the heart-lifting tower is variegated with traceried and shafted bell openings, and a pinnacled and battlemented top. See the fan-vault and panelled arches that support it inside. 19thC and 20thC alterations raised the

nave and aisle roofs. The Wadham Chapel is resplendent with light pouring through its many windows, and contains fine, early 17thC brasses of the founders of Wadham College, Oxford. 15thC Wadhams are also represented in brass. **P** nearby. *Open 07.00–18.00 Mon–Thur & Sat, to 20.00 Fri; 07.30–19.30 Sun.*

Isle Abbotts, St Mary the Virgin   **4 H4**
9m E of Taunton off A378. A magnificent tower with many of the Somerset features, as well as strong individual characteristics, and with niches retaining their statues. The beautifully proportioned chancel is of c1300 and has lovely, elaborated lancet windows and richly panelled piscina and sedilia. Outstanding Perpendicular details include the fan-vault in the S porch. The church has a restored barrel organ. **P.** *Open 09.00–dusk daily.*

Martock, All Saints   **4 J4**
6m NW of Yeovil on B3165. A golden Ham Hill stone church, whose lancet-windowed E end is 13thC, while the major part was built in the 15thC, partly through the prosperity of the cloth trade. A glorious tie-beam nave roof was added in 1513, embellished with traceried panels, angels and pendants. Below it are elaborately canopied niches, in which figures of the apostles were painted during the 17thC. Outside, near the N porch, cemented notches in a damaged buttress were one-time footholds for climbing up onto the roof to retrieve balls when fives was played below. A piece of masonry having struck a bystander on the head, the churchwardens stopped the game, and in their accounts for 1758 is an entry 'For digging up ye Fives place 3 6d.' **P.** *Open 07.00–dusk Mon–Sat, 07.30–19.30 Sun.* Among fine houses in the village is the medieval Treasurer's House.

Mells, St Andrew   **4 K5**
2m W of Frome off A362. Beside the restored Elizabethan manor house in a delightful village of grey and yellow stone cottages, wreathed by trees and lawns. The splendid 15thC tower is distinguished among Somerset towers by its triple windows at two stages and the buttress pinnacles peeping above the parapet to meet the large corner pinnacles. Every three hours one of four tunes is chimed, among them the ancient Mells Tune. See the elaborate and unusual S porch and polygonal vestry, the gift of a London draper called Garland in 1485. 19thC restoration altered

a number of features of the interior. The Horner Chapel has its original roof, an equestrian monument by Sir Alfred Munnings and E window by Sir William Nicholson. Near the church entrance is a large piece of embroidery by the lady of the manor, Mrs Horner, to a Burne-Jones design. A 16thC Horner, John, is connected with Jack Horner of the nursery rhyme on very flimsy grounds; through marriage the Asquiths now own the manor. A peacock perched above an empty tomb forms a memorial to Laura Lyttleton, d1886, by Burne-Jones, and in the churchyard are buried Roman Catholic theologian Ronald Knox, d1957, who lived in the manor, and First World War poet Siegfrid Sassoon. *Open daylight hours daily.*

St Andrew, Mells

Minehead, St Michael and   **3 G5**
All Angels
Church St. On a hillside with wide, refreshing views over the bay and up to Exmoor. Most splendid is the rood screen across nave and aisle, with lovely foliage friezes and much finely carved detail. The octagonal font has the charming feature of figures seated on a ledge at the foot of the bowl, legs dangling. Two angels help support the Elizabethan communion table in the N chapel. See the early 15thC effigy of a priest holding a chalice, under a fine, gabled canopy and the brass to a lady with high headware. **P.** *Open 09.00–18.00 Mon–Thur & Sat, from 07.30 Fri & Sun.*

St Michael and All Angels, Minehead

North Cadbury, St Michael the Archangel   **4 J5**

7m NE of Yeovil off A303. The finely proportioned Perpendicular church and the Elizabethan manor house beside it, built of the same grey stone, form a beautiful composition. The Botreaux family built the church early in the 15thC, except for the tower, paid for by the rector a few years earlier. Lady Elizabeth applied to make it a college of seven chaplains, and although it never became one, the loftiness of the magnificent chancel reflects the fact it was built to accommodate the clergy. Her effigy, 1433, wearing horned headdress, can be seen on a fine tomb-chest, together with that of Lord Botreaux, d1391. In the W window are saints in 15thC stained glass. Numerous subjects carved on the 16thC bench ends include a flute-player, a packhorse and a cat with mouse and mousetrap. The alphabet is painted in old-fashioned letters on the wall of the vestry, which must have been used as a schoolroom. Note the symmetry of the two-storeyed N and S porches, panelled above the doorways and vaulted inside. **P.** *Open 08.30–dusk daily.* Not far off is the Iron Age camp of Cadbury Castle, on a steep, grassy hill with impressive earth ramparts, thought to be the site of King Arthur's Camelot.

North Curry, St Peter and St Paul   **4 H4**

6m E of Taunton off A378. Handsome houses line the approach to the 13thC–15thC church, set in a large, well-kept churchyard, with extensive views on the N side. The octagonal tower is immediately eye-catching. Its base is of c1300 and upper stages Perpendicular. The fan-vaulted S porch, with niches over the doorway, shares its impressive elaboration with the whole of the S side. There is a Norman doorway on the N side, but fewer outstanding external features. A spacious interior with 14thC nave arcades. *Open by 08.00–dusk daily.*

Norton St Philip, St Philip and St James   **4 K5**

3m S of Bath on A36. Jeffrey Flower, a rich citizen of Norton, who died in 1644, is believed to have built the tower and much of the church according to his own design, with resulting idiosyncratic variations of the county characteristics in the tower especially – including big windows at the ground-stage. The church has much interesting detail, including a wagon roof in the porch, tower vault with a very large opening for the bellropes and three screens. **P.** *Open 08.30–dusk Mon–Sat, from 07.30 Sun.* In the picturesque village are the ancient George and Fleur-de-Lys inns and, nearby, a Tudor dovecote.

Oare, St Mary   **2 F5**

5½m E of Lynton off A39. A small, quaint building with a tower rebuilt, and chancel extended, in the 19thC. The wagon roofs are medieval, and the pulpit, box pews and reading desk pleasing 18thC work. In the old part of the chancel, W of the screen, is the window through which Carver Doone shot Lorna at her wedding. *Open daylight hours daily.* R. D. Blackmore used the tradition of a 17thC band of outlaws on Exmoor for the romantic story of *Lorna Doone* and associations are strong here in the Doone valley.

Old Cleeve, St Andrew   **3 G5**

1m SW of Watchet on B3191. John Tucker left money in his will of 1533 for building the impressive tower, and also his 'tokers shers' (the tools of his cloth-finishing trade). The church is largely 15thC and incorporates some earlier work. See the wagon roof in the nave, the brass lectern of 1911 in Arts and Crafts style, the 18thC chandelier, the E window stained glass by Comper, 1953, and that in the E window of the S aisle by Morris & Co. A large heart of cobbles lies in the porch floor together with the cobbled date 1614. **P.** *Open daylight hours daily.* On Exmoor's edge, near picturesque Dunster and

Cleeve Abbey ruins, whose refectory, rebuilt in the 16thC, has a wonderful wagon roof.

Porlock, St Dubricius 3 G5
5m W of Minehead on A39. Dubricius was a 6thC celtic missionary from Wales, thought to have founded the first church here. Romantic legend describes him as an adviser of King Arthur, who summoned him to solemnise his marriage to Guinevere. The present church is mainly 13thC–15thC and has a curiously truncated shingled spire, supposed to have been higher until damaged in a great gale of 1703. See the impressive 15thC Harington monument, with alabaster effigies of a knight who served Henry V in France, and his wife. **P**. *Open 09.00–18.00 or dusk daily*. Famous for the 'person' who interrupted Coleridge's composition of *Kubla Khan*, Porlock is beautifully situated between wild Exmoor and the sea, at the head of the Vale of Porlock; an enchanting spot nearby is Porlock Weir, a hidden quay with whitewashed cottages.

Selworthy, All Saints 3 G5
3m W of Minehead off A39. There are wonderful, panoramic views of Exmoor and Dunkery Beacon from the porch, and the thatched cottages around the green are very pretty. A Perpendicular church. The S aisle of 1538 has outstandingly beautiful window tracery and a gloriously decorated wagon roof. The fine S door-way has a linenfold-panelled door. There are a classical-style 18thC W gallery, a delightful early 19thC pew for the squire above the porch and locally carved pew ends. **P**. *Open 09.00–dusk daily*.

Shepton Mallet, St Peter and St Paul 4 J5
Peter St. Immediately on entering one feels like paying homage to the amazing and memorable 15thC wagon roof, of 350 carved panels and over 300 bosses, each one different and creating overall a floral effect. The 14thC tower is an early example of the Somerset type. A spire was planned for it but not completed. There are rough Norman nave piers and a Saxon font. The aisles were extended in the 19thC and the chancel rebuilt. Renaissance motifs such as cornucopia decorate the 16thC stone pulpit. Foliage and a trumpet-blowing angel ornament the 18thC organ case. Good monuments. **P**. *Open 08.45–dusk Mon–Thur & Sat, from 07.30 Fri; 08.00–19.30 Sun*. An interesting town with the market place and 15thC shambles at its heart.

Stogursey, St Andrew 3 H5
7m NW of Bridgwater off A39. A spacious church, whose tower has an early Norman origin, a 19thC parapet and a slated spire. The E end was a priory church from the 12thC until the priory's suppression early in the 15thC. The capitals of the tower arches have fascinating carvings of animals, leaves and a face, and the arches of the 12thC chancel aisles make a spectacular display of Norman zigzag. The nave was refashioned early in the 15thC. See the 16thC bench ends carved with vines, birds and other lively designs and good 17thC and 18thC monuments, attended by cherubs and putti. **P**. *Open daylight hours daily*.

St Andrew, Stogursey

Stoke St Gregory, St Gregory 3 H5
6m S of Bridgwater off A361. An octagonal tower, whose lower part is of c1300 and top 15thC, with a small, delightful stone spire. The earliest bell, of 1628, has the inscription 'First I call to wake you all'. The chancel is diminutive compared with the tall 15thC nave arcades and clerestory. Figures of Faith, Hope, Charity and Time are carved on the Jacobean pulpit, their corresponding symbols below. Examine the panelling on the 14thC font and the screen to the choir vestry, with carvings of the five wise virgins. There are stocks under an ancient yew in the churchyard. **P**. *Open morn–18.00 Mon–Sat, to 19.45 Sun*.

Taunton, St Mary Magdalene 3 H4
Church Sq. The church has a most remarkable and fine tower, the highest in Somerset, 163ft to the tips of its pinnacles, with three tiers of twin windows, blossoming with Somerset tracery, an extended, pierced parapet and attenuated corner pinnacles. It was built at the beginning of the 16thC and rebuilt

in exact replica in 1858–62. Outstanding too is the S porch dated 1508, adorned with statues in niches and a star-vault inside. Unusually, the 15thC–16thC church has double aisles, incorporating a 13thC arcade; there is a fine Tudor nave roof, its carvings gilded in 1968, angel capitals on the nave pillars and statue niches above, lovely fan-vaulting under the tower, a delicately traceried 19thC font and 19thC pulpit and reredos. **P**. *Open daylight hours daily*. Taunton is one of the great agricultural market towns of the west with a politically colourful past.

Trull, All Saints   3 H4
1½m SW of Taunton off A38. The medieval church is outstanding for its wood carving in the surviving parts of the rood screen, the roof bosses, bench ends and pulpit. Especially interesting are the pulpit with its figures of St John the Evangelist and doctors of the church, and the rustically carved figures on the bench ends, which would form a procession were they not separated. Panelling at the back is inscribed with the date 1560 and the name of a wood carver, Simon Warman. 15thC stained glass includes the Dragon Window, in which St Michael, St Margaret and St George each slay a dragon. Under a churchyard yew are the village stocks. *Open 09.00–20.00 or dusk Mon–Sat, 08.00–20.00 Sun*.

Watchet, St Decuman   3 G5
On a hill behind the small harbour. A colourful legend surrounds the patron saint: a celtic missionary, Decuman, sailed here on a raft; after a life of devotion he was beheaded by his enemies, picked up his head and washed it in the spring to the W of the church, still a venerated site. The church is Perpendicular with a 13thC chancel, lovely wagon roofs on angel supports and with carved wall-plates and bosses, and an impressive array of 16thC and 17thC brasses and monuments to the Wyndhams. Note too the fine carving on the 17thC pew in the Wyndham Chapel and the unusual niches in the nave pillars, complete with statues in some cases. **P**. *Open 09.00–dusk daily*.

Wedmore, St Mary   4 H5
8m W of Wells on B3139. A very impressive and large 15thC church, incorporating earlier building, including a fine S doorway of c1200. This has a door with the date 1677 nailed on, although the ironwork on it is earlier. The 16thC wall painting of St Christopher, above the ornate Jacobean pulpit, is imposed on a 15thC painting of the same subject, in which the head of the Christ child can be seen. Ships, fishes and mermaids congregate below. A brass tablet by the N door commemorates the thousandth anniversary of King Alfred's death, a reminder that the peace treaty of 878 between Alfred and the Danes was concluded at Wedmore. **P**. *Open daylight hours daily*.

Wells, St Cuthbert   4 J5
St Cuthbert St. The largest parish church in Somerset, its tower one of the tallest, with bell-openings which reflect the style of those in Wells Cathedral's W towers. Perpendicular magnificence is equally the portion of tower and church. The 13thC core had a crossing tower which collapsed in 1561. The nave pillars of that building were heightened by the later masons. See the vault and bosses under the tower and vast tower arch, the tie-beam nave roof, beautifully carved 17thC pulpit, and the remains of fine 15thC reredoses in the transepts. **P**. *Open daylight hours daily*. Nearby are the wonders of Wells Cathedral, built 12thC–14thC, and the medieval and later moated Bishop's Palace, complete with swans who have inherited the trick of ringing a bell for food from their Victorian ancestors.

◁ AVON ▷

Bath, Abbey   4 K6
There was a Saxon abbey on the site, in which Edgar was crowned first king of all England in 973. Bishop King, Henry VII's secretary, started to build the existing church in 1499, following a dream of angels going up and down a heavenly ladder, which image was transferred onto buttresses on the W front, forming an exquisite decoration, as does the spectacularly carved W door of 1617. The exterior is altogether imposing, with its declamatory pinnacles, handsome pierced parapets and flying buttresses. The church was not completed by the Dissolution and the splendid fan-vaults

inside are of different periods; the nave's is of the 19thC. Meet fashionable, Georgian Bath in the wealth of memorial busts and portraits assembled here. Sad to say, there is no representation of Beau Nash, d1761, arbiter of 18thC fashion, under whose patronage Bath rose to be the queen of English spas, merely an inscribed tablet in the S aisle. Look into Prior Bird's richly carved Chantry Chapel. *Open summer 09.00–19.00 Mon-Sat, winter to 16.30; 08.00–19.45 Sun.* The elegant Pump Room is a few paces away, the Roman baths are close by; the Assembly Rooms, redolent of the pleasure or discomforture of Jane Austen heroines, are a healthy stride away and house the Museum of Costume, which includes in its comprehensive display Byron's Albanian dress. All around is one of the finest Georgian cities in England, with matchless Bath stone terraces and crescents and beautiful public gardens.

Bristol, All Saints   **4** J6
Corn St. Norman becomes Perpendicular part-way down the nave, in pillars and arches. The early 18thC tower is topped by a cupola inspired by Wren, which was rebuilt in 1930. Putti gather round the memorial to Sarah Colston, d1701; that to Edward Colston, d1721, has a very striking, reclining figure of him by Rysbrack, his thoughts clearly intent on performing more of the philanthropic deeds for which he was famous. An imposing classical design, by Gibbs, frames a list of them above. *Open 07.30–16.30 Mon-Fri.* Bristol's port flourished most at the end of the 14thC and in the 15thC, trading in wool and cloth. Heavily bombed in the Second World War, it remains a city of charm and character, with its great cathedral, founded in 1140 as an abbey church, of which the Chapter House is renowned, the elegant suburb of Clifton and Brunel's wonderful Suspension Bridge, completed in 1864 and looking as if it has just been gracefully thrown across the gorge.

Bristol, Christ Church with St Ewen **4** J6
Broad St. In the heart of the city, the church was rebuilt by Bristol architect, William Paty, and its opening in 1791 was celebrated in a ball at the White Lion, then adjoining the church. Brought from the earlier church were the dragon vane on the spire, the Quarter Jacks of 1728, the Renatus Harris organ and fine case and the Lord Mayor's sword rest. The influence of Gibbs and Wren is

visible in the steeple and lovely white and gold domed interior. The delightful rood screen, with golden garlands twisting round white columns, formed the reredos, until Tractarian tendencies brought about its replacement by the more Gothic one in 1882. Admire the charming altar table of 1790 and the handsome hanging Art Nouveau plaque of St Michael killing the dragon. Poet Robert Southey, whose father was churchwarden, was baptised here. *Open 07.30–20.00 Mon-Fri, 09.00–17.00 Sat, 09.00–20.00 Sun.*

St Mary Redcliffe, Bristol

Bristol, St Mary Redcliffe   **4** J
Redcliffe Hill. It is touching that the church dubbed by Elizabeth I in 1574, 'the fairest, goodliest, and most famous parish church in England', includes among its remarkable features a tomb to the church cat, who was resident from 1912–27. The church was built between the early 13thC-15thC on the Avon bank's red cliffs, when Redcliffe was inhabited by wealthy merchants. The exterior is magnificent, and the interior an amazing, awesome sight, arches and pillars soaring in exquisite slenderness and grace to the ribbed vaults, which are studded with more than 1,200 bosses, each different. These were covered in pure gold c1740, when Bristol women

gave their jewellery for melting down. The fabulous hexagonal N porch, with extremely elaborate ornamentation, including much knobbly foliage, and an astonishingly ornate doorway with a hint of the orient in it, was built to crown a shrine to Our Lady within. Thomas Chatterton, 1752–70, who poisoned himself in desperation at his poverty, wrote poetry in the treasury over the porch. Coleridge's *Monody on the Death of Chatterton* laments, 'Poor Chatterton! *he* sorrows for thy fate, Who would have prais'd and lov'd thee, ere too late'. The American Chapel contains a ship's figurehead of Elizabeth I, and many fragments of medieval glass make up a window. The tomb of William Penn senior is in the S transept; his son William founded Pennsylvania. The whale rib brought back by the Cabots, who sailed from Redcliffe Harbour in 1497 and discovered Newfoundland, is under the tower. See the Royal Arms of Charles II, gorgeously coloured and framed, the two effigies of William Canynges, merchant of vast wealth, who restored the church after the spire was struck by lightning in 1446, the tombstone of his cook, with knife and colander on it, the rather fierce eagle lectern of 1638 and a brass in the chancel, showing a headdress just like that worn by a playing card queen. **P** nearby. *Open summer 09.00–20.00 daily, winter to 18.00 Mon-Sat, to 20.00 Sun.*

Chelvey, St Bridget   **4 J6**
6m SW of Bristol off A370. A lovely, small church in a pastoral setting, its tower crowned by a pretty, pierced parapet and corner pinnacles. Enter through the Norman S doorway and note the venerable benches to the left. The chancel of c1300 has a handsome 14thC E window with fragments of old stained

St Bridget, ancient benches

glass at the top, and a fine 16thC stone reredos surrounding a Victorian panel. Very tall image niches are either side. A 13thC knight with lance and sword is incised on a slab under the altar table in the early 17thC Tynte Chapel, where, too, are more ancient benches and the squire's carved Jacobean pew. The ogee-gabled recesses and piscina in the S aisle are 15thC. **P**. *Open daylight hours daily.*

Chew Magna, St Andrew   **4 J6**
4m S of Bristol on B3130. The august tower has pinnacles and parapet and gargoyles for its guardians. There is Norman stonework round the S doorway, a 13thC S aisle and 15thC N aisle. The beautifully carved medieval rood screen was restored in the 19thC. In the N chapel are 15thC effigies of Sir John and Lady St Lo and memorials to their descendents, the Stracheys, including one to Lytton Strachey, famous for his irreverent and idiosyncratic portraits of *Eminent Victorians*. The wooden effigy of a knight in 14thC armour is in a most incongruous position, as if practising a bizarre yoga posture – causing the lion on which his foot rests to sit upright instead of couchant as heraldry demands – which however occasions him no displeasure as he smiles inscrutably. The inscription on the tomb is in Victorian Gothic lettering throwing the knight's identity into doubt. Is he indeed the true Sir John de Hauteville that tradition claims? **P**. *Open daylight hours daily.* Chew Court adjacent, was once an episcopal palace and is now a private house. The early 16thC Church Ale House, at the churchyard's entrance, was used for parish festivities. Enjoy strolling round this red sandstone village of pretty Georgian houses and old inns, near the Mendip Hills. Not far off is Stanton Drew, circled by rings of prehistoric stones, and Hauteville's Quoit, which the mysterious Sir John of the effigy is said to have hurled into its present position.

Clevedon, St Andrew   **4 H6**
Old Church Rd. A romantically sited headland church with a late Norman crossing tower, which has a spectacular E arch inside, thick with lozenge and zigzag decoration. The S and W arches were altered later and are much taller. Unusually, the pillars of the 14thC S arcade have no capitals. The clerestory was added in the 15thC. Tennyson's bosom friend, Arthur Hallam, who died at 22, is buried in the church. His death

St Andrew, Clevedon

inspired Tennyson's great narrative threnody, *In Memoriam*. **P**. *Open Jul, Aug, Sep 14.00–16.00 Sun if guide available, or by arrangement*. Clevedon is a pleasant seaside resort with a 19thC profile. Close by is Clevedon Court, a medieval manor house with later alterations and beautiful 18thC terraced gardens. Thackeray stayed here while writing *Vanity Fair*. Visit the striking upstairs chapel.

**Compton Martin, St Michael   4 J6
and All Angels**
9m S of Bristol on A368. A fascinating Norman church, with one of its nave pillars twisted like a piece of barley sugar, very distinctive among its smooth companions, with whom it has in common a scalloped capital. The small and low rib-vaulted chancel is a very moving sight. See the Norman font and clerestory and the carved bosses on the N aisle roof. Perpendicular alterations and additions were made, including the aisle windows and the tower, which has diagonal pinnacled shafts at one stage. On the church's N side Norman monsters parade on the corbel table. **P**. *Open 10.00–18.00 Mon-Fri, 11.00–17.00 Sat & Sun*.

Iron Acton, St James the Less   4 J6
'Here lyeth Robert Poyntzs Lord of Iren Acton and thys stepyl maked', is inscribed on a slab of 1439 in the Poyntz Chapel, and is thought to refer to the church or churchyard cross, as the tower was built earlier. Other monuments to the medieval lords of the manor include incised slabs to Robert Poyntz's two wives, effigies of a knight and well-

dressed lady, and a fine 16thC canopied tomb. There are 16thC benches with linenfold carving on their ends, a beautiful brass candelabra of 1725, a pulpit of 1624, its sounding board delightfully carved, Communion rails erected in compliance with Archbishop Laud's order, and, in the restored chancel, a king, a pope and a bishop in stained glass, a marble and mosaic pavement, and a vividly coloured reredos designed by F. C. Eden in 1928. Eden also made the screen in classical style behind the S altar. The statue of Our Lady of Altotting was given in 1972 by a Bavarian convent of an order founded by Mary Poyntz in the 17thC. The former parish lock-up is in the tower, and the 15thC memorial cross is an impressive feature of the churchyard. The substantial tower has the singular presence looking over its N parapet of an effigy of half a knight, which was once whole and recumbent. **P**. *Open 07.00–19.00 Mon & Tue, from 09.00 Wed, from 08.30 Fri, from 08.00 Sat; 06.30–21.00 Thur, 07.15–20.00 Sun*. Picturesque village.

Keynsham, St John the Baptist   4 J6
The majestic tower with distinctive parapet and pinnacles was built in 1634, following a brief from no less a personage than Charles I, pleading for funds for the church, 'most lamentably ruinated by . . . Tempestuous weather . . . with hideous Clapps of Thunder and flashes of Lightning (which) in a moment threw down the Steeple'. The 13thC chancel with lancet windows is the oldest part, and the remainder of the church was completed by 1470. Look out for the lovely 15thC screen between chancel and S aisle, whose decoration includes a row of golden suns, the Carolean pulpit, and two interesting monuments to the Bridges, who lived in a mansion built on the abbey ruins, which was demolished in 1776. That to Sir Thomas Bridges, d1661, has a thin, regal effigy and a substantial angel looking down from chunky clouds. The church has an offertory plate inscribed, 'G. F. Handel 1750', and it is thought the musician stayed with the Bridges. He may also have given a bell which charmingly declares, 'Altho' my voice it is but small – I will be heard amongst you all'. The abbey was founded in the 12thC, to the E of the church, and suffered a lapse in discipline after the plague of 1348, when the Bishop instructed, 'the Canons are

not to play at dice with the laity'. It was dissolved in 1539. **P.** *Open 09.00–17.00 Mon-Wed, to 12.30 Fri, to 16.00 Sat.*

Thornbury, St Mary the Virgin **8 J7**
Castle St. The 16thC tower has a most sumptuously decorated crown, with handsome turrets and pierced parapet, forming a wonderful celebration of the mason's art. The clerestory is castellated and pinnacled and the church was largely rebuilt in the 15thC, incorporating Norman doorways. Note the unusual tracery in the S windows, the stone Perpendicular pulpit and the clawed pedestal supporting the font. **P.** *Open 08.00–18.00 daily.* Beside the Tudor castle, skilfully restored in the 19thC, with spectacular windows on the S side. The town's domestic architecture spans the centuries.

Westbury-on-Trym, Our Lady, **4 J6**
St Peter, St Paul and the
Holy Trinity
Formerly collegiate, the church is large and splendid, with a glorious outsize pinnacle on the tower's stair turret. Late in the 13thC, Godfrey Giffard, Bishop of Worcester, enlarged the early 13thC church, building the wide S aisle for the parishioners. Examine the fine sedilia and piscina here, and the foliage and heads decorating the capitals of the nave pillars. When John Carpenter was bishop in the second half of the 15thC, he built the chancel with its unusual three-sided apse, the N chapel and the tower, as well as new college buildings, of which the battlemented gatehouse tower and half one side remain in College Rd. See his monument, the top part of which was destroyed by the puritans and replaced in 1853. **P.** *Open 09.00–17.30 Mon-Sat.*

Weston-super-Mare, All Saints **4 H6**
St Joseph's Rd. An impressive late Victorian church by G. F. Bodley, 1898–1902, imitating Decorated and Perpendicular Gothic forms. The S aisle and Lady Chapel are the work of F. C. Eden, 1925. A spacious interior with boarded wagon roofs. The rood screen is by Bodley, as is the font, with a cover by W. H. R. Blacking. Bodley's pulpit was carved by Zwink of Oberammergau. Much stained glass. **P.** *Open 09.00–17.00 Mon-Sat, to 19.00 Sun.* A whole bevy of architectural styles is reflected in the Victorian terraces and crescents of this popular seaside resort, whose sands stretch for ever at low tide. For a wonderful view visit Worlebury Hill to the N, where there are remains of an Iron Age hill-fort.

Winscombe, St James the Great **4 H5**
9m SW of Bristol on A38. A gracious sight on a hillside, its august tower 100ft high, decorated with pinnacles and pierced parapet, repeated on the N side of the church, and with a pyramidally topped turret. Notable features include the original Perpendicular roofs in the chapels and N aisle, the tower vault, the font of unusual design and lovely medieval glass in the S chapel and chancel N window. In the E window is beautiful, vibrantly coloured glass by the firm William Morris and Co. **P.** *Open approx 09.00–20.00 or dusk Mon-Sat, from 07.30 Sun.*

All Saints, Wrington

Wrington, All Saints **4 J6**
4m SW of Bristol on A38. A magnificent, nobly proportioned tower, pinnacled square turrets at the top and a pierced parapet that is echoed on the aisles and clerestory. It inspired Sir Charles Barry's design for the Victoria Tower of the new Houses of Parliament in the 19thC. Peer back at the gargoyles assembled on tower and aisles. A charming feature is the sanctus bell turret on the nave's E end, which has the original bell inside. See the pretty statue niches at the E angles of the chancel and the bulbous tracery in the E window, a 19thC replica of a c1300 original. A lovely Perpendicular interior in which angels between the clerestory windows support the roof. Scrutinise the finely carved capitals on the nave pillars and the fan-vault under the tower. The *Church-Goer,* 1851, records 'A group of

private apartments, enclosed with red curtains, something like the dinner boxes of a city chop-house', which were swept away during restoration in 1859. What were the curtains for one wonders? The lovely rood screen was preserved. There is a lavishly carved Perpendicular font, a Victorian pulpit and a reredos designed by Sir Charles Barry in 1832. In the S porch, pay passing homage to the bust of John Locke, 1632–1704, philosopher and author of an *Essay concerning the Human Understanding*, born and baptised at Wrington, and to that of Hannah More, 1745–1833, writer and philanthropist. **P.** *Open 07.00–19.00 Mon-Sat, to 20.00 Sun.*

Yatton, St Mary the Virgin   **4** H6
7m SW of Bristol on A370. The octagonal, truncated spire is a curious and striking sight for miles around. The top half was taken down in 1595 and never replaced. The handsome tower has a graceful stair turret and pretty parapet. Lady Isabel de Chedder had the exuberantly ornamented S porch built in the 15thC, with foliage round the ogee-gabled doorway and a vault within. She built the Newton Chapel at the end of the 15thC to house the ornate tomb she shares with her husband who died in 1488, and still keeps an eye on the church as the ghostly Grey Lady. Built in the early 14thC, the finely proportioned

St Mary the Virgin, Yatton

nave and aisles were refashioned in the 15thC. Observe the wagon roof and the embroidered blue velvet pall made from two 15thC vestments. The Chapter House was built in 1975. There are graves in the churchyard to gipsies Merily and Isaac Joules. **P.** *Open 08.00–17.00 Mon-Sat, 09.00–19.00 Sun.*

THE
—— SOUTHERN ——
COUNTIES

Dorset Wiltshire Hampshire
Isle of Wight

We can learn something of importance about Dorset churches from the study of place names. It is remarkable how often the word 'minster' is incorporated – Beaminster, Charminster, Iwerne Minster, Sturminster Newton. These minsters were large collegiate churches which were not affiliated to any great monastic order. As a result they were not very rich and their daughter churches – the typical village churches of Dorset – are for the most part humble. In the south of the county there are the two famous quarries of Purbeck and Portland; the latter was used by Sir Christopher Wren for the building of St Paul's, while fonts and effigies made of Purbeck marble date back to the Middle Ages. It was at these quarries that the practice was developed of cutting the stone to its finished form on the site, so that no needless weight had to be transported. This may account for a certain family likeness in the towers of Dorset churches.

Wiltshire has a complex geological structure. In the north west natural resources (fine oolitic limestone and fat pastures for the rearing of sheep) produced both the material and the money for the distinguished churches of the county. In some cases the stone was so abundant that whole villages were built of it, as in the Cotswolds. Stylistically the builders often looked towards Wells and Gloucester for inspiration, which accounts for some of the noble towers in the region. But there are good quarries elsewhere, such as Chilmark, from which Salisbury Cathedral was built and which has been recently reopened for its repair.

The valleys running out of Salisbury Plain tend to be steep and narrow, so that the villages are closely packed and the churches rise from a cluster of roofs. The Bishop's manors seem to have set a fashion for cruciform churches with central towers as at Potterne and Bishops Cannings. Of these, Edington is undoubtedly the most distinguished. Edington was a priory church built by William of Edington, who became Bishop of the extremely wealthy See of Winchester. It is said that he was offered the archbishopric of Canterbury and turned it down with the words: 'though Canterbury be the higher rack, Winchester hath the deeper manger'. Some three hundred years separate the earliest cruciform church from the latest, which argues an impressive continuity of style.

Hampshire on the whole relates more to Sussex and Surrey than to its neighbours to the west. In the valleys of the Meon, the Test and the Itchen the simple, bucolic style, mostly in flint with squat belfries of weather boarding, is not unlike that of West Sussex. The early importance of Winchester, hallowed by Alfred, accounts for a number of distinguished Norman churches, in particular Romsey and Winchester's own St Cross, to which may be added East Meon, the only one to be built as a parish church and described by Pevsner as 'one of the most thrilling village churches in Hampshire'.

◁ DORSET ▷

Beaminster, St Mary the Virgin   4 J4
Built on an eminence, the glorious 16thC tower has a commanding position. Slender pinnacles clamber up it from many angles, some on the backs of angels or little devils, giving the tower a festive air. Sculptures decorate the W front, including figures of a pilgrim and a fuller, who possibly paid for the building of the tower. The interior is 15thC–16thC, and contains impressive monuments to the Strodes, whose family built Tudor Parnham House; that to George Strode, d1753, is a very dignified classical composition by Peter Scheemakers. *Open daylight hours daily.* The town is pleasant with plenty of pretty houses. Parnham House and gardens are 1m S.

St John the Baptist, Tudor timber roof

Bere Regis, St John the Baptist   4 K4
9m NE of Dorchester on A35. A handsome Perpendicular flint and stone chequer tower. Inside, heads decorate two of the capitals of the 12thC S arcade and nail-head adorns the arches. Enlargements and additions were made in succeeding centuries, most glorious of which is the timber roof, probably built by Cardinal Morton, Henry VII's Chief Tax-gatherer, which is carved and painted in exuberant style, with large central bosses and figures shooting out from the sides. See the Norman font and 16thC bench carvings. Fascinating to Thomas Hardy fans will be the Turberville tomb and Chapel, which Tess visits as she draws close to her lugubrious end, and which are said to have inspired *Tess of the D'Urbervilles. Open 09.00–dusk daily.*

Blandford Forum, St Peter   4 K4
and St Paul
Eminent among the distinguished Georgian buildings erected by John and William Bastard after a fire of 1731 destroyed the town centre. It has a pleasing tower and cupola and an impressive, lofty interior with a classical coolness and restraint in its details, although the chancel, added in the 19thC, is more elaborate. Tall columns with Ionic capitals support the handsome entablature and vaulted nave roof. Note the elegant W gallery, organ case, pulpit, box pews, ornate mayoral chair and the font. Among memorial tablets is one naming the Bastards' buildings in the town, and in the churchyard is their family tomb with a handsome obelisk on it. **P**. *Open 07.15–18.30 Mon–Fri, from 08.30 Sat; 07.45–20.00 Sun.*

Bournemouth, St Peter   5 L3
Hinton Rd. Buried here is the founder, ardent Tractarian Alexander Morden

Bennett, who engaged G. E. Street, best known as architect of the Law Courts in London, to build the church, which he did from 1854–79, onto an existing S aisle. The impressive steeple was the last part to be built. Look at the pulpit carved by Thomas Earp and exhibited at the Great International Exhibition of 1862, the different stones in the clerestory, the brass plaque on the back row of the choir stalls, commemorating Prime Minister William Gladstone's last communion here in 1898, and the richly embellished chancel and sanctuary, the latter vaulted and delightfully painted by Bodley with censer-swinging angels. John Keble, one of the founders of the Oxford Movement, worshipped in the Keble Chapel after retiring to Bournemouth in 1865. The stained glass in its S window is by Morris and Burne-Jones. See the Resurrection Chapel by Comper, 1925–6, in the churchyard, and the Shelley vault, where Romantic poet Percy Bysshe Shelley's heart is buried, after first being buried in Rome, and where Mary Wollstonecraft Shelley, author of *Frankenstein*, is buried in her entirety. Limited **P**. *Open 08.00– 17.30 Mon–Wed & Sun; from 09.30 Thur & Sat, to 17.00 Fri.*

St Stephen, Bournemouth

Bournemouth, St Stephen   **5 L3**
St Stephen's Way. The church is an awe-inspiring Victorian expression of Early English Gothic, by J. L. Pearson, 1881–98, architect of Truro Cathedral. The tower was built in 1907. Inside above all, it is undoubtedly beautiful and successful in recreating a sense of the old, glorious forms and colour associated with pre-Reformation worship, that the Oxford Movement sought to revive. It has a soaring, rib-vaulted nave and double aisles, an apse with ambulatory and tall, graceful lancet windows in the chancel, where a brightly coloured and gilded triptych forms the reredos. The vivid stained glass is by Clayton and Bell. Examine the fine, marble font and pulpit and the delicate wrought-iron rood screen. **P**. *Open 09.00–17.00 Mon & Wed– Sat, from 08.00 Tue & Sun.* In a dignified seaside resort, developed in the 19thC, when the omnipresent pines were plant-ed. Tree-clad ravines, known locally as chines, plunge down to the sandy shore.

Branksome, St Aldhelm   **4 K3**
St Aldhelm's Rd. E district of Poole. An elegant church by Bodley and Garner, 1892–4, with West Country characteristics, including a wagon roof uninterrupted by a chancel arch in the long nave, and no clerestory. Interesting features include the Decorated Gothic tracery in the E window and font by Randoll Blacking with a gilt cover. **P**. *Open 11.00–16.00 Thur, 10.00–11.00 Sat.* Poole, with its magnificent natural harbour and smuggler-haunted past is worth visiting.

Burton Bradstock, St Mary   **4 J3**
3m SE of Bridport on B3157. Sheltered in the Bride valley, a coastal village of great charm, thatched cottages and stone houses wandering down lanes and narrow streets. A pretty Perpendicular church with a central tower, wagon roofs and a S aisle of 1897, with singular stylistic features by E. S. Prior. **P**. *Open 07.45–dusk daily.*

Chalbury, All Saints   **5 L4**
8m N of Bournemouth off B3078. A delightful, small church on the summit of Chalbury Hill, with remarkable views on every side. Horton Tower is to the E, Wimborne Minster, Christchurch and the Isle of Wight to the S. The church's plastered walls, box pews, three-decker pulpit, W gallery and clear glass in the 14thC E lancets, all testify to a puritan fervour, untouched by any ideas of Gothic revival. A curious and appealing arched and columned construction leads through to the chancel, where there are Victorian seats which were reserved for local nobility and the rectory servants. **P**. *Open daylight hours daily.*

Charminster, St Mary the Virgin　　**4 J3**
1m N of Dorchester on A352. The river
Cerne runs beside the churchyard, in
which the early 16thC tower rises
loquaciously with its many pinnacles,
turret stair, gargoyles and the
omnipresent entwined Ts, monogram of
the builder, Sir Thomas Trenchard.
Inside are impressive Norman nave
arcades, chancel arch and clerestory
windows, medieval extensions and a
19thC chancel. Near the chancel is a
charming remnant of a medieval wall
painting of pomegranates and on one
side of the tower arch a sepia tree. See
the restored monument to Grace Pole, in
which cherubs in clouds hover above her
kneeling effigy. 'Through the Bad
Conduct of the Boys in the High Seats',
the old box pews were replaced in 1893.
P. *Open 08.00–17.00 Mon–Sat, 07.00–19.30
Sun.* Half a mile S is Wolfteton House,
16thC home of the Trenchards.

Christchurch, Christchurch Priory　　**5 L3**
Church St. An appealing legend
surrounds the priory church's Norman
origin: a plan to build the church a mile
up the Avon valley was thwarted by the
miraculous nocturnal transportation of
building materials back down to the site
of an earlier church; an extra, unknown
workman helped with the building, and
when a roof beam was cut a foot short it
was found the next morning
mysteriously in its place and the right
length. The workman was seen no more,
but was believed to be Christ, to whom
the church was then dedicated. You can
see the Miraculous Beam near the
glorious Perpendicular Lady Chapel.
Great Norman pillars process majestically
up the nave to the beautifully vaulted
chancel, whose E wall is dominated by
an ornate 14thC stone reredos. Examine
the stalls and misericords, featuring
Richard III, jesters in abundance, a
salmon, and a whole panoply of
medieval characters. Most sumptuous of
the chantries is that of the Countess of
Salisbury and her son, Cardinal Pole,
who opposed Henry VIII's break with
Rome. In the Montacute Chantry, look
for the capital showing the 12 apostles,
including two-faced Judas. Outside,
admire especially the Norman stair
turret, exquisitely embellished with
arcades and a prominent lattice pattern,
and the magnificent 13thC N porch. *Open
summer 09.30–21.00 Mon, Tue & Thur, to
17.30 Wed, Fri & Sat; 14.15–18.00 Sun;
winter closes 17.30 Mon–Sat.*

Dorchester, St Peter　　**4 J3**
High St. John White, rector from 1606–48,
and founder of Massachusetts, is buried
in the porch. Apart from the Norman S
doorway, the church is Perpendicular. In
the S chapel is a plan of the restored
church drawn in 1856 by Thomas Hardy,
author of fine but doom-laden novels,
when he worked for an architect in the
town. An unusual naturalism is
expressed in the 14thC effigies of two
knights in the chapel, who look
remarkably as if they are taking an
afternoon nap, turned slightly, with one
hand resting lightly on the chest. There
is an excellent Jacobean pulpit and a
19thC reredos of Leonardo's *Last Supper*
in alabaster. *Open 09.00–18.00 daily.* A
historic county town, with a good
museum which includes a reconstruction
of Hardy's study. Remains of Iron Age
Maiden Castle are 1½m SW.

Horton, St Wolfrida　　**5 L4**
8½m N of Bournemouth off B3078. An
abbey was founded here in the 10thC by
Wolfrida and a later priory church was
dedicated to her. The present L-shaped
church of brick, stone and flint was built
in 1722. Its Vanbrughesque tower
is a singular and exciting sight
with its heavy cornice and pyramidal
spire. The four cherubs on the striking
early 18thC reredos of coloured and
gilded plaster, are said to be the children
of a former vicar who all died as infants.
There are box pews and interesting 14thC
effigies of a wimpled lady and a knight.
Though shy, a spectre known as the
Horton nun has been seen in the church,
but her more frequent haunt is Horton
Hollow. *Open 10.15–dusk daily.* On a hill
above the village is Horton Tower, a tall
18thC folly.

Lyme Regis, St Michael the　　**4 H3**
Archangel
In a dramatic clifftop position. What is
now the porch was the nave of a
Norman predecessor, which had a central
tower. The baptistry is under the tower
with its impressive Norman E arch, and
from here extends the large, early 16thC
church. The beautifully carved Jacobean
pulpit boldly proclaims the donor from
the sounding board, 'Richard Harvey of
London, Mercer and Marchant
Adventurer 1613', and the W gallery is
inscribed, 'John Hassard built
this. . .1611'. Mary Anning, famous for
her discovery of an ichthyosaurus fossil
in 1811, is commemorated in a stained
glass window in the N aisle. *Open 08.00–*

18.00 daily. Lyme is a seaside resort of charm and restraint; its heyday was early in the 19thC, when, in Jane Austen's *Persuasion*, Louisa Musgrove had her traumatic fall on the Cobb, the 14thC breakwater. The Cobb figures in the more recent fiction and film of John Fowles' *French Lieutenant's Woman*.

Moreton, St Nicholas   **4 K3**
9m NE of Weymouth on B3390. There is great charm and grace in this Georgian version of Gothic, built in 1776, enhanced by Laurence Whistler's exquisite engraved glass windows of 1958 in the apsidal E end, which have a motif of candles wound round by ribbons. Lawrence of Arabia is buried in the churchyard a short walk away. **P**. *Open 07.30–dusk daily*.

Puddletown, St Mary   **4 J4**
3m NE of Dorchester on A35. There are vestigial Norman remains, otherwise the church is largely Perpendicular, with a chancel of 1910 in style. The nave has a panelled chestnut roof and there are 17thC box pews and W gallery, a three-decker pulpit with sounding board, wonderful Norman font and striking, painted 16thC inscriptions. Observe the monuments to medieval knights, brasses and many memorial tablets. **P**. *Open 09.00–dusk daily*. Puddletown is the Weatherbury of Thomas Hardy's *Far from the Madding Crowd*, in which the church figures prominently, and in woods bordering the W of the parish is the gamekeeper's cottage of *Under the Greenwood Tree*. Half a mile E, wound round by the river, is beautiful, medieval Athelhampton House, with a spectacularly timbered roof in the great hall and landscaped gardens.

Shaftesbury, St Peter   **4 K4**
Of the 11 medieval churches of Shaftesbury, St Peter is the sole survivor. It is Perpendicular, with an earlier foundation and later additions, including the 16thC W porch, with miniature fan-vaulting. The light, pleasing interior has a handsome, gold-lettered reredos and fine, restored oak-panelled roof. The crypt under the S aisle was once a beer cellar. *Open 10.00–16.00 Mon–Sat*. Shaftesbury no longer has the glory of the abbey founded by Alfred the Great at the end of the 9thC, nor much of its medieval splendour, but it has a spectacular hilltop position, from which picturesque, cobbled Gold Hill makes a steep descent into a lush landscape.

Excavations have unearthed what may be the relics of St Edward, hidden at the Dissolution, which can be seen in the museum in the abbey ruins, Park Walk.

Sherborne Abbey

Sherborne, St Mary the Virgin   **4 J4**
Abbey Close. A Saxon cathedral preceded the abbey church, which became parochial after the Dissolution. 9thC Wessex kings Ethelbald and Ethelbert, Alfred the Great's brothers, were buried here. Built of golden Ham Hill stone, the church is beautiful – marvellously so in the fan-vaulting, of an incredible sumptuousness, the earliest of which is in the choir (c1450), restored in the 19thC. Peep at the 15thC misericords on the Victorian stalls, which include carvings of a woman beating a man and a boy being birched. As well as the magnificent Perpendicular work, Saxon, Norman and Early English evidence is all visible, the latter most perfectly in the Lady Chapel, entered through a fine archway; it has a modern E bay and a glass reredos, daintily engraved by Laurence Whistler in 1968. The church has the heaviest ring of eight bells in the world; the tenor has the charming inscription, 'By Wolsey's gift I measure time for all; To mirth, to grieffe, to church I serve to call'. Visit St Catherine's Chapel which has an impressive late 16thC monument with putti on top and lovely medieval stained glass. And don't miss the fan-vault in the Wykeham Chapel, the 16thC tomb of Sir John Horsey, who bought the abbey at the Dissolution and sold it to the town, the brass recording the burial in 1541 of Sir Thomas Wyatt, poet and courtier, and, in the N choir aisle, the Purbeck marble mask-like head of Abbot Clement of c1150. **P** nearby. *Open summer 09.00–18.00 Mon–Sat, from 08.00 Sun; winter to 16.30*. See the 15thC almshouses at the

entrance to the Abbey Close. The fine country town is distinguished by a number of medieval and other historic buildings, among them the castle where Sir Walter Raleigh lived for 15 years.

Sydling St Nicholas, St Nicholas   4 J3
11m S of Yeovil off A37. Downland surrounds the charming village of yellow stone and thatch. The church is delightfully situated and one of its gargoyles starred in the film of Thomas Hardy's *Far from the Madding Crowd.* See the bosses on the nave's wagon roof, the box pews, the 12thC font reminiscent of a Roman capital, and the monument to Lady Smith, d1796, on which her husband rises from his tomb. The church possesses an Elizabethan chalice, the Sydling Cup. **P.** *Open daylight hours daily.*

Wareham, Lady St Mary   4 K3
This was an Anglo-Saxon church of great importance, largely rebuilt in 1842. It has a rare, Norman, hexagonal lead font, handsomely detailed with figures of the apostles under arches, a beautiful 14thC E window, and two vaulted chapels beside the chancel. Inspect the inscribed stones in the N aisle, dating from the 7thC to 9thC, commemorating British chieftains, and the 13thC Purbeck marble effigies of knights in chain mail and surcoats either side of the chancel. **P.** *Open summer 10.00–18.00 Mon–Sat, winter to 15.00 Mon–Sat; 08.00–19.30 Sun.* St Martin's Church has Eric Kennington's effigy of Lawrence of Arabia, d1935. The 9thC earth ramparts round the town testify to its part in Alfred's fight against the invading Danes.

Wimborne Minster, St Cuthberga   4 K4
7m NW of Bournemouth on A341. An 8thC nunnery, destroyed by the Danes, preceded a college created by Edward the

St Cuthberga, chained library

Confessor, of which the mighty two-towered church remains. A Norman character (with dazzling quantities of zigzag decoration in the nave arcades), distinguishes the interior, growing outwards and upwards into the 13thC and later, and culminating in Victorian insertions and restoration. Meet Moses with a neatly plaited beard on a 13thC choir arch, and then move on to the ornate Decorated sedilia and piscina with ebullient Victorian finials, the Jacobean stalls and the stained glass. The S transept houses the beautiful chained library and the organ of 1965, whose gilded trumpets blow out the sound in conjunction with the pipes. Tablets and monuments abound. Don't miss the astronomical clock, on which the earth stands still in accordance with medieval cosmology, or the engaging 19thC wooden Quarter Jack, who at some stage in his career exchanged a monk's habit for the garb of a grenadier. **P.** *Open 09.00–dusk Mon & Wed–Sat, from 07.30 Tue & Sun.*

◁ WILTSHIRE ▷

Aldbourne, St Michael   5 L6
6½m NW of Hungerford on A419. In downland scenery, and prominent on the village green among picturesque cottages, the church is scarcely the place where you would expect to come across fire engines, but here are two fascinating examples of 1778. The Norman church was remodelled in the 13thC and 15thC and restored in the 19thC. It has a magnificent, battlemented Perpendicular

tower with Somerset tracery, and S porch, chapels, transepts and fine roofs of the same period. See the brasses and imposing monuments. **P.** *Open 08.30–dusk Mon–Sat, from 07.00 Sun.*

Alton Barnes, St Mary   5 L6
6m NE of Devizes off A361. A delightful little church under Marlborough Downs, with only 13 pews in the body of the church and a Georgian gallery. The high,

narrow nave with pilasters along the wall expresses its Saxon origin, as does the long-and-short work at the W end. The brick chancel is dated 1748; the lovely nave roof and a three-decker pulpit are further distinctive features of the church where Augustus Hare, Oxford orator, was rector early in the 19thC. **P.** *Open 10.00–dusk daily.* The Kennet and Avon canal is close by, and 1m N Wiltshire's largest White Horse is poised to take off into the Vale of Pewsey at a quick canter, being quite youthful as he was cut into the chalk as recently as 1812.

Bishops Cannings, St Mary the Virgin   5 L6
3m NE of Devizes off A361. Very beautiful countryside surrounds the village, which has thatched and half-timbered cottages and a church whose grandeur reflects the fact that it was built on the Bishop of Salisbury's estate. The august 13thC tower has an elegant 15thC spire. Note the rib-vaulted S porch, the ornate arches in the transepts, the late Norman pillars and capitals in the nave and the scrolls painted on the chancel vault. There is a poorbox and most unusual is the meditation pew and a great painted hand whose inscriptions invite you to ponder sin and death. **P.** *Open 08.00–dusk daily.*

Bishopstone, St John the Baptist   5 L4
4½m SW of Salisbury off A354. In a tree-shaded setting near the river Ebble; the villagers burnt and abandoned their cottages around the church at the time of the Plague. It is a beautiful 14thC church, with a partly Norman base to its crossing tower. Before going in, visit the vaulted, miniature cloister at the end of the S transept with a tomb inside, and gorgeous stone canopy over the priest's doorway. The S transept and chancel are rib-vaulted and there are sculptured heads as well as elaborate sedilia in the chancel with vaults and bosses of their own. The richly carved woodwork in pulpit, lectern and choir stalls was given by a former rector, G. A. Montgomery, whose 19thC Gothic tomb in the S transept is by A. W. Pugin, powerful proponent of the Gothic revival. **P.** *Open 08.00–dusk daily.*

Bradford-on-Avon, St Laurence   4 K6
This tiny Saxon church is an awesome witness of Christianity, its true nature unveiled in 1856 after ages of secular use as a school and cottage. Spare of detail, with blank arcading round the outside

and two angels hovering above the chancel inside, its striking height and narrow arches form proportions of elegant simplicity and a potent memorial of Saxon England. The town has numerous interesting houses, including a sumptuous early 17thC wealthy clothier's mansion, a delightful 17thC bridge with two 13thC arches, a 14thC tithe barn and narrow, twisting streets, often connected by flights of steps as in the hill towns of Italy. Make time for the brasses, monuments and wall painting in medieval Holy Trinity Church.

St Laurence, Bradford-on-Avon

Calne, St Mary the Virgin   4 K6
A splendid Perpendicular exterior, punctuated by pinnacles, the tower built in style although it is a replacement of an earlier steeple which fell down in 1628. The 15thC N porch has a lovely vault and pendant. Round Norman pillars and scalloped capitals lead up to the graceful Perpendicular clerestory in the nave and the chancel has 17thC pillars and arches. Note the lovely timber roof, the lavish organ case by C. R. Ashbee, c1905, and the capacious Elizabethan chest. In the S porch are panels from the tomb of Inverto Boswell, known as the King of the Gypsies, who died of smallpox in 1774. **P** nearby. *Open 10.00–12.00 & 14.30–16.30 Mon, from 11.00 Tue, Thur & Fri, from 09.30 Wed; 10.00–12.00 Sat, 08.30–12.00 & 14.30–19.15 Sun.* There are handsome Georgian houses on the green

and not far away are the spectacular 18thC gardens of Bowood House, in which Capability Brown and Repton had a hand, and where a cascade inspired by Poussinesque landscape paintings makes a thrilling fall.

Castle Combe, St Andrew   4 K6
5m NW of Chippenham off B4039. The splendid, pinnacled, Somerset-style tower was paid for in the 15thC by rich clothiers who must have traded at the market cross. The church has a 13thC E wall with fine lancet windows, but is largely a restored Perpendicular building. It has a wonderful font, ornamented with arches and figures, and a 14thC tomb with a knight's effigy and mourners under a lavish veil of ogee arches. Most unusual is the chancel arch's decoration of statuettes. **P.** *Open daylight hours daily.* Although there is no longer a castle, the wooded combe embraces the village famous for its role in the film *Dr Doolittle.* Built of lovely, yellowy stone with steep-roofed cottages and with a babbling brook, it is exceedingly pretty. Manor House Hotel has some distinguishing features and is 17thC in origin with 19thC alterations.

Cricklade, St Sampson   9 L7
5½m NW of Swindon on B4040. The small-windowed Tudor tower was built by the Duke of Northumberland, who was beheaded by Queen Mary in 1553. It is a most arresting sight, boldly flourishing huge, protuberant pinnacles and making rather a heavy crown for the church. The tower's vault is impressively studded with bosses and has a splendid display of shields. It is a very interesting church in which work of several periods, from Saxon to Victorian, is visible, including some beautiful 13thC lancet windows. The fine cross in the churchyard, intact but for the absence of sculpture from the top, originally stood at the High St crossroads. **P.** *Open 09.30–16.00 Mon–Fri, except during school holidays.*

Dauntsey, St James the Great   4 K6
4½m SE of Malmesbury off A420. A 17thC tower whose gargoyles and pinnacles help to declare its Gothic intentions. Many fascinating features in the church include Norman doorways, Jacobean box pews with knobs, a 16thC Doom painting on wood, a rood screen, fragments of medieval stained glass, brasses and a variety of interesting monuments. *Open approx 09.00–18.00 daily.*

Downton, St Laurence   5 L4
6m SE of Salisbury on A338. The spacious church has an imposing presence, in which work of different periods is harmonised. The crossing tower has a chequered history of rebuilding and the S aisle was rebuilt during restoration in 1648. The earliest fabric is in the round Norman pillars and scalloped capitals at the W end of the N arcade. The 14thC chancel contains remarkable monuments to the Favershams, two of them by Peter Scheemakers, the 18thC Dutch sculptor. See the handsome table made from the sounding board of a long-lost pulpit. *Open Whitsun-Sep 14.30–16.00 Mon–Sat.* In a village on the Avon, with an interesting example of town planning of c1205 in the Borough, a broad street with grass running down the middle. 18thC Moot House has a garden dell created from the earthworks of a Norman castle and there are pretty cottages in the High St. Stuffed trout, pike and perch in the Bull Hotel are testimonies to the angling renown Downton enjoys.

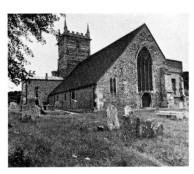

St Laurence, Downton

Edington, St Mary, St Katharine and All Saints   4 K5
4m E of Westbury on B3098. The magnificent, cruciform church, with battlements piercing the skyline, confronts smooth downs to the S and both gain grace by the encounter. William of Edington, Bishop of Winchester, built the former monastic church on a noble scale in 1351–61. The nave formed the parish church and the chancel the monastic choir. Here are concentrated the richest embellishments, including canopied niches and damaged but exquisitely detailed statues of the evangelists. Supporting the niches is a fascinating assembly of little, lively

figures. The transition from Decorated to Perpendicular Gothic can be followed in the tracery of the chancel's side windows and in that of the transept windows, where one style grows into the other. See the original stained glass filling the N transept E window and beautiful figures and fragments elsewhere. Delightful 17thC and 18thC plaster roofs are distributed round the interior, and the many monuments reward examination. George Herbert, metaphysical poet and disciple of John Donne was married here. Pay your respects to the largest and oldest yew in a Wiltshire churchyard. **P**. *Open 08.30–dusk daily.*

Great Bedwyn, St Mary the Virgin   5 L6
5m SW of Hungerford off A4. The handsome church was built in the 12thC–14thC, with a charming battlemented top to the tower. The 12thC arches in the nave dazzle with their prominent zigzag decoration and the pillar capitals are also richly carved. See the long, 13thC lancet windows in the N and S walls of the chancel, leafy ogee arch round the piscina, and the interesting monuments, including a 14thC knight's effigy and the 16thC monument to Sir John Seymour, father of Jane Seymour, Henry VIII's third wife, who had the distinction of not dying on the block. **P**. *Open 08.30–17.00 Mon–Sat, 08.00–19.00 Sun.* The village rises from the Dunn river and Kennet and Avon canal banks, and above it is Saxon Chisbury Camp, built to defend Wessex from the kingdom of Mercia. Close by is ancient Savernake Forest, where some of the magnificent trees are probably pre-Conquest and in which great avenues of beeches were laid out in the 18thC.

Lacock, St Cyriac   4 K6
3m N of Melksham off A350. The Perpendicular tower has a delightful stair turret and a porch with a battlemented top, prettily curvacious above the entrance. Further enjoyable features on the outside are the gargoyles, parapets and pinnacles and a 17thC house attached to the S transept. The Perpendicular light-filled nave has an unusual window over the chancel arch. In the S transept, discover the brass of 1501 to Robert Baynard and his wife, each of them wearing heraldic clothing, their 18 children below, the five girls wearing the kennel headdress seen on playing card queens. The Lady Chapel is a 15thC gem, gloriously vaulted and decorated with bosses and stars and ribs circling round pendants. It contains Sir William Sharington's tomb of 1566, an exuberant composition of great charm in its details of arabesques, strapwork, jaunty putti holding a shield, and small vases of flowers. **P** nearby. *Open daylight hours daily.* Lacock Abbey to the E, was founded as a nunnery in 1229, when Magna Carta was still recent news, and was bought by Sir William Sharington after the Dissolution for £763. He converted the conventual buildings into a manor house, of which much remains, with 18thC Gothick alterations, although the abbey church has gone. Parts of it are entrancing and from one of the oriel windows Fox Talbot, the pioneer of photography, made his first negative in 1835. The National Trust village is a lovely assemblage of medieval and later houses and contains the Fox Talbot Photographic Museum.

Malmesbury, Abbey   4 K6
The 12thC abbey succeeded earlier buildings and had a spire added to its crossing tower in the 14thC, which was taller than Salisbury Cathedral's. Both W tower and crossing tower and spire fell down in the 16thC, destroying much of the E and W ends, but leaving nave and aisles. Wealthy clothier, William Stumpe, bought the abbey at the Dissolution and gave it to the town as the parish church, although he also set up his looms in it at one point. The opulently carved S porch, with arch upon arch of attenuated, elegant Norman sculpture, is an unforgettable sight; inside the massive Norman pillars and arches, the gallery above, and the 14thC clerestory and vaulted roof, are of awe-inspiring grandeur. Inspect the 'watching loft' in the S aisle, which looks just like a theatre box and whose purpose is inscrutable; the pulpitum at the E end that used to cut off the nave from the monks' choir, with Henry VIII's Royal Arms on top; and the tomb of King Athelstan, Alfred the Great's grandson. In the churchyard is a tombstone to Hannah Twynnoy who, in 1703, was mauled by a tiger, which escaped from a travelling circus. *Open 10.00–dusk Mon–Sat, to 19.00 Sun.* The glorious abbey dominates the town, which is spread on a hill beside the Avon, with many gracious houses of different periods, and a spectacular, battlemented market cross of c1500, with flying buttresses and an elaborate lantern on top.

Marlborough, St Mary the Virgin   5 L6
In a prominent position, the church, founded in 1160 and with a flamboyant doorway of that period, was rebuilt after a fire devastated the town in 1653. The Perpendicular tower and walls survived, and the outstanding feature of the rebuilding, in an interior reflective of the puritan ideal of a plain preaching-house, is the elegant classical S arcade. The chancel was rebuilt in the 19thC. **P** nearby. *Open 09.00–17.00 Mon, Tues, Fri & Sat, from 07.30 Wed, from 08.30 Thur; 07.30–19.00 Sun*. Set in Marlborough Downs, serene Georgian buildings compose the town's wide High St, at the W end of which is St Peter and St Paul's Church, where Thomas Wolsey, later Cardinal and Henry VIII's Chancellor, was ordained in 1498. Now redundant, it is used in the summer as a Tourist Information Bureau and Brass Rubbing Centre.

Mere, St Michael the Archangel   4 K5
7m NW of Shaftesbury on A303. The church has a Perpendicular tower, nave arcades and clerestory, a 13thC chancel and sumptuous 14thC chapels and N porch with vault and bosses. Admire the wonderful, lofty Perpendicular rood screen, with restored coving and loft, and the chapel screens, the misericords on the stalls, which include carvings of angels and a man poking his tongue out, 17thC benches and lovely 14thC stained glass in the S chapel, where there is a brass of 1398 to the chapel's founder. **P** nearby. *Open 08.00–dusk daily*.

St Michael the Archangel, Mere

Potterne, St Mary the Virgin   4 K6
2m S of Devizes on A360. Standing out on an eminence above the village, a 13thC cruciform church, intact in its simplicity

and beauty, the plain lancet windows and pointed arches achieving great clarity of design. The Perpendicular tower is lavishly adorned in comparison, with Somerset tracery in the bell openings and a pierced parapet with pinnacles crowning it. See the Saxon font, inscribed (in Latin) round the rim, 'As a deer longs for the running brooks, so longs my soul for you, O God', from psalm 42. **P**. *Open 08.30–18.00 daily*. In the village are some delightful thatched cottages and half-timbered houses, the finest of which is 15thC Porch House, in the High St.

St Mary the Virgin, Potterne

Purton, St Mary   5 L6
4m W of Swindon on B4041. The splendid church is in a lovely, leafy setting beside the Elizabethan manor house, great tithe barn and a small thatched cottage, and has the rare distinction of two towers of equal importance: a Perpendicular W tower with an openwork parapet and a 14thC central tower with a spire. Built from the 12thC to the 15thC and restored in the 19thC, its fine details include a large number of statue niches, filled with modern sculptures by Simon Verity, evoking the original rich decoration; medieval wall paintings, including a beautiful 14thC death of the Virgin, in which a tiny figure represents her soul; a painting of the Last Supper by a Flemish contemporary of Rubens, Jacob Jordaens; and a wealth of fragments of old stained glass. **P**. *Open 08.00–dusk daily*.

Salisbury, St Thomas   5 L5
St Thomas's Sq. It is a great joy to enter this beautiful, light church and look up at the tall, panelled clerestory and wooden

nave roof, trimmed with lace-like cresting and angels. The chancel collapsed in 1450 and its rebuilding was financed jointly by the dean and chapter of the cathedral on the N and wealthy merchants on the S, whose names and symbols are carved on the capitals of the pillars. The angels carved under the roof hold their musical instruments in their left hands or upside down, so that from heaven's point of view they will be the right way up. The restored late 15thC doom painting above the chancel arch is very impressive; hell has a vast fish's mouth into which the damned are gingerly stepping, after some diabolical persuasion, while the redeemed rise from their tombs on the other side and Christ sits on a rainbow at the apex, a resplendent city either side. On looking to the right of the chancel arch one is delighted by the sumptuous 15thC Lady Chapel, built by a rich wool merchant, William Swayne, which has a beautiful roof, carved 18thC wooden reredos, exquisite iron railings and medieval wall paintings. *Open 09.00– 19.00 Mon, Thur & Fri, from 08.00 Tue & Wed; 10.00–17.00 Sat, 08.00–20.00 Sun.* Salisbury is a fascinating city to explore, rich in medieval and later buildings, some of the finest of which are congregated in the Cathedral Close, where soars above all, the majestic 13thC cathedral.

St Peter, Stourton

Stourton, St Peter   **4 K5**
3m NW of Gillingham on B3092. In an opulent setting of woods and lawns, which spread out to the gardens of Stourhead House and confronting paganism in the Pantheon across the

lake. It is a lovely Perpendicular church, with pretty 19thC pierced parapets and some early 14thC work. Monuments include an effigy of a lady of c1400 with a fascinating headdress, and those to the two Henrys Hoare, the first of whom, d1725, built Stourhead House and the second of whom, d1785, laid out the grounds. *Open 08.00–dusk daily.* The core of the grand Palladian mansion was destroyed by fire in 1902, but the rooms were reconstructed and a fine collection of Chippendale furniture is on display. The glorious gardens lavishly offer picturesque vistas, and a superb mingling of nature and artifice is achieved in the placing of the Temple of Flora, the Grotto with its nymph and other romantic constructions.

Wilton, St Mary and St Nicholas   **5 L5**
3m NW of Salisbury on A30. A bold expression of Italian Romanesque style and an amazing sight in Wiltshire, the church was built for Lord Herbert of Lea by T. H. Wyatt and D. Brandon, in 1841– 5. The rose window, and arcade below, the ornate portal and side doors, compose a façade typical of Lombardy, to which has been added the tall campanile, or bell tower, attached by a small, highly ornamented colonnade. Black marble columns separate the chancel from the nave and 2ndC BC marble columns from the Temple of Venus at Porto Venere are at the end of the side aisles. Of outstanding interest are the pulpit, converted from a 13thC shrine from St Maria Maggiore in Rome, with twisted colonettes studded with mosaic, the sumptuous stained glass from various European and English sources, including a panel from the Sainte Chapelle in Paris, and some fine monuments. **P.** *Open May-Sep 10.00–12.00 & 14.00–16.00 Mon-Fri.* Wilton House close by is one of the greatest of the English country houses built on the wealth and land of the pre-Reformation abbeys. The first earl of Pembroke was given the nunnery and lands by Henry VIII in 1544. The present house is a conglomerate of styles from the 17thC onwards and has magnificently decorated state rooms, a sumptuous art collection and lavish 18thC garden architecture. In addition, 7,000 model soldiers are on display.

◁ HAMPSHIRE ▷

Alton, St Lawrence   **5 N5**
The door, dramatically scarred with battering marks made in a Civil War battle of 1643, is a reminder of a more turbulent past. Take time to scrutinise the capitals of the Norman crossing tower arches which are decorated with axe-work carvings of animals, including a wolf and a dove. A new nave and chancel were built round the tower in the 15thC. Christopher Wolaston, falconer to Tudor monarchs, is commemorated in a brass. Admire the Jacobean pulpit with beautifully decorated columns. **P.** *Open 09.00–18.00 Mon & Thur–Sat, to 20.00 Tue, 07.00–18.00 Wed, 07.30–20.00 Sun.* Jane Austen's house is at Chawton, 1m S.

Basing, St Mary   **5 N5**
2m E of Basingstoke off A33. Large, Late Perpendicular with evidence of its early Norman origin in the arches of the crossing tower. Monuments to the Paulets lead to fine N and S chapels, built by them. Note the ornate pulpit of 1622. The church was much damaged in 1644 when Basing House nearby was besieged and destroyed by Cromwell, but luckily the lovely statue of the Virgin and Child above the W door escaped harm, probably because ivy covered it. **P.** *Open daylight hours daily.*

Beaulieu, Blessed Virgin and Holy Child   **5 M4**
Early English, it was the refectory of Beaulieu Abbey until 1538. High in the wall, the pulpit replaces the former reader's desk, and the stairway to it runs between lancet windows and a gracefully proportioned arcade on Purbeck marble shafts. **P.** *Open 08.00–18.30 daily* Adjacent attractions are Palace House, the National Motor Museum and the New Forest.

Binsted, Holy Cross   **5 N5**
3m E of Alton off A31. The Domesday Book records Binsted, or Benestede, meaning a holding of land; to this day you can see the church's Norman piers and capitals. The 14thC N transept has a monument to Richard de Westcote, a descendant of whom founded a chantry here in 1331; angels shield his head. Field Marshall Montgomery is buried in the churchyard and his knight's banner hangs in the nave. **P.** *Open 09.00–17.00 Mon–Sat, 12.00–17.00 Sun.*

Holy Cross, Binsted

Bishop's Sutton, St Nicholas   **5 N5**
7m SW of Alton off A31. Flint walls harbour a few Roman bricks. The wide nave and chancel are Norman as are the doorways, the S carved with beakheads. Four massive oak posts support the quaint 14thC shingled belfry and the late 13thC chancel has a brass of a medieval knight and lady. **P.** *Open approx 09.00–dusk daily.*

Bishop's Waltham, St Peter   **5 M4**
The church spans the centuries with a Norman foundation, 16thC and 17thC alterations and 19thC restorations; the squat tower dates from the end of 16thC. Don't miss the outstanding pulpit of 1620 and the original box pews in the 18thC W gallery. **P.** *Open 09.00–18.00 daily.* The 12thC episcopal palace nearby was much damaged in 1644, during the Civil War, and subsequently fell into ruin. Craft workshops in the Old Granary, Bank St.

Bramley, St James   **5 N6**
8m S of Reading off A33. Two weather vanes on the roof of the chapel by Soane 1802, show the Brocas heraldic crest of crowned Moors heads, which celebrates the bloodthirsty deed of a 14thC member of the family in 'overcoming the King of Morocco and cutting off his head'. The brick W tower was built in 1636. Among many notable features are: the 15thC wall painting of St Christopher opposite the church door and the 13thC painting of Becket's murder on the S wall; the three Transitional windows; exquisite fragments of stained glass of St Catherine, three musicians and three saints; Tudor panelling in the chancel; and the 18thC W gallery on fluted Ionic columns. See too the dolorous white

marble monument in the chapel, and the early 16thC Flemish glass. *P. Open 07.30–dusk daily.*

Brockenhurst, St Nicholas 5 M4
Ancient New Forest church, at home in one of the greatest remaining forest areas of England; a forest with a recorded history that goes back to 1079 when William the Conqueror designated it as hunting country for red deer. Glance up at the zigzag moulding round the Norman S doorway and at the Tudor S window with carved shield and memorable heads, probably of Henry Fitzalan and his son, Lord Matravers. Periods mingle in the brick W tower, 1763, Norman nave, late 13thC chancel and 19thC N aisle. In the graveyard (near the New Zealand First World War memorial) is the tomb of 'Brusher Mills', d1905, who followed the unusual calling of snake catcher: he is depicted about his activities in the New Forest, together with a can for serpentine accommodation. *P. Open May–Sep, 14.30–17.00 Mon–Sat.*

Chilcomb, St Andrew 5 M5
2m SE of Winchester off A31. In a secluded position under the downs, this intact and lovely Norman church, still has its original pillar piscina decorated with flat eaves. Amid its ancient walls, pore over the facsimile of a charter signed by King Alfred's son, Edward the Elder, in 908, making a grant of the Chilcomb lands. *P. Open 10.00–18.00 (or dusk) daily.* Peaceful village and countryside.

Cosham, St Philip 5 N4
Portsmouth suburb. Designed by Sir Ninian Comper and built in 1937, embracing Byzantine, classical and later styles. The focal point is the ciborium at the E end, a gilt canopy on columns with Corinthian capitals, four angels on a starry vault, and a figure of Christ resurrected above. Octagonal font with gilded ogee-pointed cover. *P. Open 09.00–18.00 Tue–Sat, 08.00–18.00 Sun.*

East Meon, All Saints 5 N4
1m W of Petersfield off A272. Nestled against a hill among the meadows of the Meon valley, with 15thC Court House nearby, the cruciform church is a pure Norman piece of parish devotion, with a powerful, spectacular tower and W doorway. The great treasure within is the vivaciously carved font of black marble from Tournai in Normandy. On one side Adam and Eve are created and on another they fall, clutching fig leaves to

their privy parts and setting about the toil to which they were condemned. Lively dragons and birds decorate the other sides. See the E window stained glass, chapel reredos and screen by Comper. *Open approx 09.00–dusk daily.* A stream courses down the charming village's High St.

East Wellow, St Margaret 5 M4
3m W of Romsey off A27. Deep in the country. The Early English church is especially known for the multitude of 13thC wall paintings including masonry patterns, each square or rectangle containing a flower; on the N wall of the nave St Christopher holds the child in his left arm, eel spear in right; a figure sits spinning and another approaches on horseback. See too the 16thC timbered aisle and picturesque porch, and the handsome Jacobean pulpit, altar rail and panels round the altar. Diminutive dovecote belfry. Look out for the memorial to Florence Nightingale in the churchyard. *P. Open summer 08.00–20.00 daily, winter to 18.30.*

Eling, St Mary 5 M4
2m W of Southampton off A35. The medieval interior has a beautiful Early English chancel arch, but extensive 19thC restoration by Benjamin Ferrey imposed a Victorian stamp on the exterior; the fine Tudor tower remains. A 16thC Venetian painting of the Last Supper forms the altarpiece. Among a variety of interesting memorial tablets are two by Rysbrack. *Open 13.00–17.00 Mon–Sat, 08.00–20.00 Sun.* Rare redbrick 18thC tide mill nearby, in full working order.

Fawley, All Saints 5 M4
10m SE of Southampton on A326. Significant features of the 12thC church remain, including the base of the tower, the fine W doorway with lively zigzag and fleuron decoration and the chancel arch. Graceful nave arcades lead through the arch to a chancel of c1300, restored by Randoll Blacking in 1954, after bombing in 1940. Scrutinise the beautiful Jacobean pulpit, carved with arches in perspective and scrolly brackets. *P. Open daylight hours Fri–Sun.* On the edge of the New Forest.

Hurstbourne Tarrant, St Peter 5 M5
5m N of Andover on A343. Hurstbourne Tarrant belonged to a Dorset nunnery in the 13thC, and the old flint church is partly Norman – see the S doorway with eagle and lion heads. Later developments include Transitional and 13thC arcades,

an early 14thC W doorway, and Perpendicular bench ends. Take time to inspect the fascinating early 14thC mural of the Three Quick and Three Dead, showing the legendary meeting of three kings out hunting with three skeletons, symbolic reminder of their mortality. Outside, note the lovely weatherboarded 15thC bell tower in three stages and the broach-spire. *Open daylight hours daily.* Historic and appealing village in the Test valley, where William Cobbett often stopped on his *Rural Rides.* The Test river is famous for its trout.

Idsworth, St Hubert　　　　　5 N4

3m N of Havant off B2149. In peaceful downland, 200 yds from the road up a grassy path. Architectural features include a Norman nave, Early English chancel and a delightful 18thC boarded bell turret. But by far the most striking attributes are the important medieval wall paintings: on the N wall of the chancel St Hubert is shown curing a case of lycanthropy in a creature with wolfish body and human head; below a zigzag line John the Baptist is thrown into prison, courtly figures feast and gesticulate, Salome dances with swords, curving backwards as though she had no bones in her body, and the Baptist's head is passed on a salver to Herod. Tremendous vitality leaps from these scenes. The Jacobean pulpit is also worthy of attention. *Open 09.00–dusk daily.*

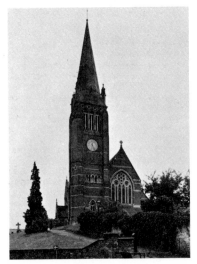

St Michael and All Angels, Lyndhurst

Lyndhurst, St Michael and　　5 M4
All Angels

Built in polychromatic brick by William White, 1858–70, on an eminence befitting its powerful Victorian presence. The exquisite E window is of the New Jerusalem, by Pre-Raphaelite Burne-Jones; Leighton's fresco below illustrates the parable of the wise and foolish virgins, harmoniously centred on the figure of Christ. Madox Brown and Rossetti also contributed to the church's marvellous stained glass. The nave roof is decorated by a fanfare of life-size angels. Alice Hargreaves, the inspiration for *Alice in Wonderland,* lies in the churchyard. *Open 08.30–17.00 daily.* Lyndhurst is in the midst of the New Forest; you can visit the 17thC house where the Verderers still meet to administer it. Numerous teashops and inns. Note the shop with antlers hanging from the ceiling, where venison faggots and sausages are sold.

Leighton's fresco

Milford-on-Sea, All Saints　　5 M4

3m SW of Lymington on B3058. Mostly Early English although there are two late Norman arches in the S arcade with robustly carved capitals. The chancel roof has impressive 17thC oak bosses. See too the fine Elizabethan oak altar table in the N chapel and the corbel frieze on top of the handsome tower. Monks from Christchurch Priory took services until the 14thC and the unusual arrangement of rooms under the lean-to roofs either side of the tower accommodated them. Two tombstones lying NS instead of EW are those of suicides, ominously inscribed, 'He departed himself'. **P.** *Open summer 07.00–18.00 daily, to 15.30 winter.*

Minstead, All Saints　　　　5 L4

10m W of Southampton off A31. Resident in a delightful New Forest village, this quaint, largely Georgian, church was untouched by Victorian restorers. The gabled porch is dated 1638 and the brick tower 1774. The windows impart a domestic air, increased by 18thC parlour pews within for the gentry, and hat pegs in the transept. Galleries, commandment boards and a three-decker pulpit help form an essentially Protestant picture. Examine the 12thC font. Conan Doyle is buried here. P. *Open 09.00–dusk daily.*

North Baddesley, St John the Baptist   5 M4

3m W of Eastleigh off A27. In rural retirement, on a hill above woods, forming a picture of charm and interest. The sturdy brick tower is dated 1674. Glance up at the window in the SE wall of the nave and descry the carvings of angels. Admire the screen and pulpit of 1602. The church was well restored in the 19thC. There are twin memorial stones in the churchyard to a poacher, hung for firing a shotgun at a gamekeeper. **P.** *Open 09.00–17.00 daily.*

North Hayling, St Peter   5 N4

3m S of Havant off A3023. The quaint fool's cap steeple contains an ancient set of bells which retain their wooden axles, and crowns a charming 12thC and 13thC church. Buttresses support the E wall which nonetheless leans. Examine the 16thC poppyheaded oak pews in the choir. Also the late 18thC–early 19thC tombstones, graced by garlands and cherubs. Princess Yourievsky, one of the last members of the Russian royal family, is buried in the churchyard; another regal presence is the 800-year-old yew tree. **P.** *Open 09.00–18.00 or dusk daily.*

Odiham, All Saints   5 O5

7m E of Basingstoke on A287. Fine 17thC brick tower, consonant with the nearby almshouses built in the same century. The early 13thC chancel arcades and tower arch, date from around the time King John tried to set out from nearby Odiham Castle to sign the Magna Carta in 1215; his barons, aided by the French, besieged the castle. Observe the late Perpendicular nave arcades, the distinctive W galleries of 1632, and pulpit of 1634, the round chalk font, and the medieval brasses. *Open 09.00–17.00 Mon–Thur & Sat, to 21.00 Fri, to 20.00 Sun.* Houses of different periods are gracefully juxtaposed in the High St.

Portchester, St Mary   5 M4

3m E of Fareham on A27. Within mighty Portchester Castle, whose walls are Roman and keep Norman and later medieval. Founded by Henry I and probably complete by 1133, the perfect Norman church is faced with ashlar inside and out. The W front is marvellously intact, with an elaborately carved doorway; the tower arches are most impressive too. The upper part of the 12thC font is said to represent the Garden of Eden, and men and animals, birds, reptiles and plants are visible in the pattern. The Arms of Queen Anne, 1710, with cherubic decoration, record her bounty in paying for restoration of the church after it was damaged by fire. *Open 09.00–dusk or 18.00 Mon–Sat, 07.30– last service Sun.* The sea is on three sides of Portchester Castle. 18thC houses in village centre to NE.

Romsey Abbey

Romsey, Abbey church of St Mary and St Ethelflaeda   5 M4

Founded at the start of the 10thC, rebuilt in the 12thC and 13thC on a magnificent scale, it became the parish church at the Dissolution of the Monasteries in 1539; the original Deed of Sale to the people of Romsey, for £100, has Henry VIII's seal upon it. The S side of the choir is considered one of the best examples of late Norman architecture anywhere. See the rare 16thC wooden reredos, painted with melancholy saints, angels celebrating the risen Christ and a portrait of the abbess who paid for it; admire the 13thC Purbeck marble effigy of a lady beneath an ogee canopy in the S transept. Also in the S transept is the 17thC St Barbe monument, and Earl Mountbatten's tomb. A beautiful Saxon rood, c1000, behind the altar in the S choir aisle, shows the cross as the tree of life. At an angle with the 12thC abbess' doorway outside the abbey is another, larger, Saxon rood; both are powerful depictions of Christ victorious over death. *Open 08.30–18.00 daily.* Broadlands, former home of Earl Mountbatten whose horrific assassination in August 1979 shocked the world, is nearby.

Selborne, St Mary   **5 N4**
4m S of Alton. The yew tree is a venerable
screen for the church. With a tower
covered in creeping tendrils and a ravine
behind, it is very much in the midst of
nature, befitting the burial place of 18thC
naturalist, Gilbert White. His tombstone
is simply inscribed with his initials and
date of death. The striking stained glass
window depicting St Francis celebrates
White's *Natural History of Selbourne*.
Powerful Norman pillars join Transitional
arches in the nave. 19thC restoration by
White's great-nephew continues the
family connection. **P** nearby. *Open
daylight hours daily.* GW's house, The
Wakes, is opposite. The Zig-Zag Path
leads to the top of the wooded hanger
where White made many of his
observations.

St Mary, Selborne

Silchester, St Mary the Virgin   **5 N5**
10m SW of Reading off A340. Although the
Roman town of Calleva Atrebatum is
buried beneath the fields, its walls stand
above, deep in the Hampshire
countryside, the church to the E.
Wooden bell turret. Take a close look at
the delightful frieze on the early Tudor
oak screen, of genuflecting angels with
leafy-looking legs, and at the long,
wimpled, 14thC effigy of a lady in the
ogee-arched recess in the S aisle. Early
13thC nave and chancel with flowers
charmingly frescoed on the splays of the
lancet windows. Fine Jacobean domed
canopy over the pulpit. **P**. *Open daylight
hours daily.*

Sopley, St Michael and All Angels **5 L4**
3m N of Christchurch on B3347. The lovely
Early English and 14thC church stands
on a hill overlooking the river Avon and
water meadows down to Christchurch.
The tower has a small snuffer spire.
Inspect the sculptured heads on the

transept arch in the N aisle and the two
corbels of angels playing a pipe and
stringed instrument at the W end of the
nave. *Open 08.00–19.00 daily.*

Southampton, St Michael   **5 M4**
and All Angels
St Michael's Sq. Out beyond the medieval
city walls and through Bargate, where
George III stands in a niche,
anachronistically dressed as a Roman
emperor. Large and rectangular, opposite
the ruins of Holy Rood church. The
Norman tower arches and Goodwin's tall
arcades of 1828 are juxtaposed. The
memorable Norman font from Tournai
has winged monstrous figures on it and
the 15thC Flemish eagle lectern is very
beautiful. **P** nearby. *Open 11.00–16.30
Mon–Sat, from 12.00 Sun.* Explore
medieval Southampton round about.

Stoke Charity, St Mary   **5 M5**
and St Michael
6m N of Winchester off A34. In rural
isolation, the beautiful little church is of
Saxon origin, but mostly Norman, its
structure scarcely tampered with in
subsequent centuries. Peer through the
double squint. The N chapel has some
original floor tiles. Tombs skilfully
repainted and regilded in 1946. Examine
the interesting headdresses worn by the
four married daughters on the 15thC
brass of Sir Thomas Hampton and the
rare iron locking staple of 1236 in the
font. The medieval sculpture of the Mass
of St Gregory is an exceptional survival
from puritanical defacement of the
figurative. **P**. *Open daylight hours daily.*

Tichborne, St Andrew   **5 M4**
6m E of Winchester off A31. Handsome
brick W tower, 1703, conspicuous on a
knoll above the picturesque village.
11thC chancel in which both Saxon and
Norman details are visible. Note the fine
Jacobean communion rails and box pews.
The Tichborne Chapel in the N aisle is a
pre-Reformation Roman Catholic enclave
within the church, where mass is said on
the day of the Tichborne Dole distribution
in testimony of royal favour. Good monuments. **P**. *Open 08.00–18.00 daily.* The
Tichborne Dole of flour is distributed
from Tichborne House on Lady Day.

Titchfield, St Peter   **5 M4**
3m W of Fareham on A27. The Anglo-
Saxon W porch, which forms the base of
the 13thC tower, dates far back to the
8thC, although there is work of many
periods here and the church as a whole
does not give a great impression of

antiquity. The Norman doorway with zigzag moulding and decorated capitals is particularly fine and the nave retains Saxon proportions. Leaves and winged figures adorn the capitals of the arches leading to the 14thC S chapel from the chancel. Within is the sumptuous late 16thC monument to the earls of Southampton, of marble and alabaster, with tall obelisks at the corners. Dating from the 15thC, the splendid N aisle has niches either side of the E window in elaborate Perpendicular style. **P**. *Open 09.00–dusk or 20.00 Mon–Sat, 07.45–20.00 Sun.* Georgian village in the Meon valley; Tudor gatehouse and ruins of Titchfield Abbey.

Warnford, Our Lady   **5 N4**
7m W of Petersfield on A32. In the wooded Meon valley. Look out for the unusual circular bell openings in the squat Norman tower, and admire the 13thC nave and chancel. The Norman font retains an iron locking staple. 17thC Neale monuments are prominent either side of the altar. See the grave, under a holly tree, of one George Lewis, who cut trees on a Sunday against all advice and was finally cut off from life by a falling branch, as the carving illustrates. **P**. *Open*

daylight hours daily. Nearby, are ruined 13thC St John House, Old Winchester Hill and the Hampshire Ridgeway, part of a prehistoric road.

Winchester, St Cross   **5 M5**
The Hospital setting is of great interest – the imposing church was once the Hospital chapel. Lofty, cruciform, in places the 12thC merges into the 13thC: aisles that are Norman at the E end become Early English at the W. The Norman chancel was restored by Butterfield in 1864. Norman rib-vaulting and zigzag decoration make a great flourish throughout the E end. Numerous features repaying more than a cursory glance include Perpendicular stone screens in the chancel; 15thC stained glass; 16thC stalls with profiles in panels; brasses; tiles in the aisles; a most remarkable eagle lectern of indeterminate date, and the unusually patterned Jacobean communion rail. **P**. *Open 09.30– 17.00 Mon–Sat.* Hospital built 1445. Much to be seen in Winchester itself, once one of England's greatest, as it is one of her most ancient cities: the cathedral incorporates Norman and later medieval styles; there is multiple evidence throughout the city of its long history.

◁ ISLE OF WIGHT ▷

Arreton, St George   **5 M3**
2m SE of Newport on A3056. Early Norman evidence survives in a doorway and windows. The church was enlarged in the 12thC and 13thC when the aisles were added and the chancel and S chapel with fine geometrical window tracery and graceful arcade built. Exceedingly imaginative monuments include two of the early 19thC by Sir Richard Westmacott. A grandson of Oliver Cromwell is buried here. **P**. *Open 08.00–dusk daily.* Nearby is 17thC Arreton Manor.

Carisbrooke, St Mary the Virgin   **5 M3**
1½m SW of Newport on B3401. A beautiful Norman and 13thC church, which had a priory attached from the 12thC–15thC, of which nothing now remains. The majestic Perpendicular tower presides over a church without a chancel, although the chancel arch still stands. The 16thC monument to Lady Wadham depicts her in the midst of six saints.

Open 07.00–17.30 Mon–Fri. Carisbrooke Castle, with a Norman keep and Tudor outer walls built as an emergency measure against the Spanish Armada of 1588, is a formidable sight. Having sought refuge with the governor after his defeat, Charles I was imprisoned here in 1647.

Gatcombe, St Olave   **5 M3**
1m S of Newport off A3020. In a wooded setting, a 15thC church with late Norman origins and a 19thC chancel. Fragments of 15thC stained glass in the S windows include an angel standing on a wheel on a chequered board, symbolising Christian conquest over fate. Exquisite glass by the Pre-Raphaelites fills the E window. There are effigies of a young soldier, d1917, and of a medieval knight, carved from oak, legs crossed to denote that he crusaded in the Holy Land. **P**. *Open daylight hours daily.* 18thC Gatcombe House and park close by.

Godshill, All Saints   **5** M3

2m W of Shanklin on A3020. There are extensive views over the island from the hilltop church and a cluster of thatched cottages at its foot. Known as the church of the Lily Cross for its beautiful and unique 15thC wall painting of Christ crucified on a triple-branched flowering lily, it is largely a 14thC double-naved rebuilding of an earlier church. The feet of Sir John Leigh's effigy, d1529, unusually rest on a pig, and at the soles of his feet are curious and fascinating 'bedesmen', bearded monks resting their heads on one hand and telling their beads with the other for the repose of Sir John's soul. Other monuments are to the Worsleys of Appuldurcombe, for 300 years from the Dissolution, Lords of the Manor. The masterly painting of *Daniel in the Lion's Den* is attributed to Rubens. **P.** *Open Mar–Oct 09.00–18.00 daily, occasionally Nov–Feb.*

Newchurch, All Saints   **5** M3

3m NW of Shanklin off A3056. Lovely wide views from here over the Arreton valley. The 13thC and 14thC church has a charming Georgian wooden upper part to its tower, a magniloquent sounding board topped by an angel over the pulpit, royal coat of arms of 1700, and a glorious gilded lectern of a pelican with three young. **P.** *Open 08.00–dusk daily.*

All Saints, Newchurch

Newport, St Thomas the Apostle and St Thomas of Canterbury   **5** M3

St Thomas' Sq. Built by S.W. Dawkes, in 1854–5 in Decorated Gothic style, the spacious church has an imposing tower, a sumptuously carved pulpit of 1636, an alabaster effigy of Sir Edward Horsey, d1582 and memorials by Baron Marochetti to Prince Albert and to Charles I's daughter, Princess Elizabeth. *Open 08.00–16.00 Mon, Tue, Thur; 06.30–*

18.30 Wed; 08.00–20.15 Fri; 08.00–12.00 *Sat.* An attractive and interesting hillside port, with some grand old buildings, including the early 17thC grammar school where Charles I lodged while negotiating a political settlement with Cromwellian commissioners.

St Mildred, Whippingham

Whippingham, St Mildred   **5** M4

2m SE of Cowes on A3021. Dedicated to an Anglo-Saxon princess and with a pre-Conquest foundation, the present Osborne Estate church was designed by Prince Albert and A. J. Humbert, 1854–62, and built at the behest of Queen Victoria. It is a right royal repository for tombs and memorabilia of the Battenberg lineage. The late Earl Mountbatten's parents are buried in the churchyard and the tomb of Prince Henry of Battenberg, d1896, and his wife Princess Beatrice, d1945, Queen Victoria's youngest child, is in the Battenberg Chapel. Princess Beatrice and the ladies of the court worked the carpet, stools and prie-dieu, and a crocheted hassock was made by Victoria herself. The beautiful Art Nouveau bronze screen is by A. Gilbert. Edward VII had the royal pew put in and in the centre is the chair used by Queen Victoria when she worshipped here; the silver spoon from which she took her last communion is preserved. There is a jewel-studded bible given by 'maidens of England' on Beatrice's marriage in the church, and the carpet in front of the altar is part of that used in Westminster Abbey for Elizabeth II's coronation. **P.** *Open Easter Mon–Oct 10.00–17.30 Mon–Fri.* Queen Victoria's favourite home, Osborne House, replete with the monarch's atmosphere, is to the N, overlooking the Solent, and in huge grounds.

THAMES
—— & CHILTERNS ——

Bedfordshire   Hertfordshire   Berkshire
Oxfordshire   Buckinghamshire

'When we reach the southern part of Bedfordshire', writes Sir William Addison, 'the question of whether churches are in Bedfordshire, Buckinghamshire or Hertfordshire becomes practically meaningless if we confine our attention to style'. The geology of the area is very mixed and the churches exhibit a profusion of styles, none of which can be identified as truly local.

The north west of Bedfordshire relates to Northamptonshire, from whence it derives some distinguished spires. The central clay vale, described by Bernard West as 'a wilderness raped for brickmaking', dictates the material of all modest buildings. In the south the Totternhoe quarries yield a clunch which weathers badly but offers a workable material for indoor carvings, some of which are excellent.

There is a great deal of flint obtainable in the chalk line of the Chilterns and Gogmagogs; chalk rubble and flint are therefore typical materials of much of Buckinghamshire. Historically the county lacks any specific ecclesiastical centre and it is chiefly famous for a group of late 12thC fonts in the neighbourhood of Aylesbury.

It might be thought that Hertfordshire, by contrast, would have profited from the presence of the great St Albans Abbey, but this was not so. 'Due to constant mismanagement of its finances and estates', writes Gordon Slade, 'the Abbey was kept in a state of chronic insolvency.' In the 17thC and 18thC, being close to London, it became a favourite county for the wealthy and many churches have been enriched with their memorials – from the starched figures of the Renaissance, or the periwigged heroes of the Glorious Revolution, to the classically draped widows weeping over some 'storied urn'. The only architectural feature to which Hertfordshire has given its name is the 'spike' – a small timber and lead spire, rising from the centre of the tower – which is often almost hypodermic in its needle-like sharpness.

Berkshire, once again, has no distinctive style and no really distinguished churches. It was a thinly populated county until the present century and its typical churches were originally almost cottage-like. 19thC wealth and Tractarian churchmanship led to many of these being rebuilt by Street, Butterfield or Gilbert Scott. The architect-built church usually owes little or nothing to local conditions for its style. One wonders again why Reading

Abbey exercised so little apparent influence upon the region, but there is no real evidence of it.

Oxfordshire partakes of its neighbours' characteristics rather than offering a distinctive landscape or a regional style. In the east, it is the Chilterns and in the west beginning to be Cotswold, where it can claim Burford, one of the finest of the wool churches in a town where almost every house deserves attention. In the north where Oxford marches with Warwickshire and Northamptonshire, it produces a russet ironstone; 'a land of little hills', writes Betjeman, 'and golden brown churches and cottages'. In the typical churches to the west, often enlarged in a Perpendicular style which is probably inspired by Gloucester Cathedral, the ample clerestory windows are usually rectangular, filled with Perpendicular tracery and topped with square hood-mouldings. Oxfordshire is a county of many large estates and it is not unusual to find the village church almost in the garden of the great house.

◁ BEDFORDSHIRE ▷

Ampthill, St Andrew **10** O8
The ironstone church is set amid undulating countryside. It dates from the 14thC and 15thC with fine nave arcades, and though much restored has preserved delightful features such as the medieval angels and gilded bosses on the nave roof. The brasses are gathered at the W end of the nave, and include one to a Merchant of the Staple and one of a 15thC lady wearing a contemporary butterfly headdress. See the dignified memorial tablet in the chancel to Richard Nicolls, who gave New York its name after it was taken from the Dutch, and who was killed at the Battle of Sole Bay in 1672, by the cannon ball now embedded in the monument. **P.** *Open 08.00–18.30 Mon–Sat, 07.30–20.00 Sun.* Henry V's uncle, Sir John Cornwall, built a castle in Ampthill Park in the 15thC, frequented by Henry VIII in the 16thC and where Catherine of Aragon was held to await her divorce. The present house was built in the 18thC and is now a Cheshire Home.

Bedford, St Peter de Merton **10** O8
De Parys Av. The church has Victorian arcades and a fascinating earlier history. The present chancel was the nave of a Saxon church and the tower once stood at the W end. Saxon long-and-short work is visible in the tower, and stones were uncovered in 1890 which suggested there had been a great fire in it, probably started by marauding Danes. See the two

monoliths behind the lectern and pulpit. The beautiful Norman S doorway is the remains of the Church of St Peter de Dunstable. A chapter house was completed in 1982. *Open 09.00–17.30 Mon–Sat, 08.00–18.30 Sun.* Bedford honours John Bunyan, who spent a fruitful time in gaol here writing the *Pilgrim's Progress*, in a statue close to the church.

Blunham, St Edmund or St James **10** O8
4m E of Bedford on A1. The church has a very distinctive 16thC tower, with four crocketed pinnacles at the corners and four smaller ones in between; its base is Norman. The church is mostly of the 14thC and 15thC and has a great treasure in the 14thC alabaster statue of the Virgin with lilting body, which though headless, is beautiful. See the bosses on the chancel roof and the Elizabethan pulpit. John Donne was Rector of Blunham when he died in 1631, as well as being Dean of St Paul's. *Open 08.00–18.00 Mon, Tue & Thur–Sat, from 09.00 Wed, 09.00–16.00 Sun.*

Cardington, St Mary **10** O8
2m E of Bedford off A603. Though it has some vestigial Norman work in the tower arch, and a late Perpendicular chancel and chapel arcades, the church is largely of 1900. It has one of the only three existing Wedgwood black basalt fonts in England, given in 1783. Between the chancel and the N and S chapels are canopied tomb-chests with interesting

brasses of Sir William Gascoigne, d1540, and two wives, and of Sir Jarrate Harvye, d1638, and his wife; Sir Jarrate is wearing decidedly anachronistic armour. The 18thC and 19thC Whitbread monuments are very fine. There is also a monument to those who died in the airship R101 crash in 1930. **P.** *Open 08.30–dusk Mon–Sat, 07.30–19.00 Sun.*

St Peter, Dunstable

Dunstable, St Peter   **10 O8**
Dunstable Priory was founded by Henry I in 1131 for Augustinian canons. There are scant remains of the priory buildings, but much of the church is intact. Its two W towers fell in a storm of 1222, after which the W front was rebuilt without towers. This has an unusual outside gallery and richly decorated Norman and 13thC portals. The present tower is 15thC. The Norman nave arcades are impressive and so is the gallery above. The nave roof was rebuilt in 1871. There is a fine, restored Norman font. It is thought that the carved 16thC wooden pillars N of the high altar, may have been given by Queen Mary when she was trying to revive Roman Catholicism. They incorporate the royal badges of England and Spain. There are several brasses and some notable 18thC monuments. **P.** *Open 07.45–17.30 Mon–Wed; 09.00–17.30 Thur; 09.00–21.00 Fri; 07.45–17.00 Sat; 07.30–19.45 Sun.*

Eaton Bray, St Mary the Virgin   **10 O7**
3m W of Dunstable off A4146. The restored 15thC exterior and modern tower give no hint of the interior splendour in the 13thC nave arcades. A Norman baron, William de Cantelou, built the N arcade

(traces of his castle moat remain 1m N). Its shafted pillars and moulded arches are spectacularly rich and the capitals ornately carved with leaves, presumably to celebrate his wealth as churches of this size are not normally graced with such elaboration. The S arcade also has beautiful leaf-carving, on capitals and brackets, and the font reflects the N arcade capitals. There is remarkable 13thC ironwork on the S door. **P.** *Open 09.00–20.00 Mon & Tue; 09.00–17.00 Wed–Sat; 07.30–17.00 Sun.*

Luton, St Mary   **10 O7**
The generously proportioned church with flint and stone chequer-patterned exterior, is a striking interlude in an industrial townscape. Its interior is expressive of the wealth of the town at the time when it was built, in the 13thC, 14thC and 15thC, and incorporates many beautiful and unusual features. Primarily these are an elaborately vaulted and carved 14thC font canopy, the tower arch rising behind it, the S door with intricate tracery, the choir stalls which are carved with animals and poppyheads with faces in them, the outstanding stone screen between the Wenlock Chapel and the chancel, the lovely, sunken, vaulted Barnard Chantry, and the four sedilia instead of the usual three. There is a number of interesting brasses and monuments. **P** nearby. *Open 09.00–16.00 Mon–Sat, 08.00–13.00 & 17.30–20.30 Sun.* Not far is Luton Hoo, a great house built in the 18thC and 19thC, with park by Capability Brown and display of Edwardian wealth within.

St Mary, Luton

Milton Ernest, All Saints   **10 O9**
3m NW of Bedford on A6. Butterfield restored this attractive church of Norman chancel, 13thC W tower, 14thC arcades and 15thC nave roof, and added some idiosyncratic touches. There is 19thC stained glass by Gibbs and a handsome 19thC iron screen in the tower arch. An unusual and charming feature is a bread

box of 1729, from which loaves were distributed until 1966. Butterfield's father is buried in the churchyard. **P.** *Open 09.00–18.00 Mon–Sat, 08.00–18.00 Sun.* Milton Ernest Hall and cottages, designed by Butterfield, are close by.

All Saints, Odell

Odell, All Saints   **10 O9**
6m NW of Bedford off A6. The prominent Perpendicular tower is on a church dating from the same period, with vaulted S porch and elegant arcades. Some lovely stained glass of angels survives in the E window of the S aisle. A fine 17thC screen with two rows of balusters is under the tower arch. Odell has the distinction of a former rector who sailed to America in 1635 and founded Concord. *Open approx 10.00–dusk daily.*

Pavenham, St Peter   **10 O8**
3m NW of Bedford off A6. Up steeply rising Church La, a 14thC and 15thC church, which has a priest's room with a fireplace over the porch. Most remarkable is the ornately carved 17thC woodwork in the

church, given in 1848, and consisting largely of panelling from chests and chimney pieces, which is profusely and effectively distributed over church and furnishings. On the Feast of St Peter an ancient custom of strewing grass over the church floor is observed. *Open summer 10.00–18.00 daily, winter 10.00–16.00 daily.* Explore this beautiful village of stone houses on the river Ouse and take the footpath to 13thC Stafford Bridge.

Shillington, All Saints   **10 O8**
8m N of Luton off A600. The church is an impressive landmark, and there is a superb view from the churchyard over a flat, pastoral scene. The old steeple fell in 1701 and was replaced by the present tower in 1750. Long and spacious, this 14thC Gothic church with a 13thC crypt and 15thC additions has some pre-Reformation pews; a fine brass of a priest, Matthew de Assheton, d1400; and a wonderful, lofty and complete rood screen and screens between the chancel and chapels. **P.** *Open 08.00–dusk daily.*

Turvey, All Saints   **10 O8**
5m NW of Bedford on A428. A richly interesting church with remains of Saxon rounded windows above the S arcade. The tower has risen in stages over the centuries, reaching its apex in 1864. There is remarkable 13thC foliated iron scrollwork on the S door. Much of the church is of the 13thC and 15thC, with a chancel built by George Gilbert Scott in 1852–4, containing an exuberant organ. Look up to the angels and bosses on the 15thC nave roof. A beautiful 13thC wall painting of the crucifixion is in the S aisle. Don't miss the impressive and inventive Mordaunt monuments and, in the churchyard, the Victorian Higgins mausoleum. **P.** *Open daylight hours daily.* In the riverside village are Jacobean Turvey Abbey and 18thC Turvey House – which can be viewed from the bridge – and 17thC agricultural workers cottages in Abbey Sq.

◀ HERTFORDSHIRE ▶

Ashwell, St Mary the Virgin   · **10 P8**
4m N of Baldock off A1. Soaring 14thC tower and spire. Broad, graceful interior, made almost stark by light pouring through plain glass onto whitewashed walls and palish stone. Old St Paul's, as it was prior to the Great Fire of 1666, is

scratched on the tower wall, showing the E rose window, which was so famous that Chaucer records in the *Miller's Tale* that women wore badges of it. Other graffiti record the violence of a plague of 1349 and a storm of 1361, which blew down Norwich Cathedral's spire,

bringing the period vividly to life.
Spindly 15thC lychgate. **P**. *Open 09.00–
dusk daily. Tower open summer Sun
afternoons*. Handsome village with timber-
framed and gabled brick houses.

Bishop's Stortford, St Michael   **10 R7**
Wind Hill. On a hillock in a historic town.
The Perpendicular W tower was
extended upwards in 1872. A whole
congregation of faces and figures carved
in wood and stone is gathered here:
corbels in the nave are of the apostles
above and grotesque creatures below,
while in the N aisle corbels of angels face
more homely figures holding the tools of
14thC trades; the misericords, which
reputedly come from Old St Paul's, are
carved with angelic, animal, and human
heads. The 15thC rood screen is
elaborately carved and the 17thC pulpit
has a false floor for short preachers to
stand on. Cecil Rhodes was baptised
here. **P**. *Open 08.00–dusk Mon, Tue, Thur;
09.15–dusk Wed & Fri; 08.00–19.00 Sat;
12.00–18.30 Sun*.

Digswell, St John Evangelist   **10 P7**
Suburb of Welwyn Garden City. A pointed
arch of c1200 and 13thC piscina, attest to
the early origins of a church which was
twice restored in the 19thC and extended
in this. There are large, remarkable
brasses in the old chancel of Richard II's
Standard-bearer, d1415, and his wife. **P**.
*Open 09.00–17.00 Tue–Sat, 08.00–12.00
Sun*. Digswell house, beside the church,
was built c1807 with classical portico.

Hemel Hempstead, St Mary   **10 O7**
Below street level, in the handsome High
St of the old town. 14thC fluted, lead
spire rises slenderly from the Norman
crossing tower. Wonderful, large Norman
interior has in the W wall of the nave an
intricately carved doorway, whose
capitals show Adam and Eve wrestling
with the serpent, a rib-vaulted chancel
and a clerestory – an unusual feature for
the period. See the 14thC brass to Robert
Albyn and his wife, against the W wall in
the S aisle. *Open 11.30–17.00 Mon, Thur,
Fri; from 07.00 Tue; from 10.00 Wed; 07.30–
11.30 & 18.00–20.00 Sun, in school term;
key obtainable other times*.

Hitchin, St Mary   **10 P8**
In a town with a medieval core,
something of the wealth of Hitchin at
that time is expressed in the church,
particularly in the two-storey, vaulted S
porch with two highly decorated
doorways – an exuberant display of the
donor's riches accumulated from the

St Mary, Hitchin

wool trade. 14thC nave. The roofs and
screens are outstanding examples of
14thC and 15thC wood carving, each
individual in design. A medieval feast all
in all. Some unusual brasses in the S
chancel chapel, including a priest with a
bleeding heart and a Merchant of the
Staple. Many other monuments. **P**. *Open
08.15–17.15 Mon–Sat, 08.00–12.30 &
14.30–16.30 Sun*.

King's Langley, All Saints   **10 O7**
2m S of Hemel Hempstead on A41. Near
street of old redbrick houses. 15thC
arcades and tower arch. The ornately
carved 17thC pulpit is decked with
delightful chanticleers. Of great interest
is the late 14thC tomb – blazoned with
alabaster shields – of Edmund of
Langley, First Duke of York and son of
Edward III, who was born in 1341 in a
palace that put the King into King's
Langley. **P**. *Open 09.00–17.00 Mon–Sat,
07.45–19.45 Sun*. Edward II's notorious
favourite, Piers Gaveston, was buried in
the 14thC friary, the remains of which
are now part of a Rudolf Steiner school.

Knebworth, St Mary and   **10 P7**
St Thomas
3m S of Stevenage on B197. Leafy setting in
Knebworth House grounds. 15thC tower
with diminutive spike. Nave and chancel
arch built early in 12thC. Prominent
among the monuments in the Lytton
Chapel – rebuilt in early 18thC to make
room for them – are two portraying half-

reclining, portly periwigged men wearing carefully observed clothes, and a stately, standing sculpture of 1710. There is a very fine brass in the chancel of Henry V's Treasurer, wearing an elaborate cope. **P**. *Open 08.00–20.00 daily.* Bulwer Lytton, the novelist, had a hand in some of the 19thC details of Knebworth House.

St Mary and St Thomas, Knebworth

St Albans, St Michael   **10** O7
Almost in the centre of what was Roman Verulanium: Roman brick is visible in the Saxon nave windows. Aisles were formed in the Saxon walls in the 12thC and there are some Decorated and Perpendicular windows. The tower and W end are 19thC work. A knight and a floriated cross are notable brass monuments. The alabaster monument of 1626 to Sir Francis Bacon, philosopher and Lord Chancellor is pre-eminent, and shows him in Elizabethan dress, seated, asleep. **P**. *Open May–Sep 14.00–17.00 Mon–Fri; Apr–Oct 14.00–18.00 Sat & Sun.* Gorhambury, Bacon's country house, is nearby; also the Roman theatre, and the cathedral.

                                              10 P7
6 miles N of Hertford on A10. In a pretty village. The detached 15thC tower is unique in the county. The nave slopes up to the early 13thC chancel, with a wide arch and dogtooth decoration. An

imposing interior. A tomb chest in the N aisle has excellent brasses of John Field, Alderman of London, d1477, and his son, standing on flowery hummocks. The pole of a Scottish banner stands beside the tomb of Sir Ralph Sadleir, d1587, who was Army Treasurer in Scotland and probably paid the army from the hefty chest in the N aisle. **P**. *Open 09.30–dusk daily.* Climb the churchyard slope for a view of the countryside.

Tring, St Peter and St Paul   **9** O7
Battlemented church and tower. Part of the chancel dates back to the 13thC. Note the unusual 14thC stone vaulting under the tower with central aperture. Work of the 15thC and 16thC is interspersed with that of the 19thC in the rest of the church. Corbels of a fabulous nature decorate the nave. Civic splendour is captured in the classical style monument to Sir William Gore, d1707, and his wife, in which he reclines against a funeral urn in an elegant fashion, wearing the robes of a Lord Mayor of London, and she reclines on the other side. **P**. *Open 10.00– 15.00 Mon, Wed, Thur; 09.30–16.00 Tue; 10.00–12.00 & 13.00–14.00 Fri; 10.00–14.00 Sat; 08.00–19.30 Sun.* Ancient town on Roman Akeman St.

Ware, St Mary the Virgin   **10** P7
A fine, large church in the centre of the town. Of the 14thC, with 15thC additions, 19thC restorations and a 1982 extension. Slender Perpendicular pillars lead to the chancel and through an arch with carvings of Edward III and Joan of Kent, who financed the 14thC rebuilding of the church. The S chapel has 17thC panelling with foliage scrolls and a piscina joined to a sedile, the heads of Henry VII and his mother sculpted either side. The 14thC font is ornately carved. **P**. *Usually open 14.00–16.00 Mon, Tue, Fri, Sun; 10.00–11.00 Wed; 10.30–12.00 & 14.00–16.00 Sat.* Many historic buildings around, including maltings, and gazebos on the river Lea. Once home of the Great Bed of Ware.

◁ BERKSHIRE ▷

Bisham, All Saints   **5** N6
4m NW of Maidenhead on A404. The Thames flows alongside the churchyard and Norman W tower. The late 16thC Hoby Chapel has six heraldic lights of

1609, and outstanding coloured monuments, including recumbent, armoured, alabaster figures of Sir Philip and Sir Thomas Hoby, Elizabethan diplomats. To the right Thomas Hoby's wife kneels in widow's weeds, three daughters who predeceased her behind and an infant lying at her knees. She is said to have beaten another infant to death for blotting his copy books and she haunts the abbey nearby, trying to wash her hands clean like Lady Macbeth. Most exquisite is the Margaret Hoby monument, with swans poised for flight at the base of an obelisk, surmounted by a heart. *Open daylight hours daily.*

All Saints, Bisham

Bradfield, St Andrew   **5 N5**
8m W of Reading off M4 (Exit 12).
Delightful approach bordered by the river Pang and brick and timber cottages. The church has an early 17thC battlemented and turreted W tower and a 14thC N aisle arcade. For his rebuilding of 1847–8, Sir George Gilbert Scott culled Transitional features from local churches: the sanctuary arch, thought to have been suggested by one at Sonning, has an outer band of ascending angels bearing scrolls, while the central boss resembles that at Tidmarsh. Overall, something of an extravaganza in that little integrity of style has been achieved. See the fine 19thC bronze memorial in the S transept, of a kneeling figure framed in strapwork. **P.** *Open 09.00–21.00 Mon–Sat, 07.00–21.00 Sun.* Bradfield College public school beside the church has a chapel by Oldrid Scott. Beautiful countryside round about.

Bucklebury, St Mary the Virgin   **5 M6**
6m NE of Newbury off A4. A Perpendicular W tower with 18thC pinnacles, diminutive spire, and carved figures on its S wall. The late Norman S doorway is wonderfully embellished with mustachio'd faces, flowers and zigzag patterns, surmounted by a rotund face, orb and Maltese cross. Inside are Georgian box pews, benefaction boards on the W gallery and an ancient iron-bound treasure chest. See the inscription on an oak tie-beam in the chancel, '1591 Francis Winchecom Esqvier build this'.

The E window by Frank Brangwyn, 1912, is brilliantly coloured. **P.** *Open 09.00–18.00 daily.* In pastoral seclusion.

Cookham, Holy Trinity   **6 O6**
4m N of Maidenhead on B4447. Beside the Thames. The churchyard was the scene of Stanley Spencer's *Resurrection.* Late Perpendicular W tower. A large church with a 12thC and 13thC core. In the N chapel is a fine memorial sculpture of 1810 by Flaxman, accompanied by a euphemistic epitaph to the drowned deceased, 'who was suddenly called from this world to a better state whilst on the Thames'. The chancel monument to the Master Clerk of Henry VI's Spicery, d1517, includes a brass of the Holy Trinity. Interesting medieval tiles on the altar pavement. **P.** *Open morn–19.00 Mon, Thur & Fri, to 20.00 Tue, to 21.00 Wed & Sat, to 20.30 Sun.* Teas on Sun in summer. Stanley Spencer Gallery *open daily Easter to Oct, weekends winter.* Attractive village, walks, Quarry Wood.

Newbury, St Nicholas   **5 M6**
West Mills. Gothick archways lead into the churchyard of the splendid Perpendicular, battlemented church. The tower pinnacles have battlements and pinnacles of their own. The nave was built on the proceeds of John Smallwood's wealth from the cloth trade

St Nicholas, Newbury

in the early 16thC; his initials are on its
roof. A great cloth master and capitalist,
his importance was sufficient for him to
entertain Henry VIII and Catherine of
Aragon at his home. The pulpit of 1607
has panels framed with luxuriant foliage.
19thC chancel arch and roof. **P**. *Open
08.00–15.30 & 17.00–18.00 Mon–Thur,
08.00–18.00 Sun.*

Ruscombe, St James the Great   5 N6
½m N of Twyford on B3024. A beautiful,
small Norman flint chancel, with faded
13thC paintings of saints on the splays of
the E lancets. The paintings of angels are
20thC work. 14thC wagon roof.
Concordant with the chancel are the
lovely redbrick nave of 1638 and W tower
of 1639. The Ten Commandments were
painted above the chancel in the late
16thC and the pulpit and sounding board
are 17thC. On the N wall is an
impressive monument to Sir James Eyre,
d1799, composed of a sculpture of a
woman beside an urn, over which a
branch of weeping willow drapes. **P**.
Open daylight hours daily.

St Denys, Stanford Dingley

Stanford Dingley, St Denys   5 M6
10m W of Reading off M4 (exit 12). In
gentle downland. The wooden bell tower
is of c1400 and the S doorway of c1200,
with stiff-leaf capitals on shafts and a
rosette in the arch. Diminutive late 12thC
N arcade; the S arcade is early 13thC and
there are some 13thC painted scroll
patterns on each. An 18thC brick chancel
with clear glass and texts, its character
harmonising with the nave. Unusual
decorated bricks in the chancel arch. **P**.
Open approx mid–morn to dusk daily. Pretty
village, with the 15thC Bull Inn for
indoor or outdoor eating.

Tidmarsh, St Laurence   5 N6
5m W of Reading on A340. The
weathervane in the form of a gridiron
commemorates St Laurence's fiendish
martyrdom on a cooking instrument. The
early Norman S doorway with zigzag
scroll and chain decoration has at its apex
a grotesque head with exceedingly big
teeth. Victorian carving on the timbers
supporting the belfry reflects the
doorway motifs. The unusual continues
in the 13thC apse of five sides of an
octagon, with an impressive central boss
of foliage. *Open daylight hours daily.*

Windsor, St John the Baptist   6 O6
High St. Built in 1820 by Charles Hollis,
and enlarged by a polygonal apse later in
the century. The slender iron piers and
roof are unusual. Mosaics by Salviati in
the apse. The beautiful railings of the S
chapel were carved by Grinling Gibbons,
originally for Windsor Castle Chapel, and
given to the church by George III. A
17thC German painting in the W gallery
vividly evokes the Last Supper. **P**. *Open
10.30–17.00 Mon–Sat, 08.00–19.30 Sun.* A
town of note, with a royal castle of an
early origin, whose present magnificent
silhouette is largely 19thC.

◁ OXFORDSHIRE ▷

Bampton, St Mary the Virgin   9 M7
13m W of Oxford on B4449. A large
church, restored in the 19thC, but in
origin late Norman with 13thC and
14thC rebuilding. Statues and small
buttresses link the tower to the lovely
spire. Note the sets of graduated lancet
windows throughout the church. The
13thC sedilia and piscina are quite richly
carved, the two-tiered 15thC Easter

Sepulchre in the chancel is exceptionally
elaborate, and the 14thC W doorway and
gabled porch have ballflower decoration.
The 19thC organ case is an enthusiastic
Gothic revivalist piece. Cherubs abound
on the Baroque monuments in the Horde
Chapel. **P**. *Open 09.00–17.00 Mon–Sat,
08.30–16.30 Sun.* There are interesting
17thC and 18thC houses to be seen in the
village.

Blewbury, St Michael   **5** M6
3m S of Didcot on A417. In a downland,
stream-watered village of great charm,
the spacious church with Norman
beginnings and later medieval additions,
has a timbered S porch, rib-vaulted
chancel and interesting brasses, including
a rare 19thC one. Ancient doors, squints,
and the royal arms of Charles II are
further testimonies of age and interest.
*Open 09.00–16.00 Mon–Thur & Sat, to
17.00 Fri, 08.00–19.00 Sun.* Narrow lanes
and the thatched walls lining a pathway,
which are thought to be Saxon in origin,
add to the delight of the village.

Bloxham, Our Lady of Bloxham   **9** M8
3m S of Banbury on A361. A church of
grandeur on a hill above the village, with
a 14thC spire of awesome slenderness.
The tower is distinguished by angle
buttresses set diagonally. The W
doorway is elaborately decorated and on
it a Last Judgement scene features in
relief. 14thC corbels outside the N aisle
include fabulous beasts and the N aisle
W window has the rare and striking
feature of figures carved in the tracery, as
in the Jesse window at Dorchester. The S
chapel is beautiful, its great windows
giving the effect of a screen of glass.
Note the star in the head of the W
window of the early 14thC S aisle. The E
window has stained glass by William
Morris and Edward Burne-Jones of angels
and saints, the heavenly Jerusalem
looking like a cross between a medieval
and Renaissance city above, and bizarre
clouds by Philip Webb in between. The
15thC rood screen has original painted
figures at the base. **P.** *Open 09.00–dusk
daily.* In the village are lovely 16thC and
17thC thatched, ironstone houses.

Broughton, St Mary   **9** M8
1m S of Banbury on B4035. Beside the
castle in the park. It was built c1300,
much of its detail expressive of the point
where Early English Gothic becomes
Decorated Gothic. The beautiful E
window was restored in the 19thC. Most
uncommon is the 14thC stone screen.
The church has effigies of knights, Sir
John of Broughton's in a fancy 14thC
recess, and of a knight and lady, which,
exquisitely detailed though they are,
belong to different ends of the 15thC.
The 19thC memorial tablets are also
interesting. **P.** *Open summer 09.00–19.00
daily.* 14thC and 16thC moated
Broughton Castle offers a feast of
medieval and later features, inside and
out.

Buckland, St Mary   **9** M7
6m E of Faringdon off A420. The wide,
12thC nave leads to a Decorated chancel,
which has a lovely timber roof with
carved bosses. Most startling is the
contrast between the unadorned N
transept and the S transept sparkling
with mosaics, with which it was
decorated at the end of the 19thC. There
are old pews, a Jacobean pulpit and
tower gallery, and 12thC ironwork on the
S door. See the triangular niche in the
chancel for the heart of William Holcott,
d1575. **P.** *Open 08.00–dusk daily.*

St Mary, S transept

Burford, St John Baptist   **9** L7
6m NW of Witney on A40. Norman and
15thC work unite strikingly in the tower,
but the church is mainly 15thC, and, in a
town made rich by the wool trade, the
money for its restructuring flowed from
that source. The three-storeyed S porch is
very rich in detail. The tower and other
parts of the church underwent Victorian
restoration. Don't miss the memorial of
1569 to Henry VIII's barber, Edmund
Harman, accompanied by vigorous
Brazilian Indians. The best monuments
are in the S chancel chapel; see that to
Sarah Bartholomew, d1689, a delightful
Baroque tablet, bursting with vitality. In
the churchyard are 17thC and 18thC bale
tombs carved with details lively and
lugubrious. **P.** *Open Apr–Sep morn–19.00
daily, Oct–Mar to 17.45.* Burford is a

St John Baptist, Burford

lovely Cotswold stone town on the river
Windrush, with a wealth of medieval and
17thC houses.

Charney Bassett, St Peter   9 M7
12 SW of Oxford off A420. In a picturesque
village. A small church with an unusual
Jacobean belfry, and a very striking
Norman S doorway, surrounded by
carved faces, their tongues sticking out.
Above the doorway inside, a man holds
a gryphon in either hand and appears
undismayed that they are biting his
arms. **P.** *Open daylight hours daily.*

Chipping Norton, St Mary   9 M8
the Virgin
In a pleasant, hillside market town, with
numerous 18thC Cotswold houses. The
W tower was rebuilt in 1825. The 15thC
nave is very fine, built on the proceeds of
the wool trade. In it, the shafted pillars
rise straight up to the roof, soaring
between the clerestory windows which
have no other division between them.
There is a very unusual hexagonal S
porch, the bosses on its vault in the
forms of devilish faces. Note the 14thC
window at the E end of the S aisle,
reputed to come from Bruern Abbey after
the Dissolution, and impressive in its
size. **P.** *Open 09.00–dusk Mon–Sat; 07.30–
19.30 Sun summer, to 17.30 winter.*

Church Hanborough, St Peter   9 M7
and St Paul
7m NW of Oxford off A4095. Admire the
needle-thin spine. Carved doorways and
small, round-headed windows survive
from the Norman fabric. There are also
some 13thC details, but the interior is
Perpendicular, with graceful, concave
octagonal pillars, and screens which
extend across aisles and chancel and
retain some of their original colour.
Examine the fine pulpit and the brasses,
among which is a 16thC brass of a
shrouded figure. **P.** *Open 09.00–dusk daily.*

Cogges, St Mary   9 M7
1½m SE of Witney on A40. A lovely,
quaintly-towered church, in origin 12thC,
but with later medieval additions. The
14thC N chapel is luxuriant in the details
of its arches, E window with white and
yellow stained glass leaf pattern in the
unusual tracery and outlandishly figured
corbels and frieze. Angels support the
pillow of a 14thC wimpled, female tomb
effigy and the dog at her feet symbolizes
fidelity. **P.** *Open approx 09.00–dusk daily.*
Cogges Farm Museum is adjacent.

Cottisford, St Mary   9 M8
9m SE of Banbury off A43. A small, 13thC
village church without aisles, with
original lancet windows in the chancel
and N wall of the nave, and an E
window of c1300. 19thC restoration was
extensive. The base and shaft of a
medieval cross stand in the churchyard.
Open 08.00–18.00 daily. The former home
of Flora Thompson, author of late 19thC
portrait of rural life, *Larkrise to Candleford,*
is in the village.

Deddington, St Peter and St Paul   9 M8
6m S of Banbury on A423. The church
tower's gilded vanes and eight pinnacles
make a colourful declaration of its
presence, overlooking the market square.
The tower replaced its medieval
predecessor which fell in 1634. The body
of the church dates from the 13thC and
14thC and was restored in the 19thC. See
the 13thC sedilia and piscina with nicely
detailed leaf capitals, in the chancel. A
17thC interpretation of Gothic is
expressed in the fan-vaulted N porch. **P.**
Open 09.00–16.00 daily. Mounds mark the
site of a 12thC castle where Piers
Gaveston, Edward II's favourite who was
hated by the nobles, was held in 1312.
Castle House is a 17thC rebuilding of a
medieval house where Charles I spent a
night, and Leadenporch House is a rare
surviving 14thC hall house.

Dorchester, St Peter and St Paul   **9** N7
3m N of Wallingford on A423. A Saxon
cathedral was founded here in 634,
which in 1170 became an Augustinian
abbey church. The Norman church
survives in the N wall of the nave and in
other parts of the masonry. There were
enlargements in the 13thC, 14thC and
17thC and restoration in the 19thC. The
greatest beauty is concentrated in the
14thC choir, most famously in the Jesse
window. Its tracery forms a tree
springing from the loins of Jesse, on
which are eloquent sculptures of his
descendants, others of whom are
depicted in stained glass. The same
masterliness is visible in the elaborate
sedilia and piscina. There is a
magnificent 12thC lead font, a shrine to
St Birinus in the S choir aisle, and an
unforgettable effigy of a knight, c1280,
drawing his sword in defiance of death.
A black, stone slab to Sarah Fletcher
records that she 'died a martyr to
excessive sensibility' in 1799. Note the
wealth of medieval and 19thC stained
glass. Impressive 19thC lychgate. **P.** *Open
09.00–dusk daily.* Willows shade the
church. The village on the bank of the
river Thame, has a High St of brick and
timber-framed inns and houses of great
charm, and lanes with thatched cottages.

Dorchester Abbey

Great Haseley, St Peter   **9** N7
12m SW of Aylesbury off A329.
Outstanding in the imposing church is
the late 13thC chancel, with fine,
geometrical tracery in the windows, and
a group of sedilia, piscina and founder's
tomb, all beautifully detailed. There are
squints through to chapels on either side,
and the church presents a panoply of
Gothic styles, as well as Norman details
in the nave arcades. Interesting brasses
and monuments. **P.** *Open daylight hours
daily.* In the village are a 17thC manor
house and pretty thatched cottages.

Hanwell, St Peter   **9** M8
1m N of Banbury on A423. This secluded,
early 14thC church is endowed with
animated carvings which are very
enjoyable. Figures of men and monsters
process round the outside of the chancel,
while figures link arms and lean out
boldly from the capitals inside. In the S
aisle is a fireplace with a pinnacle-shaped
vent. The windows range from 13thC to
Tudor. **P.** *Open daylight hours daily.* The
remains of Hanwell Castle are to the E.

Henley-on-Thames, St Mary   **5** N6
the Virgin
Hart St. In the heart of the town, its
partly chequer-patterned exterior and
16thC tower framed by two 18thC inns.
The interior is largely medieval. 15thC St
Leonard's Chapel has gargoyles on its
parapet and canopied niches beside the
altars. Lady Periam, d1621, looks out
from an imposing monument. There are
numerous Victorian additions, including
a second N aisle, and two fine stained
glass windows by Hardman in the N
chapel. There is a great view from the
tower. *Open 09.00–16.00 daily.* Tudor-style
almshouses and the fine 14thC timber-
framed Chantry House abut onto the
churchyard. The Thames at Henley is the
scene of the studied smartness and
frivolity of the July regatta.

Horley, St Etheldreda   **9** M8
2m NW of Banbury off A41. Various styles
of Gothic built on to a late Norman
church. There are dignified, tall nave
arcades, and a glorious S aisle E window
with a rose at the top. The church was
restored in 1915, and its screen and rood
loft added in 1947–50. See the lovely
18thC organ case, inlaid with brass, and
big, 15thC wall painting of St
Christopher, very striking in its details
and tapestried effect. *Open 09.00–19.00
daily.* In the churchyard is the 17thC
thatched school house; a 16thC–18thC
manor house is to the S. Attractive
ironstone village.

Iffley, St Mary the Virgin   **9** M7
S district of Oxford on A423. Visitors come
from far and wide to see this Norman
church with remarkable zigzag and
beakhead carving clustered round
doorway and windows on the restored W
front. The S doorway also displays an
explosion of carving, among which notice
the vigorously sculpted capitals. The
tower is impressively detailed too, both
outside and inside the church. The
vaulted chancel was partly rebuilt in the

13thC. Cherubim figure in 15thC stained glass in the nave. *Open daylight hours daily.*

Langford, St Matthew   **9 L7**
6m S of Burford off A361. The central tower is Saxon work of a high order, as is a robed sculpture of the reigning Christ on the porch, though this may be of a later date. The head was probably broken during the Commonwealth, but what remains has a powerful serenity about it. The elegantly proportioned aisles were built c1200 and the fine chancel in the 13thC, with Victorian lozenge shapes added above its twin lancets. 15thC screens are at the ends of the aisles. **P.** *Open daylight hours daily.* In flat, Thames valley countryside, with lovely Cotswold houses.

Longworth, St Mary   **9 M7**
9m SW of Oxford off A420. A 13thC and Perpendicular church, which has remarkable expressions of the Arts and Crafts movement, in the paintings and metal frames of the reredos and the stained glass crucifixion by Heywood Sumner, c1900. Vines are the preponderant decoration of the latter. There are 15thC brasses and a monument by Westmacott to William Bowles, d1801. **P.** *Open daylight hours daily.*

Mapledurham, St Margaret   **5 N6**
1m N of Reading off A329. In an isolated and beautiful Thameside position, with Elizabethan Mapledurham House beyond a stately 18thC gateway. William Butterfield refaced the tower with a flint and brick chequer pattern in 1863. The medieval church has a railed-off Roman Catholic S chapel, owned by the lords of Mapledurham House, and originally built to house the tomb of Sir Robert Bardolf, d1395. See the fine brass to him and the tomb effigy of Sir Richard Blount, d1628, who started to build Mapledurham House late in the 16thC. Lady Cecily Blount lies beside him with a fancy coiffure. There is 15thC stained glass in the chancel. One of William IV's children by Mrs Jordan was one-time vicar and is buried in the churchyard. **P.** *Open Easter–Sep 14.00–17.00 Sat & Sun.* There is much to see in Mapledurham House, where Martha Pope, beloved by the poet Pope, lived.

North Leigh, St Mary   **9 M7**
9m NW of Oxford on A4095. The church has a late Saxon tower and is otherwise largely medieval. Especially beautiful is the 15thC Wilcote Chapel, with elaborate fan-vaulting, an ogee-arched tomb recess decorated with pinnacles and angels, and stained glass with intriguing patterns of foliage and letters of the alphabet. The 18thC second N aisle combines classical details with Baroque. The stone chancel screen and pulpit are Victorian. Note the 15thC Doom painting. There are some ebullient Baroque details on 18thC memorials. **P.** *Open 09.00–17.00 Mon–Sat, 08.00–19.00 Sun.*

St Giles, Oxford

Oxford, St Giles   **9 M7**
St Giles St. A Norman and 13thC church with Victorian and 20thC restoration. There are unusual round-arched recesses in the aisles. The font has dogtooth decoration and colonettes at its angles. Kneeling figures from a 17thC monument are prayerfully disposed on window sills. Ancient tombstones and yews stand in the picturesque churchyard. *Open 14.30–17.00 Mon–Fri, 14.30–17.30 Sat & Sun, 09.30–12.30 Thur & Fri.*

Oxford, St Mary Magdalen   **9 M7**
Magdalen St. The N aisle, called the Martyrs' aisle, is good Gothic revival of 1841 and consonant with the Martyrs' memorial built N of the church at the same time, to commemorate the Protestant martyrs, Cranmer, Latimer and Ridley, burnt in Broad St in 1555–6. The tower was rebuilt early in the 16thC. Elaborate 14thC font and 19thC Gothic diptych memorial. Venerable chest of c1300. *Open 08.15–19.00 daily.*

Oxford, University Church of St Mary the Virgin   **9 M7**
High St. Among Oxford's dreaming spires one of the dreamiest, with its amazing display of 14thC Gothic in pinnacles upon pinnacles. The church's history is entwined with that of the university. Degree-conferring ceremonies

were held in it and the room above the Congregation House, where masters met, held the university library until c1488. The extravagant Virgin Porch of 1637, with curly columns inspired by Raphael or Bernini, incorporates classical features and a statue of the Virgin. The interior is gloriously high and light, with tall, shafted Perpendicular columns in the nave and great windows, one in the chancel nearly reaching the ground. Often the scene of religious controversy, Cranmer, Ridley and Latimer were tried here, and in 1833 John Keble preached the sermon which heralded the Oxford Movement, leading some of its followers to Rome, notably Newman, appointed Vicar of St Mary's in 1828. See the Keble window. *Open 09.30–16.30 Mon–Sat, 12.30–16.30 Sun.* Ascend the tower for a view of the renowned university and city. The colleges and other beautiful buildings are open to visitors. Famous Botanic Garden beside the river.

University Church, Virgin Porch

Stanford-in-the-Vale, St Denys 9 M7

13m S of Oxford off A420. Largely a medieval church with Perpendicular porches and 14thC arcades and aisles. The piscina in the chancel has a rare canopy over it, believed to have been a former reliquary. 14thC stained glass figures are in the heads of the chancel E and S windows. The Jacobean font is enclosed by an ornately carved wooden structure, complete with cover. **P.** *Open 10.00–16.00 Mon–Sat, 09.00–19.00 Sun.*

Sunningwell, St Leonard 9 M7

4m SW of Oxford on B4017. The unique feature of the church is the heptagonal 16thC Jewel Porch, named after John Jewel who was rector c1551. It is a delightful structure with Gothic windows and Ionic columns. Otherwise the church is mainly Perpendicular. The E window was designed by J. P. Seddon, c1877, and is reflective of the work of William Morris and the Pre-Raphaelites. See the outsize poppyheads on the bench ends. **P.** *Open daylight hours daily.* Don't miss the village duck pond.

Sutton Courtenay, All Saints 9 M7

2m S of Abingdon off B4017. A fine late Norman tower, 13thC chancel and 14thC nave arcades. Admire the brick S porch and the 17thC wooden font cover. Satisfyingly simple screens, and some box pews. George Orwell is buried in the churchyard. **P.** *Open 14.30–21.00 Fri, 09.30–18.30 Sat, 08.00–18.30 Sun.* There is a wealth of interesting houses in the picturesque village.

Swyncombe, St Botolph 5 N6

7m NW of Henley-on-Thames off B481. A small, flint and stone Norman church in a lovely, remote spot beside the Ridgeway. Medieval wall paintings in the chancel, of scroll and diaper decoration, were uncovered and repainted in the 19thC. There is a Victorian S porch and 20thC rood screen and loft. **P.** *Open daylight hours daily.* The Ridgeway walk passes the church. 19thC Swyncombe House is to the S.

Thame, St Mary 9 N7

8m SW of Aylesbury on A418. A 13thC church in origin, with later medieval additions. It was restored in the 19thC. See the flowing tracery in the Decorated aisle windows, and the elaborate vaulted S porch of the same period. The 16thC stalls in the chancel have linenfold panelling and poppyheads, and the chancel screen has prettily carved shafts. There is an impressive marble tomb in the chancel to Lord Williams, d1559, and his wife. Numerous brasses. **P.** *Open 09.00–dusk daily.* The market town has a wide main street abounding in inns and timber-framed, gabled, and patterned brickwork houses of various periods. Thame Park, 1m S, is a 16thC and 18thC house with two contrasting façades and splendid interiors.

Waterperry, St Mary the Virgin   **9** N7
13m SW of Aylesbury off A418. A delightful
pastoral setting for a 12thC and later

St Mary the Virgin, Waterperry

medieval church with a Saxon chancel
arch. There are old box pews, splendid
medieval and 16thC stained glass, a fine
14thC knight's effigy, interesting brasses
and a 19thC monument tinged with
melodrama. In the churchyard are the
base and shaft of a medieval cross. **P.**
Open daylight hours daily.

Witney, St Mary the Virgin   **9** M7
A fine, heart-lifting 13thC tower and
spire. A 13thC rebuilding of the church
incorporated Norman work, and to it was
added some luscious 14thC detail in the
chantry chapels and 15thC enlargements.
In the N transept see the beautiful 14thC
window with flowing tracery giving the
impression of an opening blossom, and
handsome tomb recesses below. Overall,
Victorian restoration has given an austere
veneer to the interior. **P.** *Open 07.30–
18.00 Mon–Fri, 09.00–18.00 Sat, 08.00–
18.00 Sun.*

◁ BUCKINGHAMSHIRE ▷

Amersham, St Mary   **10** O7
Walk down through woods from the
station to old Amersham for a view over
hills and medieval church. Solid,
Victorianised exterior and stalwart tower,
for which a new peal of bells was cast in
1983. 17thC Flemish stained glass shines
in the E window and fine medieval
brasses stud the N transept floor. Entry
to Drake Chapel, where there are
memorable monuments, by arrangement,
unless you attend 10.00 Holy
Communion in the chapel on
Wednesday. **P.** *Open 08.00–17.00 Mon–
Sat, 07.30–19.15 Sun.* Pretty, wide–
thoroughfared town with buildings
ranging from Tudor to Georgian.

Aylesbury, St Mary   **9** N7
Early English, but extensively restored in
the 19thC. The lead spirelet is an eye-
catching finale to the large, cruciform
building, approached through Georgian
Church St. The font is of beautiful,
Norman work: wide bowl on square
base, decorated with scrolls and leaves.
Similar ones in the county are known as
'Aylesbury' fonts. The 15thC oak
vestment press is of great interest. Also
an Elizabethan monument to Lady Lee in
which she kneels, her daughter behind,
and between them two babies in
swaddling clothes to show that they were
infant mortalities. A rare Victorian brass

of one Frances Squibbs. *Open 10.00–15.00
Mon–Fri, 10.00–16.30 Sat, 08.00–19.00
Sun.* Waddesdon Manor not far.

Chenies, St Michael   **10** O7
22m NW of London on A404. Above the
river Chess. This 19thC restoration of a
15thC building reflects the centuries with
a stair-turreted W tower, a Norman font,
Victorian hammerbeam roofs, and 15thC
and 16thC brasses, including one of a
lady holding her heart. Stained glass in
Bedford Chapel by Kempe, 1895–8.
Assembled in the chapel – part of the
Bedford Estate and rarely open – are very
impressive monuments to the dukes of
Bedford, some flamboyantly expressive.

St Michael, Bedford Chapel

P. *Open 09.00–dusk daily.* Tudor manor house beside church and 'model' Bedford Estate houses in village.

Fingest, St Bartholomew   9 N7
4m SW of High Wycombe off B482. The vastness of the Norman tower is made yet more extraordinary by the smallness of the church attached to it. The double-gabled roof was added much later. The body of the church is Norman and the chancel was built in the 13thC. *Open 08.00–early eve or dusk.* In a gentle rural setting, with some Georgian and timber-framed houses round about.

St Bartholomew, Fingest

Gayhurst, St Peter   9 N8
3m NW of Newport Pagnell on B526. An exotic cupola crowns the tower of the Georgian church, completed in 1728. Preserved intact are box pews, two-decker pulpit, panelling and plaster ceilings, delightfully elaborated in the chancel. The interior is further enhanced by a monument of 1728 to Sir Nathan Wright and his son Sir George, with statues of them in composed, oratorical stance, wearing minutely detailed costume of the day, including wigs; the setting of curtained canopy and Corinthian pilasters has a theatrical air. **P.** *Open winter 08.00–16.00 daily, summer to 20.00.* Late Elizabethan Gayhurst House nearby.

High Wycombe, All Saints   9 N7
The Perpendicular tower base boasts an 18thC parapet with obelisk pinnacles. Victorian restoration by Oldrid Scott outside, and Street inside. 13thC transepts are juxtaposed with Perpendicular arcades and clerestory. In the N chapel is a notable monument by Peter Scheemakers, 1754: Corinthian columns and pediment frame a sarcophagus on which the figure of Lord Shelburne reclines, dressed as a Roman,

his wife behind. Figures either side wear Roman dress. *Open 09.00–17.00 Mon–Fri, 09.00–13.00 Sat.*

Hillesden, All Saints   9 N8
3m S of Buckingham off A421. Large, Perpendicular church, a great sight at the end of a remote road. Stair turret with lantern of flying buttresses; pinnacles and three- and four-light windows. Amazing purity of style, since there are no later additions to the building. 19thC restoration by Sir G. G. Scott, to whom the church's architecture had been an inspiration as a boy. A clerestory of continuous, clear lights makes the interior very bright. Stone rows of angels border the chancel ceiling, mostly bearing scrolls, those over the altar playing musical instruments. Damaged, 16thC alabaster Denton tomb. The Dentons were Royalists in the Civil War, when their mansion nearby was razed. Bullet holes from the period are visible in the 15thC door in the beautiful fan-vaulted N porch. **P.** *Open daylight hours daily.*

Little Missenden, St John the Baptist   10 O7
3m NW of Amersham on A413. Of Saxon origin. Study the fine 13thC wall paintings – of St Christopher, fishes swimming round his feet, carrying Christ over a brook; of a crucifix and of St Catherine's martyrdom on the wheel, blades from which slay the spectators of her death. The dado is of the 12thC. Roman brick is visible in the chancel arch and crosses behind it are thought to have been made by swords of local gentry on their way to the Crusades. 12thC Aylesbury font with stylised leaf decoration. Timbers at the entrance to the 15thC porch are from a single oak, split and turned upside down. *Open 08.00–20.00 Mon–Sat, 07.30–19.30 Sun.*

St John the Baptist, Little Missenden

Newport Pagnell, St Peter and St Paul   **9** O8

Above the river Lovatt, the Tudor tower dominates, crowned by 19thC pinnacles. The vaulted N porch is of two storeys. The S porch and doorway are pure 14thC work, though much else is restored. The Perpendicular nave and clerestory, watched over by colourful, carved apostles, create a light and large interior. Savage rebuilt the S aisle in 1827–8, when the 14thC sedilia were probably moved here. **P**. *Open 07.30–17.30 Mon–Sat, 07.45–18.45 Sun.*

North Crawley, St Firmin   **10** O8

3m E of Newport Pagnell off A422. A rare testimony to the rebuilding of the chancel in the late 13thC is given by an inscription outside the E window. The 13thC tower becomes Decorated at the top. Inside, the early 14thC N arcade faces the 13thC S arcade with the variation of one arch less. Of the Perpendicular period, note the windows, clerestory and the fine painted screen. Further distinctive features are the box pews and the 17thC font cover. *Open 09.00–18.00 daily.*

Olney, St Peter and St Paul   **9** O8

5m N of Newport Pagnell on A509. Set in a riverside market town with a Georgian disposition to its houses, the church's soaring 14thC broach-spire, studded with small windows, surmounts a tall tower. Gracefully traceried high windows distinguish the early 14thC interior. Associations with 18thC poet William Cowper include the *Olney Hymn* he wrote with reformed slave trader John Newton, which is sung during the service following Olney's Shrove Tuesday pancake race; an endearing portrait in stained glass with his three pet hares and, in the churchyard, tombstones by his friend James Andrews. **P**. *Open daylight hours daily.* Cowper wrote some of his most famous poems at Orchard Side in Market Pl (now a museum) and enjoyed the quaint companionship of three hares, the subject of many letters, termed 'divine chit-chat' by Coleridge and Lamb.

Penn, Holy Trinity   **10** O7

3m NW of Beaconsfield on B474. In the village from which a famous family took its name, the creeper-clad Crown Inn is a close neighbour to the church, built on a spur of the Chilterns, and commanding magnificent views. On the N side is the Penn family's former private entrance. Remark the unusual single-handed tower clock. Inside are eyecatching 12thC coloured consecration crosses. The beautiful nave roof was raised above an earlier structure in 1380 and the church's culminating glory is the Doom painting hanging above the chancel arch, which shows Christ in Majesty, seated on a rainbow. Examine the interesting brasses and memorials of the family of William Penn, founder of Pennsylvania. **P**. *Open 09.00–dusk daily.* Bekonscot Model Village is nearby.

Stoke Poges, St Giles   **10** O6

3m N of Slough on B416. The yew under which Gray is reputed to have written his *Elegy* is opposite the SW door. Note that 'yonder ivy-mantled tower' has been divested of its cover to preserve the 13thC structure. Styles from the 12thC–16thC are married agreeably. Admire the 14thC timber S porch with ogee-headed tracery, the 17thC heraldic glass in the Tudor Hastings Chapel, the dignified brasses and the exceptional survival of the base of a 15thC altar cross. Nearby Stoke Park was built for John Penn, grandson of William Penn of Pennsylvania and the Penn vault entrance is near the font. Gray is buried near the Hastings Chapel. A rather forbidding memorial sarcophagus on a square pedestal was erected further off in 1799. **P**. *Open 09.30–17.00 daily.*

West Wycombe, St Lawrence   **9** N7

1m W of High Wycombe on A40. The church has a medieval core but was exuberantly Georgianised. Stucco garlands run between the nave columns, whose elaborate Corinthian columns rise to a frieze and painted ceiling. Gracefully decorated chancel ceiling. Some of the furnishings are reflective of the imagination and irreverence of members of the 18thC Hell-Fire Club, who met in the golden ball on top of the tower and dedicated themselves to dissipation. The bizarre Dashwood mausoleum outside is eyecatching. **P**. *Open 14.00–17.00 Sat & Sun; 14.00–17.00 Mon–Fri May–Sep.* Towards the village are the caves where unspeakable Hell-Fire frolics might have taken place, and nearby is West Wycombe Park, transformed by Sir Francis Dashwood from something rather plain into a classical symphony.

Willen, St Mary Magdalene   **9** O8

1m NE of centre of Milton Keynes. Dr Busby of Westminster School paid for the building designed by Robert Hooke, a former pupil, in 1679–80. Reverberations of Wren in W doorway in particular. It is worth paying particular attention to the barrel-vaulted nave with stucco panelling, the original furnishings which remain intact, the candle-holders at pew ends, and the organ case with cherubic accompaniment. See too the gorgeous marble-bowled font – cherubs heads here as well – with ogee-shaped cover. Apse added 1867. **P**. *Open 07.30–dusk Mon–Sat, 11.00–dusk Sun.*

Wing, All Saints 9 O8
10m NE of Aylesbury on A418. The memorable Saxon apse with pilaster strips and two original windows has a crypt of c7thC beneath. The extent of the Saxon fabric is awe-inspiring and includes the chancel arch, nave arcades and N aisle. Early 14thC S aisle. Don't miss the brass in which porter Thomas Cotes, d1648, kneels, arms raised appealingly. The 15thC is represented by an octagonal font, the bowl supported by figures of ministering angels. Monument

All Saints, Saxon apse

to Sir Robert Dormer, 1552, of sarcophagus with Renaissance motifs of garlands and ox skulls. Very grand surround of Corinthian columns and entablature. No sign of Sir Robert. *Open 09.00–18.00 Mon–Sat, 08.00–19.00 Sun.*

SOUTH
—EAST ENGLAND—

Kent   Surrey   Sussex

Kent was the point of entry into England for Roman Christianity. It was also the landing stage for successive waves of invaders and the area in which influence from the continent was likely to be felt first. Sumptuous buildings reflected the fact that it was near enough to France for the beautiful stone of Caen to be imported. Kent therefore offers a sequence of styles rather than any single style of its own.

The county is unusual in possessing two ancient cathedrals, Canterbury and Rochester, the latter being the obvious inspiration of important Norman churches as at Barfreston. In these there already occurs a theme which was to be developed locally of placing a cornice of carved heads beneath the eaves. Proximity to London also benefited Kent and it is almost certain that masons were attracted from Westminster Abbey. 13thC churches are common, and often derive from the great age of monasticism. Since monastic orders were transcontinental, these churches frequently reflected the latest styles from France. But where a lay patron financed the building – usually of the tower – he was generally more interested in rivalry with some neighbouring parish and thus a strong similarity exists among many of the towers of Kent. These towers are typically all in one style, which argues a single campaign of building.

In Sussex, by contrast, towers more often show a stratification of styles due to successive building campaigns. This is probably because Sussex was not, in the Middle Ages, a rich county. In the 18thC Horace Walpole could write that the county had 'a Saxon air and its inhabitants are savages'. The area also suffered very heavily from the Black Death and recovery was slow. Sussex churches have more often grown with the ages than been the result of notable acts of munificence. Their unity derives from the continued use of the same materials.

Horsham stone splits easily into thin slabs and has therefore been much used for roofing. Unlike the triple naves of Kent, the typical Sussex church shelters its nave and aisles beneath a single tent of roof. This admits a minimum of light with the result that the churches are subject to a dim, religious atmosphere. Wooden spires are common, and for these the appropriate covering was cleft oak shingles. This attractive form of tiling needs renewal about once a century, so do not expect to see original shingles anywhere.

Shingles are also a feature of some of the spires of Surrey. The problem of building a spire – which is to be octagonal – is that of making it 'grow' from a tower which is rectangular. The simplest way is to begin a triangle of sloping roof from each face of the tower; at a certain height these facets, together with the interstices between them, provide the eight points of departure of the spire, known as a broach-spire.

Betjeman dismisses Surrey as being a tale of 'heavy restoration, of unpretentious fabrics or of new Victorian buildings'. There are, however, considerable Norman remains among his unpretentious fabrics. The heavy restoration would in many cases be the result of using Reigate stone. This resembles Caen stone and was deemed worthy to be used on Westminster Abbey, and, indeed, on most royal buildings of the medieval and Tudor period, but it does not weather well.

◁ KENT ▷

Aldington, St Martin   **7** T5
8m W of Folkestone off B2067. A 16thC W tower of generous proportions, on a church of which Erasmus was once rector. Soaring tower arch. Vestiges of Saxon and Norman work on N side. Lavishly carved poppyheads on the chancel stalls. A priest's door side-by-side with three 14thC sedilia, and part of a 15thC rood screen help to make up a largely medieval picture. Members of the Aldington group of smugglers are buried here. **P**. *Open daylight hours daily.*

Aylesford, St Peter   **6** R5
1m N of Maidstone off M20. A ragstone church with a Norman W tower. The nave and N aisle are of equal width: there are two Decorated windows in the N aisle and the nave arcade is 15thC. The Royal Arms of William and Mary are of 1689. Among the monuments are a 15thC brass of a knight and lady, a prodigiously anachronistic memorial of c1699, in which Sir John Banks is a contemporary gentleman in wig and cravat above and a Roman in his garb below, and a tomb of c1604 whose effigies retain their original colouring. **P** nearby. *Open 09.00–17.00 Mon–Sat, 08.00–19.00 Sun.* See ancient ragstone bridge over the Medway.

Barfreston, St Nicholas   **7** T5
3m NW of Dover off A2. Small, highly ornate 12thC church. The S doorway is a scene of intense activity, with carvings of fighting animals, men charging on horseback, the labours of the months, zodiacal signs, and animals playing musical instruments. Christ sits in the centre of the tympanum. The great wheel window at the E end has colonettes for spokes and winged beasts at its

periphery. Inside, see zigzag decoration round chancel arch. There is a bell in a tree. **P**. *Open 09.00–dusk daily.*

Barham, St John the Baptist   **7** T5
6m SE of Canterbury on B2065. The tall copper spire rises from a 14thC tower. A 13thC cruciform church, with geometrical tracery in the side windows of the chancel and elaborated lancets in the E window. Crown-post roofs. 15thC brasses of a knight and lady and 18thC monuments. Lord Kitchener's name is on the Roll of Honour. **P**. *Open 09.00–19.00 Fri–Sun.* Lovely wooded backcloth to 18thC redbrick houses in the village. Flamboyantly gabled 17thC Broome Park, former home of Lord Kitchener, nearby.

Birchington, All Saints   **7** U6
District of Margate off A28. Largely a 13thC and 14thC church, with a 19thC nave roof and extensive exterior restoration. There is a memorial window to Pre-Raphaelite Dante Gabriel Rossetti, d1882, in the S aisle. A number of interesting monuments. On the 16thC tomb in the Quex Chapel to Sir Henry Crispe and his first wife, his effigy has one hand on the breast, the other on his hip, as if he would profess something from his stony state. More eloquent is Rossetti's gravestone in the churchyard, in the form of a Celtic cross by Ford Madox Brown, with imaginative carving by Jane H. Patteson on it, which includes reliefs of St Luke painting. **P**. *Open 08.30–18.30 Mon–Sat, 07.30–19.30 Sun.* 19thC Quex Park close by.

Brabourne, St Mary the Virgin   **7** T5
5m E of Ashford off A20. A 12thC church with lofty nave and chancel, beside

which the tower is squat. The chancel arch is remarkably wide and tall. Fine 13thC S aisle. In the N wall of the chancel is a Norman window with its original stained glass of flowers intact. There is a medieval oak staircase in the tower; four impressive 15thC and 16thC brasses of knights and ladies, and an elaborate heart shrine of c1300 in the chancel, are also worth seeing. **P**. *Open 09.00–dusk Mon–Sat, 08.00–dusk Sun*. A pretty village lying under the Downs, with 18thC cottages at the churchyard entrance.

Canterbury, St Dunstan   **7 T6**
London Rd. Beside the N porch is a complete Decorated chapel of 1330. The Roper Chapel is of the 15thC and 16thC and houses family tombs; but the chief fame of the church is that it enshrines the relic of Sir Thomas More's head, removed at the behest of Henry VIII for non-concurrence in his marital plans, and brought here by More's daughter, Margaret Roper. Note the beautiful, slender Perpendicular font cover. **P**. *Open 09.00–17.00 daily*. The glories of Canterbury Cathedral are close by.

Canterbury, St Martin   **7 T6**
North Holmes Rd. The oldest parish church in the country. Bede records its use for Christian worship before Augustine came here in 597 and started his mission of conversion. There is Roman brick in the nave and chancel, and blocked-up Saxon windows in the W wall. Note the early font, decorated with arches and circles interlocking. The narrowness of the chancel is unexpected at the end of the wide nave. 16thC brasses. **P**. *Open 07.15 Mon, Thur; 09.00*

St Martin, Canterbury

Tue, Wed, Fri, Sat; 08.30 Sun to approx 18.00 summer, 16.00 winter. There is a view of Canterbury Cathedral from the hill on which the church stands and the city is rich in buildings of the medieval and other ages.

Charing, St Peter and St Paul   **7 S5**
4m NW of Ashford on A20. Close to the Downs and the ruins of the medieval Archbishop's Palace. A glorious late 15thC W tower of four stages on a church of 13thC origin with transepts added in the 14thC. The two-storied porch is rib-vaulted. The roofs were replaced after a fire in 1590. Though not on display, the church possesses a unique Vamping Horn, in that of the few remaining this one alone still has its mouthpiece; it was used by the choir leader as an amplifier. **P**. *Open 08.00–dusk Mon–Sat, 08.00–19.00 Sun*. The picturesque village has some notable redbrick and timbered houses.

Chartham, St Mary   **7 TS**
1m S of Canterbury on A28. A cruciform church built at the end of the 13thC, its chief glory is the Kentish tracery of the chancel windows, in which the patterns seem to shower outwards, almost like fireworks, an effect achieved by splitting the cusps. The magnificent brass of 1306 of Robert de Septvans, is the fourth oldest in the country, and shows a knight with curly coiffure, wearing chain mail and surcoat with protruding epaulettes. The timber roofs are original. The side windows in the chancel have 13thC grisaille glass bordered with coloured leaves. A monument of 1751 by Rysbrack with serene figures of Sarah Young and her husband, includes an impressive putto – not merely decorative, but with a definite presence. **P**. *Open 09.00–15.30 Mon–Sat, 12.00–15.30 Sun*.

Chiddingstone, St Mary   **6 R5**
6m NW of Tunbridge Wells off B2027. Partly rebuilt after a fire in the 17thC. Stone faces look down from the 15thC W tower, rudely poking out their tongues; one has two noses and mouths and three eyes. The church has 14thC windows and nave arcades, an impressive roof, and an elaborate font cover of 1628. The iron grave slabs in the S aisle and nave are testimonies to the former Wealden iron industry; the earliest is of 1601, to Richard Streatfeild, ironmaster. The book rest of the Jacobean pulpit is supported on a charming cherub's head. Pyramidal roofed mausoleum in the

churchyard. **P**. *Open daylight hours daily.*
Delightful Tudor and later timber-framed
houses and early 19thC mansion,
Chiddingstone Castle, in the National
Trust village.

Cliffe, St Helen 7 S6
4m N of Rochester on B2000. A church of
great distinction. The early 14thC chancel
is built of black and white stripes of flint
and ragstone, with beautiful and
individual tracery in the N and S
windows. Vaulted 13thC W tower and
graceful 14thC screen. Unmissable
piscina and sedilia with copious carving.
There are wall paintings in the transepts
of St Edmund's martyrdom and Christ in
Majesty, and red zigzag patterns on the
nave pillars. **P**. *Open 06.00–18.30 Mon–
Fri, 09.00–17.00 Sat, 09.00–20.00 Sun.* A
most interesting setting above the lonely
marshes of the Thames estuary.

Cobham, St Mary Magdalene 7 R6
1m W of Rochester on B260. Above all else,
the 13thC and 14thC church is
outstandingly rich in brasses of the Lords
of the Manor, gathered in the lofty
chancel. Here is a noble assembly of
knights and ladies, including two early
15thC brasses of knights under elaborate
canopies, their sons on pedestals at their
feet, and one of the third Lord Cobham
holding a church; he founded a college of
priests close by in 1362 to say masses for
the souls of his forebears, which became
almshouses. The large, alabaster
monument is of 1561. The 14thC piscina
and sedilia are very ornate. **P** nearby.
Open daylight hours daily. The Leather
Bottle Inn has Dickensian associations,
Cobham Hall is late Elizabethan, and
nearby is Owletts, a 17thC house with
elaborate staircase, highly decorated
plaster ceiling and a 25-acre garden.

Cranbrook, St Dunstan 7 S5
The handsome tower clock is
surmounted by a figure of time. The
14thC S porch is rib-vaulted and has a
boss of a head in foliage, which
complements the massive oak bosses of
green men at the W end of the church,
formerly in the chancel roof, and
introducing the spirit of nature into the
large and light interior. Remarkable brass
chandelier with sunray decoration. The
total immersion font up steps in the S
aisle, was built in the 18thC to attract
baptists. Such effort deserved more than
the single recorded baptism in it. Marble
relief of 19thC painter, Thomas Webster,
shows him holding paint-brushes and

wearing a smock. Eddy memorial. **P**.
Open 07.00–dusk daily. Be sure to see the
working windmill in the town before
leaving.

Dartford, Holy Trinity 6 R6
A Norman N tower, Perpendicular at its
uppermost stage. 14thC nave and
beautiful W doorway. The exterior was
heavily restored in the 19thC. A huge
painting of St George and the Dragon
decorates the S chapel. There are some
good 15thC brasses, and a 17thC
monument to Elizabeth Spilman, German
wife of Sir John Spilman, Elizabeth I's
jeweller and founder of the first paper
mill in Dartford. **P**. *Open 09.00–10.30 Thur
& Fri, 09.30–11.30 Sat, daylight hours Sun.*

Deal, St George 7 U5
High St. Late Queen Anne and early
Georgian, built partly to serve visiting
sailors. Nelson worshipped here when
the fleet was anchored beneath the
Downs within Goodwin Sands. Captain
Parker, his 'dear son and friend', is
buried in the churchyard. **P**. *Open
daylight hours daily.* Beside the sea, Deal
has one of the impressive defensive
coastal castles built by Henry VIII to keep
Roman Catholic Europe out.

Elham, St Mary the Virgin 7 T5
5m N of Folkestone on B2065. A medieval
church in a rather enchanting village of
brick and tile-hung houses. Elements
from different periods are harmoniously
combined. The N porch has a brick gable
and a doorway of c1200 with a 17thC
wooden hood-mould. 17thC painted texts
hang in the nave. The church was
restored early this century by F. C. Eden,
who inserted a number of richly coloured
fittings. In the chancel is a singular piece
of Victorian stained glass in which
Carlyle and the singer Madame Patti
appear as Saul and David, accompanied
by Gladstone, Disraeli and three of
Queen Victoria's daughters. **P**. *Open
09.00–18.00 daily.*

Eynsford, St Martin 6 R6
6m N of Sevenoaks on A225. Grand
Norman W doorway with much lively
zigzag carving. Simplicity and breadth
characterise the whitewashed interior,
with a wide chancel arch and unusual
apsidal sanctuary. 13thC and 14thC
work, although the apse retains its
Norman form. The eight lancets in the S
transept make a striking assembly.
Medieval stone faces regard the world
from corbels. The Tudor N aisle has head
brackets, one with foliage at its mouth.

Open 09.00–dusk Mon–Sat, 08.00–19.30 Sun. Opposite, the ford and bridge over the river Darent and the timbered Plough Inn create a delightful scene.

Goudhurst, St Mary   **7** S5
9m E of Tunbridge Wells on A262. In the Weald, on a hilltop with a wonderful view to the S. Built of yellow sandstone, with an interesting mingling of Gothic and Neo-Classical details on the W face of the 17thC tower. 13thC and 14thC nave arcades and 19thC restoration. The Culpeper monuments include two distinctive 16thC coloured wooden effigies of a knight and lady in the S aisle. There is a fine 17thC Italian marble memorial to William Campion in the chancel. **P** nearby. *Open approx 09.00– dusk, or 18.30 in summer.* A very pleasing village of tile-hung and timbered houses, including weavers cottages.

St Mary, Goudhurst

Harbledown, St Nicholas   **7** S6
1m W of Canterbury on A2. A leper hospital was founded with the church c1085. 19thC almshouses now take the place of the hospital. The tower, W doorway and N aisle are Norman and the interior is beautiful and unadorned. The 14thC chancel has some original stained glass, of figures and Canterbury bells and, in the E window, censing angels and winged seraphim. 13thC stalls and

benches. Medieval relics of the hospital are on display. **P**. *Open 09.00–18.00 Mon– Sat, 08.00–19.00 Sun.*

Hawkhurst, St Laurence   **7** S5
12m SE of Tunbridge Wells on A268. The long E window has wonderfully fluid late 14thC tracery burgeoning from the centre. The chancel arch is impressively lofty. A 14thC interior and Perpendicular exterior with battlements and two- storeyed porches. **P**. *Open 09.00–16.00 daily.* The Moor, the surprisingly named village green, has one or two distinguished houses at its pleasant periphery.

St Peter, Hever

Hever, St Peter   **6** R5
6m NW of Tunbridge Wells off B2026. A 13thC and Perpendicular church overlooking the Eden valley. A slender, shingled spire. In the chancel is a brass of Margaret Cheyne, d1419, slim and elegantly dressed, genuflecting angels holding a cushion under her head. And in the Bullen Chapel is a magnificent brass of Sir Geoffrey Bullen, Anne Boleyn's father, d1538, in robes of the Order of the Garter. A Tudor fireplace and Elizabethan chest are also in the chapel. Lovely colours in the stained glass window by Hardman, 1877, with detail of foliage and mulberries, in S wall of chancel. **P**. *Open 08.00–dusk daily.* Beside Hever Castle, where Anne Boleyn was courted by Henry VIII. The pub opposite the church is named after him.

Higham, St Mary　　　　　**7** R6
3m NW of Rochester on A226. A marsh-
edge church at the road's end, in a
hamlet with two thatched cottages and
few houses. Mainly 14thC, with bands of
ragstone and flint on the outside and a
timber spirelet. Faces and flowers are
carved around the 14thC S door, a bird at
the apex, while the central part is carved
with tracery patterns like a window. The
15thC rood screen is still in place and the
beautiful 14thC pulpit leans a little with
age. Some vividly coloured 19thC stained
glass. *Open 08.00–dusk daily.* Dickens'
home, Gads Hill, ½m S.

Hollingbourne, All Saints　　　**7** S5
5m E of Maidstone on B2163. A 15thC W
tower and 14thC nave arcades. The
windows follow a transition from the
Decorated style, exemplified in the W
window of the S aisle, to Perpendicular,
fully expressed in the S windows of the S
aisle. Notice the handsome hexagonal
17thC pulpit with strapwork carving. The
Culpeper Chapel was built in 1638 to
house the tomb of Elizabeth Culpeper,
commemorated in a fine white marble
effigy. Legend has it that the lead coffins
of the Culpepers move around now and
then in the vault below. Needlework by
four 17thC Culpeper ladies, which
occupied them for 12 years, can be seen
on request. **P.** *Open 09.00–18.00 daily.*
Tucked under the Downs.

Hoo, St Werbergh　　　　　**7** S6
4½m NE of Rochester off A228. The tall
spire is a local landmark. A 13thC church
added to in the 14thC and 15thC. There
is some 15thC stained glass of angels in
the tracery of the chancel windows, and
memorial windows to Thomas Aveling.
Several good medieval brasses. **P.** *Open
09.30–16.00 Mon–Wed & Fri in school term;
08.00–12.00 & 18.00–19.30 Sun.* 2m S is
Upnor Castle, built in the 16thC to
protect Chatham Dockyards, newly built
on the other side of the river. Elizabeth I
reviewed the fleet from it in 1581.

Hythe, St Leonard　　　　　**7** T5
Numerous steps lead up to the church on
a very steep hill. Here is preserved an
extraordinary and macabre assembly of
8,000 thigh bones and 2,000 skulls. The
13thC chancel was built on a most
unaccustomedly lavish scale for a parish
church, in three storeys, signalling
considerable prosperity in Hythe at the
time when it was one of the Cinque
Ports, before the sea receded. The
processional passage at the E end makes

its way through the buttresses. The W
tower was rebuilt in the 18thC. Steps
lead up to the chancel and sanctuary.
Lachrymose putti attend the 17thC
monument to Elizabeth Beane. See the
19thC reredos in the S chancel aisle. **P.**
Open 07.30–sunset daily. Hythe is worth
wandering in, particularly on the hillside.

Ightham, St Peter　　　　　**7** R5
4m NE of Sevenoaks on A25. On a knoll.
Although there is earlier evidence, the
church was largely built in the 14thC and
15thC with a N aisle of 1639. A noble
effigy of Sir Thomas Cawne, knight, who
built Ightham Mote in the 14thC, lies
beneath a 14thC window with curly cusp
ends. Also in the chancel is a 17thC bust
of a famous needlewoman, Dorothy
Selby; the epitaph claiming her 'Arte
disclosed the Plot, which had it taken
Rome had tryumph'd & Britains walls
had shaken', credited her as the
discoverer of the Gunpowder plot.
Spacious Jacobean box pews. **P.** *Open
08.00–dusk or 18.00 daily.* Pretty village;
orchards, woods and enchanting Ightham
Mote nearby.

Leeds, St Nicholas　　　　　**7** S5
4½m E of Maidstone on B2163. A Norman
W tower of ragstone and a magnificent
tower arch. The high, narrow nave
signals an Anglo-Saxon origin and indeed
there are two Anglo-Saxon windows
above the N arcade. The Perpendicular
rood screen extends across the entire
width of the church and is carved with
finely traceried windows. Brasses and
monuments. **P.** *Open 09.00–18.00 daily.*
Nearby, battlemented Leeds Castle rises
romantically from a lake.

Lenham, St Mary　　　　　**7** S5
9m E of Maidstone on A20. Norman
beginnings are visible in the N chapel.
The Early English chancel has a 14thC
wall painting of a robed bishop, and a
stone altar, an uncommon survival.
There are 15thC choir stalls with
misericords and an ancient chest with 10
locks. Birds and vines in vases are carved
engagingly on the pulpit. A faded 14thC
painting of St Michael weighing souls is
on the S wall of the nave. 14thC effigy of
priest in mass vestments, hands joined in
prayer. **P.** *Open 09.00–dusk winter, 09.00–
17.00 summer.* Attractive and historic
houses in the village.

Lullingstone, St Botolph　　　**7** R6
2m E of Orpington on A225. Approached
through the 16thC gatehouse of
Lullingstone Castle, with which it shares

a great lawn and lake. Of flint, with 16thC brick N chapel, 18thC white porch and small bell turret. Glorious Queen Anne plaster ceilings and a lovely early 16thC rood screen on which Tudor roses flower and the pomegranate of Aragon is carved. 18thC balustrade above. Good stained glass from the 14thC to 18thC in the Decorated windows. A fine monument to Sir John Peche, d1522, in the chancel; the effigies of Sir George Hart, d1587, and his wife hold hands on a tomb-chest in the N chapel, while the W wall of the chapel is taken up by a heraldic memorial of 1738, expressive of Gothick verve. **P**. *Open 09.00–dusk daily.* Lullingstone Roman Villa close by.

Lydd, All Saints   **7** T4
A long and lofty church with a 132ft high 15thC tower, distinguished by having as its mason Thomas Stanley, senior mason at Canterbury Cathedral, and visible for miles over Romney Marsh. Lydd was cut off during a storm of 1287 which moved the river mouth from New Romney to Rye. The body of the church is Early English, of fine proportions, though the chancel was bombed and rebuilt in this century. A Saxon ingredient is to be seen in three blocked arches. There is a number of good brasses in the nave, tombstones of the shipwrecked and of smugglers, and Flaxman's first monument, 1781, to Anne Russell and her baby, who is carried up by an angel to his mother standing on a cloud. **P** nearby. *Open Jun–Sep 14.00–17.30 Wed; 10.00–13.00 Sat all yr & Nat Hols.*

Lyminge, St Mary and   **7** T5
St Ethelburga
4m N of Folkestone on B2065. An ancient Christian shrine. Queen Ethelburga founded an abbey here in 633 and traces of 7thC walling remain. Danes overran the church in the 9thC and Dunstan, Archbishop of Canterbury rebuilt it in the 10thC. A 15thC flying buttress rather dramatically supports the E end. A W tower and N aisle were added early in the 16thC. **P**. *Open 09.00–17.00 or dusk Mon–Sat, 07.30–17.00 or dusk Sun.*

Maidstone, All Saints   **7** S5
On the bank of the Medway. A former collegiate church founded in 1395, it forms a Perpendicular entity, the stalls and misericords almost intact, and lavish sedilia with gabled canopies and lantern spires. Fine nave arcades. The roofs were renewed in the 19thC. A brass depicts six generations of the Beale family from

All Saints, Maidstone

1399. Memorial to Sir John Astley, d1639, has four Carolean figures posing in shrouds, making significant but inscrutable gestures. Memorial to an Elizabethan member of the Washington family. **P**. *Open 10.00–16.00 Mon–Sat Apr–Sep; 10.00–16.00 Mon, Tue, Fri, Sat & 12.00–16.00 Wed Oct–Mar.* Medieval buildings of college, former archbishops' palace and tithe barn cluster round.

Marden, St Michael and All Angels   **7** S5
7m S of Maidstone on B2079. A low 13thC W tower with white, weatherboarded top. A remarkable studded and fluted medieval S door leads in to the vista of early 14thC arcades. See the tracery of the beautiful early 14thC windows at the W end of the N aisle, unrestored. Others were restored in 1868 and details altered. The pointed chancel arch is c1200. Figures above the capitals are defaced but for one near the font, holding a dagger. The vivid stained glass in the E window is by Patrick Reyntiens, 1962. The font of 1662 has an unusually large contemporary cover. 18thC brass chandelier. **P**. *Open 07.30–dusk daily.* Farm trails nearby in this centre for hops and apples.

Meopham, St John the Baptist   **7** R6
5m S of Gravesend on A227. The church was dedicated in 1325 and was entirely rebuilt at that time. The imposing W

tower has a Victorian W doorway and upper stage, with trefoiled lancets lower down. The pulpit of 1682 is of outstanding quality, with floral and marquetry adornments and peeping putti heads. **P.** *Open daylight hours daily.* Take a stroll S to Meopham Green and the smock windmill of 1801.

Mereworth, St Lawrence   **6** R5
7m SW of Maidstone off A26. A most arresting 18thC Neo-Classical sight in the Kentish countryside, with a spire imitating that of St Martin-in-the-Fields and intimations of Inigo Jones' St Paul, Covent Garden, in the portico. A circular vestibule below the tower leads to barrel-vaulted nave and columns supporting an entablature instead of arches. There is heraldic stained glass, a 14thC brass of a knight and beautiful 15thC alabaster effigy of a second knight. **P.** *Open summer 09.00–19.00 Mon–Sat, 08.00–20.00 Sun; winter 09.00–16.00 Mon–Sat, 08.00–16.00 Sun.* Nearby Mereworth Castle, built 1723, pays unstinting homage to Palladio. Yotes Court, a 17thC redbrick house, is also worth visiting in the vicinity.

Mersham, St John the Baptist   **7** T5
1m SE of Ashford off A20. The church has a Norman beginning, late 13thC tower and S aisle and some work of the late 14thC. The W window is a most striking sight: for its great width, with a row of shields at the foot of its 13 lights and dainty quatrefoils above, and for the top section, where the windows have been put in diagonally so that the tracery heads lie outermost. The 17thC altar rails and 18thC screen to the S chapel are notable. The Knatchbull monuments trace changing memorial fashion. *Open 09.00–17.00 daily.*

Minster-in-Sheppey,   **7** S6
St Mary and St Sexburga
Isle of Sheppey. High on the N coast of the Isle of Sheppey, stand two churches in one, the first founded in the 7thC by the Saxon queen Sexburga, as the church of a nunnery of which she was the first abbess. Parts of the original fabric remain, including Roman tiles. The chancel was rebuilt in the 14thC and the tower in the 15thC. The parish church was built in the 13thC and restored in the 19thC. One or two remarkable carved heads remain from Elizabethan alterations to the nuns' chancel. Notice the 12thC column statue of the Virgin and Child, and the early 14thC effigy of Sir Robert de Shurland, who looks as if

he is about to turn over. Two large, foreign 14thC brasses. **P.** *Open Jun–Sep 10.00–12.00 & 14.00–17.00 Mon–Sat.* Gatehouse to W.

Nettlestead, St Mary the Virgin   **6** R5
2m SW of Maidstone off B2015. Small church, set back from the road, whose 15thC windows compose the larger part of the N and S walls of the nave. Angels hold shields in medieval stained glass in the window tracery. A storm of 1763 destroyed most of the rest of the medieval glass. There are Jacobean wall monuments either side of the chancel. A squat tower and sequestered churchyard with enormous yews. **P.** *Open approx 09.00–dusk Mon–Sat, 12.00–dusk Sun.* Note the timber-framed gatehouse of Nettlestead Place to the SW; the medieval manor house to which it led is now rebuilt, though it retains a 13thC undercroft, and is private.

Newington, St Mary the Virgin   **7** S6
2m W of Sittingbourne on A2. The Perpendicular tower soars up to battlements and turret. Width and length characterise the Decorated interior. There is prettily carved 15thC panelling in the S aisle, a font cover incorporating Renaissance motifs and a bench in whose poppyheads small animals appear. Also several medieval brasses, and 14thC paintings of saints and scenes quite hard to discern. **P.** *Open summer 14.00–16.30 Sat & Sun.*

Northfleet, St Botolph   **6** R6
Nr Gravesend on A226. In a landscape worthy of Salvador Rosa, of craggy chalk cliff overlooking a wooded quarry. The original 12thC tower toppled and was replaced in 1717. There is evidence of Saxon long-and-short work, and remains of 13thC arcades within a large, early 14thC structure. The restored windows are worth looking at for their Kentish and geometrical tracery. The chancel screen of 1313 has dainty trefoil-headed lights and is a rare survival. *Open 19.00–20.00 Tue, 09.00–10.00 Thur, 10.00–11.00 Sat, 10.00–12.00 & 18.00–20.00 Sun.*

Penshurst, St John the Baptist   **6** R5
4½m NW of Tunbridge Wells on B2188. Approached through the original Leicester Square of half-timbered cottages, one, lychgate-like, forming an arch leading into the churchyard. A sandstone church with strikingly large pinnacles on the tower. Early English and 14thC nave arcades, and much 19thC renewal. A delicately carved screen of

1895. The Sidney Chapel, 1820, has a prettily painted tunnel-vault with leafy bosses. Half a Purbeck marble knight in chain mail, d1299, lies among numerous monuments. Under the tower are 13thC coffin lids with foliated Albigensian crosses, one with a figure of a fervently praying nun. **P.** *Open 08.00–dusk daily.* Beside the church is Penshurst Place, a wonderful manor house where that perfect Renaissance man, Sir Philip Sidney, was born, and a most picturesque village.

Plaxtol   **6** R5
8m W of Maidstone off A227. No dedication, because built during the Commonwealth, in 1649. The hammerbeam roof is its glory. The 19thC brought restoration and additions. The Cromwellian reredos in the S transept has a carving of the Crossing of the Red Sea, in which Israelites and Egyptians wear 17thC English dress. Two remarkable 18thC chandeliers hang in the nave. The rustic churchyard has 18thC gravestones unique to W Kent and E Sussex, of head-shaped humps carved with animated skulls. *Open 09.00–dusk Mon–Sat, 08.00–19.30 approx Sun.* A charming weatherboarded terrace of cottages curves beside the church, and interesting Old Soar Manor is a mile off.

Queenborough, Holy Trinity   **7** S6
On the Isle of Sheppey and once a port. There is a wonderful view of Kent from the turreted W tower. Edward III's exchequer paid for the church, c1350. The octagonal Kentish ragstone font of 1610 has a relief of the keep of Queenborough Castle, which was demolished later that century. The roof painting c1698 of clouds and stars, with an angel sounding the last trumpet at the E end, attended by four cherubs, has unfortunately faded. **P.** *Key available.* Interesting monuments jostle in the graveyard.

St Margaret at Cliffe,   **7** U5
St Margaret of Antioch
The clerestory is remarkable for its external arcading. There is quite a breathtaking view down the nave to the wide chancel, the nave arches on scallop capitals and the chancel arch with dogtooth and zigzag decoration. The whole is 12thC. The W doorway is lavishly moulded and carved with heads and figures. **P.** *Open 08.00–12.00 daily.* St Margaret's Bay is nearby.

St Nicholas at Wade, St Nicholas   **7** T6
5m SW of Margate off A28. A 13thC church with arches of c1200 to the chapels from the chancel. The tower is of the early 14thC. In the S arcade are late Norman arches, one of which rests on leaf crocket capitals, while the other capitals are decorated with heads spilling leaves from their mouths. Note the fancy Baroque brass chandelier. **P.** *Open 08.30–dusk daily.* Cottages and farm buildings cluster round. The remains of Reculver Roman Fort are to the N.

Sandwich, St Clement   **7** U5
A fine Norman central tower. There is much interesting carving on the capitals of the tower arches and on the doorway to the stair turret. The chancel is of the 13thC, and the nave, rebuilt in the 15thC, has an open timberwork roof, decorated with small angels. The octagonal Perpendicular font has bold and beautiful heraldic decoration and pedestals for statues in the base. **P.** *Open summer 07.00–17.00 Mon–Sat, 07.00–19.30 Sun; closes 15.30 winter.* One of the medieval Cinque Ports, the sea retreated from Sandwich in the 16thC; it is a charming town of medieval buildings, restored in the 18thC.

Sevenoaks, St Nicholas   **6** R5
At the top of a hill, with interesting historic buildings round about. Very big, 13thC and Perpendicular, with 19thC additions of battlements and clerestory. Angels abound in support of the chancel roof. A memorial of 1911 on the N wall of the chancel records that John Donne was rector of Sevenoaks from 1616–31. Stained glass by Kempe in the S aisle. There is a memorial window to William Pitt, First Earl of Amherst, in the N chancel chapel. **P.** *Open 09.00–17.00 or dusk Mon–Sat, 07.45–20.00 Sun.* Fabulous 15thC–17thC Knole House and park nearby.

Shoreham, St Peter and St Paul   **6** R6
4½m N of Sevenoaks off A225. Pinnacled flint and brick 18thC W tower. Timber S porch with Perpendicular lights. Decorated and Perpendicular. The fan-vaulted rood screen stretching right across church unusually retains its loft doors and stair. Colourful 18thC organ case, from Westminster Abbey. Burne-Jones window in S wall of nave, with lustrous figures of Joy, Creation, Love – Creation a fiery-winged angel holding a globe. *Open 09.00–17.00 Fri & Sat, 07.30–19.30 Sun.* Beamed George Inn opposite;

the Darent river flows through the village, which has Samuel Palmer associations. Wooded hills around.

Staplehurst, All Saints   7 S5
8m S of Maidstone on A229. The 15thC tower fronts the highest point of the village street. A most remarkable feature is the Saxon S door, adorned with Danish ironwork displaying an astonishing fantasy of marine life, including a cross between a fish and a bird with a curly tail near the top. The chancel has two early 14thC N windows and an anchorite's cell, beneath the squint in the N wall. 12thC and 13thC work in the nave arcade. The church also has a heart sepulchre. **P** nearby. *Open daylight hours Mon–Sat, 07.00–21.00 Sun.* The village's charm lies in its timbered Elizabethan houses.

Tenterden, St Mildred   7 S5
The beautiful W tower is a great feature of the town and was built over several decades in the 15thC. A 13thC chancel and 14thC nave, S doorway and N chapel, which has a window with the flowing tracery characteristic of the period. A medieval shafted, hexagonal font. **P** nearby. *Open 09.00–18.00 Mon, Tue, Thur–Sat; 07.00–18.00 Wed; 07.30–19.00 Sun.* An exceedingly attractive town, reputed birthplace of William Caxton in 1472, and where the Kent and East Sussex Railway runs steam trains on certain days.

Throwley, St Michael and   7 S5
All Angels
9m W of Canterbury off A251. The Norman W doorway has inventive geometrical patterns on the arch mouldings well worth studying. Otherwise a later medieval church with some 19thC work. There are imposing 16thC and 17thC tombs in the N and S chapels. **P.** *Open 08.30–17.00 daily.* Belmont House gardens, ½m NW, are open on occasion; the first Lord Harris had the house built at the end of the 18thC and there is a memorial to him in the Lord Harris Chapel in the church.

Tunbridge Wells, King Charles   7 R5
the Martyr
A dedication countering Puritan incursions around the wells. Built 1676–8 to accommodate growing numbers of visitors. Subscription list has Pepys' name on it. Enlarged later in 17thC. Outstanding plaster ceilings by Wetherel and Doogood, domed and decorated with wreaths of fruit, palms and putto

heads. **P.** *Open 08.30–dusk Mon–Sat, 07.45–19.45 Sun.* Across the road are the chalybeate springs and elegant promenade of the Pantiles.

West Malling, St Mary the Virgin   7 R5
3m W of Maidstone on A228. A Norman tower with an elegant 19thC spire. In the Early English chancel is an alabaster tomb with reclining effigies of Sir Robert Brett, d1624, and his wife in Jacobean dress, the whole brightly coloured. The nave was twice rebuilt, in the 18thC and in this. James II's coat of arms is exuberantly carved with flowers and fruit, in Grinling Gibbons's style. *Open 08.00–18.00 Tue, Wed, Fri, Sat; to 21.00 Mon, Thur; to 20.00 Sun.* St Leonard's Norman keep tower nearby; also Manor Park Country Park, with marked walks.

St Mary the Virgin, Westerham

Westerham, St Mary the Virgin   6 R5
View over Darenth valley and downs from churchyard. Partly 13thC, low tower and short spire. Perpendicular aisles, arcades and nave roof. 19thC restoration. Medieval timber spiral staircase in tower, and Edward VI's Royal Arms. Among brasses, one of a priest wearing pre-Reformation vestments after the Reformation. Exuberant Gothic revival organ case of 1871. Above memorial to General James Wolfe, who worshipped here as a boy, a

window of sumptuously coloured glass designed by Burne-Jones. *Open 08.00–18.00 Mon–Sat, to 20.00 Sun.* Chartwell, the former home of Sir Winston Churchill is nearby.

Wingham, St Mary the Virgin   7 T5
5m E of Canterbury on A257. Although there is some earlier evidence, there was major rebuilding in the 13thC, when a college of priests was founded. A spacious church. The nave was rebuilt in the 16thC, but progress was at one point halted, when a Canterbury brewer embezzled the funds in 1555. The result is an unusual wooden nave arcade instead of one of stone. 15thC reredos, which is a rarity. The misericords are distinctively carved with foliage. Imaginative monuments on which a panoply of angels and putti mourn. **P.** *Open 08.30–dusk Mon–Sat, 07.30–dusk Sun.* A handsome, large village with many interesting 18thC houses.

Woodchurch, All Saints   7 S5
4m E of Tenterden on B2067. There is great eloquence and beauty in the simplicity of the large, 13thC interior. The three long E lancets are a focal point, with shafts and moulded arches; the wide nave arches add to the sense of breadth. The 14thC brass of a fully vested priest is unusual, and the manorial pew notable. The steeple soars on the edge of the village green. *Open summer 09.00–18.00 daily, winter to 17.00.*

Wrotham, St George   6 R6
7m W of Maidstone on A25. A lichened 15thC W tower with a rib-vaulted passage through it. Battlemented two-storey S porch, and an Early English and 14thC interior. Lofty tower arch. The S aisle reredos, designed in 1907 by Comper, has a medieval-style painting of angels in azure robes. A turret stair beside it leads to the singular feature of a Nun's gallery above the wide chancel arch. Note the ballflower decoration on the piscina in the chancel. A 19thC pulpit, angels bursting forth from below. **P.** *Open 09.00–dusk daily.* On a slight incline, overlooking a house of Elizabethan origin, Wrotham Place.

Yalding, St Peter and St Paul   7 R5
5m SW of Maidstone on B2010. There is a Saxon window in the tower, a flower-pattern clock face, and an 18thC cupola on top of the round turret. A 13thC and 14thC spacious interior with broad arches. See the 17thC monument on the N wall of the chancel, from which Ambrose Warde and his wife look out at us, though they kneel at a prie-dieu as if they ought to be engaged in prayer like their children below. Near the pulpit is a memorial window to the poet Edmund Blunden, engraved by Laurence Whistler, 1979. There are two 15thC yews near the N porch. **P.** *Open 07.30–18.00 daily.* A medieval bridge spans the river Beult and there are numerous interesting houses in the village.

◁ SURREY ▷

Alford, St Nicholas   6 05
10m S of Guildford on B2133. Approach bordered by picturesque tiled cottages on right and village stocks and whipping post on left. The walled churchyard is also a beautifully kept garden. The medieval N door has a diamond-shaped framework, and massive 15thC oak timber pillars support the spire and bell turret, an impressive sight as you enter. Round piers and pointed arches form the late 12thC S arcade; the more refined N arcade is early 14thC. Fine, large Norman font. Jacobean pulpit with sounding board. The ancient altar stone is of Sussex marble. Though half the pre-Christian yew opposite the N door has fallen, the remaining half is going strong. **P.** *Open daylight hours daily.*

Blechingley, St Mary the Virgin   6 P5
3m E of Redhill on A25. 12thC and 13thC work mingled with that of the 15thC and 19thC. A masterly early 18thC monument to Sir Robert Clayton, Lord Mayor of London, shows him and his wife before a classical-style background, their clothes exquisitely detailed, their stance eloquent and restrained, the whole composition expressive of the reign of Queen Anne. Tomb of Sir Thomas Cawarden, d1559, Master of the Revels at the Tudor court, who, wisely from the point of view of keeping his head, shifted religious allegiance according to that of the reigning monarch. Site of 13thC cell of Roger the Hermit in S chapel. Devilish gargoyles. **P.** *Open 09.30–dusk Mon, Thur, Fri; from 07.15 Tue & Wed; from 08.00 Sat*

St Mary the Virgin, the Claytons

& Sun. Delightful village of timber-
framed and tile-hung houses, remnants
of a Norman castle, and N Downs
beyond. Place Farm, 1m N, now mostly
18thC, was Anne of Cleves' home after
her divorce from Henry VIII.

Burstow, St Bartholomew   **6** P5
3m NE of Crawley off M23 (exit 9). Norman
origin, but largely of the 15thC. The most
remarkable feature of the church is the
beautiful medieval timber tower. Tower
and broach-spire are finely shingled, as
are the four corner pinnacles. Wealden
resources of wood and iron are also
evident in the large, impregnable, iron-
bound chest. John Flamsteed, first
Astronomer Royal, was rector during the
Restoration. **P**. *Open 08.00–18.30 daily.*

Chaldon, St Peter and St Paul   **6** P5
1½m W of Caterham off B2031. Mostly of
the 12thC and 13thC, with a very ancient
bell. The pulpit is one of the few to be
made in the country during the
Commonwealth, and is dated 1657. An
outstanding and rare 12thC wall painting
shows in the centre small, naked bodies
climbing up the ladder of salvation to
heaven, while others tumble down to
hell. Fearful torments, including a
cauldron, attended by demons, await the
fallen, while above in purgatory, the

devils have angels to contend with,
including the Archangel Michael, who is
winning in the weighing of souls. **P**.
*Open approx 10.00–dusk Mon–Sat, 07.30–
19.30 Sun.*

Chiddingfold, St Mary the Virgin   **6** O5
5m S of Godalming on A283. Interesting
18thC redbrick, arched tombstones in the
churchyard. The shafts of the 13thC nave
arcades were lengthened in the 15thC.
Unusually long 13thC lancet windows in
the S wall of the chancel. At the end of
the S aisle, fragments of original
Chiddingfold glass form a lancet
window, commemorating the local
medieval glass-making industry, at its
height during the 14thC. Heavy
restoration, 1869. Bells and handbells are
rung – there is one pre-Reformation bell.
P. *Open 09.00–18.30 Mon–Sat; 07.30–20.00
Sun.* The medieval Crown Inn opposite is
notable, as are many of the tile-hung
houses round the village green. Walking
sticks and wally sticks for shepherds are
made locally.

Chipstead, St Margaret   **6** P5
2½m S of Coulsdon off A23. In a slight
hollow, surrounded by gentle downland
and opposite the village green. Though
suburbia is close by, it is invisible. A
13thC church with rib-vaulted crossing
tower and tasteful Victorian additions by
Norman Shaw and Rev P. Aubertin.
There are unusual triangular heads to the
chancel lancet windows, and stone
chancel seats with a classical Grecian
overtone to the scroll and leaf decoration
on the ends. See the different tracery
patterns carved on each panel of the
14thC font. Monument to Sir Edward
Banks, d1835, commemorates his rise
from obscurity to builder of London,
Southwark and Waterloo bridges. *Open
14.30–16.00 Sat & Sun, 09.00–11.00 Sat
summer.*

Compton, St Nicholas   **6** O5
3m SW of Guildford on B3000. The
beautiful, plain Saxon tower has a 14thC
shingled broach-spire. A nave of 12thC
pillars and arches made of hardened
chalk and of dazzling whiteness, leads
the eye down to the surprise of the
unique double sanctuary, with Norman
stone vaulting and early stained glass of
Virgin and Child in the lower sanctuary,
and elegant wooden rail of the same
period in the upper. 12thC mural above
the chancel arch. **P**. *Open 09.00–18.00
Mon–Sat, 07.00–20.00 Sun.* Curious Watts
memorial chapel nearby, and picture

St Nicholas, Compton

gallery with over 100 paintings by G. F. Watts, the Victorian painter. Also 16thC Loseley House, and a farm inviting you to fish for trout.

Dunsfold, St Mary and All Saints   6 O5
8m S of Guildford off B2130. In the Weald close to the Sussex border. Built between 1260 and 1320 above a stream, where there is a 'holy' well, on what was probably a sacred spot in pre-Christian times. Massive 14thC oak door. Rare oak pews of c1300 with holes for tapers at their ends. The chancel slopes slightly to the N to symbolise the attitude of Christ's head on the cross. Triple sedilia for three orders of clergy – priest, deacon and sub-deacon. In the walls outside are wooden plugs on chains, once used to drain the church when water was sluiced over the floor. The medieval altar stone lies under a huge 1000-year-old yew. *Open approx daylight hours daily.*

East Clandon, St Thomas   6 OS of Canterbury
3m E of Guildford on A246. A delightful, small village church. The 13thC chancel has an E window of two lancets instead of the usual three, and a 14thC low side window from which the sanctus bell was rung. A 12thC nave with Perpendicular windows. The pretty belltower and the aisle are late Victorian. *Open 09.00–17.00*

Mon–Sat, 08.00–17.00 Sun. Hatchlands, handsome 18thC house decorated by Robert Adam, nearby.

Ewhurst, St Peter and St Paul   6 O5
7m SW of Dorking on B2127. Cruciform, sandstone church of the 12thC and 13thC; the tower was well rebuilt in Norman style after falling down in 1838. The Norman S doorway is plainly moulded yet very distinctive, as is the church as a whole. Finely carved 17thC altar rails. *Open 09.00–18.30 Mon–Sat; 07.00–20.00 Sun.* In an area designated one of outstanding natural beauty.

Farnham, St Andrew   6 NS
A large church, mostly of the 15thC, when it was partly rebuilt after a fire. Exterior restored 1855. Quite an imposing W tower. The 12thC chancel, restored in 1848, has finely detailed sedilia and piscina and refined 17thC altar rails. The E window is by Pugin and was shown at the Great Exhibition of 1851. Memorial in the tower to William Cobbett, author of *Rural Rides*, who was born in Farnham. *Open 08.00–dusk Mon–Sat, 07.30–20.00 Sun.* Much Georgian architecture to be enjoyed in the town and Farnham Castle, frequented by royalty from Edward I to Queen Victoria, is worth a visit.

St Andrew, Farnham

Frensham, St Mary the Virgin   6 N5
3m S of Farnham off A287. Remarkable, large W tower, late 14thC. The enormous three-foot-wide copper cauldron inside the church is claimed to be a genuine witch's cauldron, used by one Mother Ludlam, who lived in a cave near Waverly Abbey at a time difficult to specify. **P.** *Open 09.30–dusk Mon–Sat, 07.30–19.00 Sun.* Frensham Ponds, Great and Little, are here, amid heathland, the Little Pond covered by water lilies in the season.

Great Bookham, St Nicholas   **6 O5**
2m SW of Leatherhead on A246. A
beautifully inscribed stone records that
the chancel was rebuilt in 1341 by the
Abbot of Chertsey. The weatherboarded
W tower is supported on massive oak
timbers and has a 12thC flint base.
Scalloped capitals decorate the 12thC
nave pillars. There is a notable brass of
1598 of a sagacious-looking Tudor couple,
Henry and Elizabeth Slyfield. Other
notable monuments include one to Col
Thomas Moore, d1735, in Roman garb
and attitude, a 19thC memorial backed
by a weeping willow that overwhelms
the chancel wall, and one to Cornet
Geary who died in an ambush during the
American War of Independence. *Open
08.00–17.00 Mon–Thur & Sat, to 18.00 Fri
& Sun.*

Guildford, Holy Trinity   **6 O5**
High St. Rebuilt in a classical style in the
18thC, after the tower collapsed, with
further 19thC alterations. An impressive
and spacious interior. Marble pedestals of
piled-up books support the columns and
canopy over the tomb of Archbishop
Abbot, d1633. Abbot's Hospital, founded
by him early in the 17thC, is opposite
and has a remarkable gatehouse, with
almshouses and chapel beyond. **P**
adjacent. *Open approx 06.00–18.00 Mon–
Sat, 06.00–20.00 Sun.*

Guildford St Mary   **6 O5**
Quarry St. Anglo-Saxon central tower
remains, but this ancient church was
enlarged in the 12thC and 13thC, partly
to accommodate the royal court at
Guildford Castle. Steps punctuate
progress up the nave, adding further
interest to an unusual interior. Until 1825
the rib-vaulted chancel had an apse,
removed in order that the street might be
widened for George IV to drive his coach
and four to Brighton. The N and S
chapels retain apses. Slanting openings
through the chapels were made to allow
processions to pass round the altar.
Prominently moulded 13thC N doorway.
SPCK bookshop at W end. **P.** *Open
09.00–17.30 Mon–Wed, Fri & Sat.* Remains
of castle nearby. Exceptionally interesting
17thC Guildhall and clock in the cobbled
High Street.

Hascombe, St Peter   **6 O5**
3½m SE of Godalming on B2130. In a
lovely village embraced by hills. Built by
Woodyer in 1864 in late 13thC style, the
revival of medieval coloured decoration
makes the interior very remarkable. In

the gilded apse, stained glass by
Hardman and Powell and surrounding
paintings depict biblical scenes with
angels present, and the painting round
the nave walls of the miraculous draught
of fishes culminates on the E wall, where
the disciples drag in the net. The 15thC
rood screen has been transformed into a
fervent Victorian expression of colour
and, in places, of sentiment. **P.** *Open
09.00–18.00 daily.*

Lingfield, St Peter and St Paul   **6 P5**
3m N of East Grinstead on B2028. A
Perpendicular church in which the N
aisle is almost as wide as the nave,
dating mostly from 1431, when Sir
Reginald Cobham founded a college for
chaplains, clerks and 13 poor persons.
The monument to the first Lord Cobham,
who fought at the Battle of Crecy and
died in 1361, shows him in full plate
armour, a colourful Saracen lounging at
his feet. There are impressive alabaster
effigies in the chancel of the third Lord
Cobham, d1446, and his wife, and
excellent brasses of the second Lord
Cobham and his wife in the N chapel.
Numerous other notable medieval
brasses, including two of priests in full
mass vestments. 15thC screen, and
misericords with carved heads. Chained
bible on double-desked lectern. *Open
07.30–19.30 daily.* Pretty 15thC–18thC
houses surround the churchyard. 18thC
lock-up in village centre.

Puttenham, St John Baptist   **6 O5**
4m SW of Guildford off A31. In a pretty
village, beside the N Downs Way. The
15thC tower is much restored, gaps in
the brickwork frequented by doves. The
12thC S doorway has scallop decorations
and a moulded arch. Pleasingly simple
interior, in which the bases of the huge,
12thC pillars rise towards the E, as if the
floor had sloped originally. Restored in
1861 by Henry Woodyer, who inserted
dormer windows on the N side. *Open
08.30–dusk daily.* Fine 18thC Palladian
mansion to the S.

Seale, St Laurence   **6 O5**
3½m NE of Farnham off A31. The setting,
at the head of the valley below the Hog's
Back, is a beautiful one. Restored in the
19thC in keeping with the original
medieval building, of which vestiges
remain. The polychrome tower with
pyramidal spire is an interesting
Victorian expression of a more sober
original. The wooden S porch is
medieval. Memorial in the N transept to

Ensign Long, drowned in 1809, has the distinction of a verse written by Long's school friend, Byron. The altar painting is attributed to Cima. *Open 07.30–20.00 daily*.

Shere, St James　　6 O5
4½m SE of Guildford off A25. A handsome 13thC shingled spire on a Norman tower. There is striking Norman zigzag decoration on the S doorway arch, a Purbeck marble font of c1200 and some beautiful medieval stained glass, including Chiddingfold glass in the S aisle. The 13thC chest was placed here to collect money for the Crusades, in conformity with an order of Pope Innocent III. It is sobering to peer through the quatrefoil and squint in the chancel and ponder the life of the anchoress Christine, who was enclosed but for these openings and a grating through which food was passed. *Open daylight hours daily*. Afterwards you might welcome convivial refreshment in one of the inns in this pretty place, or a stroll beside the Tillingbourne.

Stoke D'Abernon, St Mary　　6 O6
3m NW of Leatherhead off A245. On the bank of the river Mole. Numerous interesting details remain, despite drastic 19thC restoration. Here is the oldest figure brass in England, of Sir John D'Abernon, d1327, of outstanding quality. By its side, that of his son, shorter, and demonstrating changing armorial fashion. In the chapel are life-size, recumbent, coloured Tudor effigies, propped up on one elbow, and a rare pre-Reformation fireplace. There is fine rib-vaulting in the 13thC chancel and 17thC furniture. The Jacobean pulpit is a little loud, but balanced by the simplicity of the 13thC alms chest opposite. Italian statue of madonna and child, c1500, and

St Mary, Stoke D'Abernon

notable medieval stained glass. Look for the 12thC faded fresco of a crucifix on a nave pillar, and the outline of a doorway high in the S wall, once the private entrance of a Saxon lord. **P**. *Open 14.00–18.00 Sat & Sun*.

Walton-on-Thames, St Mary　　6 O6
The 15thC tower was reshaped by 19thC restoration. Largely built in the 14thC, although five Norman pillars remain from an earlier church. Roubiliac's magnificent memorial of 1755 to Viscount Shannon, depicts him with the appurtenances of a military career, including large tent, flag and gun. His daughter is sculpted below, her clothing beautifully detailed down to her shoes. Elizabeth I's gamekeeper at Oatlands Palace, John Selwyn, d1587, is commemorated in a brass, stabbing a stag, which he is said to have done at the feet of H.M. **P**. *Open 09.00–17.15 Mon–Sat, 07.45–20.00 Sun*. Manor Road opposite leads to the Old Manor House, c1500. River towpath nearby.

West Horsley, St Mary　　6 O5
4½m NE of Guildford on A246. Slightly detached from the village which has some pretty timbered houses, and close to West Horsley Place, a big house of medieval origin. Mostly 13thC and earlier. Some good 13thC stained glass in the central and N lancets in the chancel. Admirable 18thC monument to John Kendal in the S aisle has a relief of a rose tree with a single fallen bloom. Sir Walter Raleigh's head is buried here. **P**. *Open 09.00–16.00 daily*.

Witley, All Saints　　6 O5
3m SW of Godalming on A283. A Saxon window survives in the S wall. The carved S doorway is 11thC; tower, chancel and S transept early 13thC. In the latter are lovely lancet windows. Of the 12thC paintings on the S wall of the nave, the Marriage at Cana is most visible. Unfinished memorial in the sanctuary to a servant of Edward IV's brother, the Duke of Clarence, he who was drowned in a butt of Malmsey wine. The barrel roof and alabaster reredos in the chancel are Victorian additions, as is the N aisle. The Victorian water-colourist, Birkett Foster, is buried in the churchyard. *Open approx daylight hours daily*. Picturesque tile-hung cottages in village and old White Hart pub opposite. Hammer ponds and Witley Common with nature walk are in the vicinity.

St Mary the Virgin, Worplesdon

Worplesdon, St Mary the Virgin 6 O5
2½m NW of Guildford on A322. The substantial, Perpendicular stone tower is prominent above the village. An inscription inside records that Richard Exfold built 14ft of the tower, for which he left money in 1480. The cupola on top comes from the old rectory stables. A medieval interior which contains some 14thC glass; of particular interest are two richly coloured canopies with figures in the N aisle. The 17thC pulpit and font are from Eton College. A deep and ancient well stands in the churchyard. **P.** *Open 09.00–18.00 Mon–Sat, 07.30–19.30 Sun.*

◁ SUSSEX ▷

Alfriston, St Andrew 7 R4
3m N of Seaford on B2108. The 14thC church stands on an Anglo-Saxon mound on the Tye, or village green, and is built of fine flintwork, in the form of a Greek cross. Especially striking are the fluted piers of the tower arches. Notice the unrestored Decorated windows in the N transept and chancel and the huge modern E window. The Easter sepulchre and the sedilia and piscina are remarkable features in the chancel. Take the path round to the E end for a sylvan scene of considerable charm, edged by the Cuckmere river. **P.** *Open daylight hours daily.* Visit the 14thC Clergy House beside the church, *open Apr–Oct.* Medieval inns in the village recall its proximity to the ridgeway, travelled from ancient times.

Arlington, St Pancras 7 R4
3m SW of Hailsham off A22. A remarkable and ancient flint church in rural retirement, on the line of a Roman road. The nave is Saxon and the N chapel Norman. Unusually, the shingled spire of the 13thC W tower begins below the ridge of the nave roof. Edward III's head is carved above the Decorated E window. Traces of painted foliated crosses are visible either side of the chancel arch. **P.** *Open 10.00–dusk daily.* Restored 13thC Michelham Priory 2m NE.

Arundel, St Nicholas 6 O4
A late 14thC church. The elegant stone pulpit is also Perpendicular, though restored in the 19thC. Wall paintings of the Seven Deadly Sins and Seven Works of Mercy are still discernible. The Fitzalan Chapel at the E end is separated from the nave by a rare late 14thC iron grille and later wall, and is entered from the castle grounds. A quite amazing array of impressive monuments to the dukes of Norfolk is assembled in it. *Open summer 09.00–18.00 daily, winter 10.00–dusk daily.* An attractive town and riverscape below the Downs, with a castle of considerable romance from the distance; close to its image is tarnished when the medieval castle is revealed as a 19thC imitation, but it contains wonderful furnishings and paintings.

St Nicholas, Arundel

Battle, St Mary the Virgin 7 S4
A large church with 12thC nave arcades and 13thC and later medieval work. There are two 15thC brasses, a 16thC tomb with Renaissance motifs, and a Norman font with a charming Perpendicular cover. **P.** *Open 09.00–dusk Mon–Sat, 07.30–20.00 Sun.* Beside the

church are the magnificent remains of
Battle Abbey, built by William the
Conqueror on the spot where Harold got
one in the eye, and consecrated in 1094.

Bishopstone, St Andrew   **6 R4**
10m E of Brighton off A259. In the Downs,
a most unusual and lovely church. Part
of the nave and the S *porticus*, or side
chamber, possibly date from the 8thC.
Among the Norman additions are the W
tower with monsters and heads looking
out from it, and the S doorway into the
porticus. Above the doorway is a Saxon
sundial with the name Eadric inscribed
on it. See the 12thC coffin lid, beautifully
carved with a cross, lamb and cross and
two big birds drinking uncomfortably
from an urn. **P.** *Open daylight hours daily*

Bosham, Holy Trinity   **6 N4**
3m W of Chichester off A27. A wonderful
but slightly formidable interior, a
reminder that churches were resorted to
as defensive fortresses in early days, with
windows high up in the wall to prevent
arrows or stones penetrating, like the
three small circular Saxon windows. The
massive horseshoe-shaped Saxon chancel
arch is an amazing and impressive sight
and the five lancets seen through it very
beautiful. It is believed that King
Canute's daughter is buried here, even
though it is disputed whether he tried to
rule the waves from here or from
Southampton. Definitely, Harold prayed
here before setting sail for Normandy in
1064, as evinced by the Bayeux Tapestry
where he appears, hefty hawk in hand,
before the church, which is remarkable
however in bearing no resemblance to it
at all. The tower arch is a very good
example of Saxon long-and short work
and the tower has an original Saxon
window with baluster. *Open 08.00–17.00
daily.* The creekside setting is delightful
and you will certainly want to explore
the village.

Brighton, St Peter   **6 P4**
York Pl. A grand work of Gothic revival
by Sir Charles Barry, completed in 1828,
for which the late 14thC choir of York
Minster was the inspiration. The spire he
designed was never built, but the tower
itself is very impressive with unusual
recesses at its lower part. Slender piers in
the lofty interior. Barry's chancel was
replaced by a larger one in 1906, whose
ceiling was brightly painted in 1967–9 to
echo the style of a medieval church
interior. **P.** *Open 10.00–16.00 Mon, Tue &
Thur; 10.00–11.15 Wed; 07.30–14.30 Sat;*

St Peter, Brighton

09.00–11.30 & 17.00–19.00 Sun. The
church overlooks the Steine where the
atmosphere of Regency Brighton still
prevails, with the Royal Pavilion nearby
as its most ebullient expression.

Chiddingly, dedication unknown   **7 R4**
4½m NW of Hailsham off A22. On the
periphery of the Weald. The fine 15thC
W tower has one of the three remaining
ancient stone spires in the county, lofty
and pinnacled. The Pelham Buckle,
badge of the Pelham family, is carved on
the tower doorway. The church is mainly
of the 13thC, 14thC and 15thC with a
19thC chancel. There is an astonishing
alabaster monument in the S transept to
Sir John Jefferay, d1571, on which he
reclines in legal robes, his wife below,
while a younger couple look down their
noses from niches, the lady wearing
prominent ruff and farthingale. Were
cheeses really placed before the proud
pair as stepping stones from their
mansion, Chiddingly Place, to church, as
tradition has it? At any rate, the stone
drums they stand on represent the
cheeses. **P.** *Open 09.00–19.00 or dusk
Mon–Sat, 08.00–20.00 or dusk Sun.*

Church Norton, St Wilfrid's Chapel 6 O3
6m SW of Bognor Regis off B2145. The nave
was moved from here to a new parish
church in Selsey in the 19thC, leaving the
13thC chancel at Church Norton, in rural
seclusion and close enough to the shingle
beach to be reached by seaspray on a
windy day. It has an aumbry and piscina
of Caen stone and a Tudor tomb on

which man and wife kneel face to face, reliefs of their patron saints beside them. *Open summer 09.00–dusk daily, winter Sat & Sun only.*

East Grinstead, St Swithun   **6 P5**
The tower of the former church collapsed in 1785, destroying the nave as well. The church was rebuilt in 1789 by James Wyatt, in battlemented Perpendicular style. The oldest dated iron tomb slab in the country, 1570, lies in front of the chancel and together with one of 1616 forms a testimony to the Sussex iron industry of the past. Included in the stained glass is an Oxford Movement centenary window by Burlison and Grylls, 1933. *Open 08.00–18.00 Mon–Sat, 07.30–20.00 Sun.*

Eastbourne, St Mary the Virgin   **7 R4**
Church St. In old Eastbourne, removed by a mile from the seaside resort. Round and octagonal piers alternate in the handsome nave arcades, c1200. The substantial tower is 14thC, as are the screens. An ogee-arched Easter Sepulchre faces sedilia and piscina in the chancel. *Open 07.30–dusk daily.* Timber-framed 16thC and elegant 18thC houses around the church embody the original Eastbourne. The former manor house contains the Towner Art Gallery of 19thC and 20thC British paintings.

St Mary the Virgin, Eastbourne

Folkington, St Peter   **6 R4**
5m NW of Eastbourne off A27. A small, delightful church of great simplicity, at the end of a road beneath a steep wooded hillside. There is a sense of nature brimming over around the flint nave and chancel and wooden belfry. Inside are old box pews and two elegant memorials attended by putti. **P.** *Open daylight hours daily.* A footpath leads up to the S Downs.

Hastings, All Saints   **7 S4**
Old town. Early 15thC church in medieval Hastings, with a W tower partly of flint

and stone chequer. There is a Doom painted above the chancel arch, showing Christ seated on two rainbows, wearing a red mantle, and with stars at his feet. The heavenly Jerusalem has unfortunately disappeared, but a very picturesque devil presides over the torments of the damned, consisting in hanging from gallows. Only one gallows is complete with lost soul. The church has a Father Willis organ. *Open daylight hours daily.* William began his Conquest here. Much of the medieval castle is under the sea but the ruins can be visited, as can the nearby smugglers' caves. Timber-framed and Georgian redbrick houses lead down to the fishing harbour and the unique tall, wooden huts once used for drying nets. Victorian and present day Hastings stretches along the shore.

All Saints, Dacre tomb

Herstmonceux, All Saints   **7 R4**
8m N of Eastbourne off A271. Two miles from the village, on an eminence overlooking the sea to the south. The tower and W wall are the earliest parts, built c1180; otherwise the church is of the 14thC and 15thC. There is a fine brass of a knight in the chancel, Sir William Fiennes, d1402, offering 120 days pardon to anyone who says a *pater noster* and *ave* for his soul. His son began building Herstmonceux Castle in 1440. Outstanding is the 16thC repainted Dacre tomb, in exuberant late Gothic style, with 15thC effigies of two knights, probably bought from Battle Abbey at the

Dissolution and representing a saving for the Dacre purse. **P.** *Open daylight hours daily.* Moated and turreted, Herstmonceux Castle entrance is opposite the church.

Mayfield, St Dunstan　　　　**7** R5
7m S of Tunbridge Wells off A267. Dunstan is reputed to have built a wooden church here in 960 and in his nearby forge enterprisingly pinched the Devil's nose with red-hot tongs. Gabled and timbered houses lead up the High St to the church, the 13thC tower of which is all that remains of the church prior to a fire of 1389. It is otherwise Perpendicular. The two-storeyed S porch is rib-vaulted and imposing. Note the four Sussex iron tomb slabs, one of 1668 and another of 1708, the two striking 18thC candelabra and the fine 15thC oak roofs in the S and N aisles. **P** nearby. *Open 08.00–dusk daily.* A girls school is in the remains of a palace of the Archbishops of Canterbury beside the church, which has a great medieval hall.

New Shoreham, St Mary de Haura　**6** P4
A commanding portside church with Norman tower and transepts, a choir transitional between Norman and Gothic, and a ruined nave. No-one has solved the mystery of why the magnificent choir should have Norman pillars and arches on the N, while a Gothic character asserts itself in the shafted pillars on the S, though not built much later. Nonetheless, there is a sense of vivacity in the whole conception, harmonised by the rib-vaulting. *Open 08.00–17.30 Mon–Sat.*

Newick, St Mary　　　　　　**6** P4
6m SE of Haywards Heath on A272. The very pleasing Perpendicular tower has a handsome W door with heads on the hood-mould. There is Norman evidence in the S wall and a restored 14thC porch. The nave was lengthened in 1886–7 and the 13thC chancel rebuilt and decorated with frieze, wagon roof and beautiful tiles. The organ with casework by John Oldrid Scott was made by the Casson Positive Organ Company in 1889, very advanced for its day and still intact. Near it is a stained glass window by Burne-Jones. *Open approx 09.00–17.30 daily.* Several historic houses in the village including the late 17thC Old Rectory.

Rodmell, St Peter　　　　　　**6** P4
7m E of Brighton off A26. A lovely, small Norman church whose early 13thC tower has a pyramidal spire and an unusual annexe adjoining, used as a baptistry.

The ornate Victorian chancel arch imitates its predecessor, which is thought to have been made of stones from Lewes Priory, carved with late Norman motifs. A N wall window contains medieval stained glass of the Trinity. See the round central pier of the S nave arcade with fine carving of foliage on the square capital. *Open daylight hours daily.* Adjacent Monks House, retreat of Virginia Woolf and coterie, is open to visitors.

Rotherfield, St Denys　　　　**6** R5
7m S of Tunbridge Wells on A267. Near a pretty triangle of houses, a large, early 13thC church with a 15thC tower and two-storeyed N porch. There are box pews, an elaborate 16thC font cover and a spectacular Jacobean pulpit, backed by two bold eagles in profile. Also, a Doom of c1300, showing Christ and angels and a most characterful and circumspect St Michael weighing souls, one wing askew. And a beautiful E window by Burne-Jones of the angelic choir. **P.** *Open 08.30–16.30 Mon–Sat, 07.00–19.30 Sun.*

Rottingdean, St Margaret　　**6** P4
4m W of Brighton on A259. The church is mostly Early English and has a beautiful, though squat, central tower with long lancets. Glorious stained glass was designed by Burne-Jones and made by William Morris, including the E window of the archangels Gabriel, Michael and Raphael, and windows in the tower of Jacob's Ladder and the Tree of Jesse. *Open 08.45–18.30 daily.* There is a delightful green and pond in front of the church and some handsome houses in the village, including the Elms where Rudyard Kipling lived for five years, and North End House, Edward Burne-Jones' home.

Rye, St Mary the Virgin　　　**7** S4
The church is at the summit of the picturesque hill town and one time Cinque Port, with an 18thC water-house in the verdant churchyard and houses comfortably propinquitous to it. The church, as the town, suffered from French raids, most drastically in 1377, but Norman and medieval work remains. And what was probably the greatest loss to the church, of the W door, occurred in the restoration of 1882. The early 13thC nave arcades contrast with the slender Perpendicular chapel arcades. Simple and appealing 15thC screens stand between transepts and chapels and the 13thC Clere Chapel contains an elaborately carved 18thC mahogany altar. There is

much vivid modern stained glass and a window by Burne-Jones in the N aisle. Enchanting golden, chubby cherubs act as quarterboys on the tower clock, whose pendulum swings inside the church. *Open 09.00–18.00 Mon–Sat, 07.30–19.30 Sun.* The tower is *open on summer weekdays* for a view out to sea. Though smuggling receded with the sea in the 16thC, you can sense its salty history keenly in the cobbled streets and timbered inns, especially in Mermaid St.

St Mary, Sompting, in its ivy days

Sompting, St Mary   6 O4

2m NE of Worthing off A27. It is exciting to see the Saxon tower with the only 'Rhenish Helm' spire in England, and the church's position on downland overlooking the sea is lovely. The tower arch has scrolled and jagged decorations on the capitals and the whole church is rich in interesting carvings, such as the curious face on the corbel in the N transept, the abbot complete with crozier and architectural features in the 12thC S transept and the Saxon and Norman carvings on the N side of the nave. **P.** *Open 08.30–dusk Mon–Sat, 07.30–dusk Sun.* Benches outside for the weary, or those who want to admire the view.

South Harting, St Mary and   5 N4
St Gabriel

3½m SE of Petersfield on B2146. Under the Downs on the Hampshire border, this imposingly large church with a copper spire is of the early 14thC. New roofs were built in it after a fire in 1576: the nave and transept roofs are unexceptional, whereas the chancel's is superlatively embellished with carved baluster posts, wall posts and pendants.

Complementary to this example of Elizabethan carpentry is the ingenious 19thC spiral staircase in the N transept. Eric Gill designed the churchyard war memorial. *Open 08.00–17.45 Mon–Sat, 07.30–dusk Sun.* Ascend the hill to visit Uppark, late 17thC redbrick mansion with 18thC interiors, once the home of Lord Nelson's mistress, Lady Hamilton, and retaining its original furnishings.

Steyning, St Andrew   6 P4

5m NE of Worthing on A283. A truly majestic, late Norman church, although the chequered tower of c1600, replacing a former central tower, is out of character with the rest. Ethelwulf, King Alfred's father, was buried here in 857 and the Saxon tomb slab in the porch may be his. The huge S doorway still has its Norman hinge. Each arch and capital in the church is carved with such a wealth of individual decoration that a brilliant statement of the creativity of the period is conveyed. *Open 08.00–19.00 or dusk daily.* From the churchyard there is a view of the Downs and Chanctonbury Ring. Numerous medieval timber-framed and tile-hung cottages and later gabled houses make Steyning a delightful place to wander in.

West Chiltington, St Mary   6 O4

8½m NW of Worthing off B2139. A 12thC church with massive pillars and scallop capitals to the aisle, the original bell clappers in the N porch and a pretty, shingled spire of 1602. There are two fine 14thC windows in the S wall, an exceedingly long squint from aisle to chancel and a dignified linenfold-panelled pulpit. Above all, there is an astounding quantity of wall paintings: those in the Lady Chapel are of the 12thC and show angels and apostles in adoration; the 13thC paintings in the nave are of the Passion on the S (see how devilish the flagellators look) and the Nativity on the N. Of the 14thC are the figure of Christ in the nave N window and the decoration of the soffits of the arches. Though faded, they give a strong impression of the impact colour and narrative originally made. *Open summer 09.00–17.00 daily, winter 10.00–16.00 daily.*

Wilmington, St Mary and St Peter   7 R4

5½m NE of Seaford on A27. Deep in downland seclusion and tree-shaded, not least by a yew of great girth and antiquity. Delightful oak-shingled belfry. The Norman chancel has two original windows and stone seats used by monks from the adjoining priory. In the 13thC N chapel (squeeze past the organ) is a charmingly idiosyncratic stained glass window of St Peter surrounded by six butterflies, three moths and a bee, all but one of which are identifiable. The nave was rebuilt in the 14thC and the chancel arch in the 19thC. The Jacobean pulpit has a steepled sounding board. 18thC and 19thC table tombs were placed near the porch to accommodate the distribution of bread and beer, willed to the poor by those beneath. **P.** *Open daylight hours daily.* The 231ft-high Wilmington Long Man, who might be prehistoric or might not, is a dramatic hill figure opposite the churchyard, long since deprived of his privy parts for prudery's sake. Museum in the remains of the medieval priory *open Apr–Oct.*

St Mary and St Peter, Wilmington

Winchelsea, St Thomas a Becket   7 S4
Edward I gave land for a new town in 1288, after a storm changed the course of the river Rother, inundating old Winchelsea, and the church was planned on a magnificent scale. It was never completed and besides was damaged in French raids. What remains are chancel, side chapels and ruins of the transepts. These have remarkable grandeur of architecture and decoration. The three black marble effigies in the N chapel, beneath ogee arches and gables carved with feathery foliage, and the two stone effigies in the Alard Chantry – one holding his heart – are beautiful and memorable. The modern stained glass by Douglas Strachan is vibrantly coloured. Millais' daughter Effie posed for two paintings by him in the large box pew at the SW end. **P.** *Open 08.00–dusk daily.*

Early in the 15thC the harbour silted up and Winchelsea's population contracted, giving an air of desertion to the spacious half-built town, which it still retains.

Wisborough Green, St Peter ad   6 O5
Vincula
8m SW of Horsham on A272. In a beautiful setting on a hill overlooking undulating meadows. The 13thC tower was either built over an 11thC nave with exceptionally thick walls, or onto the keep of a castle; the doorways are high enough for a mounted knight to gallop through. The impressive and well-preserved 13thC wall painting in a recess right of the chancel arch is of St James above and the crucifixion below, where Christ shares the crossbar with one of the thieves. Note the exceedingly ancient altar stone, the lancet windows and old benches in the 13thC chancel and lovely timber N porch. *Open 08.00–dusk daily.* Generous village green and tile-hung, brick and half-timbered houses of charm.

Withyham, St Michael and   6 R5
All Angels
4m NW of Crowborough on B2110. Rebuilt in the 17thC after being struck by lightning in 1663, and incorporating part of the 14thC fabric. Family monuments are assembled in the Sackville Chapel, the most arresting of which is a white and grey marble monument by C. G. Cibber, to Thomas Sackville, d1677 aged 13. He reclines on the tomb-chest, holding a skull, while his life-size parents kneel on cushions either side, as if they had that moment come to mourn, giving great immediacy to the whole conception. **P.** *Open 08.30–dusk Mon–Sat, 07.30–after Evensong Sun.* Part of Old Buckhurst, former Sackville mansion, remains ½m SW, and the village has the attractive weatherboarded Dorset Arms and 16thC timber-framed, former ironmaster's house, Duckings.

Worth, St Nicholas   6 P5
2m E of Crawley off B2036. An Anglo-Saxon church on a grand scale, whose powerful presence is felt in numerous features, such as the large chancel arch with semi-circular columns and cushion capitals, and the transept arches; the apsidal chancel, the pilasters on the exterior, and three twin-arched nave windows divided by balusters. There is a pretty 16thC restored lychgate and a 19thC tower. *Open 07.30–dusk Tue, Wed & Fri–Sun, from 09.00 Mon & Thur.*

LONDON

The London basin, embracing the whole of the Thames-Kennet valley from Newbury to Southend, and reaching up the eastern side of Suffolk into Norfolk, is an area of clay, sand and gravel. London clay produces bricks of a dependable quality and a browny-yellow colour; stone had to be imported. Since London is on a navigable river, this was easily done and stone came from as far afield as Caen in Normandy and Purbeck or Portland in Dorset. Portland stone – the type habitually chosen by the 17thC and 18thC architect – has a way of weathering both dark and light that looks like a shadow projection and often gives the buildings the appearance of being in the sun when they are not.

Of nearly a 100 medieval churches in the City, only a few survived the Great Fire of 1666. St Bartholomew, Smithfield is by far the most important. Across the river, magnificent St Mary Overy became Southwark Cathedral.

The great rebuilding after the fire gave London over 50 churches by Sir Christopher Wren, of which only 16 survive. These are enough, however, to demonstrate the truth of Sir John Summerson's words: 'the glory of the City churches is, first, in their original and daring variety of planning in which one sees Wren's keen experimental mind at work; and, second, in the lovely additions their steeples made to London's Georgian skyline'.

Not all the classical spires are by Wren. James Gibbs – who wrote 'steeples are indeed of a Gothic extraction, but they have their beauties when their parts are well disposed' – added the very fine spires of St Mary le Strand and St Martin-in-the-Fields. Nicholas Hawksmoor, who might be regarded as Wren's understudy, must also be remembered. Queen Anne's Act for the building of 50 London churches gave him his opportunity. His greatest works were at St Mary Woolnoth and St Alfege's Greenwich, where the tower, however, is by John James of Greenwich. John James also gave us the beautiful little church of St Lawrence, Stanmore. This was the parish church to the Duke of Chandos' fabulous house, Canons Park, and it contains a fine memorial to the Duke by Carpenter. Rich patronage often drew distinguished architects into the environs of London in this way.

In 1818 an Act of Parliament voted a million pounds for the building of an unspecified number of churches to catch up with the steady enlargement of the capital and heralded the mammoth 19thC programme of church construction. Churches were put up for £15,000–£20,000 and the Board of Works employed their three architects – Nash, Soane and Smirke. None of these was really a church architect and the results were often disappointing, but Nash's well-known All Souls, Langham Place makes a fitting climax to the vista of Regent Street.

In the 20thC, population shifts have left the inner city churches subject to the pressures of reduced congregations, while the new suburbs have created a demand for places of worship. H. G. Wells described London as 'stupendous in her pregnant totality'. It is always producing something new and may have surprises for us in the churches yet to be built.

◁ THE CITY ▷

Barking-by-the-Tower, All Hallows **6** P6
Byward St EC3. Pepys went up the tower,
built 1658, to watch the Great Fire of
London, until he 'became afeared to stay
there long and down again as fast as I
could'. Fire caused by Second World War
bombs left only tower, crypt, undercroft
and two walls standing and the church
was subsequently beautifully rebuilt.
There is evidence of a church founded in
675 in an archway discovered during
rebuilding. Fascinating history unearthed
in the undercroft includes the remains of
a 2ndC Roman mosaic pavement. Also
on display in the undercroft museum are
parts of two Saxon crosses. **P.** *Open
08.30–18.00 Mon–Wed & Fri; to 19.30 Thur;
10.00–18.00 Sat & Sun.* Weekly music. A
brass rubbing centre and a restaurant are
attached to the church. Next door is the
Tower of London.

All Hallows, Barking-by-the-Tower

Bishopsgate, St Helen **6** P6
Great St Helen's EC3. Set back from the
main thoroughfare, the church has a
battlemented W front with wide 15thC
windows, medieval doorways and
charming 17thC belfry. To a 12thC
church was added a conventual church in
the 13thC, now called the Nuns' Choir,
which became part of the parish church
at the Dissolution. See the night staircase
which led up to the nuns' dormitory.

There are a number of interesting brasses
and a magnificent Jacobean pulpit. Many
important citizens are buried here,
including Sir Thomas Gresham, d1579,
who founded the Royal Exchange; see
too the spectacular Elizabethan tomb of
Sir William Pickering, d1574, ambassador
to Spain under Elizabeth I. *Open 09.00–
17.30 Mon–Fri; some weekends.*

Cheapside, St Mary-le-Bow **6** P6
EC2. Wren's magnificent steeple of 1678–
80 was his most expensive, costing
almost as much to build as the rest of the
church. From it ring the famous Bow
Bells, whose predecessors recalled Dick
Whittington to be thrice mayor of
London, and whose sound defines the
boundaries of the City, so much so that
only those born within their range are
true Cockneys. The Norman arches, or
bows, in the crypt give the church its
name and the Archbishop of
Canterbury's ecclesiastical Court of
Arches is held under them. Walls and
steeple survived the 1941 bombing, and
the interior was restored by Laurence
King, with symbolic gifts of furnishings
from Germany and Norway and fine
stained glass by John Hayward. *Open
09.00–16.00 Mon–Fri.* Live and recorded
music weekly.

St Mary-le-Bow, Cheapside

Cornhill, St Michael   **6** P6

EC3. The church was rebuilt by Wren in 1670–7, the tower to Hawksmoor's design, in 1722, with large turrets and pinnacles at the corners. Classical and Gothic are combined in the interior, which was restored in the 19thC by George Gilbert Scott. Scott's full-flowered Gothic revival N porch does not blend harmoniously with Wren's style. See the beautifully detailed bench ends, carved by W. G. Rogers in the 19thC. The lectern won him a prize at the Great Exhibition of 1851. Thomas Gray, author of the *Elegy in a Country Churchyard,* was born in Cornhill in 1716 and baptised here. *Open 08.00–17.00 Mon–Fri, 10.00–14.00 Sun.* Regular concerts and *Mon* organ recitals.

Eastcheap, St Clement   **6** P6

Clements La, King William St EC2. A Wren church restored by Butterfield in the 19thC and by Comper in the 20thC. His are the richly coloured and gilded pictures on the reredos. The Baroque organ was built by Renatus Harris in 1696 and the casework is original. Magnificent pulpit and sounding board decorated with cherubs and swags of leaves. The church claims to be the St Clement's of the *Oranges and Lemons* nursery rhyme, since the churches named therein are all City churches, and because of the proximity of London Bridge where Spanish barges unloaded their cargos of oranges. *Open 09.00–16.00 Mon–Fri. Closed Aug.*

Fleet Street, St Bride   **6** P6

EC4. Layers of history lie beneath Fleet Street's cherished parish church. A Roman ditch and part of a mosaic pavement can be seen in the crypt museum, and evidence of Saxon, Norman and medieval churches has also been uncovered. Wren built a new church after the Great Fire of 1666, whose five-tiered spire has been the model for a million wedding cakes, and was called by Henley 'a madrigal in stone'. Godfrey Allen restored the church after war damage, and furnished it in Wren's style. *Open 09.00–17.00 Mon–Sat.*

Fore Street, St Giles Cripplegate   **6** P6

Barbican EC2. The 16thC walls and nave arcades survived incendiary bombs in 1940; restoration by Godfrey Allen was completed in 1960. A bastion of the ancient City wall is behind the church, probably a medieval rebuilding of a Roman one. St Giles was the medieval patron saint of cripples; Cripplegate, however, stems from *crepel,* Anglo-Saxon for a covered way, which went from the gate to a watch tower. Cromwell was married in the church and Milton is buried in it. Their busts stand under the organ loft with those of Daniel Defoe and John Bunyan. The tower, 15thC below and 17thC above, is crowned by an unusual cupola. *Open 10.00–14.00 Mon & Wed–Fri; to 17.00 Tue; 14.00–17.00 Sat & Sun.* The church forms an oasis in the midst of the gigantically scaled Barbican Arts Centre and tower blocks.

Foster Lane, St Vedast   **6** P6

EC2. Delightfully varied surfaces lead up to the obelisk spire of the church, built by Wren and restored after war damage. The 18thC organ case and ornately carved pulpit come from other City churches. There are facing pews, a striking black and white floor and a ceiling glittering with silver, aluminium and gilt. *Open 06.00–18.00 Mon–Fri, 06.30–09.00 Sat, 07.00–12.00 Sun.* Music *Tue lunchtime.*

Garlick Hill, St James Garlickhythe **6** P6

EC4. Wren rebuilt the church in 1676–83, and added the delightfully inventive spire of curves and angles in 1713–17. The many windowed interior led to its being called 'Wren's Lantern'. Rich in its furnishings, the panelled church has a beautifully carved pulpit and sounding board with wig peg, an organ case complete with trumpeters, and iron hatstands on the pews. *Open 10.00–15.00 Mon–Fri, 12.00–15.00 Sat.* Lunchtime live and recorded music.

Holborn Viaduct, St Sepulchre   **6** P6

EC1. The 19thC witnessed the addition of outsize pinnacles to the stately 15thC tower of this large and light church, rebuilt in gracious Wren style after the Great Fire of 1666. Look up at the lovely vault as you enter through the restored 15thC porch. Notice the capacious churchwardens' pews at the W end of the nave, the garlands and open-mouthed cherubs delectably carved on the font cover, and the gilded angels reclining on top of the organ case. Harboured in the church is the sinister Execution Bell, rung by St Sepulchre's bellman outside the condemned cell at Newgate on the eve of execution – lest the prisoners should be sleeping – and followed by a verse urging repentance. Elizabeth I's tutor, Roger Ascham, was buried here in 1568 and John Smith, first governor of Virginia, in 1631; Sir Henry Wood, founder and conductor of the Proms is commemorated in the Musicians' Chapel. *Open 09.00–16.00 Mon–Fri.*

Lombard Street, St Edmund the King　　　　　　　**6 P6**
EC3. Rebuilt by Wren after the Great Fire of 1666, with gracefully detailed steeple. Joseph Addison, poet and essayist, was married here in 1716. There is elegant panelling on walls, lectern and stalls, and fine carving on the pulpit. The marble font is enclosed by a railing. Either side of the Commandments on the reredos are 19thC paintings of Moses and Aaron by William Etty. See the beautiful iron sword rest. *Open 08.30–16.30 Mon–Fri.*

Lombard Street, St Mary Woolnoth　6 P6
EC3. Brilliantly built by Wren's pupil Nicholas Hawksmoor in 1716–27. Its tower is unique and striking, the columned principal stage leading up to two separate turrets on top. The rusticated façade and bold N front add to the imposing effect. Immediately impressive inside are the altar canopy supported on twisted columns and the giant columns in groups of three. From the pulpit John Newton, reformed slave trader, and rector from 1780–1807, denounced the slave trade and inspired Wilberforce to bring about legislation against it. Newton's memorial is on the N wall. 17thC organ case encloses a Father Smith organ. *Open 09.00–16.45 Mon–Fri.* The church is used for meditation and relaxation at lunchtimes.

Ludgate Hill, St Martin of Tours　　6 P6
EC4. The delightful lead spire creates an elegant balance with St Paul's dome as you approach from Fleet St. The church was rebuilt by Wren in 1677–84, incorporating part of the medieval city wall on its W side, and stands close to the site of Ludgate, which was the curfew gate, the first to be closed at night. A small model of the gate is carried in procession on special occasions. Inside is much richly carved woodwork: see especially the beautiful carvings round the doors. Captain William Penn, father of the founder of Pennsylvania, was married here in 1643. *Open 10.00–16.00 Mon–Fri.* Frequent music recitals.

St Mary Abchurch, St Mary the Virgin　　　　　　　**6 P6**
Abchurch La. EC4. Although a church stood on the site in the 12thC, the present building is by Wren, 1681–6. The lead spire is charming but the interior is a revelation, a great dome supported on walls and arches and painted in 1708 by William Snow. The garlanded reredos was carved exquisitely by Grinling Gibbons and there is other fine carving by craftsmen contemporary with him. Some of the pews from the period remain, and wrought iron sword rests are on the two front pews, to hold the civic sword when the Lord Mayor attends a service. *Open approx 11.00–16.00 Mon–Fri.*

St Mary-at-Hill, St Mary　　　　6 P6
EC3. A Wren church, partly rebuilt by James Savage in the 19thC. It has a beautiful, domed interior with lavish plasterwork and excellent 17thC and 19thC woodwork, including the pulpit, lectern, W gallery and the only box pews to survive intact in a Wren church. See too the wonderfully intricate wrought iron sword rests. Although Billingsgate wholesale fish market has departed its ancient site in Lower Thames Street, just down the hill, its traders still come here for the annual Harvest of the Sea Thanksgiving on the *second Sun in Oct. Open 13.00–14.00 Tue-Thur.* Regular musical recitals are held.

Smithfield, St Bartholomew-the-Great　　　　　　**6 P6**
EC1. Founded as a priory church in 1123 by Rahere, a courtier (turned monk) of Henry I, together with the adjoining hospital. Remaining are choir, transepts, part of the cloister, and glorious W gateway. The path between the gateway and porch follows the former nave, with part of the nave wall on the right. Perpendicular and 19thC additions have been made, but the overwhelming impression of the interior is of the beauty of the great Norman arcades and galleries, in which the later canopied tomb of Rahere and Prior Bolton's oriel window are delightful intrusions. The tangible sense of a hallowed place perhaps stems from the legend of Rahere, who is said to have had a vision of St Bartholomew saving him from a monster about to drop him into a dark chasm, and promising God's vigilance over the proposed church 'night and day, that the asker in it shall receive, the seeker shall find. . .'. The only pre-Reformation font in the City is here. **P.** *Open 08.30–16.30 Mon–Thur & Sat, 11.00–16.30 Fri, 08.30–20.15 Sun.* Regular concerts and recitals are held.

◁ CENTRAL LONDON ▷

Covent Garden, St Paul 6 P6
Bedford St WC2. The imposing portico
faces the piazza and makes a fitting
backcloth for street entertainers' acts, not
least because it is known as the actors'
church. Confusingly, this is the E end,
not the entrance, and the grand doorway
is false. Inigo Jones completed the church
in 1638 and it was restored by Thomas
Hardwick after a fire in 1795. There are
memorials to Marie Lloyd, Boris Karloff,
Sybil Thorndike and Lewis Casson. The
one to Grinling Gibbons is a wreath of
flowers carved by himself. **P.** *Open 09.00–
16.30 Mon–Fri.* Frequent lunchtime and
evening concerts. Covent Garden Market
Hall, transformed from its former lusty
self to a shopping arcade surrounded by
restaurants, is fun though some of the
prices are fancy.

Euston Road, St Pancras 6 P6
NW1. Directly based on the pagan temple
of the Erechtheum on the Acropolis at
Athens, the church is a splendid
celebration of classical forms, and was
built by H. W. and W. Inwood in 1819–
22. Wasn't the congregation affronted by
the distinctly non-Christian caryatids
outside the church? The tower of two
octagons is imposing, as is the large
galleried interior with Ionic columns in
the apse. **P.** *Open 07.45–18.30 Tue–Fri, to
12.00 Sat.* Organ and chamber orchestra
recitals *Thur lunchtime.*

Langham Place, All Souls 6 P6
W1. Cleverly designed and positioned by
Nash in 1822–4, when he was building
his way up from the elegant curve of
Regent's Street to Regent's Park, it is
now under the shadow of Broadcasting
House. The circular portico of great
Corinthian columns and spire ringed
with smaller columns nonetheless form a
landmark. *Open 09.00–21.00 Sun–Fri,
09.00–13.00 Sat; Aug to 17.00 Mon–Fri.*
Occasional organ recitals and Christian
folk music.

Margaret Street, All Saints 6 P6
W1. The church, sequestered in a
courtyard and flanked by the vicarage
and former choir school, forms a
compelling and admirable composition,
together with the tall, proud spire.
William Butterfield's Early English Gothic
design of 1850 sought to exemplify
Cambridge Camden Society ideals.

Inside, the display of Victorian
decoration is marvellously sumptuous, if
a little loud in parts. Tile pictures,
coloured marbles and the vast gilded and
painted reredos are deeply impressive.
Ninian Comper's reredos and canopy of
1911 in the Lady Chapel are of the same
opulent character. *Open morn–19.00 daily.*

Piccadilly, St James 6 P6
W1. A redbrick exterior and an amazingly
light interior, created by huge windows.
Built by Wren in 1676–84 and restored
after war damage. Galleries and tunnel-
vaulted nave with accurately reproduced
plaster ceiling. Swags carved by Grinling
Gibbons swing flamboyantly across the
reredos. The lovely font is one of
Gibbons' rare sculptures in marble and
has as its base the Tree of Knowledge,
with Adam and Eve either side. The
organ case, with angelic and cherubic
figures on top is also by Gibbons. *Open
08.00–21.00 Sun–Fri, to 01.00 Sat.* The
Wren coffee house adjoins the church,
and the London Brass Rubbing Centre is
to the E. Wide-ranging events, including
lectures, seminars, concerts and prayer
meetings are held daily. In the heart of
the West End, near theatres and shops.

Queen's Gate, St Augustine 6 P6
SW7. In high Victorian Gothic, with
pointed towers and soaring bellcote, this
is a prominent church that demands
notice. It was built by William Butterfield
in 1865–71. The wide, colourful interior,
restored from its 1920s whitewash, is
lavishly embellished by Martin Travers'
reredos and Stations of the Cross. *Open
08.00–19.00 daily.* Nearby is a most
impressive array of Victorian architecture,
in the cathedral-like Natural History
Museum, extravagantly detailed Victoria
and Albert Museum, Baroque-style
Brompton Oratory, and, further N, the
Albert Memorial and Albert Hall.

St Giles High Street, 6 P6
St Giles-in-the-Fields
WC2. Connected with the foundation of a
leper hospital in 1101 by Queen Matilda,
whose grandfather, Duncan I, was
murdered by Macbeth, it became a parish
church in 1200. The present church was
built by Henry Flitcroft in 1731–3. It has
an unusual spire and a tunnel-vaulted
interior, containing the top portion of the
pulpit used by John and Charles Wesley

for 40 years in the former Wesleyan chapel in nearby West St. The poets Andrew Marvell and George Chapman are buried here. Those condemned to execution at Tyburn stopped at St Giles for a last cup of ale, and many were brought back for burial, among them 12 17thC Roman Catholic martyrs, including Oliver Plunket, canonised in 1975 and his exhumed body since parted from his head for burial in Downside and Drogheda respectively. *Open 09.00–16.00 Mon–Fri; 07.30–08.45, 10.00–12.45 & 18.00–20.00 Sun. Mon lunchtime organ recitals.*

Strand, St Mary-le-Strand　　　**6** P6
WC2. Traffic thunders by this small, perfect Baroque church in the middle of the road. Designed by James Gibbs in 1714, its semicircular portico and daintily detailed tower are exquisite compositions. Grace characterises the exterior and interior carvings. Cherubim, clouds and gilt rays stand out above brilliant sky-blue stained glass windows in the apse, and the nave ceiling is sumptuously coffered. Examine the shapely pulpit with fine carvings and look back along the nave to admire the elegant W balcony. *Open approx daylight hours Mon–Fri, 10.30–12.30 Sun.*

Trafalgar Square,　　　**6** P6
St Martin-in-the-Fields
WC2. Gibbs' great classical portico and inventive Portland stone steeple of 1722–6 make an elegant angle with the

St Martin-in-the-Fields

National Gallery and Trafalgar Square. This is the parish church of Buckingham Palace (though not used as such) and above the chancel is a royal box, complete with fireplace. There are panelled walls and box pews, and above, galleries and graceful plaster ceiling. See the delicately carved staircase to the pulpit and the fine font cover and rails. *Open 07.30–20.00 daily.* There are regular lunchtime concerts in the church and a folk club in the crypt. The church focuses on aid to young people and to the homeless.

◀ OUTER LONDON ▶

Battersea, St Mary　　　**6** P6
Battersea Church Rd SW11. This charming 18thC brick church with classical details, has poetic associations. Here William Blake married the daughter of a Battersea market gardener in 1792, and its commanding view over the Thames inspired Turner to paint sunsets from the vestry window. The E window has rare 17thC heraldic glass. There are some interesting monuments of an earlier date than the present church, including one to a 17thC Samson of whom it is said, 'Thrice-twenty mounted Moors he overthrew, Singly on foot, some wounded, some he slew Dispers'd ye rest; what more could Samson do!' What indeed. **P.** *Open 12.00–14.00 Mon–Fri, 15.00–18.30 Sun summer.* It is hoped that

St Mary, Battersea

the de Morgan collection of pottery and pre-Raphaelite painting in Old Battersea House will eventually be open to the public.

Chiswick, St Nicholas 6 P6
Church St W4. Off gracious 18thC riverside Chiswick Mall, the church has a fascinating history drawn from its former position beside a ford crossing the Thames, making it the recipient of gifts from rich travellers and merchants. After a number of additions and restorations, the church was rebuilt between 1882–4 by J. Loughborough Pearson, and its 15thC tower restored in 1936. In the churchyard are the urn-topped tomb of William Hogarth, d1765, with Garrick's epitaph, 'Farewell, great painter of mankind . . .' and tombs of painters P. J. de Loutherbourg, d1812, and Whistler, d1903. **P.** *Open 14.00–16.00 Fri, 10.00–12.00 Sat, 14.30–17.00 Sun.* Walk up picturesque Church St and turn left to see the house on which Miss Pinkerton's academy for young ladies was based in Thackeray's *Vanity Fair*, into whose garden a furious Becky Sharp hurled the parting gift of Johnson's *Dictionary*. A left turn further up into the incessantly roaring Great West Road, leads to Hogarth's House and elegant Palladian Chiswick House and gardens.

St Alfege, Greenwich

Greenwich, St Alfege 6 P6
Greenwich Church St SE10. The medieval church on the site was built in commemoration of Archbishop Alfege's martyrdom under the Danes in 1012. The present church is a massive and bold classical conception built by Nicholas Hawksmoor, 1711–14, with a tower by John James added in 1730. It is the burial place of General James Wolfe and of the 16thC musician Thomas Tallis, of whom it was lamented in contemporary song, 'Tallis is dead, and music dies'. **P.** *Open 10.00–12.00 & 14.00–16.00 Mon–Wed, 10.00–12.00 Sat, 08.00–12.00 Sun; May–Oct 14.00–16.00 Sat & Sun.* Greenwich is outstanding for the most magnificent assemblage of 17thC buildings in England, set at the foot of rising ground where Greenwich Park fronts the Thames. They include the Royal Naval College and National Maritime Museum.

Hampstead, St John 6 P6
Church Row NW3. A handsome finale to one of Hampstead's loveliest Georgian streets, the wrought iron gates and railings, castellated tower and great clock making contributory, individual statements. Built in 1745. Surprisingly, Gothic revivalist George Gilbert Scott, drew up a petition against an extension to the church which would have involved rebuilding the tower, with names on it like Norman Shaw, William Morris, Edward Burne-Jones and Anthony Trollope. The large, galleried interior has arches on Ionic columns and was restored in 1872. A bust to John Keats, whose house in nearby Keats Grove can be visited, was erected 'by Americans' in 1894. John Constable's tomb is in the verdant churchyard, from which there is a very good view over London. *Open 07.30–17.00 Mon–Sat, 07.30–19.30 Sun.*

Hampstead Garden Sub 6 P6
St Jude-on-the-Hill
NW11. Imposingly positioned, E. L. Lutyens' church of 1909 forms part of his grand design for Central Sq and is balanced by the Free Church opposite. The tower and spire are highly impressive and the steeply sloping roofs remarkable. Byzantine overtones distinguish the design. Domes, barrel vaults and heavily timbered aisles form an unusual assortment in the spacious interior. The decoration is well worth studying and includes frescoes by W. P. Stamer; women form the theme of the Lady Chapel frescoes and Queen Alexandra, Edith Cavell, Florence

Nightingale and Elizabeth Barrett Browning are featured among many others on the W dome. *Open daylight hours daily.*

Harrow on the Hill, St Mary   **10** P6
High St. Take in the magnificent view and pay passing homage to the Peachey Stone in the churchyard, where Romantic poet Byron sat for hours when a boy at Harrow School. John Lyon, d1592, founder of the famous public school beside the church, is commemorated in a brass and in a monument of 1815 by Flaxman. Restored by Scott in the 19thC, the core of the church is 13thC and the tower is Norman at the base. Admire the fine font and 17thC pulpit. **P**. *Open 08.30–18.30 Tue–Sun.*

Kilburn, St Augustine   **6** P6
Kilburn Park Rd NW6. Built on an ambitious scale by J. L. Pearson, 1870–80, the redbrick church is in Early English Gothic style, variegated by French features. Outside, turrets, spirelet and the magnificent steeple extend the aspiring lines of the pointed lancet windows, and inside soaring vaults achieve an awesome loftiness.

Compelling perspectives are created by the gallery tunnelling through the buttresses, the tall, narrow aisles, and the ambulatory. Wall paintings and stained glass by Clayton and Bell add further interest. *Open 09.30–11.00 Sat, before and after services Sun.*

Little Stanmore, St Lawrence   **6** P7
Whitchurch La. Sheltered behind a stately Tudor tower and elegant Georgian exterior, is a sumptuous Baroque ensemble of painting by Bellucci and Laguerre, with a flourish of gilded woodwork by Gibbons. The church was built by the Duke of Chandos on his estate of Canons in 1715. Presiding over the vaulted nave, arrayed with box pews, is the Duke's Gallery, in which Bellucci's copy of Raphael's *Transfiguration* forms a cloudy canopy above the ducal box. In the Chandos Mausoleum, the bewigged Duke stands dressed as a Roman between his two kneeling wives, and trompe l'oeil architectural and sculptural paintings round the walls effectively deceive the eye. As composer for the Duke from 1717–21, Handel doubtless played the organ here. *Open 14.30–17.30 Sat & Sun.*

THE HEART OF
———ENGLAND———

Gloucestershire   Hereford and
Worcester   Leicestershire
Northamptonshire   Shropshire
West Midlands   Warwickshire

There used to be an expression 'as sure as God's in Gloucestershire', which
was coined on account of the great multitude of churches in that county.
With the important Norman foundations of Gloucester and Tewkesbury to
inspire them, many date back to that period. But the later Middle Ages was
the great age for the Cotswolds. As Clifton-Taylor wrote: 'they had the
money (from the fleeces of their innumerable sheep), they had the masons
and, most important of all, they had the stone'. The only fault in this
attractive oolitic limestone is that it is not resistant to the pollution of a
smoky town; it is a rural stone *par excellence*. One immediately thinks of the
beautiful villages of the Cotswolds and Northamptonshire where every
house is built of this warm, golden stone which attracts a silver lichen. It
also attracted the finest craftsmen. There is surely no coincidence in the fact
that the only phase of the Gothic style to originate in England was born at
Gloucester – the Perpendicular, with its complex tracery, its intricate fan-
vaulting and its delicate chiselled ornament. We naturally associate
Cotswold stone with the Perpendicular style.

The short, tender grass of the treeless uplands supported sheep; on their
fleeces the great 'wool' churches, of which Northleach and Chipping
Campden are perhaps the most remarkable, were founded. Even the
tombstones offered a special opportunity to the stone carver, and the
churchyard at Painswick is justly famous.

If, instead of following the oolite belt north east from the Cotswolds, we
travel north and west, we enter a fertile, fruit farming country much
favoured by the monastic movement. It is a well wooded area and many of
the old houses are timbered. It is not unusual in Hereford-Worcester to find
the same domestic style applied to the humbler churches. Some four-fifths
of Herefordshire, however, is of old red sandstone, which at its best, can
preserve intricate Celtic carvings, such as those at Kilpeck, for 800 years.
The highly decorated exterior of Leominster has also survived, although its
provenance is of various periods.

Leicestershire is another county well endowed with churches: between
1150 and 1250 the villages in the limestone country round Ketton and

Clipsham were busy building. 'No region in England can show as many fine churches in such a small area', as Dr Hoskind so appositely remarked. The best stone here is a strip of marlstone, running roughly between Market Harborough and Melton Mowbray, which possess the two finest churches in Leicestershire.

In many ways Northamptonshire resembles the Cotswolds. The same stone offers the same building opportunities – one thinks immediately of Oundle, and of Collyweston slates, the stone tiles which are so typical a feature of the county. The quarries of Barnack, Weldon and Helmdon have provided stone for buildings all over south east England, as well as for the great houses of the region – Burghley, Kirby, Drayton and Boughton. But although the stone resembles that of the Cotswolds, the style does not. Northamptonshire is famous for its spires. It has also retained a complete sequence of styles, starting right back with Brixworth, which dates from the 7thC, and the Saxon tower at Earls Barton.

Calamitous times were frequent on the Welsh Marches, and some of the churches of west Shropshire are built, like the castles, of undressed stone, with strong, squat towers, obviously intended for defence. Although there are few significant remains of pre-Norman architecture, nearly half the churches in Shropshire have round churchyards, which nearly always betokens a Saxon foundation.

A 'new' neighbour to the east, the West Midlands was awarded county status in the local government reshuffle which gave official recognition to the commercial and industrial heartland of Birmingham and its overspill. Alterations to medieval churches reflect the changes which came with the growth of city centres, first in the 18thC (classical influences), and then in the Industrial Revolution of the 19thC and the Gothic Revival of the Victorians.

Moving over the border into Warwickshire, we find the county divided unevenly by the river Avon, south of which the oolite of the Cotswolds is still found, but north of which there is only red sandstone. North Warwickshire was poor and thinly populated in the Middle Ages, and produced no great churches, but the centre of the county boasts Stratford-upon-Avon and the seasonal influx of tourists may be as interested in the font in which the Bard was probably baptised as in ecclesiastical architecture.

◁ GLOUCESTERSHIRE ▷

Ampney Crucis, Holy Rood   8 L7
2m E of Cirencester off A417. The restored churchyard cross and 15thC sanctus bellcote are splendid features outside the church, which has a Norman zigzag decorated chancel arch inside, the remains of a Saxon N doorway, a Norman pillar piscina, a 13thC S door with original ironwork, stone seats in the porch, 14thC wall paintings and Jacobean pews. Impressive among the diverse monuments are the Elizabethan effigies of George Lloyd and his wife, accompanied by five sons and seven daughters. **P**. *Open daylight hours daily.* A private, gabled, partly-Tudor manor house lies picturesquely to the W and a mill and water gardens are delights close by.

Avening, Holy Cross   8 K7
3m S of Stroud on B4014. Lovely Cotswold scenery enshrines the cruciform Norman church, which has a very imposing, big

N doorway with twisted pillars and sculptured capitals and a 16thC doorway within it. Notice the small Norman aisle, the beautiful rib-vaulted Norman chancel with a harmonious 14thC extension and windows and the nave altar with an oak Commonwealth table of 1657. In the 13thC N transept is the kneeling effigy of Henry Bridges, d1615, notorious pirate, smuggler and highwayman, and be sure to look behind the organ in the S transept at 17thC monuments carved with great vitality. **P**. *Open 09.00–dusk daily.*

Berkeley, St Mary the Virgin   **8 J7**
A magnificent, large church on a bosky hill overlooking the castle, with a separate tower built in Gothic style in 1753. The church is resonant with historical associations, not least because many of the lords of Berkeley Castle are buried here; see the alabaster effigy of the eighth Lord Berkeley, d1361, into whose charge Edward II was given and subsequently murdered with a red hot poker. And inspect the door in the 14thC rib-vaulted porch, which has bullet holes and axe marks from the Cromwellian siege of church and castle in 1645. The 13thC nave has beautiful arcades, high chancel arch, a wonderful 15thC stone rood screen, and soaring lancet windows at the W end. Look up at the carved heads in nave and aisles and the toad perched on the heads of two gossiping women on a pillar in the nave's S arcade. There are medieval wall paintings, including a fragment of a Doom above the chancel arch. Among fine table tombs and gravestones in the churchyard is one to the Earl of Suffolk's jester who was killed during revels at the castle in 1725 and whose epitaph was written by Swift. **P** at castle. *Open summer 09.30–dusk daily, winter to 17.00.* The Norman keep dominates 14thC Berkeley Castle, which has a great timber-roofed hall, rooms containing 18thC gilt furniture, tapestries and silver, terraced gardens and a deer park.

Bibury, St Mary the Virgin   **9 L7**
13m SE of Cheltenham on A433. Standard roses in the tree-embowered churchyard and the gables of 17thC Bibury Court close by, provide a glorious setting for the Cotswold stone church, which is of Saxon origin and has a fine Saxon carving of interlocking circles outside the N wall of the chancel. Examine the late Norman N doorway, exuberantly carved with beaded zigzag and stylised palm leaves and the lovely 14thC windows ·

either side. Inside, one's glance is immediately drawn to the exquisite, arcaded 13thC E lancet windows, seen through the narrow 13thC chancel arch with Saxon masonry below, and between the impressive late Norman and 13thC nave arcades. The chancel is lavishly supplied with aumbries, or wall cupboards, and also has 13thC stained glass in a small S window. The nave has a fine timber roof and the square font is extremely beautiful in the simplicity of its lines and decoration. In the churchyard are substantial table tombs enlivened by cherub heads. Limited **P**. *Open 09.00–dusk daily.* The picturesque Cotswold village shows local architecture at its most beautiful and typical. Once occupied by weavers, Arlington Row is a group of 17thC steep-roofed stone cottages hailed as architectural classics by William Morris in the 19thC. Arlington Mill houses a folk museum.

St Mary the Virgin, bale tombs

Bourton-on-the-Hill, St Lawrence   **9 L8**
15m NE of Cheltenham on A44. A lovely church of Norman origin, with 14thC and 15thC additions. Pause to admire the wonderful gargoyles on the N side and the parapet round the chancel before entering the limewashed, light-filled interior with its 18thC N gallery and a 19thC Winchester peck and bushel made of bell-metal. Seats for the weary or picnickers in the well-kept churchyard. **P** *Open daylight hours daily.* 17thC cottages and other interesting buildings clamber pleasingly up a steep hill in the pretty village. Indian-inspired early 19thC Sezincote House and gardens and late 19thC Batsford Park and arboretum are nearby.

Bourton-on-the-Water, St Lawrence   **9 L7**
In a golden Cotswold stone picture-book village on the river Windrush, the church

was founded in 709 and has a Norman crypt, a charming, Neo-classical balustraded tower of 1784 and a fine Victorian Gothic S porch, N aisle and superbly roofed nave by T. G. Jackson. During the 18thC and 19thC rebuildings, the rectors refused to pay for a new chancel so that built by Walter de Burhton in 1328 remains, with the unusual feature of a sedilia in a window in the S wall. The chancel roof was exquisitely painted with coats of arms in 1928 by F. E. Howard, who also designed the reredos and rood screen. The stone coffin near the S wall of the churchyard, where there is also a number of interesting table tombs, is probably Walter de Burhton's. **P**. *Open summer 09.00–dusk Mon–Sat, winter to 17.00; 07.30–19.30 Sun.* As well as the delights of the delicate stone bridges spanning the river and the 17thC and 18thC houses, Birdland and the famous model village are here.

Chipping Campden, St James the Great 9 L8

In a flawless example of a Cotswold wool town, the church represents an outpouring of wealth and piety during the 14thC and 15thC. It has a splendidly decorated W tower, and tall nave arcades whose concave pillars grow into curving capitals, with light flowing down on them from the clerestory and window over the chancel arch. The pulpit and lectern were given by Sir Baptist Hicks, benefactor of the church and town, whose fabulous tomb has 12 Egyptian marble columns and effigies of himself and his wife clad for a state occasion, with coronets and conspicuous ruffs. See the beautiful 15thC altar hangings, brasses, including that to wool merchant William Grevel, d1401, and the muniment room. **P**. *Open 08.00–dusk daily.* The town's gracious buildings invite a leisurely perambulation.

Cirencester, St John Baptist 8 L7

Market Pl. Graceful Georgian buildings, in which the interesting Cotswold town is rich, frame the magnificent Perpendicular wool church, which is one of the largest in England and which displays a porch more dazzling in its size and ebullient array of oriel windows and niches than any in the country; it was used as the town hall after the Dissolution. The fine, panelled tower was built on a barbaric foundation: the heads of rebellious earls Kent and Salisbury, executed in the market place in 1400 for

St John Baptist, Perpendicular porch

trying to restore Richard II to the throne; the contents of their treasure chest, awarded the townspeople by a grateful Henry IV, paid for its erection. A brass of Reginald Spycer, d1442, who led the beheading party, and his four wives is in the Trinity Chapel. See the filigree openwork stone parapets round the church and fascinating carvings. One marvels at the height of the clerestoried, sumptuous nave of 1515, with noble looking angels displaying the arms or marks of the merchants who built it. Henry VIII's arms are above the chancel arch window. A beautiful cup made for Anne Boleyn in 1535 is on show and chancel and chapels are rich in monuments, stained glass and, in the case of St Catherine's Chapel, fan-vaulting of 1508. The pre-Reformation wine-glass pulpit has unique openwork tracery and the bold figure of a bluecoat boy is by the S door. **P**. *Open summer 09.30–18.30 Mon–Sat, winter to 17.00; summer 12.30–18.00 Sun, winter to 17.30.*

Coates, St Matthew 8 K7

3m W of Cirencester off A419. The lovely church has a glorious battlemented and pinnacled 14thC tower, its bell openings embellished by ogee arches. Be sure to see, on its W side, the noisome anthropophagus, a giant-like figure, half-way through swallowing someone, legs first. Note the carved Norman S doorway, the 13thC lancet windows in the S aisle and the flowing tracery in the Decorated E window of the chancel, where there is a narrow 13thC priest's door. The baptistry has some interesting inscribed 17thC brasses and stone seats round the walls, and in the nave is a dainty 19thC chandelier with a dove on top. **P**. *Open daylight hours daily.*

Elkstone, St John Evangelist   **8** K7
6m S of Cheltenham off A435. The church is outstanding for the richness and completeness of its Norman work. Don't miss the fascinating carvings on the corbel table outside the nave, and, on the S doorway, a magnificent Christ in Majesty on a cushioned throne, surrounded by beak-head carving, in which an upside-down figure seizes the snouts of its neighbours. Inside, one is drawn at once to marvel at the spectacular zigzag decoration on the two arches leading to the chancel, which supported the original tower. The chancel has a Norman vault with grotesque faces in the centre and a very ornate E window. There is the most unusual feature of a dovecote over the chancel. The W tower of 1370 has gargoyles on its parapet and quaint figures on the buttresses with musical instruments. It has a majestic arch inside and a vault decorated with angels and bosses. *Open daylight hours daily.* See the two fine 17thC table tombs in the churchyard.

Fairford, St Mary the Virgin   **9** L7
17m SE of Cheltenham on A417. The splendid Perpendicular church was built at the end of the 15thC by John Tame, wool stapler and cloth merchant, except for the base of the tower, built by the earls of Warwick. Remark the grotesque figures with swords guarding the tower at the corners, beneath padlocks, and the unusual paired pinnacles at the top. Among lively carvings round the church, look for that of a charming jester or boy about to jump from the string course, near the porch. Carved stone angels abound in the interior, whose graceful, unified design is the result of being built all at one time, but the greatest glory is in the 28 windows of opulently coloured glass, contemporary with the church, which may be the work of Barnard Flower, Henry VII's master glass painter, and which includes a memorable, restored Last Judgement in the W window, ablaze with colour and incident. The glass is a sublime sight, unparalleled in England's parish churches. See the

animated carvings on the choir stalls' misericords and the beautiful screens, rare in the county, under one of which is a brass of John Tame and his wife, with brasses to his son Edmund and two wives nearby. **P**. *Open 09.00–dusk Mon–Sat, 07.30–19.30 Sun.* There are fine 17thC and 18thC houses in the market place, an old mill on the river Coln and a picturesque dovecote of c1600.

Gloucester, St Mary de Crypt   **8** K7
Southgate St. Outstanding in this fine Perpendicular church with a Norman foundation, is the restored chancel, sumptuous in its details of soaring E window, sedilia and piscina with ogee canopies, statue niches, stone screens with ogee-arched openings which grow into pillars supporting the chancel arcade, 16thC clerestory and roof with bosses and angels. The lavish 16thC wall painting of the adoration of the magi on the chancel's N wall was restored in 1982. Also of interest is the pulpit from which George Whitefield, famous 18thC evangelist, preached his first sermon, the S chapel commemorating Robert Raikes, founder of the Sunday school movement, and the handsome monument by Peter Scheemakers with a chubby, tearful putto. The beautiful tower's pinnacles and battlements were taken down as unsafe in 1908. *Open summer 09.30–dusk Mon–Sat, to 16.00 winter.* Roman and medieval Gloucester are close by. The magnificent cathedral, whose 14thC cloisters and choir form exquisite symphonies in stone – the latter vividly lit by the glorious E window which was the largest in the world when it was built – is the burial place of Edward II, murdered in Berkeley Castle, and of Edward Jenner, 18thC discoverer of vaccination, whose father was vicar of Berkeley.

Leonard Stanley, St Swithun   **8** K7
1m SW of Stroud off A419. The substantial Norman tower and its taller 14thC square turret overlook a farmyard with remains of former priory buildings and a Saxon chapel with a charming 14thC chancel, as well as a beautifully kept churchyard. The 12thC priory church has fascinating Norman work in the elaborate doorways decorated with crocodile-like animals and in expressive carvings on capitals in the chancel of the nativity and of Mary Magdalene wiping Christ's feet. And see Adam and Eve depicted as animals over an aumbry in the chancel, a most curious

composition. Also notable are the 18thC font and cover, the 14thC wagon roof, benches made from Stuart altar rails and stained glass by Morris & Co, 1922, in the 15thC W window. **P.** *Open 08.00–dusk daily.* Permission needed to visit farmyard buildings.

Little Barrington, St Peter 9 L7
3m NW of Burford off A40. In a Cotswold village of great charm, with 17thC houses and cottages of character and a brook running across the green. It is a small and lovely church, whose battlemented and pyramidal topped sanctus bellcote over the chancel arch is a delightful feature. Enjoy the Norman carving outside the N aisle of Christ in Majesty, with angels extending protective wings, the memorial tablet of 1702 outside the porch with earlier figures sculptured either side, two of them holding hands, and the lively decoration round the Norman S doorway presided over by a monstrous head. The Norman, 14thC and 15thC interior has pretty window tracery in the N aisle, where there are statue niches at the E end and fragments of medieval stained glass above. *Open daylight hours daily.*

Minchinhampton, Holy Trinity 8 K7
3m SE of Stroud off A419. The singular 14thC truncated spire was reduced to its present height in 1563 and prettily crowned with pinnacles and battlements. The most glorious display of masonic artistry is in the early 14thC transept, supported inside on pierced stone ribs and lit with myriad windows, including a spectacular rose window. Below this are two highly ornamented canopied tombs with effigies of a knight and lady, most likely the furnishers of funds to build the transept. The vaulted tower has graceful shafts and interesting bosses. Apart from transepts and tower, the church was rebuilt in 1842. William Burges designed the amazing E window tracery in 1865 and F. C. Eden the chancel's fine painted wagon roof and the rood screen. **P.** *Open 07.30–18.00 daily.* A small Cotswold town of charm and interest, built on wealth from wool and cloth.

Northleach, St Peter and St Paul 9 L7
A magnificent 15thC Cotswold wool church, it has a striking showpiece in its S porch, with original statues under canopied niches, great crocketed pinnacles and a stair turret crowned with a charming spirelet. Peer inside the elaborately vaulted porch at the corbel of

a cat fiddling to three mice. The plain, substantial tower breaks into ogee decoration and a panelled battlement at the top. The splendid clerestory, with its Cotswold window over the chancel arch, was added by John Fortey, a prosperous wool merchant, d1459, commemorated in a fine brass, his feet resting on a woolpack. And as Thomas Fortey's brass, d1447, records that he was a 'restorer of roads and churches', it is thought that he contributed to the building of the nave, whose arcades have the same impressive concave pillars and capitals as those at Chipping Campden. There are other outstanding brasses to the town's medieval clothiers, their feet resting on sheep and woolpacks, the source of their wealth. Relish the beautiful goblet-shaped pulpit and the 14thC font with carved heads and angels playing medieval instruments. *Open 09.00–dusk Mon, from 07.00 Tue, from 07.30 Wed–Sat, from 07.45 Sun.* An attractive small town with buildings dating from its wool trading days.

St Mary the Virgin, Painswick

Painswick, St Mary the Virgin 8 K7
2m S of Gloucester on B4073. The beautiful, restored medieval church, with a fine porch built in 1969, is famous for its superlative collection of 17thC and 18thC table tombs, many of them erected for the gracious Cotswold village's rich clothiers. The masons' great expertise and inventiveness is displayed in the varied Renaissance and Baroque decoration, which includes bulging cartouches and curvy scrolls, chubby-cheeked cherubs, shells, torches, festoons and podgy putti, as well as more lugubrious motifs such as bat-winged

skulls, one among which has teeth. A plain pyramidal tomb commemorates John Bryan, d1787, who carved many of the others. Follow the fascinating tomb trail, mapped out in leaflets on sale in the church, among the 99 luxuriant yews, planted c1792, whose smoothly clipped outlines, by the bye, bear no relation to the annual Clipping Service, when the dedication of the church to the Virgin Mary is celebrated. As early as 1779 the churchyard was 'a place of resort, in fine weather, for the ladies and polite inhabitants of the Town'. The iron stocks of c1630 are known locally as 'Squire's specs'. *Open approx 09.00–18.15 or dusk Mon–Sat, 07.30–19.15 or dusk Sun.*

Pauntley, St John the Evangelist　8 K8
3m NE of Newent off A417. From the church you can see the dovecote of Pauntley Court, an 18thC house, not open to the public, whose predecessor was the birthplace of the fabled Dick Whittington, thrice Lord Mayor of London. The delightfully embroidered tale relates to the real Richard Whittington, d1423, who was three or four times Lord Mayor of London, though he wasn't a poor orphan and quickly became a successful mercer. The family arms appear in medieval stained glass in the N window of the chancel and tower W window. The church's visual focal point inside is the wonderful explosion of Norman zigzag carving round the chancel arch and grotesque heads and scrolls on the capitals, and outside the equally fantastic S doorway with a fishscale pattern effervescing beneath the zigzag arch. On the other side is a 14thC timber-framed porch and a 13thC doorway. Gargoyles survey the scene from the satisfyingly dumpy tower. Note the plastered wagon roof in the chancel, corbel heads in the nave, the 16thC Flemish triptych and the impressive monuments and brasses. **P.** *Open daylight hours daily.* In rich, red Leadon vale farmland.

St Briavels, St Briavel　8 J7
6m N of Chepstow on B4228. High above the Wye valley, with glorious scenery unfolding at every turn in the road, this beautiful Norman and Early English church confronts the august gatehouse of a 13thC castle, used as a fortified hunting lodge during King John's reign and now a youth hostel. An excellent organ of 1922, a Norman font with a stone frill and interesting effigies from an Elizabethan monument are all worth

spending time over. The fine chancel was rebuilt in the 19thC and the Norman tower replaced in 1830. **P.** *Open by 10.00– dusk daily.* If you are in the village after Evensong on Whit Sunday, you may catch a piece of bread and cheese thrown by a local forester, a 700-year-old custom which used to be conducted from the church.

Slimbridge, St John the Evangelist　8 K7
4m SW of Stroud on A38. The stately 13thC tower with fine openwork parapet and the slenderest of 14thC spires rises impressively from Berkeley vale. Gargoyles lean out from the N aisle. Spectacular Early English carving surrounds the S doorway and the nave arcades display a wonderful array of carved foliage capitals. See the intriguing corbel heads in the aisles, the prettily adorned font of 1644 and the fragments of medieval stained glass in the N aisle E window and chancel. **P.** *Open summer 09.00–19.00 daily, winter to 16.00 daily.* The Wildfowl Trust is nearby.

Tetbury, St Mary the Virgin　8 K7
Church St. Set against a verdant backdrop, the church was built in 1777– 81 by Francis Hiorn, and its 15thC steeple rebuilt in 1891. It is a graceful expression of Gothic revival, with strikingly attenuated wooden columns with iron cores supporting the high vault, vast windows and cloister-like passageways leading into the church. The 18thC atmosphere is retained in the original furnishings of box pews and galleries and the two wonderful, spidery brass chandeliers of 1781, their 36 branches elegantly extending in the nave. An 18thC painting by Benjamin West is in the centre of the reredos. **P.** *Open 06.30–18.00 Mon–Sat, to 19.15 Sun.* The

St Mary the Virgin, Tetbury

handsome town is famous for the proximity of the Prince and Princess of Wales' home.

Tewkesbury, Abbey church of St Mary the Virgin   8 K8

Church St. Near the rivers Severn and Avon, one of England's most magnificent Norman churches was preserved intact at the Dissolution, when the townspeople bought it for £453. The massive tower, embellished with arcading, is of unparalleled splendour and the W front arch breathtakingly high. Giant Norman pillars process up the majestic nave to the 14thC choir, whose vault showers out exquisite patterns in stone and incorporates gilded suns to commemorate the Yorkist victory in the Wars of the Roses. The Prince of Wales, slain at the Battle of Tewkesbury in 1471, lies beneath the choir. Hugh Despenser, d1348, and his wife, Elizabeth Montacute, lie looking up at the choir, whose glories they paid for, while their nephew, Edward Despenser, d1375, kneels memorably on top of his chantry, facing the altar in gilded effigy. Hugh Despenser's mother, Eleanor de Clare, paid for the unique gallery of jaunty medieval knights with animated expressions in the 14thC stained glass. A great array of medieval nobility is commemorated in effigies and chantries of marvellous intricacy, which form a chaplet around the E end; among them the Beauchamp Chapel is the most dazzling expression of Perpendicular. *Open summer 07.30–18.00 Mon–Sat, to 19.00 Sun; winter closes 17.00 Sat.*

Upleadon, St Mary the Virgin   8 K8

7m NW of Gloucester off B4215. The sight of the unusual and delightful half-timbered Tudor tower of c1500 is very exciting, with its distinctive vertical timber strips outside and dramatically curved and crossed supporting timbers inside, on which the workmen's adze marks are visible. The tower windows have rare timber tracery, and the 16thC nave roof repeats the timber theme handsomely. The nave is Norman and the chancel 19thC. Observe the vigorous carving round the Norman N doorway

and how the string course loops over the arch. **P.** *Open daylight hours daily.*

Winchcombe, St Peter   9 L8

The masons went to town on devilish gargoyles, which leer, full of evil intent, from this stately, largely 15thC, wool church. Its building was financed by Abbot William of the abbey which stood to the E of the church, profits from the local woollen industry and by Sir Ralph Boteler, who built nearby Sudeley Castle, and who is depicted in a grotesque head near the S porch. Gaze up at the splendid gilded weathercock, which came from St Mary Redcliffe in Bristol in 1874, lording it from the top of the tower. The border of the altar cloth on display near the N door is thought to have been embroidered by Catherine of Aragon, Henry VIII's first wife, and the carving of the fine organ case is also worth examining. Look on the beautiful 15thC rood screen for the Winchcombe imp, a charming and humorous insertion among the carved roses, vines and lizards, and beyond it at the lavishly carved sedilia and piscina. **P.** *Open 09.00–dusk Mon–Sat, 07.00–20.00 Sun.* There are many interesting buildings in the town and ½m S is elegant Sudeley Castle, where Henry VIII's widow, Katherine Parr, lived and died in childbirth.

St Peter, Winchcombe

◁HEREFORD AND WORCESTER▷

Abbey Dore, St Mary 8 H8

2m N of Pontrilas on B4347. In the lyrically named Golden Valley, the beautiful 12thC–13thC church, long divested of its nave and monastic buildings, originally formed part of a Cistercian abbey. In 1634, Lord Scudamore restored the church, built the tower and added furnishings of a distinctive Jacobean character, including the screen with prominent coats of arms and obelisks on top, stalls, pulpit and gallery. Admire the resplendent 17thC stained glass, and walk around the exquisitely proportioned ambulatory, amid slender, shafted pillars branching out into the vault. Finely carved capitals and sculptural fragments abound. **P.** *Open daylight hours daily.*

Bredon, St Giles 8 K8

1m N of Tewkesbury on B4080. The lovely church has a glorious setting beside black and white thatched cottages, an Elizabethan rectory, 18thC Manor House and a 14thC stone tithe barn, in a village fringed by Bredon Hill and the river Avon. The central tower's slender spire is a landmark across the vale. A fine Norman N porch leads into a Norman nave and early 14thC chancel, where there are heraldic tiles and exquisite stained glass of the period. Also an unusual and ornate monument set in the wall, with strong heads of a man and woman above a crucifix. The 13thC Mitton Chapel has beautiful windows and an impressive Jacobean monument. **P.** *Open 09.00–dusk daily.* There are two inns which provide local interest: the 16thC thatched Fox and Hounds and 17thC Royal Oak.

Brinsop, St George 8 J8

4½m NW of Hereford off A480. This quaint, tiny 14thC church, crowned by a Victorian bell turret, stands in an orchard, deep in rural seclusion. The striking and vigorous Norman carving is by the Herefordshire School, characterised by a balance of fluidity and tension in the lines. Greet St George in the tympanum. Comper made the fine alabaster and gold reredos, rood screen figures and two stained glass windows in the 1920s. There is a window commemorating William Wordsworth and the E window has wonderful 14thC stained glass of St George. **P.** *Open daylight hours daily.*

Broadway, St Eadburgha 9 L8

Snowshill Rd. The pretty, medieval church has a rather wistful air of removal from the famous village, whereas it was at the hub of things when the main Worcester to London road passed down Conygree La close by. Handsome Jacobean woodwork in the chancel includes a communion rail with nice knobs on. There is an ancient stone font and by the pulpit with traceried panels, stands an unusual pillar alms box. *Open Easter-Sep 09.00–dusk daily.* There is much to enjoy in the charming village, not least the amber-coloured stone cottages, twinkling with dormer and mullioned windows or stretching out picturesque gables from steep roofs; all contrive to make Tudor, Stuart, Georgian and later statements most agreeably.

Dilwyn, St Mary 8 H8

6m SW of Leominster off A4112. The church's building history is a puzzle in that a 13thC rebuilding of nave, aisles and chancel blocks half the tower arch of c1200, creating an odd asymmetry. The 15thC S porch is tall and magnificent. See the screens, glorious 14thC stained glass with censing angels and knight's effigy in the chancel. **P.** *Open 09.00–22.00 daily.* The village is attractive and there are some delightful buildings round about.

Elmley Castle, St Mary the Virgin 8 K8

4m SW of Evesham off A44. Near the pretty Queen Elizabeth inn, whose sign records that monarch's visit to the Savage family mansion in 1575. The path to the church leads through a beautifully kept churchyard with a fascinating ancient sundial, which has the Savage arms on it. The church's 11thC origin is evident in herringbone masonry in the chancel. The sturdy tower was built in the 13thC and the church grew over the centuries. Spot the naive but charming carvings of a pig and a rabbit on stones in the porch. The Perpendicular font bowl, decorated with shields, sits on an amazing 12thC base of sinuous, ferocious dragons. Marvellous details of Stuart dress in the 1631 alabaster tomb effigies of William and Giles Savage and the latter's wife. She holds a tiny baby and four sons kneel at their feet. Notice the wig, lace cravat and buckled shoes on the first Lord Coventry's effigy of 1700. It was refused admittance to Croome d'Abitot church, the earl's burial place, by his son, on the grounds that the earl's second wife who had it made was the daughter of a turner and sister of a waterman and not of noble descent as inscribed on the monument. **P.** *Open 08.30–dusk daily.* Set among wooded hillocks and sloping pastures snuggling up to Bredon Hill, the village of black and white cottages and babbling brook is delightful. The 11thC castle after which it is named was in ruins by the 16thC.

Garway, St Michael 8 J8
10m S of Hereford off A466. The river Monnow caresses the Welsh border below the fortress-like tower, which would have been a place of refuge when the village was under attack. The nave is connected to it at an odd angle by a 17thC passage. The church started off as a 12thC round Knights Templars nave and chancel, whose foundations have been excavated and can be seen. Of interest are the impressive Norman chancel arch with richly carved zigzag patterns, from the Knights Templars church, the 13thC chapel, fine chancel roof, and substantial 17thC benches in the nave. **P.** *Open daylight hours daily.* A circular dovecote, inscribed with the name of the builder and the date 1326, is among farm buildings nearby, complete with accommodation for 666 doves.

Great Malvern, Priory church of 8 K8
St Mary and St Michael
Church St. Looking out to the Malvern hills, in a beautiful churchyard of lawn, yews and cedars, the panelled tower, with ogee gables and lovely openwork battlements and pinnacles, is a majestic sight. The townspeople bought the priory church for just £20 after the Dissolution. The Norman nave pillars are in striking contrast to the magnificent Perpendicular clerestory, chancel and huge E and W windows. Attention is drawn immediately to the softly glowing 15thC stained glass, of which there is more than in any other church in the country. The glass of the Magnificat in the transept N window was given by Henry VII in 1501. In it, the central figure of Mary radiates golden rays, encircled by a star-studded blue cloud, and Henry VII and his son Prince Arthur, who died in 1502, kneel below, surrounded by exquisite angel musicians. Fascinating 14thC and 15thC misericords include the beautifully carved Labours of the Months. The subtly coloured medieval floor and wall tiles (the only ones in

England) were manufactured in kilns rediscovered nearby in 1833 and 1902. Of the fine monuments, see in particular the alabaster Elizabethan effigies of the Knotsfords in the chancel. The survival of the glorious glass on such a scale has much to do with the church's position, protected by hills and the dense forest of Malvern Chase. Restoration was well done by Scott in 1860. *Open 08.00–17.00 or dusk daily. Sometimes closed 13.15–14.15.*

Great Malvern Priory

Hereford, All Saints 8 J8
Broad St. The 13thC–14thC church has a stately tower with slender lancet windows and a spire with gabled lucarnes. Perpendicular additions include the E window, charming porch and handsome roofs. Inspect the highly decorated Jacobean pulpit of 1621, the wonderful canopied 14thC stalls with ogee arches, exquisite tracery and misericords delightfully carved with quaint monsters and other curiosities. See too the Queen Anne reredos and enticing chained library in the S chapel, the bread shelf of 1683 and the 14thC oak chest, whose carvings include two dragons. Famous actor David Garrick was baptised in the 14thC font in 1717, when his parents were visiting the town.

Open 09.00–17.00 Mon, Tue & Thur, from 07.30 Wed & Fri, from 09.30 Sat; 09.00–19.00 Sun. The beautiful cathedral, with many marvellous features, is close by. Parts of the impressive medieval city wall and ornate black and white buildings make the ancient county town worth exploring.

Hoarwithy, St Catherine   **8 J8**
6m S of Hereford off A49. Medieval southern Italy, influenced by Byzantium, has wafted into the Wye valley as air wafts through the church's cloister walk. J. P. Seddon wrought the transformation of a brick church of 1843 into a reflection of Italy's rich past, at the end of the 19thC. The culmination is in the E end, where marble columns crowned by Byzantine capitals support a cupola and a gold mosaic of Christ Pantocrator shimmers from the apse. Jewel-like mosaic floors and beautiful stained glass complete a lustrous interior. **P.** *Open 08.00–dusk daily.* Wonderful Wye valley scenery meanders round the picturesque village.

Holt, St Martin   **8 K9**
4½m N of Worcester off A443. The wood above the church may be a descendant of that which gave the village its name. The 12thC church and 14thC–15thC castle have joined ranks with a few houses to form a picturesque hamlet, while the village has developed further off. The church, with a mounting stone at its lychgate, is like a hidden treasure trove of Norman carving, enchanting and monstrous. A monster with teeth, another biting its tail and a man whose mouth streams with foliage, await your attention on the capitals of the S doorway, while zigzag dances in the arch above. And there is abundant decoration elsewhere, not least round the font with wonderfully detailed monster heads whose gaping mouths are linked by swags. A 19thC replica of a mosaic of the Good Shepherd from the Mausoleum of Galla Placidia at Ravenna is over the chancel arch. Note the Virgin's jewelled cloak in 15thC stained glass in the Decorated chapel and the effigy of a medieval Beauchamp lady. **P.** *Open daylight hours daily.*

Kilpeck, St Mary and St David   **8 H8**
8m SW of Hereford off A465. Beside the motte of a Norman castle, it is an unforgettable experience to visit the. 11thC red sandstone church in its fantastic beauty and completeness. An

St Mary and St David, Kilpeck

incredible array of animal, human and monster heads surveys the scene all round the outside and among carvings on the spectacular S doorway are the Tree of Life, terrible dragons of Viking extraction and warrior figures. Haloed apostles, carved by a different sculptor, stand above one another on the chancel arch and the rib-vaulting of the apse beyond is decorated with zigzag. See the extraordinary carving on the holy water stoup and the massive font. Little has been added to the Norman work, just a Victorian bellcote and chancel windows of c1300. **P.** *Open daylight hours Fri–Sun.*

Ledbury, St Michael and All Angels   **8 J8**
Church La. The beautiful church is a 13thC–15thC refashioning of a Norman foundation. It has many unusual and fine features, including a detached 13thC tower, whose spire was added in 1733, 12thC turrets either side of the carved, Norman W doorway, and a 14thC baptistery, whose exquisite window tracery is lavished with ballflower decoration. Set aside time to examine the splendid monuments assembled here, including the 13thC effigy of a priest, whose eloquent prayer is almost audible. The reredos is a 19thC copy of

Leonardo's *Last Supper*. **P** nearby. *Open approx 08.30–dusk daily*. Cobbled Church La has some of the black and white houses of varying degrees of splendour that adorn the market town.

St Michael and All Angels, Ledbury

Leominster, Priory church of　　8 J9
St Peter and St Paul
The former priory church was built on a grand scale and is an imposing sight. See the wonderful Norman W portal and the intricately carved capitals with birds, animals and men face to face. The fine 13thC S porch has beautiful doorways and the S aisle windows burgeon with lovely ballflower decoration. The former monastic N nave is massively Norman and to its S is the former parochial nave with a marvellous, great Perpendicular W window. A fire of 1699 destroyed most of the furnishings, but see the handsome organ case of 1739, the exquisite pre-Reformation chalice, and the ducking stool, which was used to punish scolds and sellers of shoddy goods until 1809. **P.** *Open approx daylight hours daily*.
Explore the lovely town which has many charming black and white buildings.

Little Malvern, Priory　　8 K8
2m S of Great Malvern on A449. Wooded Wynd's Point forms a glorious backdrop for the mellow stone panelled tower and chancel, all that remains of a priory church founded in the 12thC and rebuilt

by Bishop Alcock in 1480–2. Ruined 15thC transepts and chapels crumble picturesquely to either side and reach out to the Court, which incorporates the Prior's Hall or refectory of the former monastic buildings, with a wonderful medieval timber roof. The fine E window stained glass, inserted by the bishop, forms a portrait gallery of the contemporary royal family, including the princes who were murdered in the Tower of London in 1483. Look at the rood screen and richly carved rood beam, the charming carvings of pigs and little faces on the stalls from which Cromwell's troops hacked the misericords, and the tiles adorning the chancel floor. **P.** *Open daylight hours daily*.

Madley, Nativity of the Blessed　　8 H8
Virgin Mary
6m W of Hereford on B4352. In a village fringed by the river Wye and the Black Mountains, the original Norman church was refashioned in the 13thC and 14thC into the present spacious and splendid edifice, culminating in an unusual polygonal apse. The clerestoried and aisled interior, is ablaze with light pouring through the many clear windows. The nobly-proportioned 13thC nave arcades lead the eye down to the E window, with brilliant, jewel-like roundels of 13thC stained glass and 14thC figures below. Of considerable interest are the sedilia ornamented with ballflower, the medieval choir stalls, the capacious font and the crypt. And if you fancy climbing a flight of 89 steps, the lovely tower-top view is open to you – on request for the key from the vicarage. *Open 09.00–dusk Mon–Sat, from 08.00 Sun*. See the 16thC timber-framed Town House in the village and the space-age satellite station.

Much Marcle, St Bartholomew　　8 J8
4½m SW of Ledbury off A449. The apricot-coloured stone church has beautiful 13thC nave arcades with a clerestory of single lancet windows. There is a number of marvellous tomb effigies, including that of Lady Grandison, d1347, in an arcaded and canopied recess in the chancel. Her skirt trails realistically over the tomb-chest and her face, hands and clothes express an exquisite grace. Late 14thC effigies of a knight and lady are accompanied by puppies tugging at her skirt hem and feathered angels at her pillow, while charming, long-fingered angels hold shields below. The lady on the 17thC Kyrle tomb wears a gown with

ruff, slashed sleeves and a brocaded underskirt, and her feet rest on an alarmingly large paw. It is riveting to come face to face with a franklin, or landowner, of Chaucer's England, wearing a jerkin and long, pointy shoes, in the rare oak effigy of Walter de Helyon. **P.** *Open 08.30–sunset daily.* Here is your chance to revisit childhood and sit inside a tree trunk; the ancient churchyard yew has proper seated accommodation for seven. 50 yds N is the great mound of Mortimer's Castle. There is a profusion of black and white houses in the parish and the Old Vicarage is a Queen Anne brick house of 1703. A dovecote of 1641 stands near Hellens, a mullion-windowed Jacobean brick manor house. Much Marcle cannot be left without a word about the 'wonder landslide' of 1575, when Marcle Hill got up and moved 400 yds in three days, uprooting trees and destroying a chapel.

Newland, St Leonard   **8 K9**
2m NE of Great Malvern on A449. Forming a social symphony, almshouses and church were built together for the Beauchamps in 1862–4, by P. C. Hardwick. Marble columns create an impression of grandeur in the interior, which is bright with wall paintings, tiles, polished marbles and stained glass windows. Stand at the gabled oriel window, behind which you might imagine a romantic heroine receiving a serenade, which communicated with the infirmary. *Open 08.00–18.30 daily.*

Pembridge, St Mary the Virgin   **8 H9**
6m W of Leominster on A44. There is a marvellous view from the churchyard on a knoll overlooking the Welsh Marches. What next arrests attention is the impressive 14thC detached belfry, of Scandinavian descent, which looks like a short, plump pagoda. It has a stone base, with slits for firing arrows through during early border skirmishes and roofs interspersed with weatherboarding. Inside is a forest of great timbers. The building of the beautiful church, between 1320–60, was held up by the Black Death of 1349. There is a cavity behind the N door in the fine, vaulted N porch for an oak beam to secure the church in times of siege. In the nave are elegant arcades and flower-like cinquefoiled clerestory windows. Dragons curl neatly in the Jacobean pulpit panels and on the lectern. See the carved altar rails, the four 14thC effigies and the medieval wall decoration in the S transept. *Open 09.00–*

St Mary the Virgin, belfry

dusk Mon–Sat, from 08.00 Sun. Picturesque black-and-white timbered cottages jostle round the market place. If visiting the Tudor New Inn, near the 16thC oak-pillared Market Hall, watch out for the ghost of a red-coated soldier with sword, who occasionally puts in an impromptu appearance.

Pershore, Holy Cross Abbey   **8 K8**
The first abbey church was destroyed by the Danes and rebuilt only to be twice damaged by fire and rebuilt in the 13thC. The nave was pulled down at the Dissolution, and its arcades are now poetically marked out by trees. But the townspeople saved the choir and transepts by buying them for £400. The shafted pillars and carved capitals of the choir are magnificent, and so is the crowning vault, studded with beautiful foliage bosses. An apse was added in the 19thC. Stand under the glorious 14thC lantern tower for a thrilling view of windows with two layers of tracery, stone panelling, and the ringing platform, built by Scott in the 19thC and suspended on beams. The S transept is the earliest part of the abbey and houses a colourful monument to Thomas Hazelwood, d1624, in which his widow wears a remarkable hat. See the striking modern altar frontals by Pat Russell, the

13thC effigy of a knight, Victorian stained glass telling the story of the abbey, and the font. *Open summer 09.00–18.00 Mon–Sat, winter to 16.00, 07.30–19.30 Sun.* Close by is the church that served the parishioners when the abbey was monastic. The delights of Pershore include Georgian brick houses with verandas and Venetian windows. The middle arch of the medieval bridge was wrecked by Royalist soldiers fleeing from the Battle of Worcester, to hamper Cromwell's men who were in hot pursuit.

Pershore Abbey

Shelsley Walsh, St Andrew　　8 J9
9m NW of Worcester off B4204. Lawn, trees and the river Teme are the natural embellishments of this enchanting small church, close to 16thC Court House. The Norman nave is entered by a zigzag-arched doorway and medieval oak door. The medieval woodwork captivates above all: the 15thC rood screen is exquisitely traceried and carved with vine leaves and tendrils, and turns to the S to form a chantry chapel. And the rare 15thC rood beam, surmounted by a 19thC Celtic cross, is equally richly carved. Look up above to the starry chancel roof, with remarkable carved beams; the 14thC nave roof is striking, too. In the chancel are 15thC floor tiles and the unusual wooden tomb of Francis Walsh, d1596. The church was restored in 1859 and the

pretty bell turret rebuilt. **P.** *Open daylight hours daily.* A 17thC Walsh, Sir Richard, of Court House, was High Sherriff of Worcester at the time of the Gunpowder Plot and instrumental in arresting the conspirators.

Shobdon, St John the Evangelist　　8 H9
6m W of Leominster on B4362. Here is a bewitching expression of that form of 18thC Gothic explored in Strawberry Hill by Horace Walpole, who converted the church's builder, Richard Bateman, to the style. Gothic, Rococco and oriental features are delightfully and extravagantly combined to produce the hybrid, Gothick, in an interior decked out in white and blue, with the piquant contrast of crimson velvet hangings on the altar and three-decker pulpit. The pulpit's pretty sounding board echoes the striking pendant ogee arches which separate the nave from transepts and chancel. See the Gothick chairs in the chancel, 18thC stained glass, and the unnerving lions parading round the Norman font. **P.** *Open 09.00–dusk daily.* The chancel arch and doorways from the church's Norman forebear were erected ½m N in the 18thC, and gables and pinnacles added to them. The carvings are of the spectacular Kilpeck kind, though much damaged by exposure, and include dragons and acrobatic angels.

Stoke Prior, St Michael　　8 K9
12m N of Worcester on B4091. The magnificent 13thC tower with fine lancet windows, makes a great impact, its sturdiness complemented by the graceful, shingled spire. The Norman N arcade also gives an impression of strength with its round pillars and arches. Built of local Bromsgrove sandstone, the church was restored in 1895 by John Corbett, owner of the nearby salt works, and the present S porch was built. But the handsome doorway is Norman and has beside it a Saxon carved stone, relic of an 8thC predecessor. The beautiful 14thC E window in the 13thC chancel is filled with glass of 1860, commemorating the abolition of female labour at the local salt works, and gives a sense of the integration of the life of the community into the church. The altar rails and reredos were designed by Eric Gill. **P.** *Open 09.30–dusk Sat, 08.30–20.00 Sun; Mon–Fri by request.*

Weobley, St Peter and St Paul　　8 H8
9m NW of Hereford on B4230. The great steeple looks down augustly upon a feast

of timber-framed black-and-white cottages and inns. The tower is 14thC and the spire, with prominent panelled and crocketed pinnacles, was rebuilt in the 19thC. The church's Norman start is visible in the zigzag-arched S doorway. Note the lovely 14thC nave arcades and clerestory and the scissor beam roof. Follow the range of 14thC tracery patterns on the octagonal font. Colonel John Birch, d1691, Roundhead Commander in the Civil War, still commands attention through his white marble, armoured statue in the 13thC chancel. **P.** *Open 09.00–dusk daily.* This is a most enjoyable village to wander in.

Wickhamford, St John the Baptist   9 L8
2m SE of Evesham off A44. In an entrancing setting beside the picturesque 16thC manor house, the church has a 17thC tower and 13thC chancel, married agreeably by an earlier Stuart nave. The interior belongs to the 17thC and has been little tampered with since. Hence a three-decker pulpit holds sway, to whose 17thC panelling carved saints and cherub heads have been added. In the chancel are 17thC altar rails and a magnificent painted alabaster monument to the Sandys, father and son, who both died in 1626. Recumbent effigies of them and their wives lie under a rich canopy, prayerful children below. Here too is the tomb of Penelope Washington, an ancestor of American President George Washington. See the box pews with linenfold and Flemish carved panels and the W gallery with fine 17thC carvings. *Open approx 08.00–dusk daily.* Cream teas are served in the village hall during the summer.

◀LEICESTERSHIRE▶

Ashby-de-la-Zouch, St Helen   13 M10
Drama is provided by the proximity of the castle ruins and serenity by the churchyard. Lord Hastings built the impressive church in 1474, at the same time as building the castle's mighty Hastings Tower. Outer aisles were added in the 19thC. Monuments in the Hastings Chapel include a grand table tomb with effigies of the second Earl of Huntingdon, d1561, and his wife, and a fine sculpture by J. M. Rysbrack of the ninth earl's widow. Notice the interesting medieval stained glass here and in the chancel, the spectacularly carved reredos of 1679 and the dreaded finger pillory near the tower, 'for the prevention of indecorous behaviour', used until the 19thC. **P.** *Open daylight hours daily.* Smouldering memories linger in the castle of Mary Queen of Scots who was imprisoned here and Charles I who stayed here on his way to Naseby.

Barkby, St Mary   13 N10
2m N of Leicester off A607. A lovely 13thC church with a 14thC broach-spire and many carved heads inside and out. The nave windows are remarkable for their idiosyncratic tracery and two side windows in the chancel for wooden doors with decorative hinges. See the old musicians' gallery and organ gallery and the restored 18thC clock. The memorial tablet to Charlotte Pochin, d1732, is by Rysbrack; ivy grows picturesquely on a Gothick arch over a sarcophagus on Mary Pochin's monument, d1804. The dangers attendant on a country life are evident from the registers which record deaths at the end of the 18thC by falling from a load of straw, from a horse, from a tree and in the case of one young man, 'by the wheels of a wagon going over his head'. **P.** *Open 08.30–dusk Mon–Sat, 07.30–20.00 Sun.* The pleasant village has a handsome, gabled vicarage.

Bottesford, St Mary the Virgin   13 N11
6m W of Grantham on A52. The river Devon tinkles under a footbridge of c1600 S of the churchyard, which is dominated by the very tall and splendid Perpendicular spire, dotted with lucarnes and with crockets climbing up it. Be sure to greet the lively gargoyles guarding the church before going inside, where your attention will be irresistibly drawn to the chancel, crowded out with eight (recumbent or upright) consecutive earls of Rutland in marble and alabaster effigy. They lie beside their wives on tombs of varying degrees of magnificence, Elizabethan, classical and Baroque styles making the most spectacular display. The sixth earl, d1632, shares the most sumptuous monument with his two wives and on it sinister reference is made to children killed by sorcery, for which witches were hanged. Grinling Gibbons

sculptured the monuments to the seventh and eighth earls. **P**. *Open 09.00–dusk Mon–Sat, 07.30–19.30 Sun*. Romantic 19thC Norman-Gothic Belvoir Castle lords it over the nearby Vale of Belvoir. The first castle was built by Robert de Todeni, who carried William the Conqueror's standard at the Battle of Hastings, and its successor has many fascinating features, including the king's rooms, which were used by George IV when he visited the castle as Prince Regent and have hand-painted Chinese wallpapers, the dining room whose coffered ceiling is worth stretching your neck for, and Gobelin tapestries and estimable paintings.

Breedon-on-the-Hill, St Mary   13 M11
and St Hardulph
5m NE of Ashby-de-la-Zouch on A453. The Bulwarks, remains of an Iron Age fort, are on one side, and to the E a limestone quarry drops precipitously down, creating a breathtakingly picturesque setting for the church. A 7thC or 8thC monastery on the hill was sacked by the Danes and was succeeded by a 12thC priory, part of the Norman fabric of which remains in the tower and whose 13thC chancel forms the present church's nave. From the monastery survive marvellous Saxon sculptures, including friezes with vine scrolls, some of which have fabulous birds and beasts and warriors kneeling or on horseback. At the E end of the S aisle is a half figure of the Virgin giving a Byzantine style blessing, and the greatest treasure of all, which can be seen by arrangement, is the ringing chamber Breedon Angel, also giving a Byzantine blessing – a powerful and beautiful sculpture whose inspiration shines through the centuries. Admire too the fine 15thC font, the grandiose monument to Sir George Shirley, d1588, and his family, and the vainglorious Shirley pew of 1627, an opulently carved private box which would have blocked the view of lesser mortals. **P**. *Open approx 09.00–18.00 Tue–Thur & Sat, from 10.00 Mon, from 07.30 Fri, from 11.00 Sun*. Nothing blocks the matchless panoramic views from the hill.

Brooke, St Peter   13 N10
2m S of Oakham off A6003. In a village of 27 people, upland circling round, the delightful church has a 13thC tower and a vigorous Norman doorway. An Elizabethan gem is lodged within in the fascinating and faithful period expression given by screens, box pews, pulpit and

stalls and the unchanged windows and arches of the N aisle and chancel of c1579. **P**. *Open 09.00–17.00 daily*.

Edith Weston, St Mary the   13 N10
Virgin
15m NW of Peterborough off A6121. The village, named after Edward the Confessor's wife Queen Edith, laps part of the manmade lake, Rutland Water. The church's elegant steeple with lucarnes looking out is 14thC. There is interesting Norman decoration on the chancel arch and capitals of the nave N arcade. The S arcade is 13thC and a chapel was added in the 19thC. Examine the 18thC chamber organ in a mahogany case and the Arts and Crafts reredos by Sir George Frampton. **P**. *Open approx daylight hours daily*. Fishing and sailing can be enjoyed on the lake. St Matthew's church, half a mile along the bank, stands mysteriously above the water's surface, raised before the meadow where it stood was metamorphosed into a lake.

Egleton, St Edmund   13 O10
17m E of Leicester on A6003. The 14thC tower is 18thC at the top. On the S doorway is a spectacular display of Norman carving, with ornamentation clustered round and under the arch, up columns and on capitals, all vibrant with life. The chancel arch is equally dazzling. See the 14thC roof corbels, the 13thC font decorated with crosses, poppyhead benches and a mural of St Edmund. **P**. *Open winter 10.00–16.30 daily, later in summer*.

Empingham, St Peter   14 O10
3m W of Stamford on A606. The church has a wonderful 14thC tower with an air of enjoyable flamboyance in its outsize pinnacles and crocketed spire. Otherwise it is largely of the 13thC, with graceful lancet windows and lovely sedilia and piscina with modest leaf ornamentation. Medieval red floral and foliage patterns are painted on parts of the walls and Perpendicular details include the roof with carved angels. **P**. *Open summer 09.00–18.00 daily, closes earlier in winter*.

Leicester, St Margaret   13 N10
St Margaret's St. A beautiful medieval church, with a 13thC S arcade and doorway and a stately Perpendicular tower, finely detailed outside and vaulted within. Perpendicular too are the clerestory, fan-vaulted S porch and magnificent chancel with statue niches and other exquisitely harmonised

decorations. The church was restored in the 19thC. *Open approx daylight hours daily.* A further dignified expression of medieval Leicester is in the Guildhall of 14thC origin. The late 18thC County Rooms and 19thC Town Hall and Corn Exchange are handsome civic symbols of later prosperity.

Leicester, St Mary de Castro　　**13** N10

Castle St. In a wonderful setting beside the remains of the Norman castle above the river Soar, in the city's centre, the church was founded in 1107 by the first Earl of Leicester as a collegiate chapel. Its spire, rebuilt in 1783, makes a dramatic impact, with crockets leaping up its great height and little windows, or lucarnes, looking out. Acrobats were once wont to slide down a rope from the top of the spire to the castle green. The late Norman chancel is the church's most glorious feature, and in particular the sedilia, with ingeniously carved capitals and rows of zigzag seeming to scintillate in the arches. There are also excellent 13thC sedilia and windows with fine geometrical tracery. **P.** *Open Easter–Oct 14.00–17.00 Mon, Tue & Sat.*

Leicester, St Nicholas　　**13** N10

St Nicholas Circle. A compelling and evocative composition is formed by the church's great Norman tower, the Roman Forum and Roman Jewry Wall. The tower has Roman brickwork and later blank arcading. Inside the church's Saxon origins are visible in two windows above the Norman N arcade. Interesting 13thC, 16thC and Victorian additions have been made, but the early work is the most memorable. The Jewry Wall Museum is devoted largely to the city's Roman remains.

St Nicholas, Leicester

Loughborough, All Saints　　**13** M11

Steeple Row. The lovely town church has a very handsome Perpendicular tower and is otherwise largely 14thC, although Victorian restoration was rather heavy handed. It has a 'weeping' chancel, out of alignment with the nave to represent the inclination of Christ's head on the cross. The most glorious feature is the 15thC regilded nave roof, built as so often on wool wealth. Bosses of weird creatures and caricatured faces look down from it and at the sides are 18 delightful, celebratory angels crisply carved and playing musical instruments. Interesting, embroidered new vestments may be seen on request. **P.** *Open Apr-Oct 10.30–16.00 Sat, or by prior arrangement.*

St Dionysius, Market Harborough

Market Harborough, St Dionysius 9 N10

High St. In a town established as a market by Henry II in the 12thC and without a churchyard because the church fell within another parish when it was built, which reserved burial rights and fees. Tower and spire form a masterpiece of graceful 14thC design, making a distinguished and gracious impact on the market square and surrounding streets, which have in parts an elegant Georgian and Victorian character. The 14thC chancel windows have splendid, restored geometrical tracery on the verge of reaching the flowing stage. The handsome chancel roof is embellished with bosses and tracery. Look back along the 15thC nave arcades with distinctive galleries to admire the vivacious Royal Arms over the tower arch, celebrating the Restoration in 1660. *Open 09.00–15.30 daily*. The charming, timbered and gabled old grammar school of 1614 to the S, was built on posts to accommodate the Butter Market below.

Melton Mowbray, St Mary　　**13** N11
Burton St. From the green on the SW, feathery tree fronds frame the large, majestic church and the tower shows off its Perpendicular crown to magnificent effect. The beautiful early 14thC Galilee Porch has luxuriant ballflower ornamentation in the W portal and from the fine inner doorway stretches a wonderful view of nave and transepts, with distinctive double aisles, built between 1280–1320, and of the striking 48-window clerestory of c1500 which admits a great influx of light. Further light is thrown on the transepts by the splendid 18thC chandeliers, when they are lit at Christmas and Easter. Near the font is the curious feature of a water pump and in the window above fragments of fine medieval stained glass are gathered. Look out for the effigies of a crusader, c1300, and a late 14thC lady in alabaster. G. G. Scott restored the church in the 19thC, and Sir Malcolm Sargent was organist here. **P**. *nearby. Open summer 10.00–12.00 & 14.00–17.00 daily, winter to 16.00*. Resounding to the ring of horses' hooves, this pleasant market town has been the centre of fox-hunting in the shires since the early 19thC. The Mowbrays were lords here in the Middle Ages. Currently it is the home of the pork pie and Stilton cheese.

Oakham, All Saints　　**13** N10
Church St. High ground to the W and S offsets the country town, whose school, founded in 1584, and market with picturesque cross evoke the Tudor and Stuart world. The 14thC church tower is paramount in the townscape and has a very distinctive W front, although its parapet is rather inelegant and the bell-openings on the S side are off-centre to accommodate the staircase. Glorious in the light-filled interior are the rare,

carved stone capitals in the nave, on which biblical scenes, foliage, grotesques and animals appear, engrossing to study. The work by Ninian Comper is also notable. **P**. *Open 06.30–19.00 Mon, to 18.00 Tue & Thur, to 20.15 Wed, to 21.00 Fri; 07.00–18.00 Sat, 07.00–19.30 Sun*. The 12thC hall of Oakham Castle is an extraordinary survival; the corbels against the walls and the capitals in its church-like arcades are excellently carved.

St Peter, Norman chancel arch

Tickencote, St Peter　　**14** O10
2m N of Stamford off A1. The restored and partly rebuilt church retains its essential Norman features. The E front is immensely variegated with intersecting arches, and much zigzag. Inside are two veritable marvels of Norman construction: the unforgettable chancel arch is one, formed of order upon order of extravagant decoration, including beak-head, curious animal and human heads and zigzag, the patterns seeming to scintillate outwards. And the other is the magnificent vault in the chancel, zigzag running up its ribs and a rare Norman boss of a monk's head and two muzzled bears in the centre. A wooden effigy of an armoured knight lies near the altar, thought to represent Sir Roland le Daneys, who fought in the French wars during Edward III's reign. The beautiful 13thC font is studded with starry ornament and faces at its angles and has foliage and interlaced arches on the sides. A pre-Reformation bell hangs in the churchyard. **P**. *Open daylight hours daily*.

Uppingham, St Peter and St Paul 13 N10
The porch leads off the market place and the 14thC tower and soaring spire pierced with lucarnes make an impressive statement in the attractive churchyard. The N aisle has pretty

Decorated detail outside and a new chancel was built in the 19thC. There are some very beautiful late Norman sculptures of an expressive Christ giving a blessing, a saint and angels. The Elizabethan pulpit is an interesting

feature. **P** limited on market day. *Open 08.00–18.30 daily*. Uppingham School, founded in 1584, is close by and opposite it a fine Tudor house. The lovely Rutland landscape and Rutland Water stretch beyond.

◁ NORTHAMPTONSHIRE ▷

Aynho, St Michael and All Angels 9 M8
5m SW of Brackley on A41. The charmingly detailed medieval tower is rather startlingly attached to a church whose shape and symmetry of central pediments and projecting end bays give it the air of a villa. It is a transformation of 1723–5 into the classical mode, and is furnished with pulpit, box pews and a distinguished W gallery of the period. Memorial tablets abound. **P**. *Open 09.00–18.00 daily*. Steep lanes, apricot trees trained fan-shape against limestone cottage walls and the former manor house, Aynhoe Park, give the village a delightful character.

Barnwell, St Andrew 10 O9
2½m SE of Oundle off A605. Yews and hollies lead up to the 13thC church with a tall, 14thC spire. On the N doorway leaves spring from a carved face. Faces also nestle in the wonderful Decorated stone reredos, which has extravagant ogee arches flourishing foliage. G. G. Scott refashioned the chancel in 1851. *Open 08.00–dusk daily*. The church nods to medieval Barnwell Castle down the hill and to the manor house built by the Montagus, both of which now belong to the Duke and Duchess of Gloucester. Willows weep and bridges crouch over the stream leading through the village to the chancel of All Saints, all that remains of a church demolished in 1825. Monuments to the Montagus are congregated here, including an obelisk on big human feet dripping mud to

three-year-old Henry, who drowned in a pond in 1625. Dressed as a Jacobean manikin, his effigy holds a scroll with a pathetic echo of his end in the words 'Lord, give me of ye Waters'. And the feet say, 'Not my feete only' and 'but also my hands and head'.

St Andrew, Saxon turret

Brigstock, St Andrew 10 O9
4m SE of Corby on A6116. It is thrilling to see the knobbly Saxon tower, contrasting with the smooth 14thC spire, and turret, the purpose of whose impressive substantiality nobody knows; a mere stairway would not need nearly so much space. The colossal tower arch looks upon an interior to which much has been added over the centuries: Norman arches confront a 14thC arcade; the S doorway and the sedilia are 13thC, while the beautiful screen to the N chapel and the porch with a pretty turret are Perpendicular. **P**. *Open summer 07.15–dusk Mon & Wed–Fri, from 09.00 Tue; winter to 18.00; 09.30–18.00 Sat, 07.30–19.00 Sun.*

St Andrew, Barnwell

Brixworth, All Saints 9 N9
7m N of Northampton on A508. Built in the
Dark Ages, when Roman Britain was
dead and the Anglo-Saxon world not
fully emerged, the church is a most
awesome survival. A monastery in the
7thC, until it was partly destroyed in
9thC Danish raids, it is surprisingly
sophisticated for its date and used bricks
from nearby deserted Roman villas. The
impressive outsize stair turret, of the
same type as that at Brigstock, was
added in the 10thC. Although the church
was extensively added to in the medieval
period its ancient feeling prevails. A
square E end replaced the 10thC apse in
the 15thC, but the apse was rebuilt in
1865. **P**. *Open approx 09.00–17.00 Mon–
Wed & Sat, to 21.00 Thur, from 07.30 Fri,
from 08.00 Sun.*

Bugbrooke, St Michael and 9 N9
All Angels
6m SW of Northampton on B4525. Set
amidst trees and grassland, the church
has a 14thC tower and spire. A
Perpendicular clerestory lights the fine,
13thC arcades. The beautifully carved
15thC rood screen burgeons into coving
at the top. **P**. *Open 08.45–dusk Mon–Fri,
from 09.00 Sat; 08.00–19.30 Sun.* There are
some dignified houses in the village.

Crick, St Margaret 9 N9
4m SE of Rugby on A428. Fascinating
carvings in this beautiful Decorated
church include the figures supporting the
Norman font, which has a knobbly bowl
and a crocketed spire-shaped cover.
Heads hold up the chancel arch and
monsters and animals the chancel
window arches. Examine the slim lady's
effigy of c1300, the unusual window
tracery, the organ of 1819 from the
Chapel Royal, and the shelter to keep the
rain off the priest at funerals. Lucarnes
look prettily out of the broach-spire. *Open
09.00–dusk Mon–Fri, from 10.00 Sat, to
19.00 Sun.*

Denford, Holy Trinity 10 O9
8m E of Kettering on A605. Delightfully set
on the bank of the river Nene, this is a
fine, 13thC church with impressively
enriched tower and broach-spire. Gape
back at the lively 14thC gargoyles
decorating the S side and the many
enjoyable heads carved inside the
church. Note the interesting arcading in
the chancel and the 16thC and 17thC
Flemish stained glass, glowing yellow
and orange in the Lady Chapel. **P**. *Open
10.00–16.00 Mon–Sat, 08.00–19.00 Sun.*

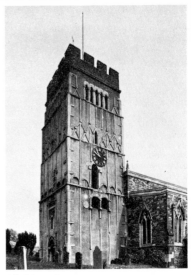

All Saints, Saxon tower

Earls Barton, All Saints 9 N9
4m SW of Wellingborough on B573. The
mighty Saxon tower is an unforgettable
sight, highly decorated with pilaster
strips, some of which fan out to form
triangles, windows with wonderfully
sturdy balusters and long-and-short work
clambering up the angles. The fact that
the tower is such a commanding and
individual presence makes it difficult to
turn one's attention to anything else,
although interesting Norman additions
include the S doorway and blank
arcading in the chancel with dazzling
zigzag decoration. **P**. *Open 09.00–17.00
Mon–Fri & Sun, to 16.00 Sat.*

Easton Maudit, St Peter and 9 O9
St Paul
8m E of Northampton off A509. A
Decorated church, restored in the 19thC,
whose elegantly detailed spire throws out
openwork flying buttresses to the tower
pinnacles. Pay attention to the graceful
18thC font, the 19thC pulpit carved with
foliage and the elaborate monument to
Sir Henry Yelverton, d1631, and his wife,
where they recline rather uncomfortably
on their elbows and cowled, bearded
bedesmen stand, caryatid-like, either
side. Dr Johnson worshipped in the
church when he visited Thomas Percy,
who was vicar from 1753–82 and
published the *Reliques of Ancient English
Poetry* in 1765. **P**. *Open 09.00–dusk daily.*

Everdon, St Mary the Virgin   **9** N9
4m SE of Daventry off A361. A dignified
14thC church of great breadth and
height, with a view over fields and hills
from the S porch. Amidst its pure lines, a
focus of rich display is the S doorway,
whose opulent carving includes a
profusion of foliage and flowers outside
and faces inside. Another is the E
window of the S aisle with its sumptuous
tracery. See too the delightful tracery of
the 14thC rood screen and the grinning
faces which charmingly appear in its
carving. A brass in the chancel
commemorates Timothy Dod, a 17thC
cleric who was too large to climb into the
pulpit. Poet Thomas Gray visited the
churchyard and church where his uncle
was rector. **P.** *Open 08.30–21.00 Mon–Sat,
07.45–20.00 Sun.*

St Mary and All Saints, Fotheringhay

Fotheringhay, St Mary and   **10** O10
All Saints
4m NE of Oundle off A605. The loveliest of
lantern towers, with the gilt falcon,
emblem of the House of York, flying
above, overlooks water meadows fringing
the river Nene and the mound where
Fotheringhay Castle stood until the
17thC. A collegiate church was founded
here by Edward, Duke of York, in 1411,
who died at the Battle of Agincourt in
1415. Its great choir was demolished in
the 16thC, but the tower and nave, with
graceful flying buttresses, are splendid.
Windows stretching to form walls of
glass create an interior brimful with light.
See the fine roof, the Perpendicular font
and pulpit with a glorious vaulted
sounding board, the tower's beautiful
fan-vault and monuments to the second

and third dukes of York, erected by
Elizabeth I in 1573. *Open daylight hours
daily.* A sublime melancholy haunts the
site of the castle where Mary Queen of
Scots was executed in 1587, and where
thistles, legendarily planted by her, grow
each year.

St Mary the Virgin, Gayton

Gayton, St Mary the Virgin   **9** N8
5½m S of Northampton off A43. The lovely
church has a distinguished neighbour in
a Tudor manor house. A Norman tower
base was wedded to a pinnacled and
crenellated crown in the 19thC. Look
down the 13thC nave arcades to the fine
E window with flowing tracery.
Also in the chancel are an early 16thC
linenfold-panelled reredos, and
misericords with interesting carvings,
including the Virgin sheltering two little
nude figures under her robe, a fighting
lion and dragon and a figure riding
through a rocky wood. An oak effigy of a
knight, Sir Philip de Gayton, d1316, lies
on an elaborate tomb-chest and in the N
chapel Francis Tanfield, d1558, is
commemorated in alabaster with his wife
and 18 children, eight of whom advanced
in life no further than infancy, as shown
by their swaddling clothes. French or
Flemish Renaissance stained glass in the
chapel was brought from France after the
Napoleonic wars. **P.** *Open 09.00–dusk
Mon–Sat, to 19.30 Sun.*

Geddington, St Mary Magdalene   **9** O9
3m N of Kettering on A43. Arcading from
the earlier Saxon nave can be seen above
Norman arches in the N aisle of the
12thC–14thC church. The beautiful E
window's tracery is reflected in the
former rood screen of 1618, where
exuberant twirls are captivatingly carved

in between the tracery. The stained glass in both the chancel and Lady Chapel E windows is by Comper, made early and late in his career. Inspect the stone reredos, the inscriptions recording the builders of the chancel and Lady Chapel, the brasses, and the King's Door in the N aisle, which was once the entrance to the church from the royal hunting lodge. **P.** nearby. *Open 08.00–19.30 daily*. The late 14thC tower is elegantly complementary to the Eleanor Cross. Of the three that still remain, this is the best preserved of the original 12 crosses which marked the places where the funeral cortege of Queen Eleanor, Edward I's beloved wife, halted on the way to London from Harby in 1291. Thatched stone cottages and a medieval bridge are picturesque accompaniments.

Great Brington, St Mary the Virgin 9 N9
6m NW of Northampton off A428. Among the multitude of poppyheads flourishing on the bench ends in this handsome medieval church, be sure to look for that of a guardian angel and child trampling a colossal dragon, near Laurence Washington's tomb, in the chancel. He, by the way, was the great-great-great grandfather of the first President of the USA, George Washington. The vivid stained glass in the huge E window is by Morris & Co. Sumptuous and mighty monuments form an amazing congregation in the Spencer Chapel. Canopies studded with rich embellishments shield effigies of armoured knights and ladies, some of whom wear extraordinary engulfing ruffs and hoods and one of whom is encased in a heraldic coverlet. A most singular monument shows a bust of Sir Edward Spencer, d1655, rising like a genie from an urn and looking unsuitably pompous considering the oddity of his situation. **P.** *Open 09.00–19.00 Mon–Sat, from 08.00 Sun.*

**Higham Ferrers, Blessed Virgin 10 O9
Mary**
Off Market Sq. The church is the centre of a group of ecclesiastical buildings exemplifying medieval religious and social integration, such as Pugin would have judged the true significance of Gothic. A school and striped bedehouse for 12 poor old men, built by Archbishop Chichele, are in the churchyard. Members of the college founded by the Archbishop in 1422 were intended to teach grammar and singing. The doorway of the 13thC tower is splendidly carved and the bell-openings lavishly

Blessed Virgin Mary, Higham Ferrers

shafted. Above is a dainty Decorated frieze, openwork flying buttresses and elegant crocketed spire. The 13thC and 14thC interior has a number of carved screens, stalls with misericords from the time of the college and fascinating brasses, including an exquisite brass of a priest, Laurence St Maur, d1337, whose soul is held in a napkin by angels above his head. Work by Comper includes the rood loft and crucifix. Outside is the 14thC churchyard cross. **P.** *Open 07.00– dusk daily*. Ruins of Archbishop Chichele's college are in the attractive market town.

Irthlingborough, St Peter 10 O9
2m N of Rushden on B571. A most striking 14thC lantern tower, all but detached from the church, surveys the town and riverscape of the Nene, crossed by an impressive 14thC bridge. You can do the same, as a guided tour will take you to the very top. The 13thC is reflected in the nave arcades and lancet windows and the 14thC in windows with reticulated and flowing tracery. Look out for the alabaster effigies, the stalls and the Perpendicular font. **P.** *Open 07.30– 17.30 daily*.

King's Cliffe, All Saints 10 O10
6m NW of Oundle off A43. The beautiful Norman and 13thC steeple and stately medieval church are in an attractive valley village, crowded with interesting foundations by theologian Rev William

Law, 1686–1761, of schools, a library and widows' and spinsters' almshouses. His tomb in the churchyard is in the form of a desk. Inside are a lovely Perpendicular roof, 15thC bench ends and fragments of medieval stained glass depicting angels with musical instruments. **P**. *Open daylight hours daily*. The dignified Georgian rectory is the former Mill House.

King's Sutton, St Peter and St Paul 9 M8
4m SE of Banbury off A423. The 14thC spire ascends from the handsome tower with exquisite grace. A band of pinnacles is linked to it by dainty flying buttresses and prominent crockets process up between lucarnes large and miniscule. Down below is the pretty village green, with stocks, inn and 17thC manor house. The church's Norman chancel incorporates Victorian details, including the screen, which formed part of G. G. Scott's restoration in 1886. Earlier relics are the Norman font and the elaborate Decorated tracery in the E window of the S aisle. The ghastly skeleton on the plaster monument to T. L. Freke, d1769, rather distracts from the presences of the comely angel and triumphant Christ. **P**. *Open 08.00–18.00 daily*.

Kislingbury, St Luke 9 N9
4m W of Northampton on B4525. In a lovely river Nene village setting, beside the handsome, early 18thC rectory. The fine steeple and church are 14thC. The S doorway is charmingly decorated, but most beautiful is the chancel, with marvellous window tracery and ornate N doorway and sedilia and piscina. **P**. *Open 08.00–20.00 daily*.

Lamport, All Saints 9 N9
8m S of Market Harborough off A508. The 12thC and 13thC church has an elegant 17thC N chapel, which echoes the details of Stuart Lamport Hall close by. In it are vigorously carved tablets to the Ishams, owners of the Hall. Classicised further in the 18thC, the church has delightful plasterwork and an imposing E window filled with powerful, early Victorian stained glass of the Resurrection. **P** at Lamport Hall. *Open daylight hours daily*.

Middleton Cheney, All Saints 9 M8
3m E of Banbury on A422. The 14thC–15thC church, restored by G. G. Scott in 1865, has a beautiful tower and spire. But above all, it is resplendent with glorious stained glass by a galaxy of Pre-Raphaelites and Arts and Craft proponents – Burne-Jones, Rossetti, Ford Madox Brown, Morris and Webb – put in when a friend of Burne-Jones' was rector. See too the medieval S door, benches and screen, which has a canopy by Scott, and the lovely roof. **P**. *Open 07.30–17.30 Mon–Sat, to 19.00 Sun*.

All Saints, Middleton Cheney

Northampton, St Peter 9 N9
Marefair. The Norman tower was rebuilt in the 17thC. This is a beautiful Norman church with no structural separation between nave and chancel. Its intricate detailing includes much zigzag in arches and carving on capitals; pillars alternate in shape in the distinctive nave. See the Saxon and Norman sculpture and the Victorian reredos. **P**. *Open 10.30–16.00 Mon–Fri*. Much of medieval Northampton was destroyed in a fire of 1675, but another fortunate survival is the rare round Norman Church of Holy Sepulchre, built by a returned crusader in 1100. 19thC St Matthew's Church, Kettering Rd, contains a serene *Madonna and Child* by Henry Moore, and a perturbed *Crucifixion* by Graham Sutherland. Since King John brought a pair of boots in Northampton for ninepence in the early 13thC, the boot and shoe trade has flourished mightily.

Oundle, St Peter 10 O10
North St. The glorious Decorated tower and spire are breathtaking elements in the finely composed town on the river

Nene, which has some fascinating buildings and a famous public school. Graceful bell-openings meet a delicate frieze, above which battlements and turrets make a more solid impression before the crocketed spire makes its slender ascent, accompanied by lucarnes. The 13thC church's Perpendicular porch is a sumptuous affair, and beyond its handsome door, with tracery panels, it is exciting to glimpse the pulpit, repainted in 1965 in its original colouring. See too the medieval screens and lectern and the interesting monuments. *Open 07.30–18.30 Mon–Sat, to 19.00 Sun.*

Passenham, St Guthlac   **9** N8
1m SW of Stony Stratford off A422. The hamlet of 10 houses is graced by a 14thC tithe barn and later medieval barn, as well as by this delightful 13thC and 17thC church. Sir Robert Banastre, d1649, who appears in the church in a wreathed niche, rebuilt the chancel in 1626. The complete set of 17thC furnishings of W gallery with a frieze, box pews, pulpit, stalls with misericords quaintly imitative of their medieval predecessors, and wall paintings of prophets and the evangelists, lend the interior great distinction. **P**. *Open daylight hours daily.*

Rockingham, St Leonard   **9** N10
1½ NW of Corby on A6003. The church, below the hilltop castle built by William the Conqueror, and separate from the village, was a casualty of the Civil War. Rebuilt later in the 17thC, a small tower was added and the church enlarged in the 19thC. Of greatest interest are the fine monuments to the Watson family, residents of the castle since the 16thC. Figures sculptured by P. Scheemakers form part of a monument to the first Earl of Rockingham, d1724, on which a dancing putto holds a wreath and trumpet. *Open Easter–Sep 14.00–18.00 Thur & Sun.* The fortress of Rockingham Castle, which received a host of royal visitors, including King John, Henry II, Edward III and Henry V, was converted to a private residence in the 16thC. Charles Dickens used it as a model for Chesney Wold in *Bleak House.* Among its attractions are the hefty procession of elephants in the 400-year-old yew hedge, lovely gardens and stupendous views from the tower. The village of 17thC-18thC stone cottages has charm.

Rothwell, Holy Trinity   **9** N9
The tower lost its spire when struck by lightning in 1660. The size of the

beautiful 13thC church was curtailed in 17thC alterations, but it is still immensely long, longer than any other in the county, and its fine nave arcades are impressive. It is famous for the charnel house in the rib-vaulted crypt, but the stalls with misericords and the interesting brasses are worth making time for, too. **P**. *Open 08.30–18.00 or dusk Mon–Sat, 07.00–17.00 Sun.* Of note in the agreeable town are the market house built by Thomas Tresham in the 16thC and Jesus Hospital, founded in 1591.

Sulgrave, St James the Less   **9** M8
5m NW of Brackley off B4525. The medieval church, with a Saxon doorway in the tower, was much altered in the 19thC. It contains a brass to Laurence Washington, d1584, and his wife and the 17thC Washington family pew. **P**. *Open 09.00–dusk Mon–Sat.* George Washington's ancestral home, Elizabethan Sulgrave Manor, was built by Laurence Washington, wool merchant and Mayor of Northampton, and sold by the family in 1659. With a Queen Anne wing and 20thC work, it now forms a shrine to George Washington, containing his black velvet coat, among other things.

Titchmarsh, St Mary the Virgin   **10** O9
5½m S of Oundle off A605. The magnificent Perpendicular tower has a celebratory air in the lavish array of statue niches and pinnacles and the friezes opulently distinguishing each stage of its ascent. The medieval interior has a bust of the poet John Dryden, who was brought up at Titchmarsh. A most unusual feature is the ha-ha bounding the churchyard. **P**. *Open 08.00–19.30 daily.*

Wellingborough, All Hallows   **9** O9
Market Sq. The medieval church in a tree-shaded setting is remarkable for the brilliant and bold stained glass of 1961 by Patrick Reyntiens to the design of John Piper; the symbols of the evangelists are brought vividly into focus by background colours of flame, emerald, gold, and sapphire. Note too the splendid Decorated E window, the 15thC screens and stalls with misericords. **P**. *Open 09.00–16.00 daily.* The Elizabethan grammer school is now the church hall. Be sure to visit St Mary's, built by Sir Ninian Comper in 1908–30 in lofty Perpendicular style; stalactite-like pendants decorate the elaborate fan-vaulted nave roof and the rood screen is very fine.

Whiston, St Mary the Virgin   **9** N9
7m E of Northampton off A428. The 16thC
church and ironstone and ashlar banded
tower, bristling with gargoyles and other
carvings, stand strikingly on a hilltop,
apart from the village. The interior is
graceful, though it has no structural
chancel. The timber roof is richly carved
with bosses and shields. There are
monuments sculptured by Nollekens,
one of which has a tearful cherub in
attendance. *Open daylight hours daily.*

◀ SHROPSHIRE ▶

Alberbury, St Michael and   **12** H10
All Angels
7½m W of Shrewsbury on B4393. A large
church in a small village, dramatically
contiguous with Alberbury Castle ruins.
The great medieval saddleback tower
makes additional visual impact. The nave
has a magnificent roof, a striking SW
window of 1897, reflecting the influence
of Burne-Jones and notable monuments.
Examine the W window in the form of a
spherical triangle and unusual 19thC
Gothic revival brasses in the beautiful
early 14thC Loton Chapel. **P.** *Open 09.00–
18.00 daily.*

St Michael and All Angels, Alberbury

Clun, St George   **8** H9
4½m S of Bishop's Castle on A488. This
Welsh border church on rising ground
has a fortress-like Norman tower, with
the smallest of windows peeping out,
whose sturdiness is complemented by
the picturesque 17thC tiered pyramidal
top. The Norman arcades with circular
pillars and scalloped capitals, enter the
Transitional style in their pointed, zigzag-
moulded arches. The 14thC N aisle roof
and restored nave roof are most
impressive. Admire the fine, medieval
canopy, studded with bosses, over the
altar and the Jacobean woodwork. The
church was restored by G. E. Street in
1876, and the handsome timber lychgate
of 1723 was rebuilt in 1956. **P.** *Open*
daylight hours daily. Cross the river Clun
by the medieval bridge and pay respects
to the imposing ruins of the Norman and
13thC castle.

Hodnet, St Luke   **12** J11
5m SW of Market Drayton on A53. In a
lovely hilltop position, its three gables set
off by black and white houses below, the
church of Norman origin has a
christening gate and wedding steps, and
a rare 14thC octagonal tower. The font is
an intriguing 17thC resurrection of
Norman style and motifs, animated by
carvings of foliage and rosettes, a
peacock, an eagle, a cock and a lion.
There is an interesting chained library
and the 19thC Heber Percy Chapel
contains a fine portrait head sculptured
by Chantrey, of Bishop Heber, d1826,
author of several well-known hymns and
onetime rector. The poet Robert Southey
wrote the epitaph. Other excellent
monuments include the recumbent effigy
of Blanche Emily Heber, d1870 and the
wreathed urns and cherubs' heads
commemorating Henrietta Vernon,
d1752. *Open daylight hours daily.* Hodnet
Hall gardens offer nature gloriously
landscaped, although the house is not
open to the public.

Leebotwood, St Mary   **12** J10
7m S of Shrewsbury on A49. In a glorious,
elevated position, a sense of timelessness
is felt in the ancient church, with a
fragmentary medieval wall painting of
the adoration of the kings and a lovely
beamed roof whose carved dragons are
visible from the gallery. An E window
with Victorian stained glass, box pews
with hat pegs and a Georgian tower
enforce the impression. **P.** *Open daylight
hours daily.* The seat in the peaceful
churchyard invites you to drink in views
over hills and valleys and the thatched
Pound Inn is an attractive enticement to
another kind of refreshment. Or follow
the road beside the church up into the
heathery Longmynd hills.

Ludlow, St Laurence   **8 J9**
College St. Soaring up from the hilltop town and vying with the castle for visual supremacy, this is a beautiful Perpendicular church with an earlier foundation, twice restored in the 19thC. It has graceful nave arcades and tower arches, and timber roofs with bosses creating multitudinous points of focus. The 14thC Decorated hexagonal porch is handsome and singular, but for that at St Mary Redcliffe in Bristol, and there is delightful tracery and ballflower decoration in the N aisle windows of the same period. Scrutinise the engaging misericords on the stalls of 1447, whose subjects include a fox dressed as a bishop preaching to geese, and the carvings nestling in the poppyheads on the S side, the screens, splendid medieval stained glass, a fine 18thC organ case and interesting monuments. *Open summer 09.00–17.00 Mon–Sat, from 12.30 Sun, winter to 16.00.* The impressive castle ruins look down on ribboning rivers and include a massive keep, whose great stone steps have been echoing with footsteps for 800 years, a circular, battlemented chapel with much of its Norman detail remaining, and a great hall, in which Milton's masque, *Comus*, received its first performance in 1634. Black-and-white gabled and orieled houses abound in the town; the most delightfully exhibitionist of which is the Jacobean Feathers Hotel, with a beautiful plaster ceiling inside.

Melverley, St Peter   **12 H10**
9m W of Shrewsbury off B4393. In a tree-embowered churchyard, the small medieval black-and-white timber-framed church is unimaginably delightful, meadowland beyond stretching down to the river Vyrnwy. It has a diminutive belfry and rustic porch and interior, with vigorous beams criss-crossing up to the

St Peter, Melverley

roof and the embellishment of a W gallery. Restoration took place in 1878 when the dainty E window was added. **P**. *Open daylight hours daily.*

Much Wenlock, Holy Trinity   **8 J10**
A fascinating Norman church with interesting later medieval layers added, such as the impressive 13thC doorways in the porch, the 14thC chapel, intricate Decorated tracery in windows here and there, and a Perpendicular E window with statue niches. Mermen with the extravagance of two tails appear rather incongruously on the Jacobean pulpit. Notable 16thC brass with kneeling figures. **P**. *Open 09.00–dusk daily.* Visit the spectacular, soaring ruins of medieval Wenlock Priory and see the lovely timber-framed buildings in the town.

Shrewsbury, Holy Cross Abbey   **12 J10**
Abbey Foregate. The W front is magnificent, with its great Perpendicular window, sumptuously traceried and extended by a crocketed ogee gable up to the statue of Edward III, in whose reign the building of the tower began. The Norman interior with its massive nave pillars was restored in the 19thC and the chancel built by J. L. Pearson in 1887 in Early English Gothic style. The remains of a shrine to St Winifred, a precious part of the former abbey, are towards the back of the nave. Very fine among the many monuments is that with a priest's effigy under a foliated cross. Outside, to the S, is an exquisite lantern-shaped 14thC stone pulpit, which was originally inside the abbey refectory and from which lessons were read while the monks ate. It has a vaulted roof with a beautiful boss of the Crucifixion. **P**. *Open 10.00–12.00 & 14.00–16.00 Mon–Sat, 08.00–12.00 & 14.00–17.00 Sun.* St Mary's is another important Norman church and has wonderful medieval stained glass. The castle was first built in the 11thC, by William the Conqueror's relative, Roger de Montgomery, founder of the abbey, and its remains are imposing. This border town has been on the hotline of historic incident: David, the rebel Welsh prince, was executed here in 1283, Percy Hotspur was killed in the Battle of Shrewsbury in 1403 and Charles I stayed here in 1642. Tudor alleyways and crooked streets of black-and-white houses are delightful to explore.

Stokesay, St John the Baptist   **8 H9**
6m NW of Ludlow on A49. Almost a mile from the village, in an enchanting setting

beside 13thC moated Stokesay Castle, the solemn defensiveness of whose S tower battles with the gatehouse's carefree 16thC timber top. Much of the Norman and later medieval church was rebuilt during the Commonwealth, a very unusual date for church building, and immediately after. Its pulpit and sounding board, and box and canopied pews date from the same period, as do the textual wall paintings. **P** when castle open. *Open daylight hours daily.*

Tong, St Bartholomew 12 K10
7½m S of Newport on A41. The tower of the Perpendicular church, which has vestiges of a predecessor, whimsically abandons its square shape for that of an octagon, flourishing pinnacles, battlements and spirelet above all. The Golden Chapel, has a gilt fan-vault and the nave a lovely timber roof ornamented with bosses. It is well worth exploring the choir stalls for their carvings, but all the while the magnificent array of monuments presents effigies clamouring for attention with varying degrees of eloquence. Among the most successful are the exquisitely serene ones of Sir

Richard Vernon, d1451, and his wife, she decked in beautiful robes and headdress, he in armour. Henry VI's Knight Constable, Sir William Vernon, d1467, is represented in brass on a richly decorated tomb chest. Bedesmen, saints and angels are attendant on some of the others. **P**. *Open 09.00–dusk Mon–Sat, 10.00–19.30 Sun.* Little Nell, of Dickens' *Old Curiosity Shop*, is reputedly buried in the churchyard.

Whitchurch, St Alkmund 12 J11
A handsome Georgian church, replacing one which collapsed in 1711. The semicircular porch, pretty balustrades and pinnacles, the Earl of Bridgewater's arms and the clock on the tower's S side, make a fine show outside, while the grand, classical columns help to create a noble interior, to which the angel trumpeting from the top of the superb 18thC organ case introduces further harmony. The tomb of John Talbot, first Earl of Shrewsbury, d1453, is in the church, his heart in the porch. **P**. *Open 07.30–19.00 Tue–Sun, from 09.00 Mon.* Georgian and other interesting old houses are in the attractive market town.

◀WEST MIDLANDS▶

Berkswell, St John the Baptist 9 L9
5½m W of Coventry off A4023. The church is a jewel radiating great charm and quaint beauty, in a setting reflecting the same qualities. The Norman chancel with shafted windows and a tiny peephole under the gable is intact, as is the double crypt of the same period. The timber, two-storeyed porch is prettily gabled and the rare S gallery, box pews and dainty screens are delightful furnishings; the wonderfully winged angels clasping one another on a monument of 1818 by Westmacott and a captivating putto on another add to the enchantment. *Open when verger is on duty, and May–Sep Sat & Sun afternoons.* Close by are a square, stone well and the 17thC old rectory and, on the leafy green stand the village stocks. An 18thC shop and the ancient Bear Inn, guarded by a Russian cannon from the Crimean War, are further distinctions.

Birmingham, St Martin 9 L9
Bull Ring. Deeply associated with Birmingham's origins, when a

predecessor stood on what was then the village green. A market was established here in the 12thC by the lord of the moated manor house, Peter de Birmingham, which is continued in the markets of the redeveloped Bull Ring. Three 14thC de Birminghams can be met in effigy in the church, whose much restored medieval sandstone pinnacled tower and pointed spire make a welcome contrast to nearby rectangular buildings. The last restoration of the spacious church was after bombing in 1941, but its 13thC beginnings remain in the stones at the base of the tower. The beautiful hammerbeam roof was inspired by that in Westminster Hall and the exquisite window in the S transept was designed by Burne-Jones and made by William Morris. See too the fine reredos, the porch carved with fruit and vegetables, presented by the market traders after the war, and the extravagantly rude gargoyle poking out its tongue at the dustbins at the back. *Open 09.15–16.30 Mon–Sat, 09.00–20.15 Sun.* Though it tempered 10,000 swords for Cromwell's men, it was the Industrial Revolution of the 18thC that made Birmingham the great centre of the canal and road network and confirmed its rise to greatness. Old buildings are few, though there is some fine Victorian architecture. The 18thC cathedral church of St Philip has magnificent windows by Burne-Jones and the 19thC Roman Catholic cathedral of St Chad, by A. W. N. Pugin, is a fascinating early exploration of his Gothic revival ideals.

Coventry, St John the Baptist   9 M9

Fleet St. The Perpendicular church with a central vaulted tower was built by Queen Isabella as a chantry to Edward the Black Prince, to both of whom there are commemorative windows. It is distinguished by unusually long and narrow windows and by beautiful nave arcades. Restored by Sir G. G. Scott in the 19thC; the rood screen was made by J. O. Scott in 1886 and the rood added in 1908. Post-war restoration was completed in 1951. *Open 08.30–19.00 Mon & Wed, to 17.00 Tue, Thur & Fri, to 12.00 Sat, to 14.00 Sun.* A phoenix risen from the ashes of war, the city has few old buildings. But it has a fascinating past, because in the Middle Ages it was one of the most important towns in England. Coventry originally developed around a 7thC convent (hence the name) and later around an 11thC Benedictine priory, founded by Leofric and Godiva. It is not certain whether Lady Godiva's famous ride ever took place, or whether she was naked merely of her expensive ornaments and jewels, but she and Leofric were buried in the now-ruined priory. The Cathedral is a moving symbol of the devastation of the Second World War and of the challenge of building anew, and it is filled with a wealth of modern artistic jewels.

Hampton-in-Arden, St Mary and St Bartholomew   9 L9

3m NE of Solihull on B4102. In a leafy village in the heart of the ancient Forest of Arden, the lovely church has a Perpendicular tower which lost its spire in 1643, a Norman and 13thC nave, and a Norman chancel. The chancel is entered through an arch adorned with crockets and carved heads and has some medieval blue and white tiles in the floor. **P.** *Open 09.00–18.00 daily.* Eden Nesfield, who built the church vestry in 1878, also built a row of beetle-browed, prettily ornamented cottages in the village and Hampton Manor House, with

an exciting pyramid clock tower. Hampton-in-Arden is said to have been the setting for Shakespeare's *As you like it* and the sunlit rural world of the play is perfectly mirrored in these delightful streets and in buildings like the 16thC timber-framed house W of the churchyard.

St Alphege, Solihull

Solihull, St Alphege   9 L9

The Square. On a hill, this beautiful church has unusual and notable features. The 13thC chancel has enchantingly pretty window tracery, foliage corbels drawn by John Constable who often stayed nearby, and Jacobean-style altar rails made locally in 1679, with charming twisted balusters and pierced leaf decoration. The lovely Chantry Chapel of St Alphege was built by Sir William de Odingsells in 1277 and a priest employed to say masses for the souls of his parents. The priest lodged in the impressive crypt below, with a fireplace for warmth. Hanging in the nave is a delightful candelabrum of 1706. **P.** *Open 08.00–18.00 Mon, Wed, Thur & Fri, from 07.00 Tue, Sat & Sun.*

Stourbridge, St Thomas   8 K9

Market St. The elegant church of local brick with stone dressings was built in 1728–36, and apse and porches added in 1890. Viewed from under the handsome tower, the classical columns soar up resplendently to vaults touched with gold. The beautiful Holy Ghost plaque, surrounded by cherubic heads, is a close copy of that in St Peter's, Vere St, London, designed by James Gibbs. The galleries, pews and W windows are of 1838 and the organ is by a celebrated 18thC maker, G. P. England, restored to its original state in 1983. **P**. *Open summer 10.00–20.00 Fri, 10.00–17.00 Sat.*

◈WARWICKSHIRE ▷

Kenilworth, St Nicholas   9 L9
Abbey Fields. Beside the ruins of a medieval abbey, destroyed in 1538. See the 'pig' of lead inside the church, weighing 10¾ cwt, which was melted down from the abbey roof and stamped by Henry VIII's commissioner, but overlooked. The magnificent Norman doorway, framed by an unusual floral frieze, is thought to have come from the abbey church. When the Earl of Leicester repaired the chancel in 1580, he placed his crest of the bear and ragged staff outside it. The cost was a mere five shillings in '1646, for making fayre the church after General Cromwell's army was here'. His army's bullet marks are on the N side. Announced on the font is its date of 1664. There are fine monuments by Nollekens and Westmacott. **P**. *Open 09.00–15.30 daily.* Cromwell ordered 12thC Kenilworth Castle's destruction after the Civil War and now it is an impressive ruin, with stark red walls about which you may scramble, imagining its floors and roofs. Henry II built the keep. John of Gaunt built the great hall in the 14thC and Robert Dudley, Earl of Leicester, entertained Elizabeth I here with great pomp in 1575.

St Nicholas, Kenilworth

Lower Braiales, St George   9 M8
8½m W of Banbury on B4035. Standing splendidly in the rolling, open countryside, with Brailes Hill towering close by. The 14thC was the period when the church was enlarged and glorified, as prosperity from the wool trade increased, although the stately tower belongs to the 15thC. Admire the lovely openwork parapet and carved animal heads and monsters on the S side, and the delightful Victorian bellcote harbouring a medieval bell. Notice the sedilia with stone arms in the chancel, the delicate net tracery in the E window and the different tracery patterns adorning the octagonal font, with ballflower ornament beneath. **P**. *Open 09.00–dusk daily.*

Preston-on-Stour, St Mary   9 L8
3½m S of Stratford-upon-Avon off A34. On a mound dominating the lovely village, whose green is prettily spread before the church, with rolling views beyond. An avenue of close-ranked yews leads to the church, remodelled in 1752–64 by Edward Woodward for James West of Alscot Park. The chancel was given the most complete Georgian expression, and has a delicately panelled and arched ceiling. Saints and patriarchs, Jonah and the whale and the Last Supper, are interspersed with death-oriented scenes in the E window of medieval European stained glass. There are some interesting monuments. **P**. *Open daylight hours daily.* There are several delightful timber-framed houses in the village, including the handsome black-and-white one close to the church, and others built as part of a model village in 1848 by James West. 18thC Gothic revival Alscot Park, ½m NE, occasionally opens its gardens.

Salford Priors, St Matthew   8 L8
8m SW of Stratford-upon-Avon, on A439. The handsome tower had a Norman start and a Perpendicular finish. The battlemented stair turret on the S side is charming, while memorably quaint gargoyles include one of a hooded figure holding his toes and riding a dragon and another of a woman poking her tongue out. The Norman doorway is exuberantly patterned all over. Fishscales, stars and

rosettes are carved beneath the arch whose zigzag decoration seems to pulsate. The 13thC chancel with pointed E lancet windows is nicely framed by the pointed arch, and in the nave is a showpiece Decorated window with dazzling flowing tracery. A striking monument of 1631 has a touching effigy of a small boy with a toy sword hanging from his shoulder, surrounded by great shields and classical pilasters, and a child who died aged three and a half in 1640, is commemorated by a little figure in a shell niche. **P.** *Open 08.30–dusk Mon–Sat, 08.45–after Evensong Sun.*

Snitterfield, St James the Great   9 L9
3m NE of Stratford-upon-Avon off A46. The progress of the tower was probably determined by visitations of the Black Death and consequent reductions in funds and population. It had reached 10ft before the first onslaught c1349, and attained 72ft early in the 15thC, following the plague of 1361 and two further periods of building. The chancel walls lean slightly outwards, which they are no doubt entitled to do after standing since the end of the 13thC. Shakespeare's father, John, was born in the village in 1529 and was almost certainly baptised in the marvellous 14thC font, complete with engaging faces peeking out from beneath. The pretty 18thC pulpit and the Y-shaped tracery in some of the windows are a delight. Renaissance and Gothic detail mingle in the two Tudor bench ends, with lusciously carved poppyheads, balusters and tiny mermaids; and two of the choir stall fronts are carved with winged and nude figures, wearing caps that were fashionable in Henry VII's reign. **P.** *Open 08.00–dusk daily.* Visit the hallowed spots associated with John's son William Shakespeare, including his tomb, at Stratford-upon-Avon, just 3m away.

Stratford-upon-Avon, Holy Trinity   9 L8
Old Town. A grand avenue of limes leads to the beautiful 13thC–15thC church with rose windows in its fine tower. Boats bob and swans stretch their elegant necks on the river flowing beside the chancel where William Shakespeare is buried. It is a wonderful Perpendicular chancel, with light bursting through great windows, and contains the font in which Shakespeare was probably baptised, very impressive statue niches either side of the E window and sumptuously carved sedilia and piscina. See too the misericords of c1500, carved with all

kinds of lively scenes and figures, the green marble pulpit and the splendid Victorian Gothic organ case. *Open Apr– Sep 08.30–19.00 Mon–Sat, 14.00–17.00 Sun, Oct–Mar to 16.00.* The bridge over the Avon was built in the 15thC, as was the old grammar school where Shakespeare studied, its timber framing and red walls a fascinating expression of medieval and Tudor England. The houses associated with Shakespeare, though much restored, are charmingly maintained and have very pretty gardens. The Royal Shakespeare Theatre was completed in 1932. It is hard to divest Stratford of Shakespeare and see what else it has to offer, but out of season it is easier to sense the atmosphere of the flourishing medieval midland market town.

Tredington, St Gregory   9 L8
9½m SE of Stratford-upon-Avon on A34. The 14thC tower and 15thC spire make a majestic impression, in a picturesque village of tiled and thatched grey stone cottages, smooth lawns and pretty flowerbeds. The honey-coloured stone porch leads into a spacious and beautiful interior, with Norman nave arcades and intriguing remains of 10thC Saxon windows and doors, high above the ground. The doors were possibly reached by ladders, which were then drawn up as protection against Danish raiders. Among the furnishings are lovely late 15thC pew fronts and bench ends, a delightful rood screen with little faces peeping out, the kind of wonderfully lavish pulpit and sounding board – of the time just before Cromwell became Protector – that you feel like shouting your very best respects to, stone benches in the 14thC chancel, and brasses of pre-Reformation priests, one of them chaplain to Henry V. **P.** *Open 09.30–dusk daily.*

Warwick, St Mary the Virgin   9 L9
Old Square. Elegantly arched over the street, with Georgian houses jostling closely round, the imposing tower was built together with nave and transepts, after a fire in 1694 destroyed these parts of the earlier church. Queen Anne contributed £1,000 to the rebuilding. On summer Sats and Suns you can get up among its exuberantly Gothic pinnacles for royal views of the castle and river, Leamington Spa and beyond. The spacious nave where Gothic and classical mingle, is lit by glinting green glass windows. There is an impressive Norman crypt. In the middle of the

14thC chancel, Thomas Beauchamp, Earl of Warwick, d1369, and his wife lie in alabaster effigy, holding hands and above them flare the ribs of a sumptuous vault. Through an impressive portal is the opulent 15thC Beauchamp Chapel, at whose centre lies the splendid copper-gilt effigy of Richard Beauchamp, Earl of Warwick, d1439, who left money for the building of the chapel. He also tried and condemned Joan of Arc to death. The colourful tomb of Robert Dudley, Earl of Leicester, d1588, Elizabeth I's favourite, and his wife Lettice, is not so fine. Richly detailed and coloured sculptures of angels and saints surround the E window, which has original glass reassembled after Roundheads smashed it in 1641. Be sure to look up at the tracery in the side windows, where myriad enchanting angels survived the puritan attack. In brilliant colours, they hold music scrolls or play musical instruments, some with feathery legs and crosses on their heads. *Open summer 10.00–18.00 daily, winter to 16.00.*
Warwick is perhaps more full of historic interest than any town of comparable size in Britain. To stand on its steep heights, overlooking the gabled medieval houses in the huddled streets, and explore the formidable castle where Warwick the Kingmaker plotted his successive changes of allegiance during the Wars of the Roses, is to understand instinctively the medieval world.

Whitchurch, St Mary   **9** L8
5m NW of Shipston on Stour, between Crimscote and Wimpstone off A34. The church stands by the river across a field, in tree-arboured rural seclusion. The village, deserted after enclosure during Henry VII's reign, has a ghostly presence in house sites and ponds around the field and in the yet visible ridge and furrow of medieval cultivation. The 12thC doorway was reset during 17thC restoration and has a lamb and cross carved over it and

the 17thC bellcote above has lichened to a silvery green. 11thC fabric composes the W half of the nave and the E end is 12thC, with a chancel remodelled in the 15thC, where lots of small suns scintillate from the stained glass. A tomb incised with cross, chalice and bible commemorates a rector who died in 1442. There is a sizeable Jacobean pulpit. **P** outside field gate or in field with sheep. *Open Easter–Christmas daylight hours daily.*

St Peter, Wootten Wawen

Wootten Wawen, St Peter   **9** L9
6m NW of Stratford-upon-Avon on A34. The core from which this beautiful church radiates, is the tower, which is two-fifths Saxon and makes a Perpendicular statement at the top. The church itself reflects most centuries and styles; in particular note the delightful decoration round the chancel's E window, the parclose screens, pretty remnants of medieval wall painting in the 14thC S chapel, the 15thC pulpit, faces looking out from the 14thC font, brasses, and a medieval knight's alabaster effigy. **P.** *Open 09.00–dusk daily.* Stately, late 17thC Wootten Hall can be admired from the outside and among interesting houses in the attractive village is a black-and-white timbered 15thC pub.

PEAK
—— & PENNINES ——

Derbyshire   Staffordshire   Nottinghamshire

Carboniferous limestone produces some of the loveliest scenery in England, with rocky outcrops forming deep gorges, steep cliffs with rushing burns and waterfalls and an alternation of high moors and grassy dales. The two main areas, the south Pennines and the Peak District, therefore resemble each other. Stone is so abundant that the boundaries between fields are made of dry stone dykes. Somehow the buildings in such areas have a curious affinity with the landscape.

This stone is hard and intractable and does not lend itself to finely chiselled ornament, but its rough finish is the quality which allies it to the landscape, and its most typical use is in the remote farmhouses of this underpopulated countryside. But it was used extensively for Haddon Hall, a building which fits beautifully into its setting. Later mansions such as Hardwick, Chatsworth and Kedleston were built in the sandstones which also abound in the county. They are often a pinkish grey and the most typical Derbyshire churches are also of this colour. Derbyshire also produces an alabaster which was much in demand for monuments in the 18thC and 19thC, but it was quarried as early as the 14thC and used extensively for fonts.

The Peak District overlaps considerably into Staffordshire, and the architecture therefore continues to reflect that of Derbyshire. In other parts of the county one is struck by the number of churches which have grown steadily with the ages and offer a sequence of styles, so that there is, as Sir William Addison has said, 'nothing in the general run of local design that can be called distinctive until the 18thC'. Among local architects of this date, there are five generations of Trubshaws recorded. Developing industry meant continued church building in the Victorian era and some of the best work of Street, Bodley, Pugin and Norman Shaw is to be found in Staffordshire.

Southwell only became a diocese in 1884. Until then Nottinghamshire was one of the many archdeaconries of York. The grander churches – Southwell itself, St Mary's, Nottingham and St Mary Magdalene, Newark – look to York for architectural inspiration and many of the smaller churches in the north of the county do the same. The Newark area, however, looks to Lincoln, for in the Middle Ages it was one of the manors of the Bishop of Lincoln. Where geological influence is not dominant ecclesiastical fashion is more in evidence.

◀ DERBYSHIRE ▶

Ashbourne, St Oswald   **13** L11
Mayfield Rd. The church is magnificent
and its slender spire heart-lifting.
Macabre skulls support obelisks on the
pillars of the elegant, wrought-iron
churchyard gates. The beautiful 13thC
chancel has a multi-moulded S doorway
and there are impressive heads and
foliage capitals on the nave pillars. A
great throng of monuments filling the N
transept includes brasses and alabaster
effigies and the famous, marble, life-size
sleeping figure of Penelope Boothby, a
five-year-old prodigy said to have been
able to speak in the four languages
inscribed on her tomb. Medieval and
interesting 19thC and early 20thC stained
glass deserves attention. The churchyard
dazzles with daffodils in spring. *Open
09.00–dusk Mon–Sat, 07.30–20.00 Sun*.
Wander down gracious Church St and St
John's St and relish the almshouses, the
grammar school of 1585 and the mansion
opposite, where Dr Johnson and Boswell
stayed.

Holy Trinity, Ashford-in-the-Water

Ashford-in-the-Water,   **13** L12
Holy Trinity
12m SW of Sheffield on A6. The poetic
village name stems from the river Wye,
crossed near the church by narrow
Sheepwash Bridge. The pretty church
was largely rebuilt in 1869, but retains
some Decorated features and a Norman
tympanum over the S doorway, carved
with a tree of life, a wild boar and what
is arguably a wolf or a lion. Suspended
from the N aisle roof are four faded
maidens' garlands, or crants, made of

white paper rosettes, which were carried
at the funerals of young virgins. The
oldest dates from 1747 and the last was
carried in 1801. Don't miss the fine
Annunciation in stained glass of 1880 by
William Morris, at the W end of the aisle.
P. *Open 09.30–dusk daily*. There are lovely
18thC and 19thC stone houses in the
village, including dignified Ashford Hall.
The annual custom of well-dressing is
observed here, as in many Derbyshire
villages.

Ashover, All Saints   **13** M12
4m NE of Matlock on B6036. Prominent in
the attractive valley village, the tower
and spire of the 14thC and 15thC church
were built by Thomas Babington, d1518;
he can be met in a splendid effigy, a
capacious purse at his waist, beside his
wife, who wears a kennel headdress, like
a playing card queen. In 1511 he gave the
lovely rood screen. The church's greatest
treasure is the Norman lead font, with
duplicated, gesturing figures all around.
A bell which cracked while ringing out
the news of Napoleon's abdication in
1814 is ringing still. **P**. *Open 09.00–19.00
Mon–Sat, from 08.00 Sun*. The churchside
Crispin Inn has interesting inscriptions.

Bakewell, All Saints   **13** L12
Gracing the hillside, the 14thC octagonal
steeple, rebuilt in the 19thC, is an
arresting sight, and surveys the Wye
Valley down to Haddon Hall. Vine scrolls
whirl on the Saxon cross in the
churchyard and Saxon and Norman
fragments of gravestones congregate in
the S porch, incised with symbols of
trades. The W doorway is Norman and
the Norman nave arcades were rebuilt in
the 19thC. The S transept was referred to
as the 'new work' when it was built in
the 13thC and its name remains
'Newark'. It was rebuilt in the 19thC and
a screen put up in 1983. In the Vernon
Chapel in the Newark are impressive
monuments to the Vernons and
Manners, including that of Sir George
Vernon, d1567, and two wives; he was
known as the King of the Peak on
account of his extravagant lifestyle at
Haddon Hall. And in the S aisle are
exquisite half-figures of 1385 of Sir
Godfrey Foljambe and his wife, he in
armour and she wearing an elaborate
reticulated headdress. *Open summer
09.00–17.00 daily, winter to 16.00*. Famed

All Saints, Bakewell

for puddings (not tarts, please) and spa waters, the town is well mannered and sprightly enough to warrant a leisurely visit. Jane Austen stayed at the Rutland Arms while writing *Pride and Prejudice*. You can still see her room and it is believed that the town of Lambton in the novel is Bakewell. The peakland palace of Chatsworth, an Elizabethan house transformed at the end of the 17thC into classical grandeur, has magnificent state rooms with painted ceilings; the park and gardens include an arboretum, a cascade and the Emperor Fountain, built for Tsar Nicholas I's visit, which can throw a water jet 296ft high. Haddon Hall, 2m SE, is like a courtly medieval tapestry come to life.

Baslow, St Anne　　　　**13** L12
3m NE of Bakewell on A623. In an enchanting riverside setting, the 14thC church was restored in the 19thC and the chancel rebuilt in 1911. The handsome tower and broach-spire are 13thC. One of the clock's dials patriotically reads 'VICTORIA 1897' instead of numerals. A Saxon cross shaft fragment is in the porch and there is a 13thC coffin lid with a fine floriated cross. What may be a unique curiosity from the past is the dog whip, for the ejection of those quadrupeds unsusceptible to silence and serenity. **P**. *Open daylight hours daily.* See the stone tollhouse of dwarfish dimensions by the pretty bridge over the river Derwent.

Castleton, St Edmund　　　　**13** L12
13½m W of Sheffield on A625. In a wild, romantic High Peak setting, with the restored ruin of 11thC and 12thC Peveril Castle glowering above. A Perpendicular,

battlemented and pinnacled tower was added to a Norman church, whose character – most vigorously visible in the chancel arch – was tamed in 19thC restoration. The church is handsomely distinguished by 17thC box pews. *Open 09.00–dusk Mon–Sat, from 08.00 Sun.* Of the four spectacular caverns in the area, Peak Cavern is the closest. Blue John Cavern is named after the amethyst-like, semi-precious stone shot with a spectrum of magical colours and found nowhere else in the world. From the Iron Age hill-fort of Mam Tor, 1m NW, called the 'shivering mountain' because the shale on its E side is continually slithering away, stupendous views stretch over the Hope and Edale valleys.

Chesterfield, St Mary and　　　**13** M12
All Saints
Church Way. Visit the tower for a panorama of the town and Derbyshire hills, and to get a close-up view of the curious crooked spire, which appears more fabulous than real, but owes its twist to the whimsical warping of wood and lead. The spacious, graceful 13thC and 14thC church was restored by Gilbert Scott in 1843 and again in 1961 after a fire gutted the N transept. Branching out of the chancel are vistas of chapels refulgent with stained glass, gilt and coloured reredoses, beautiful 18thC candelabra with exquisite wrought iron twirls for decoration and medieval screens – one with slender crocketed arches beneath fan-vaulting and the other crowned by a frieze of angels with outstretched wings. Members of the Foljambe family are magnificently represented in brass and alabaster in the Lady Chapel. The effigies of Sir Godfrey, d1594, and his wife are overlooked by an elegant Renaissance screen; close by is an unnamed Foljambe, tied in a sack-like shroud, surmounted by representations of death, old age and a very chubby childhood. Enjoy the expression of refined opulence in the Jacobean pulpit. **P** adjacent. *Open 09.00–16.30 daily.* At Whittington, on the town's N periphery, is the restored 16thC Revolution House, where conspirators met in 1688 to plot the overthrow of James II in favour of William of Orange.

Dale Abbey, All Saints　　　　**13** M11
6m NE of Derby off A6096. The soaring arch of a 12thC abbey, a hermit's cave and a windmill are the interesting companions of this tiny, glorious gem of a rustic church, which shares its roof

with a farmhouse. The 12thC church was altered in the 15thC, and its 17thC furnishings form a unique arrangement. Pulpit, reading desk and clerk's pew are behind the 'cupboard' altar – with door and shelves for storage of communion plate and linen – against whose sides an eager proliferation of pews presses. The Visitation is the most visible of traces of medieval wall paintings. *Key available when not open.*

St Lawrence, 8thC cross

Eyam, St Lawrence   **13** L12
5m N of Bakewell on B6521. Eyam was the village infected with plague by contaminated cloth sent from London to the local tailor in 1665; the 13thC–15thC church was restored in the 19thC, and contains reminders of the great heroism of the rector, William Mompesson, and the villagers, who cut themselves off from the outside world to prevent the plague spreading. The grave of plague victim Mompesson's wife is in the churchyard and inside is a copy of the plague register, a cupboard supposed to have been made from the plague infested clothes box and Mompesson's chair, dated 1665. Be sure to see too the 17thC wall paintings of emblems of the 12 tribes of Israel, the magnificent 8thC cross in the churchyard, carved with bold vine scrolls and angels, and the 18thC sundial. *Open 09.00–dusk daily.* In the attractive village are memorials to bravery in the plague cottages and graves, the

spot where open air services were held and Mompesson's well, where neighbouring villages left supplies.

Hathersage, St Michael and   **13** L12
All Angels
9m N of Bakewell on A625. Prominent above the village, with dramatic hills behind, the handsome, battlemented church has a discreetly crocketed spire and some cheeky gargoyles keeping watch. Little John's grave is in the tree-embowered churchyard of his reputed birthplace, far from Sherwood Forest to which television and Hollywood have always consigned Robin Hood and his merry men. The church's medieval fabric was restored by W. Butterfield in 1849–52. In the chancel are a number of fine brasses to the Eyres, medieval lords of the manor, including the exceedingly dashing and elegant figures of Robert Eyre, d1459, and his wife. **P.** *Open daylight hours daily.* Drink in the view of the Derwent Valley. Charlotte Brontë stayed at the vicarage with her friend Ellen Nussey in 1845 and transformed Hathersage into Morton when she wrote *Jane Eyre,* borrowing the name Eyre for her heroine. A pilgrimage can be made to the novel's poignant places round about.

Repton, St Wystan   **13** M11
5m NE of Burton-upon-Trent on B5008. In what was the capital of Saxon Mercia, the church has deep roots in history. A 7thC

St Wystan, Saxon crypt

abbey was destroyed by the Danes in the 9thC, but the crypt, once the mausoleum of Saxon kings, remains like a precious casket containing the past. It has a vault on round arches and pillars wreathed in narrow spiralling bands. Until King Cnut moved his body to Evesham in the 11thC, the crypt formed a shrine to St Wystan, martyred in 849 and the steps down are worn by pilgrims' feet. The chancel and E end of the nave are also Saxon. Additions were made from the 13thC–15thC and the elegant tower and spire are 14thC. *Open 08.00–dusk Mon–Sat, 07.30–19.30 Sun.* A 12thC priory gateway leads to Repton School, founded in 1557 and incorporating the priory's scant remains. The attractive village has an ancient cross.

Tideswell, St John the Baptist   **13** L12
6m E of Buxton on B6049. In a village in a High Peak hollow, the splendid church is all of the 14thC, its building halted for some years by the Black Death of 1348–9. The great pinnacled turrets at the corners of the imposing tower look rather ponderous, but stand beneath the tower arch, opening into the nave and beauty of proportion prevails, culminating in the gracefully soaring chancel. Here, tall side windows and the large E window, which has flowing tracery and 19thC stained glass of the Tree of Jesse, create a fountain of light. Fine woodcarving in the church includes the statues made by J. Harris in 1950, under the lovely canopied stone niches in the chancel. The unusual brasses and interesting monuments should not be missed. *Open 07.30–dusk daily.*

St John the Baptist, Tideswell

Wirksworth, St Mary the Virgin   **13** L12
Here is a 13thC church on a majestic scale, restored by Scott in 1870–6. The sculptures on an 8thC Saxon coffin lid seem imbued with life in their crowded New Testament scenes – so crowded that the angels have difficulty in assisting Christ's Ascension. Inspect the capacious Norman font and Norman sculptural fragments from the church's predecessor, the beautiful stained glass by Morris and Burne-Jones in the N transept, and the Renaissance-style monument to Anthony Lowe, d1555, with adorably animated putti holding a shield. **P**. *No regular opening times.* The hilly market town, with a Georgian character and a web of lanes, is an ancient lead mining centre. Inside the Moot Hall of 1814 is a 14-pint oblong brass dish for measuring lead ore. Much of George Eliot's *Adam Bede* was set here.

◁ STAFFORDSHIRE ▷

St Nicholas, Abbots Bromley

Abbots Bromley, St Nicholas   **12** L11
9m E of Stafford on B5234. The august Queen Anne tower, crowned with balustrade and urns, replaced one which fell down in 1688. The fine, spacious 13thC church was restored extensively in the 19thC, when Burlison and Grylls made the beautiful stained glass in the great E window. Housed in the Hurst Chapel are the ancient reindeer horns, which are taken on the annual Horn Dance through the village and around farms and hamlets. The picturesque ritual is thought to be of Saxon origin and to form a part of a pagan hunting rite,

associated with Needwood Forest, which formerly lay all around. **P.** *Open 07.30–dusk daily.* A cluster of black-and-white cottages and the 17thC Butter Cross contribute to the village's charm.

Alrewas, All Saints   **13** L10
5m NE of Lichfield on A513. Doorways remain from a Norman church, to which the beautiful chancel was added in the 13thC. The fine tower and present nave were built in the 14thC, the clerestory and handsomely carved timber roofs in the 16thC and the N arcade in the 19thC. See the pulpit of 1639, the glorious stained glass in the E window, made by Henry Holiday in 1877, the grooves and holes outside on the S wall, made in the Middle Ages by men sharpening arrows for compulsory archery practice, and the graffiti of two deer on the same wall. **P.** *Open 09.00–17.00 Mon–Sat, from 07.30 Sun.* The Trent and Mersey canal and Trent river run through the village, which has delightful thatched, timber-framed cottages.

Burton-upon-Trent, St Chad   **13** L11
Hunter St. In something of a backwater, this splendid late flowering of G. F. Bodley's genius was designed in 1903 and completed in 1910 by C. G. Hare, who added the octagonal vestry. The fine, slender tower stands a little apart, joined to the church by a vaulted passage. There is an admirable chasteness about the proportions of the spacious interior, which however is filled with beautiful carving in stone and wood. Note the barrel vault, the rood screen through whose tracery the green, blue and purple stained glass glows, and a copy of Leonardo's *Last Supper* forming the reredos below. Doctors of the church carved on the pulpit have the backing of angels carved below the organ and the Lady Chapel reredos is an eloquent piece of sculpture. **P.** *Open 09.00–18.00 Mon–Sat, later in summer, 08.00–20.00 Sun.* Fascinating examples of industrial archaeology exist in the town's 19thC breweries and maltings, including those erected by Bass, whose head, Lord Burton, built St Chad's. The Bass museum is devoted to the brewing process.

Checkley, St Mary and All Saints 12 L11
5m NW of Uttoxeter on A50. You are met by the 600-year-old yew, and those ancient witnesses to christianity, the carved Saxon cross shafts outside the S porch. The Norman tower has a charming Perpendicular top. In the lovely 14thC chancel fine features include heads either side of the windows, particularly those of Edward I, Queen Eleanor and a jester, the gem-like medieval glass, the red Indians and Tudor rose carved on a 16thC stall and the knight's effigy with legs crossed to show he was a crusader. The chapel screen and window are by Ninian Comper, and the 13thC nave has a 17thC clerestory. Arrows sharpened for medieval archery practice have left their marks on the buttresses of the chancel. Examine the priest's doorway at the same time. **P.** *No regular opening times.*

Hoar Cross, Holy Angels   **13** L11
8m W of Burton-upon-Trent off A515. The splendid church stands half a mile from the village, beside 19thC Hoar Cross Hall, on a steep hilltop overlooking the remains of Needwood Forest. The building and its history are like a medieval refrain: G. F. Bodley's lyrical Decorated Gothic design was made for the young widow of H. F. Meynell Ingram, who built the church in her husband's memory in 1872–6. Thirty-three years after his death she joined him in the Chantry Chapel, where their alabaster effigies lie under rich stone and oak canopies. Glorious scale and brilliant decoration are concentrated in the soaring, vaulted chancel, with statues under canopies, crocketed ogee arches, sumptuous reredos, organ case and window tracery. See, too, the black and white marble floor, the stained glass filling all the windows, creating a dim glow and the Stations of the Cross by carvers from Antwerp. **P.** *Open daylight hours daily.*

Ingestre, St Mary the Virgin   **12** K11
2m E of Stafford off A51. The façade of Ingestre Hall makes a grand Jacobean flourish near the church, which was probably built to Wren's design in 1676, one of only two or three outside London. The exquisitely elegant interior has an opulent stucco nave ceiling and the charming light fittings of 1886 were the foremost electrical installations in a parish church. The Royal Arms make an ebullient declaration above the majestic screen, as does the pulpit close by. Look out for the garlanded reredos in the barrel-vaulted chancel beyond, and the multiple monuments to the Chetwynds and Talbots, earls of Shrewsbury from 1856, whose former seat was Ingestre Hall. **P.** *Open summer daylight hours daily, winter key available.*

Mavesyn Ridware, St Nicholas   **12** L10
2m E of Rugeley off A513. A medieval
gatehouse is a venerable neighbour to the
church, whose nave of 1782 is joined to a
13thC aisle and Perpendicular tower.
Besides genuine medieval effigies
including a cross-legged knight and one
other, a fascinating galaxy of monuments
incised centuries after the deaths of the
Mavesyns commemorated is gathered
here, as though family pride all at once
determined the picture must be
complete. Hatchments and shields are
prominent in the church. **P**. *Open 09.00–
20.00 daily.*

St Mary, Stafford

Stafford, St Mary   **12** K11
St Mary's Gate. The Perpendicular,
lantern-shaped tower's spire collapsed in
1594. The fabric of the spacious, formerly
collegiate, 13thC church with a Decorated
N transept, is finely fused with G. G.
Scott's work of 1841–4, which partly
restored and partly replaced what was
there. Note the Tudor roof and
interesting Victorian pew ends in the
impressive and beautiful nave. In 1593,
Izaak Walton, author of the *Compleat*

Angler, was baptised in the startling
Norman four-lobed font, which is
protected by lions with a Byzantine air
who stalk round its base. Fine Georgian
organ case, carved with drapery. *Open
09.00–17.00 Mon–Sat.* The site of a Saxon
church is to the W. Visit impressive,
restored Norman St Chad, fine public
buildings, 16thC timber-framed High
House of four storeys and the Swan
Hotel which quenched the thirst of
Charles Dickens and George Borrow.

◁ NOTTINGHAMSHIRE ▷

Blyth, St Mary and St Martin   **13** N13
4m N of Worksop on B6045. A Georgian
staging post, the village has three former
coaching inns, and the majestic church

St Mary and St Martin, Blyth

stands N of its green. The Perpendicular
tower is crowned by a charming chain of
gables, linking its battlements, and eight
knobbly pinnacles, in great contrast to
the austere and primitively beautiful
Norman nave, dating from the
foundation of a priory here in 1088. The
nave is an amazing sight, with gallery
and clerestory preserved on one side,
and a 13thC vault. At the end of the
13thC the Norman S aisle was replaced
by a wider one to form the parochial
nave. The monastic E end was pulled
down in the 17thC, and its skeleton
stood in the garden of Blyth Hall,
demolished in 1972. Pay attention to the
screens, the 17thC font with cherubs
heads and the painting of St Mary
Magdalene by Fra Bartolomeo. **P**. *Open
09.00–dusk daily.*

Bunny, St Mary the Virgin   **13** N11
7m S of Nottingham on A60. In a very
interesting village, this is a lovely,
lavishly detailed 14thC church with a
crocketed spire, fine porch and ornate
sedilia and piscina. Thomas Parkyns,
d1741, builder of the manor house,
Bunny Hall, and of the school beside the

church, appears on his tomb memorably poised to perform a pugilistic feat. He was a baronet and lawyer who had a penchant for wrestling and for collecting stone coffins. Other Parkyns are gathered here. **P**. *Open 08.00–19.45 Mon, to 21.00 Tue, to 16.30 Wed–Fri; 09.00–18.30 Sat, 08.30–19.45 Sun.*

Gringley on the Hill, St Peter and St Paul   13 N13

3m W of Gainsborough on A631. The church is the focus of a picturesque, ridge-riding village, with spectacular views. The tower-top and other Perpendicular details characterise the church, but there is also Norman evidence and a 13thC arcade and shaft piscina with a beautifully decorated capital. **P**. *Open daylight hours daily.* Yet higher is Beacon Hill, at the E end of the village, site of a prehistoric hill-fort and of Prince Rupert's camp in 1644, before the relief of Royalist Newark during the Civil War.

Holme Pierrepont, St Edmund   13 N11

4m E of Nottingham off A52. Much restored 17thC Holme Pierrepont Hall is a handsome neighbour to the church, in which Gothic and classical details mingle with a certain unease. The arcade, however, makes a quite separate and self-contained statement of its 13thC identity. A quantity of interesting monuments include a gorgeous curvy cartouche, decorated with swags, to poet John Oldham, d1683. Two Henry Pierreponts, who died in 1499 and 1615, are here in alabaster effigy, the latter accompanied by wife and seven children. **P**. *Open 10.00–19.30 Sun.*

Hucknall, St Mary Magdalene   13 M11

Market Sq. The beautiful old tower with narrow lancets, is crowned by 14thC battlements and pinnacles and the lovely 14thC timber porch was carefully rebuilt when it had to be moved to accommodate the building of the S aisle in 1872. A general rebuilding took place when the transepts were added in 1888. From that time date the 27 fine stained glass windows by Kempe, offering an unrivalled opportunity to study his early work. The sealed Byron family vault is under the chancel. A former rector lifted Byron's coffin lid and ascertained that it houses the embalmed body of the poet, d1824, who is commemorated above by a tablet and portrait in profile and by a slab of marble sent by the King of Greece in 1881. **P**. *Open 09.00–17.00 Mon–Sat,*

07.30–20.00 Sun. Newstead Abbey, the Byron family seat, given by Henry VIII in 1539, is a few miles N. Lord Byron dragged his lame foot round the crumbling estate inherited from Mad Jack Byron and wondered how he could sell enough poems to pay for it. Preserved are his bedroom and personal belongings, the huge brass collar of his beloved dog Boatswain, whose memorial is in the grounds, letters, miniatures, locks of hair and the helmet he designed for the Greek campaign against the Turks in which he died. The delightful gardens include waterfalls, a Japanese water-garden and a teahouse, Monk's Stew Pond, and rare shrubs and trees.

Langar, St Andrew   13 N11

9m SE of Nottingham off A52. An august, cruciform 13thC church looking into the Vale of Belvoir. Handsome woodwork includes the Jacobean pulpit with book rests on brackets and the 17thC balustered altar rail. A throng of Elizabethan lords and ladies and their descendants, recumbent on fine monuments, await resurrection in the transepts; among them are exquisitely sculptured Thomas Lord Scroope, d1609, and his wife, their bearded son kneeling at their feet. **P**. *Open daylight hours daily.* Samuel Butler spent the unpleasant childhood he describes in *The Way of All Flesh* at the former rectory.

St Peter and St Paul, Mansfield

Mansfield, St Peter and St Paul   13 M12

Church Side. A wonderfully sturdy Norman tower grows into a 14thC crown and a spire of 1669. The fine 13thC nave leads to the Norman chancel with Perpendicular arcades into the N and S chapels. Don't overlook the Elizabethan altar in the latter, the interesting monuments and the organ, built from an organ of 1911 from Clare College Chapel,

Cambridge. **P**. *Open 09.00–17.00 Mon–Sat,
07.30–20.00 Sun*. Elegant public buildings
preside over the Market Pl and nestling
in alleys behind are some 16thC and
17thC stone cottages.

Newark-on-Trent, St Mary　　**13** N12
Magdalene
Market Sq. Near the hub of the town, the
church makes a grand impression. It is of
magnificent, cathedral-like dimensions
and the 13thC tower soars up to an
exquisitely tapering 14thC spire.
Gargoyles and saints abound. Elegant
lines of lofty pillars process up the 15thC
nave to chantry chapels and chancel,
where Comper's reredos of 1937 glitters
goldly through the delicately carved late
15thC rood screen. Examine medieval
humour, devotion and quirky
observation in the carvings congregated
on the misericords of the choir stalls,
including a dragon, an owl, angels and
quarrelling men. See the fine medley of
medieval stained glass in one large
window, the transepts which look as if
they have walls of glass, the vast brass of
a Newark merchant, Alan Fleming,
d1363, and the 12thC crypt. *Open 08.30–
17.00 Mon–Sat; summer 14.00–17.00 Sun*.
In the fascinating market place, figures of
angels and saints peer out from gables on
the 14thC former White Hart Inn, and
the colonnaded onetime coaching inns,
the Saracen's Head and Clinton Arms,
were both frequented by Walter Scott
and Gladstone. See too the 18thC town
hall, the half-timbered Governor's House,
more Tudor houses in Kirkgate, elegant
Georgian brick houses and the jovial
Victorian Ossington Coffee House, built
to promote temperance. The craggy
remains of the clifftop castle, where King
John died in 1216, and where Royalists
withstood Parliamentarian siege
during the Civil War, are impressive.

Nottingham, St Mary the Virgin　**13** M11
High Pavement, The Lace Market. A
glorious Perpendicular vision among the
tall, commercial buildings of the Lace
Market, the church is exquisitely
decorated with panelled battlements,
pinnacles, feathery ogee arch and gables
and multitudinous windows. John
Samson, d1416, whose alabaster effigy
lies under a canopy in the S transept,
built the sumptuous S porch and left £10
towards the building of the church, as
well as his best horse and its saddle and
bridle. A bronze door of 1904 leads into
the spacious, slender-pillared nave and
the transepts which, like those at

Newark, have walls filled with glass, to
dazzling effect. Colour stems from
Victorian stained glass throughout the
church, from the chancel screen and
great gilded reredos of 1885 by Bodley
and Garner, the latter hiding a memorial
window of 1863 to Prince Albert, and
from the chancel roof, gracefully painted
in blue and gold leaf in 1965. And the
gilt and coloured splendour of the right
royal lion and unicorn of c1708 must not
be missed. An epitaph in the N transept
commemorates a 10-year-old prodigy,
Henry Plumptre, d1719, who had
mastered 'Jewish, Roman and English
History, the Heathen mythology and the
French Tongue and was not
inconsiderably advanced in the Latin'.
The S chapel of 1916, by Temple Moore,
contains a 15thC Nottingham alabaster
panel. **P**. *Open 08.30–17.00 Mon–Sat,
08.15–20.00 Sun*. The Lace Market was
never a market with stalls and jostling
customers, but an enclave of Victorian
lace manufacturers' offices and
warehouses. The continuous row of
windows on top floors gave maximum
light for mending and finishing.

Nottingham, St Peter　　**13** M11
St Peter's Gate. The chancel was
destroyed when the Roundhead garrison
at the nearby castle cannoned Royalists
out of the medieval church during the
Civil War, and was rebuilt in 1670 and in
1878. Tudor roofs resting on half figures
of angels and the organ case of 1770,
decorated with acanthus scrollwork and
two cherubs, are delightful features. *Open
11.00–14.00 Mon & Tue, 10.00–15.00 Wed–
Fri, 10.00–13.00 Sat*. The Baroque palace,
built in 1674 on the site of a castle
demolished after the Civil War, was
gutted by fire during Reform Bill riots in
1831. But it was restored and made into
the first municipal museum outside
London in 1875. Caves honeycomb the
castle's underparts and the best known is
Mortimer's Hole, through which
murdering conspirators crept towards
their aristocratic prey in 1330. The
ancient Trip to Jerusalem Inn was the
stopping place of crusaders from the
Holy Land. Earthy odours emanate from
its rooms and cellars cut back deep into
the castle rock.

West Stockwith, St Mary　　**13** N13
the Virgin
12m NE of East Retford off A161. In a brick,
riverside village, the Georgian church of
1722 is of great charm and simplicity,
distinguished by a delightful bell turret.

William Huntingdon, a ship's carpenter, who paid for the church, is commemorated in an eloquent reclining effigy of 1742. **P**. *Open 09.00–17.00 Mon–Sat, 08.30–16.30 Sun.*

Wollaton, St Leonard   **13** M11
Wollaton Rd, 3m from centre of Nottingham.
This is an extemely handsome and interesting 14thC church, with a S aisle of 1885. Its most gorgeous furnishing is a reredos of c1660, the time of the Restoration, which has Corinthian columns and exuberant details, but be sure to see too the small, stained glass window in the Lady Chapel, a sparkling insertion of 1972. Monuments to the Willoughbys abound, although Sir Francis went bankrupt in building Wollaton Hall and has no memorial. Robert Smythson, d1614, 'architector and surveyor' of the Hall, does. Fine brasses of Richard Willoughby, d1471, and his wife are in the chancel, a splendid canopy above and cadaver below. What seems a rather excessive number of four wives have been reduced to half the size of Sir Henry Willoughby, d1528, in order to share his tomb-chest. The former open arches under the tower were glazed to create a porch during restoration in 1970. **P**. *Open 09.00–17.30 Mon–Sat, 08.00–19.30 Sun.* See the medieval house outside the churchyard. Wollaton Hall is a giddy mixture of towers, pinnacles, busts in niches and gables laden with strapwork. Flamboyant tycoon Sir Francis Willoughby built this Elizabethan showpiece in 1580–8 from the industrial profits of coal. It now houses Nottingham's Natural History Museum.

Where Francis, his wife, 12 daughters and 32 servants once ate and argued, cuddled and connived, are stuffed gorillas, pickled jellyfish and Brazilian butterflies.

Worksop Priory

Worksop, St Mary and   **13** N12
St Cuthbert
Priorswell Rd. Outside, spareness of detail in the fine tower and E end of 1974, by Laurence King, unifies them with the lovely, attenuated lines of the restored 13thC Lady Chapel, and august twin-towered Norman W front. Inside, it is exciting to look down the magnificent Transitional nave of alternate round and octagonal columns, with its unusual gallery of major and minor arches and profuse nail-head decoration, to the startling contrast the 1974 chancel makes. Here the great corona, modern stained glass, shining pipes and elegant case of Peter Collins' organ, create a striking focus. **P**. *Open 07.15–16.30 Mon–Fri, to 17.30 Sat; 07.30–17.00 Sun.* See the beautiful 14thC gatehouse to the former priory, to the S.

EAST ANGLIA &
—————— THE FENS ——————

Essex   Suffolk   Norfolk   Cambridgeshire
Lincolnshire

Accessible material has always been one of the controlling influences upon architectural style. High class craftsmen will not work in indifferent stone. Essex, offering a not very enviable choice between pudding stone and clunch, is typically provided with churches in a local vernacular style, which often made use of Roman tiles and any other material that came to hand. In the neighbourhood of the great forests timber belfries were common; Thaxted boasts the only medieval spire of stone. What the county does possess is clay and clay makes bricks. Bulmer Tye still provides 'Tudor' bricks for the repair of churches and great houses all over England. The lovely towers of Ingatestone and Castle Hedingham show what distinguished use can be made of this homely material.

But there is no distinctively 'Essex' style. The great churches all borrow ideas from neighbouring centres of architecture, such as Ely or Bury St Edmunds. Saffron Walden is near enough to Cambridge to be influenced by St Mary's, but the most outstanding example is Waltham Abbey which, alone among churches in the south, reflects the architecture of Durham Cathedral.

There are only six round towers in Essex, compared with 41 in Suffolk and the 129 originally built in Norfolk: with high-set doorways that had to be reached by ladders, which could then be withdrawn, they were undoubtedly strongholds. Their flint and rubble walls and their thatched roofs formed a striking contrast with the great 'wool' churches of the region; 'they were to East Anglia what the pele towers were to the North' – Sir William Addison. East Anglia is for the most part flat and its wide skies must have stimulated a quest for light. The churches are lofty, the windows enormous and the interiors flooded with an ample illumination. This impression of height is greatly enhanced by the hammerbeam roofs so typical of the area. Flint and stone patterns, called flushwork, add extra distinction to Suffolk and Norfolk churches.

There were three likely sources of munificent patronage in the Middle Ages – the great monasteries, the aristocracy and the rich wool merchants. All three may be seen at Lavenham (Suffolk), where the crossed keys of St Peter, the crossed swords of de Vere, Earl of Oxford, and the merchant mark of Thomas Spryng all appear on the tower. Puritan iconoclast, William Dowsing, dedicated his energies to desecrating Suffolk churches during the

Commonwealth period, and evidence of his fervour is everywhere apparent. Norfolk itself still possesses an astonishing 659 medieval churches. As Sir John Betjeman has written 'Norfolk would not be Norfolk without a Church Tower on the horizon or round the corner up the lane'.

Think of Cambridgeshire, and the automatic image is of the University city. The magnificent colleges and grounds overshadow the rest of the county. It was from St Mary the Great that the Cambridge men (including Cranmer and Latimer) who led the Reformation first preached, and it was in Cambridge, in 1839, that the Cambridge Camden Society originated. Their precepts spread country-wide to leave a lasting impression on church buildings. They argued for a return to a pre-Reformation approach to ecclesiastical architecture, and Cambridgeshire churches fell particularly subject to Victorian restoration.

A great abbey or a great cathedral often inspired a local style, and this is certainly true of Ely: octagonal towers are more common in Cambridgeshire than anywhere else.

There is an octagon lantern on the very fine tower of Boston in Lincolnshire, righly acclaimed as the most magnificent of 'wool' churches. The fine quality of the Ancaster stone – a honey-coloured oolitic limestone – made possible the delicacy of the ornaments and tracery in such important churches as the one at Grantham, as well as providing ashlar for Lincolnshire's celebrated spires. Of these Louth must always have pride of place. It was one of the last to be built – between 1501 and 1515 at a total cost of £308 8s 5d. It is described by Patrick Cormack as 'the finest autumn flower of the medieval Gothic'. Lincolnshire also possesses some 60 Georgian churches, which have been described as 'protestant preaching houses'. Their furnishing certainly reflects the spirit of the age when the Ministry of the Word was emphasised at the expense of the sacraments. High box pews and three-decker pulpits were the order of the day.

◁ ESSEX ▷

Bradwell-on-Sea, St Peter-on-the-Wall　　**11** S7

7m NE of Burnham-on-Crouch off B1021. (2m NE of village). A track over fields leads to one of the rarest and most ancient of churches in isolation beside the sea wall. Standing on the wall of a Roman fort, the nave has been a witness to Christianity since St Cedd built it with bricks and ashlar from the fort c654. Porch and chancel have been shed over the ages. Its simplicity and vulnerability to North Sea gales make its impact all the more moving. **P.** *Open daylight hours daily.* The brooding atomic power station is in strange contrast on the coastal marsh. In the village St Thomas's church has a tower of 1706 and Tudor Bradwell Lodge an elegant Georgian extension, crowned by the brightest of belvederes.

Brightlingsea, All Saints　　**11** T7

On an eminence removed from the town, and set in a tree-clad churchyard with fine views over Alresford Creek to the river Colne. The stately Perpendicular exterior has distinctive flushwork decoration on the tower, S porch, vestry and N chapel. The Beriffes, wool merchants, who were responsible for the grandeur of the Perpendicular additions, are commemorated in interesting brasses. Their house, Jacobes, is in the High St. Roman brickwork in the roundheaded recess to the left of the door as you enter, is evidence of an earlier church. In the 13thC chancel is an extravagant Rococo monument to Nicholas Magens, d1764, with a globe in its centre, an angel of resurrection on one side, a putto on a cornucopia of impressive proportions, and an anchor, on the other. A series of tiles commemorates those lost at sea since 1872. **P.** *Open Easter–Sep 14.00–17.00 daily.* The waterfront is the focal point of the town and yachting one of the pleasures for which it is famous.

Castle Hedingham, St Nicholas   11 S8
6m SW of Sudbury on B1058. A Tudor-style brick tower consorts unexpectedly with a marvellous late Norman nave and chancel. Notice the Norman doors and doorways. Thick foliage furls on the capitals of the pillars, which form a bold procession up the nave to the exuberant zigzag chancel arch. Spectacular details in the chancel include a rose window. The nave's double hammerbeam roof is a splendid medieval insertion, as is the rood screen. An imposing black marble monument to John de Vere, 15th Earl of Oxford, d1539, and his wife, is a reminder of the castle connection, for the de Veres built the mighty Norman castle that still lords it over the village and Colne valley landscape. **P.** *Open 09.00– dusk Mon, Tue & Thur–Sat, from 10.30 Wed, 07.45–after evensong Sun.* The wonderfully intact castle keep commands admiration from its mound and, with a little imagination, Elizabeth I can be pictured galloping over the Tudor bridge that spans the moat on her visit in 1561. The medieval and Georgian village is a delight to explore.

St Nicholas, Castle Hedingham

**Clavering, St Mary and   10 R8
St Clement**
7m SW of Saffron Walden on B1038. Paths winding about the churchyard provide picturesque views. Look N to the tussocky, moated site of Clavering Castle, bordered by the river Stort and by the Bury, a gabled 17thC house with a medieval core. The crenellated Perpendicular church has delightful

features, including angels and saints in 15thC stained glass in the N aisle, carved heads supporting the 15thC roofs, saints on the rood screen, whose engaging presence was uncovered by the removal of black paint, and a 13thC knight in chain mail. Elizabethan brasses display the costumes of the fashionable, and the history of Haynes Barlee, d1696, can be traced on memorials to himself and his wives, the first of whom had 13 children and the second 'no issue, but a great fortune'. *Open summer 08.00–approx 19.00 daily, winter to dusk.*

St Peter ad Vincula, Coggeshall

Coggeshall, St Peter ad Vincula   11 S7
5m E of Braintree on A120. Church Grn. A big jutting gable on the timber-framed 15thC Woolpack Inn admits to a nodding aquaintance with the tree-enshrined church opposite. The 15thC tower and N side of the lovely, spacious church were rebuilt after bombing in the Second World War. Charming details outside include the ironwork on the vestry door, in the SE corner of the tower, which shows a cock crowing to represent dawn, a blazing sun for midday and star and crescent moon for night. And the pelican feeding her young on the boss in the S porch vault is joined by swallows nesting and feeding their young each summer. Mary Honywood's monument records that she left a prodigious 367 descendants when she died in 1620. The fine Paycocke brasses commemorate wealthy medieval wool merchants. **P.** *Open 07.30–dusk daily.* Visit a marvellous example of Tudor domestic architecture in the half-timbered house built by Thomas Paycocke c1500, displaying rich carving and pretty oriel windows.

Dedham, St Mary the Virgin   11 T8
6m NE of Colchester on B1029. Set in the midst of delectable buildings, the Perpendicular church testifies to the prosperity of the 15thC cloth trade in its Suffolk-like sumptuousness. A

passageway under the impressive tower flourishes tracery, the Tudor rose and portcullis on its vault, and the trademark of Thomas Webbe, the wool merchant who helped build the church. His monument inside displays a profusion of quatrefoil friezes. *Open 09.00–dusk daily.* Dedham is possibly the most attractive of all Essex villages, situated in the Constable country of the Stour valley. Constable was born across the river in Suffolk, but used to come each day to school in Dedham. Dedham watermill was one of the many in the area owned by his father, Golding Constable.

Finchingfield, St John the Baptist   10 R8
6m NW of Braintree on B1053. In the ideal village, whose picturesque houses dip down towards the duck pond and old coaching inn, the churchyard on a gentle hill is entered through the gateway of the long, timber-framed Guildhall. The 18thC cupola appears a charming frivolity on top of the substantial Norman tower. Interesting window tracery and clerestories in nave and chancel distinguish the 13thC and 14thC interior, as does the sumptuously detailed rood screen. Notice the carving on the 14thC S door and the handsome monuments. **P**. *Open 09.30–19.00 or dusk daily.* A windmill stands N of the village and Elizabethan redbrick Spains Hall is 1m NW.

Great Bromley, St George   11 T8
4½m E of Colchester on B1029. The majestic tower and flushwork panelled S porch make a wonderful display outside, as does the marvellous double-hammerbeam roof inside. Examine the carving on the capitals of the S arcade pillars, the 15thC brass of a priest and the fine tracery on the W and N doors. **P**. *Open daylight hours daily.*

Great Canfield, St Mary the Virgin 10 R7
9m NW of Chelmsford off B184. Fittingly, the mound of a Norman motte and bailey castle is a close companion. The Norman church has an elaborate S doorway with zigzag decoration and a 13thC wall painting of the Virgin and Child, expressive of great sweetness. Notable brasses and monuments. **P**. *Open summer 08.00–20.30 daily, winter to dusk.*

**Great Sampford, St Michael   10 R8
the Archangel**
10m NW of Braintree on B1053. Gabled houses make charming neighbours to the 14thC church with a 13thC chapel remaining from a predecessor. The capitals of the arch leading into the

chapel from the aisle have a snail, a barn owl and a face bitten by a dragon carved on them. The chapel formed the village school until the 19thC, and the schoolmaster's desk and cupboard are in the nave. The large E window lights a spectacular array of 26 seats in the fine chancel. **P**. *Open 07.30–19.00 daily.*

Great Tey, St Barnabas   11 S8
7m W of Colchester off A604. The mighty Norman tower with eye-catching Roman brickwork is a thrilling sight, despite the loss of the church's nave in 1829. Be sure to look at the fine window tracery in the beautiful 14thC chancel and N transept, as well as the 15thC carved bench ends and priest's stall, and the unusual chest on wheels. **P**. *Open 08.00–dusk daily.*

Greensted Juxta Ongar, St Andrew 10 R7
1½m W of Chipping Ongar off A414. In a sylvan setting of fields and woods is the sole surviving Saxon oak-log church, dating from c845. It is a moving example of forest art that suggests the sacredness of trees to an early community. Marks of the carpenters' cutting tools are visible, as are holes low down in the N wall, once thought to be apertures for lepers to look through from outside. King Edmund's body rested here in 1013, on its way to Bury St Edmunds. Later additions are the Tudor brick chancel, the weatherboarded tower with a shingled spire, the pretty dormer windows and Victorian porch. **P**. *Open 09.00–dusk daily.*

Halstead, St Andrew   11 S8
In the middle of the small town. The tower, built in 1850, is a handsome counterpart to the 14thC church. Impressive, canopied tombs shield medieval effigies of members of the Bouchier family, and a brass of Bartholomew, third Lord Bouchier, d1409, shows him with his two wives, who wear distinctive and different headdresses. Take stock of the interesting Victorian stained glass and wall paintings. The reredos was designed by Sir A. Blomfield in 1893. In the belfry is a delightfully bulbous ringers' jar, surprisingly dated 1658, at which time puritans forbade the ringing of church bells. **P**. *Open 08.00–18.00 Mon, Fri & Sat, to 20.00 Tue, Thur & Sun, to 19.00 Wed.*

High Beach, Holy Innocents   10 P7
2½m SE of Waltham Abbey off A121. In the tranquil setting of Epping Forest and seen through a cathedral of silver birches from the E. The church, designed by Sir A. Blomfield in Early English Gothic

style, was built in 1873. It has an apsidal
E end and a soaring steeple. Embroidery
on kneelers and altar linen introduces
forest creatures into the Children's
Chapel. *Open summer 09.00–18.30 daily,
winter to dusk.*

Ingatestone, St Edmund and   **10 R7**
St Mary
3m N of Brentwood off A12. An
unforgettably glorious redbrick tower,
diapered by dark brick, is united to a
church whose Norman core incorporates
Roman brick, and which has 15thC–
17thC additions. The Petre family built
the S chapel in 1556 and among excellent
monuments in the church is one to
powerful Sir William Petre, d1572,
Secretary of State and Privy Councillor to
Henry VIII, and his wife. Their effigies
are full of character and resolve. There is
a fine portrayal of John Troughton,
d1621, in an oval niche. **P**. *Open daylight
hours daily.* Tudor Ingatestone Hall, the
Petre home, has a charming 18thC bell
turret, and 16thC–18thC houses form an
agreeable ensemble in the High St.

Lawford, St Mary the Virgin   **11 T8**
5m NE of Colchester on A137. Above the
sinuous Stour, the 14thC church has a
masterpiece in its chancel, probably built
by Sir Benet de Cokefield, lord of the
manor c1340. It displays elaborate and
inventive window tracery and enchanting
carvings round the window arches,
including chains of dancing, music-
making figures, charged with vitality,
and birds and animals nestling in
knobbly leaves. Equally exuberant are the
carvings round the splendid sedilia and
piscina. Observe Edward Waldegrave,
d1584, who built Lawford Hall, and his
wife, who was secretary to Katherine
Howard, Henry VIII's fifth wife, kneeling
face to face. **P**. *Open 09.00–dusk daily.*

Little Maplestead, St John   **11 S8**
the Baptist
13m NW of Colchester off A131. The church
is fascinating as one of the only four
remaining round churches in England,
built c1335 by the Knights Hospitallers,
in imitation of the Church of the Holy
Sepulchre in Jerusalem. Heavy 19thC
restoration does not detract from the
interest of its unusual form. See the very
ancient font. **P**. *Open daylight hours daily.*

Maldon, All Saints   **11 S7**
High St. Facing the Blue Boar, whose
Tudor timbers hide behind an 18thC
façade, and with the delightful 15thC
timber-framed vicarage at the rear, the

church stands picturesquely on a hill
above the Blackwater, its unique 13thC
triangular tower making a memorable
impact. The hexagonal shingled spire has
diminutive duplicates of itself in three
spirelets and a charming 15thC canopy
sheltering a sanctus bell. Statues were
put into the niches in the buttresses of
the S aisle early this century. Inside, the
S aisle is the showpiece of the church,
with beautiful 14thC two-tier arcading
and lavish ornamentation. Below is a
vaulted crypt. The chancel and chapels
are 15thC and the nave 18thC. **P**. *Open
09.30–17.00 Mon–Sat, 07.00–20.00 Sun.*
The Moot Hall and Plume Library, on the
site of the ruined Church of St Peter, and
retaining some early 18thC fittings, are
interesting features in the pretty town.

All Saints, Maldon

Saffron Walden, St Mary   **10 R8**
the Virgin
Beautifully set on a hill which
emphasises its magnificence; John
Wastell, mason at King's College Chapel,
Cambridge, contributed to the grandeur
of the 15thC–16thC rebuilding of the
church. The stately tower, to which the
spire was added in 1832, is 193ft high.
The lofty nave arcades, with richly
decorated spandrels, the glorious
clerestory, and fine roofs are impressive
expositions of the Perpendicular.
Interesting brasses are gathered in the N
aisle, under elaborate canopies from the
preceding church. A sumptuously carved
coat of arms accompanies the tomb of
Lord Chancellor, Thomas Audley, d1544,
in the S chapel. The Perpendicular font is
prettily detailed. **P**. *Open summer morn–
approx 18.30 daily, winter to dusk.* Some of
the most delightful medieval houses in
this lovely town are to be seen as Church
St joins Market Hill. Gables and 17thC
plaster ornamentation are just part of
their charms.

St Mary the Virgin, Saffron Walden

Steeple Bumpstead, St Mary   **10 R8**
the Virgin
2m S of Haverhill on B1054. Of Norman
origin, the church has later medieval
features and was restored in the 19thC.
Study the medieval graffiti and the grand
monument to Sir Henry Bendyshe,
d1717, on which he reclines in graceful
fashion, a little baby at his side. Barley
sugar columns spiralling either side
support a lavish pediment. **P.** *Open
08.00–17.00 Mon–Fri, from 09.00 Sat &
Sun.* The Guildhall imitates that at
Thaxted.

Thaxted, St John the Baptist,   **10 R8**
St Mary and St Lawrence
5m SE of Saffron Walden on A130. Past the
silvered oak beams of the splendid 15thC
cutlers' Guildhall, and up a cobbled lane,
soars the glorious spire of the 14thC–
16thC church. The spire was faithfully
rebuilt after being blown down by
lightning in 1814. Bold gargoyles and the
embellishments on the turreted N porch
reward examination. Light and spacious,

the interior contains beautiful carved
roofs, including angels in the aisles, a
15thC font cover of marvellous
elaboration, a 17thC pulpit decorated
with luscious garlands and screens to the
chapels carved with foliage scrolls. A
host of carved stone heads looks down
from the nave arches and in the N
transept an exquisite reredos shows
Christ with censing angels either side.
See the brass of a priest in the chancel.
Open daylight hours daily. The village
vistas of half-timbered and plastered
houses and the windmill are captivating.

Waltham Abbey, Holy Cross   **10 P7**
and St Lawrence
Founded in 1030, when a cross that
wrought a miraculous cure in King
Harold was brought from Montacute in
Somerset. Refounded by Harold c1057,
the church was rebuilt in the 12thC. The
war-cry of the Saxons at the Battle of
Hastings in 1066 was 'Holy Cross', but
Harold was defeated and his body
brought back here. The spot where he
was buried is marked at the E end of the
churchyard. Rich and important until the
E parts were destroyed at the
Dissolution, what remains of the Norman
church is breathtakingly magnificent.
Zigzag-decorated arches, supported by
pillars spectacularly grooved with spirals
and zigzag, tower up to the gallery and
clerestory. William Burges refashioned
the E wall in somewhat cumbrous style
in the 19thC, and designed the reredos
and the sumptuous nave ceiling, which
was painted by Edward Poynter. The
stained glass in the E window, designed
by Burne-Jones in 1861, is vibrant with
life and intense colour. The 14thC Lady
Chapel has a 15thC Doom painting. Fine
monuments. The tower, with some
striking flint and stone chequer work was
built, unusually, during the reign of
Queen Mary, in 1556. **P.** *Open summer
10.00–18.00 Mon–Sat, from 12.00 Sun;
winter to 16.00.* The 14thC abbey gateway
survives from the monastic buildings.

◀ SUFFOLK ▶

Aldeburgh, St Peter and St Paul   **11 U9**
The sea sparkles below the long, open-
sided S porch of the handsome church,
built in the 16thC, on the brink of the
Reformation, except for the 14thC tower.
The broad nave once accommodated ship

auctions and a payment to the Earl of
Leicester's travelling players is recorded
in 1573. The church remembers the
town's two most famous 'sons': George
Crabbe, commemorated in a bust of 1847
by T. Thurlow; and Benjamin Britten, in

a memorial window of intensely coloured stained glass, designed by John Piper in 1979 and made by Patrick Reyntiens. The poet, the composer and the town are inextricably bound together – *Peter Grimes*, one of the tales told about the town by Crabbe in *The Borough* of 1810, became Britten's first opera. See the fine font and magnificent Carolean pulpit – from which Crabbe preached as curate in 1781 – luxuriantly carved with grape clusters, arabesques and neatly curled dragonish creatures. Notice too the pretty W gallery, where singers perform during the Aldeburgh festival, and the Elizabethan brasses. 19thC feminist, Elizabeth Garrett Anderson is buried in the churchyard , as is Benjamin Britten. **P.** *Open 09.00–16.30 Mon–Fri, to 18.00 Sat; summer Sun 07.00–19.30, winter to 16.30.* In this town with a Regency air, visit the 16thC Moot Hall, stranded by the caprices of the sea and the Martello tower, built in the 19thC to keep Napoleon at bay. In 1948, Britten initiated the famous Aldeburgh music festival, whose main concert hall is in the Maltings at nearby Snape.

Bacton, St Mary the Virgin   11 T9
5¹/₂m N of Stowmarket off B1113.
Interesting features combine to create an unusual exterior, where the Decorated tower is joined to a 16thC brick stair turret, inscriptions on the S aisle record a bevy of Tudor donors, and flushwork decorates the clerestory. Inside, sumptuous 15thC timber roofs, restored by W. Butterfield in the 19thC, include the double hammerbeam nave roof with prominent flowers at its edges. See the indistinct Doom painted above the chancel arch, the screen, and through it the E window stained glass by Morris & Co, two carved benches and the font with shield-bearing angels and flowers. **P.** *Open daylight hours daily.*

Badingham, St John the Baptist   11 U9
5¹/₂m NW of Saxmundham off A1120.
Standing on a knoll, converted from a site sacred to pagans, the church's tower is Norman at the base, the nave 13thC and the chancel 19thC. Flushwork confers distinction on the porch, built in 1486, as do the lively dragon and a weathered wodehouse, or wild man, over the door. In the nave, which slopes uphill, is a beautiful hammerbeam roof, whose decoration includes angels added in 1900, replacing 'sixteen superstitious cherubims', destroyed by William Dowsing's Puritan zeal. The Seven

Sacraments are wonderfully illustrated on the 15thC font; see the baby being dipped in the font for baptism and the expulsion of a horned and winged fiend during penance. **P.** *Open daylight hours daily.*

Bildeston, St Mary Magdalene   11 S8
4¹/₂m NW of Hadleigh on B1115. On a hill, half a mile from the delightful, unspoilt village of half-timbered buildings; the church's Perpendicular tower collapsed, ironically, on Ascension day 1975. Note the elaborately decorated doorway, the priest's chamber inside the church above the S porch, the beautiful nave arcades and fine roof of alternating hammerbeams and tie-beams. **P.** *Open approx 10.00–16.00 Mon–Sat, 08.00–17.00 Sun.*

Blythburgh, Holy Trinity   11 U9
3¹/₂m W of Southwold on A12. The church is a majestic sight from the creek, where it rises tree-enshrined, or from the S where you are greeted by a lacy openwork parapet, presided over by prominent grotesques and figures, and by a porch guarded by angels. Next to the porch is an ornamented stoup. The 14thC tower makes an austere impression beside the long, unbroken flow of nave and chancel, with flushwork details and glorious clerestory. The toppling of the spire during a storm of 1577 is attributed to a visitation of the devil, whose exit left scorch marks on the N door. A more corporeal, but still fiendish, visitation by Cromwellian William Dowsing in 1644, left hundreds of bullet marks in both the ancient, traceried doors. Highlights of the beautiful, sparsely furnished, interior are the roof, whose magnificent long-winged angels (bathed in light from the clerestory) and beams retain enough of their colouring and delicate decoration for one to imagine their former splendour; the vivid figures carved on the bench ends, including Avarice sitting on his money chest, Greed with a fat stomach and the other Deadly Sins; the stalls with carved figures of apostles and saints; the screen; and the delightful, rosy-cheeked Jack-o-the-clock, who tired of striking the bell after a century or two, but whose mechanism is working again now. **P.** *Open approx 08.00–dusk daily.*

Boxford, St Mary   11 S8
5m E of Sudbury off A1071. The road dips into the charming streamside village. Heavy-lidded timber-framed houses in Butcher's La look down to the church

and its dainty towertop spirelet of lead. The lovely 14thC timber N porch contrasts with the flamboyantly detailed 15thC stone S porch. Fine doors lead into the Perpendicular interior. Inspect the fascinating 17thC font cover, which has doors that fold back to reveal painted texts, the 18thC pulpit, the touching brass to a child who died in 1606, shown sleeping in his cot, with his pattens underneath, and the modern stained glass in the E window. An 18thC tablet conveys an odd notion of curtailment in recording that Elizabeth Hyam, four times a widow, 'was at last hastened to her end in her 113th year'. **P**. *Open 08.00–17.00 daily.*

Bramford, St Mary the Virgin   **11** T8
3m W of Ipswich on A1100. The 14thC tower with an 18thC lead spire is a handsome adjunct to the lavishly decorated Perpendicular N side of the church, with panelled stone parapets and carved figures, including a monkey wearing a monk's cowl and hurling stones. The dramatic presence of boulders round about is thought to indicate a pagan sacred site. Lovely Perpendicular hammerbeam roofs stretch along nave and chancel of the 13thC and 14thC interior. William Dowsing, appointed Parliamentary Visitor of Suffolk Churches in 1643, smashed 'superstitious images' here, as testified by the headless angels. The medieval stone rood screen has a Victorian top, and the beautiful 16thC font cover doors that fold back. **P**. *Open 09.00–17.00 Mon; 07.00–18.45 Tue, Wed, Fri & Sat, from 08.30 Thur, to 19.30 Sun.* Picturesque houses delight close by.

Bungay, Holy Trinity   **11** U10
Trinity St. The fascinating 11thC round tower lends great distinction to the church, which also has a turret decorated with flushwork at an angle of the 14thC S aisle. The chancel was rebuilt in 1926. Observe the handsome S chapel and the pulpit of 1558, adorned with arabesques. Thomas Scheemakers sculptured the putto lamenting by an urn, on account of the death of Thomas Wilson in 1774. **P** nearby. *Open 09.00–17.00 Mon–Sat, 08.00–19.00 Sun; later in summer.* Visit St Mary's Church, with ruins of a nuns' choir at its E end and a magnificent Perpendicular tower. The town boasts comely Georgian houses and the 17thC Butter Cross, whose 18thC figure of Justice commands respect. 12thC Bungay Castle is a shadow of its former defensive self, but retains an

extraordinary mining gallery, which would have been shored up with timbers and set alight upon the arrival of assailants to bring the building toppling down on them.

Bures, St Mary the Virgin   **11** S8
5m SE of Sudbury on B1508. The dignified medieval church is distinguished by a beautiful S chapel, with a pier's doorway ensconced in a buttress. Praiseworthy features include a Tudor brick S porch, in which a stoup is upheld by a bishop and one other, a handsome traceried door, a 14thC timber N porch, an excellent 14thC wooden effigy of a knight, and a Perpendicular heraldic font. **P**. *Open approx 08.30–17.00 Mon–Sat, 07.30–19.30 Sun.*

Bury St Edmunds, St Mary   **11** S9
Crown St. In a historic market town, whose great medieval abbey enshrined the relics of St Edmund, martyred by the Danes in 870. The beautiful 14thC–15thC church is lit by myriad tall windows. Admire the 15thC porch bequeathed by John Nottyngham, the hammerbeam roof, wonderfully embellished with angels, saints, dragons and unicorns, and the illuminated roof of John Baret's (d1467) Chantry Chapel, on which his motto, 'Grace me Governe', appears. Among brasses and monuments, note that to Mary Tudor, d1533, Henry VIII's sister and wife of Louis XII of France. *Open Mar–Oct 10.00–17.00 daily; Nov–Feb to 15.00.* Of the splendours of the abbey little remains, except the mighty Norman and 14thC gateways.

Cavendish, St Mary   **11** S8
5m NW of Sudbury on A1092. In a village to be savoured, with vineyards, immaculate cottages whose ornately ridged thatched roofs have a sculptured air, a perfectly barbered green and Tudor Nether Hall among its timber-framed houses. The tower's ringing chamber is furnished as a living room, with window seats in the casement windows and a fireplace, whose chimney makes an idiosyncratic appearance perched on the impressive 14thC tower. A winsome bellcote sits on top of the stair turret. Striking flint and stone patterns, or flushwork, decorate the stately clerestory. Sir John Cavendish, Chief Justice of the King's Bench, beheaded during the Peasants' Revolt in 1381, left a bequest towards the rebuilding of the fine chancel. See the graceful nave arcades, the 15thC roof with 17thC pendants in

the N aisle, remains of medieval stained glass, an 18thC Spanish statue of St Michael the Archangel and a 16thC relief of the Crucifixion in the S chapel. *Open 09.00–18.00 daily.*

Clare, St Peter and St Paul   **11** S8
High St. The 13thC tower is united with an elegant, lofty Perpendicular church. Notice the distinctive rood-stair turrets with crocketed spirelets above the E end of the nave, and the carved bosses in the vaulted 14thC S porch. Castellated capitals, crocketed arches and angels line the nave in the lovely, light interior. The chancel was practically rebuilt in 1617, but forms a Perpendicular expression in harmony with the earlier fabric. The E window contains heraldic glass of the same date. Pay attention to the fine screen at the E end of the S aisle, the delightful Jacobean gallery pew, the extra-large eagle lectern and the earthenware ringers' jar of 1729. **P** nearby in Country Park. *Open summer 09.00–18.30 or dusk daily, winter to 16.30.* The Ancient House Museum is close to the church. Audacious pargetting – intricately patterned plasterwork – decorates its exterior. The beautiful town has numerous handsome houses, the fragmentary remains of a 13thC castle and part of a medieval priory in fine grounds.

Cockfield, St Peter   **11** S9
7m SE of Bury St Edmunds off A1141. The fine, large medieval church makes an impressive display on the S side with flushwork and niches ornamenting the porch and elaborate battlements decorating the aisle, as well as a beautiful interior roof. Flushwork chequers the tower buttresses. In the 14thC chancel is a spectacular Easter Sepulchure. **P.** *Open 08.00–18.00 daily.*

Earl Soham, St Mary   **11** T9
9½m W of Saxmundham on B1119. The lovely Perpendicular tower is decorated by flushwork on the battlements, base and buttresses, on which inscriptions record the builders. A fine double hammerbeam roof, with figures at the sides, distinguishes the nave, as does the font, guarded by a contingent of lions, which are interspersed with angels round the bowl. Figures kneel and sit among the enticing carvings on the ends of the medieval benches. The pulpit and altar rail are Jacobean. **P.** *Open daylight hours daily.* Notable in the pretty village is moated Earl Soham Lodge.

Eye, St Peter and St Paul   **11** T9
4m SE of Diss on B1077. The marvellous 15thC tower, sumptuously decked with the flushwork typical of East Anglia, is crowned by a tall, stone-panelled parapet with surprisingly sober pinnacles. Observe the flushwork elsewhere on the exterior and notice where flint has been replaced by brick on the S porch. Remark too the parapet of brick and terracotta on the S chapel and the priest's door tucked intriguingly into a flying buttress. Inside the S porch, no longer used as an entrance, is a fine 13thC doorway and a bread shelf of 1601. The handome restored nave roof has a colourful canopy above the glorious gilded rood screen, where paintings of kings and saints congregate – sweetly decorative but without character. Comper added the loft and rood in 1925, including the elegant seraphim and scaly dragons. See the carving of the Virgin and Child, 1973, in the ornate 14thC tomb recess, the identical tombs of 1568 and 1569, with a hint of the Renaissance, and the relief of the Good Samaritan on the memorial to a naval surgeon, John Brown, d1732. **P.** *Open 10.00–18.30 Mon, Wed & Thur, from 07.45 Tue, Fri & Sat; 07.45–dusk Sun.* Neighbours are a restored timber-framed 16thC Guildhall, and the 11thC castle mound with a Victorian folly on top. There are vestigial remains of an 11thC priory at Abbey Farm to the E.

Framlingham, St Michael   **11** T9
6m W of Saxmundham on B1119. In a lofty position, the church is a forceful expression of Perpendicular majesty. The tower is embellished with flushwork and sitting lions form alternative pinnacles at the corners of the battlements. Ornate fan tracery at the sides makes the hammerbeam roof of the nave magnificent. Rebuilding of the chancel and chapels was started by the cruel and powerful Tudor statesman Thomas Howard, third Duke of Norfolk, to form a family mausoleum. Its completion was ordered by Edward VI. The third duke's, d1554, is the most splendid of the outstanding Renaissance monuments: eloquent figures of the apostles stand round the sides, under shell niches with leafy balusters between; it was erected at a surprising juncture in history, when religious images were being taken down. While Thomas Howard kept his head, his son Henry Howard, the 'Poet Earl' of Surrey, was beheaded in 1547, during the power struggle at the close of Henry

St Michael, the 'Poet Earl'

VIII's reign, and is commemorated in alabaster effigy with his wife and kneeling children. On the frieze on the tomb of Henry Fitzroy, d1536, illegitimate son of Henry VIII, witness the peremptory expulsion of Adam and Eve from Paradise and the way all but the head of Lot's wife has turned to a pillar of salt. Sir Robert Hitcham, d1636, who bought the Howard castle and manor in 1635, has four exquisitely handsome angels supporting his black marble tomb slab. See the glorious 17thC organ case and reredos with its sacred painting. **P.** *Open 08.00–18.00 daily.* Nearby, Plantagenet Framlingham Castle glowers over its lengthy past.

Fressingfield, St Peter and St Paul 11 T9
8m W of Halesworth on B1116. The lovely 14thC and 15thC church stands on rising ground at the village's centre. Look up to the fine clerestory and the additional window at the E end of the nave, above which sits an exquisite Sanctus bellcote, with miniature buttresses and a cross on a central pinnacle. The 15thC porch, built by Catherine de la Pole in memory of her husband, who died of dysentery at the Siege of Harfleur, and her son, who was killed at Agincourt, is gorgeously adorned with crowns and fleurons, flushwork and niches. Inside are a handsomely decorated roof and a set of 15thC oak benches, wonderfully carved and traceried – a delight to pore over. **P.** *Open 08.30–dusk Mon–Sat, 10.00–18.00 Sun.* Picturesquely contiguous to the churchyard is the brick and timber 16thC Guildhall, now the Fox and Goose restaurant.

Great Bricett, St Mary and 11 T8
St Lawrence
5m S of Stowmarket on B1078. The remains of an Augustinian priory church, built in 1110, which once had transepts. See the Norman N doorway, with zigzag decoration in the arch, the square Norman font, ornamented with arches, the lovely 14thC stained glass and the pulpit. **P.** *Open daylight hours daily.* Adjacent Bricett Hall was part of the priory and retains interesting early timber work.

Halesworth, St Mary 11 U9
The 15thC tower battlements are decorated with flushwork. The church has 14thC arcades and many Victorian additions. But in the chancel are interesting fragments of a 9thC Saxon frieze, discovered during restoration in 1889. The two medieval doorways in the chancel are notable; fleurons, shields, an angel and a monk preside over one, while the other has a lion at the apex and the appeal in Latin, 'Pray for Thomas Clement and Margaret his wife who had this vestry built for you'. Inspect the wooden collecting shoe with a handle and the typical East Anglian font, which has symbols of the evangelists and angels on the octagonal bowl and four lions and four wild men below, three of whom hold their clubs up to show they are regenerate, while the fourth holds his down to show he has some way to go. A memorial of 1930 commemorates Sir William and Sir Joseph Hooker, first directors of Kew Gardens in the 19thC. **P.** *Open 07.00–18.00 Mon–Sat, 07.30–20.00 Sun.* There are some agreeable buildings in the little market town, including the delightful Maltings.

Hawstead, All Saints 11 S9
3m S of Bury St Edmunds off A134. A sombre sarcophagus forms part of the grand monument to Sir Robert Drury, d1615, whose arms appear above the W doorway of the Perpendicular tower. Norman doorways with zigzag arches are either side of the nave, whose window sills form seats. Glance up at the restored angel roof and the Perpendicular chancel roof, decorated with arabesques and the monogram of Jesus. A fine 13thC crusader knight lies in a lushly foliaged niche in the chancel. See the Drury brasses and other interesting monuments, including 18thC and 19thC tablets accompanied by urns, among which is an excellent one of 1793 to Lucy Metcalfe. **P.** *Open 09.00–dusk daily.*

Hoxne, St Peter and St Paul 11 T9
4m SE of Diss on B1118. The richly adorned, stately Perpendicular tower was built by John de la Pole, the second Duke of Suffolk, in 1450. The chancel was

rebuilt in the 19thC. Dragons spring from a tree in a medieval wall painting of the Seven Deadly Sins. St Christopher and the Seven Works of Mercy are also depicted. Seven locks secure the 14thC iron-bound elm chest. There is an impressive monument to Thomas Maynard, d1742; the tower screen was made from Edmund's oak, which fell in 1848, and shows scenes of his martyrdom. **P.** *Open 07.30–dusk daily.* Hoxne is the legendary place of King Edmund's martyrdom in 870 by a flight of Danish arrows, after betrayal by a newly married couple who saw his spurs glinting under Goldbrook Bridge. An old arrowhead was found buried in the tree where he was shot, whose site is marked by a stone cross.

Kersey, St Mary   **11** S8
2m NW of Hadleigh off A1141. The fine church and 15thC tower, with a delightful flushwork parapet, look back to a larger population, but still dominate the picturesque village. The S porch makes a glorious display, with flushwork and crocketed pinnacles outside and exquisite traceried panels forming the roof inside. The 14thC nave arches are charmingly decorated, and in the N aisle is part of a 15thC screen, painted with prophets and kings. The chancel was rebuilt in the 19thC. Spot the buttressed lectern. **P.** *Open summer 08.00–19.00 Fri–Sun, winter 10.00–16.00 Fri–Sun.* Enjoy the series of enchanting intaglios which make up the village: medieval weavers' cottages in The Street, with twinkling diamond panes; a tail on the gable of the former horse doctor's house; and the River House flaunting its audacious Elizabethan porch beside the ford. Ruins of a 13thC Augustinian priory crown the slope opposite the church.

St Mary, Kersey

Lakenheath, St Mary   **10** R9
9½m W of Thetford on B1112. Outstanding in this interesting church of many periods are the glorious angel roof, the Norman chancel arch, the prominent 13thC font, decorated with foliage and gabled arches, and the bench ends, where charming animal carvings nestle, including those of a tiger and a unicorn. Along the bench backs run intricate friezes. Take a look at the 14thC wall paintings, too. **P.** *Open 08.00–17.30 Mon–Thur & Sat, to 20.00 Fri, 07.45–19.30 Sun.*

St Peter and St Paul, Lavenham

Lavenham, St Peter and St Paul   **11** S8
6m NE of Sudbury on A1141. Set at the end of the matchless and miraculously intact timber-framed Tudor wool town, the marvellous church was built by rich clothiers to celebrate the end of the Wars of the Roses in 1485. The arms of the chief of these, Thomas Spryng and the Earl of Oxford, appear on the majestic tower; the Oxford boar presides over the sumptuous S porch and an inscription on the Spryng Chapel pleads for prayers for the souls of Thomas and his wife. Inside, the screens of their early 16thC chantries are exquisitely, even fabulously, carved and detailed. Beautiful wood carving can be found too in the 14thC rood screen with flowing tracery and in the vivacious figures on the misericords. Mourn over the tiny, tragic baby brass of 1631. Though not usually open, the vestry contains a fascinating 'resurrection brass' on which Thomas Spryng, his wife and children emerge from their shrouds. **P.** *Open 10.00–18.00 daily.* Quaint streets will

lead you into enchanting medieval prospects, including those of the Guildhall in the market place, the Old Wool Hall, Tudor shops, and Woolstaplers in Prentice St.

Laxfield, All Saints　　　**11** T9
6½m SW of Halesworth on B1117. In the birthplace of Puritan iconoclast William Dowsing. Flushwork distinguishes the Perpendicular tower and a fine roof the nave. Take time over the font on which the Seven Sacraments are illustrated, the screen, box pews and the delightfully. ornate benches with animals and a tower carved on the arms. **P.** *Open summer 08.00–19.00 daily, winter to dusk.* Opposite is the interesting Laxfield Museum.

Long Melford, Holy Trinity　**11** S8
3m N of Sudbury on A134. Elizabethan pepperpot-turreted Melford Hall is an aristocratic neighbour on the Green to the grand, nobly proportioned church. A great chorus of petitions inscribed on the walls beg for prayers for the families of the 15thC clothiers who built the church. The fine tower was built at the end of the 19thC by Bodley. A miracle of grace and lightness is achieved in the flushwork decoration and the soaring clerestory. Kneeling donors figure in 15thC stained glass, with which the interior is refulgent; among them, look for stout Elizabeth Talbot, Duchess of Norfolk, artist John Tenniel's model for the Duchess in *Alice in Wonderland*. The Clopton Chantry Chapel is a glorious gem, in which the chief rebuilder of the church, John Clopton, d1497, is buried. A poem ascribed to the monk, John Lydgate, borders the roof. Sir William Cordell, d1580, builder of Melford Hall and Speaker of the House of Commons, lies in splendid alabaster effigy in the chancel. See the Lady Chapel with its distinctive ambulatory. **P** on Green. *Open*

Holy Trinity, Long Melford

08.00–dusk Mon, Tue & Thur–Sat, from 09.00 Wed; 09.00–dusk or Evensong Sun. Enjoy the straggling main street of gracious and pretty houses. When Sir William Cordell entertained Elizabeth I at Melford Hall in 1578, '200 young gentlemen in white velvet, 300 in black and 1,500 serving men', were in attendance.

Lound, St John the Baptist　**11** U10
4½m NW of Lowestoft off A12. Impact is made outside the restored church by a Norman round tower and inside by ebullient gilded furnishings. The rood screen has a 14thC base with charming curvaceous tracery, to which Comper added the opulent loft and rood. He also designed the organ case and the font cover, beneath which lions predominate over shield-bearing angels round the Perpendicular font. See too the 20thC wall painting of St Christopher. *Open 07.15–dusk Mon–Fri, from 07.30 Sat, from 09.15 Sun.*

Lowestoft, St Margaret　　**11** U10
St Margaret's Rd. The spacious church, removed from the old town, has an imposing tower of c1300 and much flushwork decoration. Lions and angels wait at the entrance to the S porch, which is rib-vaulted inside. Graceful arcades line the continuous nave and chancel. Admire the fine E window, and the stained glass of 1819 in the window to its right, by Robert Allen, who worked at the Lowestoft china factory, which enjoyed a transient existence from 1756–1803. See too the medieval brasses of skeletons in shrouds. **P.** *Open 08.30–17.00 Mon, Wed & Thur, from 07.00 Tue & Fri, 07.30–20.00 Sun.* Birthplace of composer Benjamin Britten and of Elizabethan playwright Thomas Nashe, Lowestoft is an interesting fishing port and holiday resort. Lanes called the Scores lead down from the High St and lose themselves among what curing houses remain.

Mendlesham, St Mary the Virgin　**11** T9
5½m NE of Stowmarket off A140. Fine flushwork ornaments the tower and porches of the lovely medieval church. Crowned Ms on the S porch refer to the dedication of the church and the N porch is presided over by the startling presences of two lions and two wild men. They guard the armoury on the upper floor, created in 1593 for defence against Philip II of Spain. This is a fascinating and uncommon feature and

contains accessories, including an Elizabethan long bow, as well as armour. Twenty-three wide-eyed gargoyles are also on guard outside the church. Immediately striking inside is the unusual Jacobean font cover, with elegant columns beneath a forest of pediments and prickly-looking obelisks. But also pay attention to the Jacobean pulpit, the 17thC holy table in the N aisle with one leg askew, medieval benches, stained glass and the brass to John Knyvet, d1417. **P.** *Open 08.45–16.30 Mon, Tue & Thur-Sat, from 07.00 Wed, 08.45– 12.00 Sun. Tower and armoury open July– Sep 14.00–17.00 Sun.*

Metfield, St John the Baptist   11 T9
6½m SW of Bungay on B1123, Sir William Jermy, d1385, left 100 shillings towards the building of the handsome tower, whose parapet was added in 1712. Gargoyles protect it and the S porch, whose front is panelled in flushwork, and entrance presided over by crowns, a bishop's head, lions' heads and fleurons. Inside is a wooden vault with Christ in glory in the central boss. The working turret clock is a venerable 17thC presence of great interest. Angels and lions decorate the 15thC font. Magnificently intact, the painted canopy of honour once crowned the rood; the base of the rood screen remains. Carved brackets ornament the chancel roof. **P.** *Open daylight hours daily.*

Mildenhall, St Mary   10 R9
High St. The large, impressive church is a landmark across the fens. Pinnacles climb out of shafted buttresses and make their way up the tower, though there are none on top. Flushwork chequers the N aisle and fine panelled battlements crown the elaborate N porch which has niches in its buttresses, and a vault inside studded with carved bosses. The hammerbeams of the delightfully traceried nave roof are gloriously arrayed with angels with spiky, outstretched wings. A multitude of smaller, scroll-bearing angels are on the tie-beams and wall plates. Though the roof escaped the worst Puritan ravages through its great height, it was peppered with shot, while the angels in the N aisle roof were defaced and are without wings. Biblical scenes, saints and fabulous beasts hold their own in the spandrels. Notice the fine, 13thC chancel arch and the exquisite E window tracery in which quatrefoils seem to dance round the rim. **P** nearby. *Open 09.00–16.30 daily.* The Mildenhall Treasure of Roman silver

tableware was ploughed up in a field during the last war and is on display in the British Museum.

Nayland, St James   11 S8
6m N of Colchester on A134. The fine porch, unusually attached to the 14thC tower, was built by rich clothier, William Abell, in 1525, and rebuilt in the 19thC. Inside, handsome nave arcades and clerestory lead up to the altar painting of *Christ blessing the bread and wine,* by John Constable. **P.** *Open 09.00–dusk Mon–Sat, 07.30–20.00 Sun.* In the picturesque village, gabled and timber-carved Alston Court makes a splendid medieval display and a 17thC pronouncement in its big doorway, while houses with over-hanging timber storeys are on nodding acquaintance with their neighbours.

Orford, St Bartholomew   11 U8
5m SW of Aldeburgh on B1084. Picturesque ruins of a Norman chancel extend from the Decorated church, whose tower top fell in 1830 and was replaced in 1971. The magnificent 14thC font has four proud lions and four wild men round the stem, and boldly sculptured signs of the evangelists, angels, the Trinity and a pietà above; an inscription on the top step commemorates the donors, John Cockerell and his wife. Look out for the 16thC Italian altar painting of the *Holy Family with St John and a donor,* the Tudor brasses and the pretty tracery in the aisle windows. **P.** *Open 08.00–dusk daily.* The brick and timber quayside village has some charming corners and a nautical air, although the giant gravel bank, Orford Ness, has swallowed up the former seaport. Scale the hummocky ramparts and climb to the top of the powerful, polygonal 12thC castle keep for a vertiginous view over coast and countryside. Smugglers and coaches frequented the King's Head.

Rougham, St Mary   11 S9
4m SE of Bury St Edmunds off A45. The lovely church stands almost alone, because villagers burnt their houses to try and stem the plague of 1349–50, and rebuilt them half a mile away. An intricate frieze skeins below the Perpendicular tower's splendid flushwork parapet. Ogee-arched open tracery windows distinguish the fine 14thC S porch. Read the inscriptions on the N aisle buttresses, which include the date of building, 1514, and a direct appeal from the Middle Ages, 'We pray you to

remember us that causyde ye yle to be made thus'. A profusion of poppyheads on beautifully carved 16thC benches fills the nave, where angels, alas headless, decorate the hammerbeam roof. An excellent brass shows Sir Robert Drury, d1400, as a knight in shining armour with his wife Margery. **P.** *Open 09.00–17.00 Mon–Sat, 08.30–12.00 Sun.*

Rumburgh, St Michael and St Felix   **11** U9

3m NW of Halesworth off A144. Built as part of a Benedictine priory, the church has an extraordinary wide and short 13thC tower, with impressive lancet windows and weatherboarding below a tiled roof. Inside, the medieval colours of the finely traceried rood screen shelter beneath later accretions. The pulpit is Jacobean, and some benches have old poppyheads. **P.** *Open daylight hours daily.* The site of the priory's refectory has been swallowed by Abbey Farm which, together with the churchyard, is surrounded by a moat.

St Michael and St Felix, Rumburgh

Shelland, King Charles the Martyr   **11** T9

4½m W of Stowmarket off A45. Rurally retired, a charming ogee-topped bell turret decorates the otherwise plain exterior of this small, extremely engaging 18thC church, with its rare dedication. Furnished in perfect 18thC fashion, the church has box pews, a three-decker pulpit and the convenience of wooden pegs for gentlemen to hang up their wigs in hot weather. It is believed that the variety of colours in which the interior is painted either reflects the jewels of the heavenly Jerusalem, or the local wainwright's experience in painting hay-wagons. Note the delightful cornice in the chancel and the bold foliage on the panels of the 14thC font. Above all, the church is graced by a barrel organ of 1817, regularly used during services and recently restored. **P.** *Open daylight hours daily.*

King Charles the Martyr, Shelland

Stoke-by-Clare, St John Baptist   **11** S8

4½m SE of Haverhill on A1092. The large, handsome Perpendicular church has a 14thC tower. Castellated capitals crown the nave pillars and poppyheads the benches. The pulpit is a small and perfect Perpendicular gem. See the medieval Doom painted in the N chapel, the windmill in 15thC stained glass in the S transept, and the Tudor brasses. **P.** *Open approx 09.00–dusk daily.* Delightful timber-framed and plastered cottages stand by the green, and remains of a medieval college for clergy are incorporated into Stoke College.

Stoke-by-Nayland, St Mary the Virgin   **11** S8

5m SW of Hadleigh off A134. Deep in Constable country, above the Stour valley and the views that enchanted the landscape painter, the grand, Perpendicular church figures in several of Constable's paintings. Local merchants left money to build the sumptuous tower. Tendring and Howard shields appear in the W doorway and on the font inside. Lion heads and leaves emerge from the doorway, canopied niches are ensconced in the buttresses and battlements, and pinnacles crown the tower. Tracery and a Tree of Jesse decorate the door inside the rib-vaulted S porch. Behind a Perpendicular screen, medieval brasses in the S chapel include those of a knight in shining armour with a curly beard, Sir William Tendring, and Lady Howard, ancestress of Katherine Howard and Anne Boleyn, who were to lose their heads as Henry VIII's spouses. **P.** *Open 07.00–dusk daily*. The timber-framed and plastered buildings in the village are a sheer delight; the 16thC Guildhall and Maltings are particular gems. Bed and breakfast are offered at the Tudor and Queen Anne vicarage.

Stowmarket, St Peter and St Mary   11 T9
Station Rd. Overlooking the market place, a Perpendicular tower and porches are married to a 14thC church with beautiful, flowing window tracery. A painting of Dr Young, tutor to 17thC poet John Milton is in the church and so is a remarkable iron wig stand of 1654. An inscription on a touching 17thC brass of Ann Tyrell, wearing a small shroud, records: 'By Reason and Religion Shee at Seaven, Prepar'd her selfe & Found her way to Heaven'. **P.** *Open 09.00–17.00 Mon–Sat, 07.30–19.30 Sun*. Georgian houses strike an elegant note in the town, including a hospital in Onehouse Rd, built as a workhouse and accused in 1810 of having 'more the appearance of a gentleman's seat than a receptable for paupers'. The fascinating Museum of East Anglican Life should be visited.

Sudbury, St Gregory   11 S8
The Croft. Close to the gateway of the college founded by Simon of Sudbury in 1375, and the green, or Croft, the gracious Perpendicular church has a distinguished, stair-turreted tower, restored in 1978. Notice the tracery and prettily carved border on the S door and the chapel attached to the porch. The spire-like font cover is a glorious 15thC survival. Chancel ceiling and rood canopy are gorgeously decorated but the sole remaining panel from the rood screen is now in Gainsborough's House. It shows Master Schorn, a Bedfordshire rector, conjuring a devil into a boot, a singular cure for gout. Don't miss the ornate, former gas brackets on the pillars, and the heads carved on stalls and misericords. Archbishop of Canterbury and Richard II's Chancellor, Simon of Sudbury was beheaded during the Peasants' Revolt of 1381 and his skull is locked in the vestry of the church, which he helped rebuild. It appears from an 18thC document recording that 'the sexton of the parish often puts in fictitious teeth', these were popular relics. **P.** *Open 09.00–16.30 Mon–Sat, 08.00–18.30 Sun*. There are two other medieval churches in the market town, each with ornate parclose screens. Painter Thomas Gainsborough was born

at 46 Gainsborough St, now an interesting museum, and appears in bronze on Market Hill.

Walberswick, St Andrew   11 U9
1½m SW of Southwold on B1387, across ferry. By sea and heath where birds congregate, this little medieval church was once as grand as those at nearby Blythburgh and Southwold. It was dismantled in 1696, leaving the fine tower and S aisle, which exert a tangible charm and character. **P.** *Open 08.00–dusk daily*.

Walsham-le-Willows, St Mary   11 S9
9m NE of Bury St Edmunds off A143. Diamond-patterned flushwork decorates the N porch, which has wood panelling inside. The Perpendicular nave is distinguished by concave-sided pillars and an exquisitely detailed tie-beam and hammerbeam roof. The coved and crested rood screen, dated 1441, has charming paintings of flowers on red and green at the base. Through it see the fragments of medieval stained glass in the E window. **P.** *Open daylight hours daily*.

Woodbridge, St Mary   11 T8
Church St. In a dignified market town, the church's 15thC tower and N porch are sumptuously detailed with flushwork, including friezes of initials and tracery. Delightfully ornate pinnacles crown the porch. Nave and chancel are one. The font is of a type found only in Suffolk and Norfolk, depicting the Seven Sacraments. Each tableau is framed by rays and butterfly headdresses are worn; the Crucifixion appears on the eighth panel. Some painted panels survive from a 15thC rood screen given to the church by John Albrede, a twill-weaver and Agnes his wife. There is interesting 20thC stained glass by Martin Travers in the E window and a candelabrum of 1676 in the nave. Thomas Seckford, d1587, who built the Seckford Chapel, as well as almshouses and the elegant Shire Hall in the town, is buried in the chancel. He became Master of the Court of Requests at the beginning of Elizabeth I's reign, and although she complained once about the odour of his boots, rose to great power and wealth and, as lord of the manor, built the Abbey in 1564 on the lands of a 12thC priory. *Open daylight hours daily*. Edward FitzGerald, the Victorian poet and translator, lived in a house near Market Hill and his many famous friends, including Lord

Tennyson, stayed at the Bull Inn. In its stable is a memorial to ostler George Carlow, who chose to be buried there in 1738. The Crown Hotel was the birthplace of the extraordinary John Fox, in 1528. Captured and held in slavery for 14 years by the Turks, he became something of a celebrity after his escape.

Woolpit, St Mary the Virgin 11 S9
5½m NW of Stowmarket off A45. The 15thC S porch shows an eye-catching stone face, sumptuously decorated with an ogee gable stretching up to statue niches and a lacy openwork crest. Bosses decorate the vault inside. A glorious host of feathery angels rests against the marvellous double hammerbeam roof, with wings spread as if they had only flown there recently. See the beautiful canopy at the E end. Angels abound in the aisle roofs too. There are benches with saints and animals on the arms and traceried ends and a lectern said to have been given by Elizabeth I. **P.** *Open 09.15–dusk Mon–Sat, 07.30–19.30 Sun.* The village's Tudor character asserts itself in prominent chimneystacks and timber-framed houses with diamond panes, and the 19thC declares itself in the charming, canopied pump.

Worlingworth, St Mary 11 S9
10m SE of Diss off B1118. Gleaming flint and stone chequer the buttresses of the lovely Perpendicular tower and a more splendid display of flushwork is made on the S porch. Originally thatched, the 13thC chancel was re-roofed in 1866. The Perpendicular nave has a beautiful double hammerbeam roof. Truly admirable features include the handsome set of benches of 1630, the Jacobean pulpit with a suspended sounding board and the magnificent 15thC font cover, restored and regilded in 1963, on which crockets and buttresses make a glorious ascent to nearly 20 ft. A fire engine of 1760 and a 17thC collecting shoe are also part of the furnishings. A graceful monument by Coade to Dame Ann Henniker, d1792, has delightful details, including an urn and a winged cherub's head, and that to the Dowager Duchess of Chandos, d1813, is remarkably sculptured by John Bacon. *Open 10.00–18.00 daily.*

◁ NORFOLK ▷

Attleborough, Assumption Blessed Virgin Mary 15 T10
14m SW of Norwich on A11. The 14thC church with a Norman and 13thC tower maintains an august presence, despite the neighbouring hurly-burly of a main road. A great cause for rejoicing is the 15thC rood screen, stretching across nave and aisles in almost its marvellous entirety. Delightfully cusped openings, painted figures and ornament and, above all, the loft, give a rare chance to appreciate the rood screen as it was when it formed the dominant feature of all medieval church interiors. See too the 14thC four-petalled flower tracery in the W window, the wall paintings above the tower's W arch, the 18thC pulpit and cast-iron snakes under the lectern handrails.

Bedingham, St Andrew 15 T10
4m NW of Bungay off B1135. A light and spacious medieval church whose distinctive round tower has an octagonal top. Attractive features include the lavishly carved rood screen, the medieval benches, box pews, garlands decorating the pulpit and the prettily twisted balusters of the 17thC altar rail. **P.** *Open daylight hours daily.*

Binham, Our Lady and the Holy Cross 15 S11
8m NE of Fakenham off B1388. Amid monastic ruins stand the eloquent remains of a priory church, founded in 1091 by William the Conqueror's nephew. They include the glorious if broken rhythms of the 13thC W front, manifesting the earliest example of bar tracery in England. The pretty bellcote sits rather incongruously on top. The church's E end was demolished in 1540,

Our Lady and the Holy Cross, Binham

but the galleried and clerestoried Norman nave is a splendid sight. Note the benches with poppyheads and tracery. **P** in farmyard. *Open daylight hours daily.*

Blakeney, St Nicholas   **15** T11
8m W of Sheringham A149. The church looks out to marsh and sea. Its tall, slim E tower was built as a beacon and is a curious companion for the great Perpendicular W tower. And the lofty Perpendicular nave contrasts with the beautiful, low-vaulted 13thC chancel. Graceful ribs meet in leaf bosses and a fine array of lancets form the E window. Examine the carvings on stalls and misericords, and look out for flying, trumpeting angels on churchyard tombstones. **P.** *Open 10.00–dusk daily.* Georgian Red House is a distinguished building on the Quay in this village of flint and brick cottages. Marshy creeks make their way to Blakeney Point and the National Trust's shoreside naturalists' paradise from the Quay.

St Nicholas, Blakeney

Castle Acre, St James the Great   **15** S10
4m N of Swaffham off A1065. The priory ruins and outer bailey of the castle are either side of the 13thC and Perpendicular church. The stately tower is crowned by a castellated, flushwork parapet. Saints wearing opulent ruby and deep blue robes and cloaks, gesticulate eloquently on the base of the early 15thC rood screen, gleaming with gold ornament. The doctors of the church painted on the pulpit hold streamer-like scrolls. Admire too the 14thC stalls with painted panels and misericords, the small animals and poppyheads carved on 14thC benches, and the font cover in the form of an ornate spire surmounted by a gilded dove. *Open 09.00–dusk Thur–Tue, from 09.30 Wed.* Castle Acre commands the point where Roman Peddars Way crosses the river Nar. The 13thC gateway still makes a strong stand, but otherwise

a massively impressive mound is all that remains of the stronghold started by William the Conqueror's son-in-law, William de Warenne. His son increased its defensive properties and also founded a priory in 1090. The priory ruins, in lush green meadows, include a spectacular W front with multitudinous intersecting arches. The charming Tudor prior's house is decorated with chequer flushwork and a timber-framed gable.

Cawston, St Agnes   **15** T11
10m NW of Norwich on B1145. The chancel precedes the lofty Perpendicular church, begun by Sir Michael de la Pole in 1414 and completed by his widow. An impressively austere, grey stone tower contrasts strikingly with the magnificent nave roof, richly carved with bosses and angels fixed in flight. A wild man and a dragon make two appearances – above the W door and on a piscina in the S transept. Pore over the saints painted on the fine rood screen, including a bespectacled St Matthew, and the lovely medieval chalice case. **P.** *Open daylight hours daily.*

Diss, St Mary the Virgin   **11** T9
A delightful, half-timbered neighbour in the market place turns a gable to the medieval church, whose 13thC tower is distinguished by processional arches to N and S. A dainty structure for the weather vane sits on top of the tower and a charming bellcote over the E end of the nave. Gargoyles survey the scene from the clerestory, and the fine Perpendicular S porch is decorated with flushwork panelling. John Skelton, poet and tutor to Henry VIII, was rector from 1504–29, as recorded.on the list of rectors by the S door. Inside are 14thC nave arcades and 19thC chancel. Spot the little figures carved in the tracery and panels of the 15thC W door and Moses and Aaron on the 17thC Commandment board. **P.** *Open Jul–Aug 09.00–20.00 Mon–Thur, from 08.30 Fri & Sat, from 08.00 Sun; Sep–Jun to 18.00 Mon–Sat, to 19.00 Sun.* Diss is a pretty town built around a mere. Close to the church are picturesque Mount St and the Victorian Shambles.

Great Yarmouth, St Nicholas   **15** U10
Church Plain. The largest parish church in England has a 12thC foundation and an impressive 13thC W front, with distinctive octagonal pinnacled turrets. The nave is much narrower than the later aisles. Bombed and gutted in 1942, the neo-Gothic interior is by S. Dykes Bower,

1957–60. See the colourful organ case he designed, the E window stained glass by B. Thomas, and the 18thC pews and pulpit. The pulpit's sounding board serves as cover to the Norman font. There are several interesting tombstones in the churchyard. Limited **P**. *Open summer 09.00–18.00 daily, winter to 13.00.*

Great Yarmouth's fortunes were first founded on herrings, as testified to by the gracious procession of distinguished houses along South Quay, where 'the greatest herring merchant in Europe' built what is now the Customs House in 1720. The town developed as a seaside resort in the 18thC and 19thC and has a brightly illuminated 20thC presence and extensive beaches. On one of them Mr Peggotty, in Dickens' novel, entertained his sister Peggotty and her young charge, David Copperfield, in his cosy, ship-shape boathouse, to which a conglomeration of crabs, lobsters and crawfish imparted a fishy smell from the outhouse.

Heacham, St Mary the Virgin   **14** R11
2½m S of Hunstanton off A149. The impressive 13thC crossing tower has lost its transepts and bulky buttresses take their places. The seats round the 13thC nave pillars, the Perpendicular clerestory and the handsome rood screen are all worth looking out for. A colourful piece of local Jacobean history, attracting many American pilgrims, is commemorated in a modern memorial to the Red Indian Princess Pocahontas, who married Heacham's squire, John Rolfe, in 1614. And that's not all: a descendant of her son, who settled in the USA, married President Woodrow Wilson. **P**. *Open 10.00–dusk daily.*

King's Lynn, St Margaret   **14** R10
Saturday Market The opulence resulting from the medieval port's export trade in wool and cloth, is reflected in the two W towers, begun in the 12thC and with a glorious, wide window in between. A lead spire was blown down in a storm in 1741, necessitating the rebuilding of the nave. Colossally impressive are two lavishly detailed 14thC Flemish brasses. All parties wear extravagantly pointed shoes and the women wimples; small dogs snuggle in the hems of their robes, while Robert Braunche appears to be standing on a querulous bird, and his pointed toes invade the tableau of the peacock feast offered by him to Edward III in 1349. Fine leaf capitals crown the 13thC chancel pillars, and the reredos of

1889 is by Bodley. See the stalls and misericords, the 14thC screens with crocketed gables, the marvellous Baroque pulpit, ornate Snetzler organ case of 1754 and the moon clock. **P** nearby. *Open 07.00–18.30 daily.* A popular café in the S transept is *open Easter-Oct on market days, daily during the Jul festival.*

King's Lynn, St Nicholas   **14** R10
St Anne St. The long Perpendicular church was built at the beginning of the 15thC and has a 13thC tower with a charming Victorian lead spire. The S porch is like a magnificent stone fanfare of niches and panelling, taken up in wood in the nave's angel roof. Among monuments to Lynn merchants is Robinson Crusoe's grave. **P**. *Open Easter-Oct afternoons.* The lovely Georgian brick market town rewards exploration. Be sure to see the 17thC quayside Customs House, the chequer-patterned guildhall of 1421, which houses the exquisite gold and enamel King John's Cup, decorated with lords and ladies engaged in courtly pursuits, and medieval St George's Guildhall, used as a theatre.

North Creake, St Mary the Virgin 15 S11
5½m NW of Fakenham on B1355. The beautiful medieval church has a handsome Perpendicular tower. The restored chancel, built by one William Careltone in 1301, retains richly crocketed, curved and cusped sedilia, piscina and Easter Sepulchre. Near the altar, the brass figure holding a church may be the wealthy contributor to the 15thC rebuilding, Sir William Calthorpe. Wonderfully detailed, the hammerbeam nave roof is bordered by angels. Try and discern the now dim Doom painted above the chancel arch. **P**. *Open 08.00–18.00 daily.* Remains of 13thC Augustinian Creake Abbey are 1m N. All its monks died of plague in one week in 1504, saving Henry VIII the trouble of dissolving it later in the century.

North Elmham, St Mary the Virgin   **15** S11
5m N of East Dereham off B1110. The imposing Perpendicular tower is attached to a church of Norman origin, with a grand 13thC nave and a 16thC restored chancel. Notice the 13thC leaf-decorated capitals reset above the N doorway. There are beautiful paintings of saints on the rood screen, poppyheads and animals carved on benches, some medieval stained glass, handsome monuments and a pulpit of 1626, made

by the parish clerk, whose labours were rewarded by £5.3s.4d. **P.** *Open approx 09.00–dusk daily.* N of the church are the interesting ruins of an 11thC Saxon cathedral, once the seat of the bishops of Norfolk, converted into a moated manor house in the 14thC by Bishop Henry le Despencer.

North Walsham, St Nicholas   **15** T11
Market St. A craggy ruined tower forms a picturesque accompaniment to the lofty, restored medieval church. The 14thC S porch is elaborated by fine flushwork panelling and shields. Sir William Paston, a member of the family from which the famous *Paston Letters* issued, figures on a spectacular monument of 1608, of his own design, propped up on an elbow, looking out. A pelican presides over the tall, Perpendicular font cover. See the screens and the curious Communion table. **P** except summer Thur (market day). *Open Apr–Oct 10.00–16.00 Mon–Fri, 10.00–13.00 Sat, 08.00–12.00 Sun; Nov–Mar 10.00–13.00 daily.* Gardens and houses back up to the church, close to the hub of the Market Place with its octagonal timber cross. Horatio Nelson was a pupil at Paston Grammar School from 1768–71.

St Peter Mancroft, Norwich

Norwich, St Peter Mancroft   **15** T10
Market Pl. The 15thC church stands in splendour above the Market Place, with a lavishly panelled, substantial tower arched over the street. It is crowned by nice turrets and a charming Victorian Gothic spirelet which is a little lost amid the spectacle. The clerestory forms a magnificent wall of light in the lofty interior, meeting the wonderful boss-studded roof in which the hammerbeams are covered by coving. A fine panoply of 15thC stained glass fills the E window. Allow time for the impressive canopy over the font, the brasses and monuments, including that to Sir Thomas Browne, author of *Religio Medici*, and the outstanding Mancroft Heritage Exhibition, displaying objects of great interest associated with the church. **P.** *Open 10.00–17.00 Mon, Tue & Thur-Sat, from 07.00 Wed; 08.00–19.30 Sun.* With its twisting streets and alleys, the great castle keep or the cathedral spire rising up from around every corner, Norwich is the ideal place to explore on foot. The magnificent Norman cathedral was begun in 1096 by Herbert de Losinga on the Pope's order, as a punishment for the sin of simony and the prelate performed his penance superlatively.

Ranworth, St Helen   **15** U10
9m NE of Norwich off B1140. The fine Perpendicular church and tower command wide views across the Bure valley Broads. A gracefully soaring tower arch heads the nave, at the end of which the 15thC rood screen gives a glowing testimony to medieval craftsmanship. It is carved with delicate cusps and opulently gilded and painted with apostles and saints wearing richly coloured robes. To either side are equally beautiful altars, divided from the rood screen by painted projecting wings, which are joined to posts by dainty flying buttresses. Note St Michael's flame-coloured wings and robe and gold-feathered legs and arms. A further treasure is the cantor's desk, with a plainsong Gloria painted on the front and an eagle and the opening words of St John's Gospel on the back. Also in the church's possession is an exquisite medieval illuminated Antiphoner. *Open (inc tower) 09.00–one hr before dusk daily.*

Salle, St Peter and St Paul   **15** T11
10m NE of East Dereham off B1145. A marvellous church built on a grand scale by local magnates, including the Boleyns,

in the 15thC. Rich ornamentation distinguishes the tower. There are fine, turreted two-storey porches (that on the N the most ornate), an angel-studded nave roof and bosses with biblical scenes on the boarded chancel roof. Faces and monsters are carved on the stalls, faces and flowers on the misericords. See too the poppyhead benches, medieval stained glass, screens, the Seven Sacraments font – its amazing 12ft cover complete with pulley – a Perpendicular pulpit with Jacobean extensions and notable 15thC brasses, all forming a perfect picture of the period. **P.** *Open daylight hours daily.*

Shelton, St Mary   **15** T10
7m W of Bungay off A140. Sir Ralph Shelton built the stately Perpendicular church late in the 15thC and left orders for its completion in his will. Of distinctive redbrick, divided into diamonds by dark bricks and emphasised by pale stone dressings, it contrasts with the earlier flint tower. Outsize gargoyles stare out from the S aisle and the clerestory is very imposing. 15thC donors make a prominent appearance in stained glass in the wonderfully harmonious interior, and the Royal Arms of William III sumptuously proclaim his regality. Close connections are said to have existed with Henry VIII's court and Elizabeth I visited here. **P.** *Open 09.00–17.00 daily.*

Snettisham, St Mary   **14** R11
4m SE of Hunstanton on A149. Originally a cruciform church, the magnificent tower and spire stand at the E end, without the chancel which once extended 40ft beyond. Exquisite Decorated tracery flowers in the W window, creating a memorable front together with the side turrets and porch. *The Shrimp and the Anemone* by L. P. Hartley describes its impact. See the seats circling the tall nave pillars, the 13thC saunce, or sanctus bell, the wafer oven, formerly used for baking the Communion bread, and the Jacobean family brass. **P.** *Open 09.30–19.00 Mon–Sat, 08.00–20.00 Sun.*

South Creake, Our Lady St Mary   **15** S11
5m NW of Fakenham on B1355. A beautiful, spacious church in a streamside village. The hammerbeam roof has splendid angels at its brim, gazing into the white, light-filled Perpendicular nave, their wings and colour restored to them in recent years. The 15thC rood screen has a richly

embellished ogee arch and delicate, crisply carved tracery, complementing the E window tracery of the 13thC chancel. Chests of iron and oak stand under the tower. Also preserved is a funeral bier, for which £1.6s.6d. was paid in 1687, and 15thC stained glass in the aisles. **P.** *Open summer 08.00–20.00 daily, winter to 16.30.*

South Lopham, St Andrew   **11** T9
5m W of Diss on B1113. A central Norman tower of substance and powerful presence presides over the largely 14thC church, Perpendicular flushwork battlements crowning its four arcaded stages. There is evidence of a preceding Saxon church. Examine the fine tracery on the font and the carved bench ends. **P.** *Open 09.00–17.00 or dusk daily.*

St Peter, Walpole St Peter

Walpole St Peter, St Peter   **14** R10
5m NE of Wisbech off A47. This magnificent marshland village church was built late in the 14thC. A richly detailed exterior includes rood-stair turrets with tiny windows, panelled battlements, gargoyles, a splendid S porch and a vaulted processional passage at the E end. N and S doors are decorated with tracery. Delightful features congregate in the chancel, where the windows have prominent ogee-arched niches between them and small bosses decorate the sedilia and piscina. Remarkable screens include the lovely parclose screen and the 17thC classical style screen. Jacobean furnishings include benches and box pews, the pulpit, and the marvellous font cover. Not to be missed either are the chandelier of 1701 and the sentry box style moveable shelter for the rector's accommodation at wet funerals. **P.** *Open 08.00–dusk Mon–Wed, Fri & Sat, from 07.30 Thur & Sun.*

Wickhampton, St Andrew   **15** U10
8m W of Great Yarmouth off B1140. Seated
figures form pinnacles on the 14thC
tower, which commands a view across
the marshes towards Great Yarmouth.
Delightful heads are carved either side of
the S doorway, whose door has an
ironwork foliated cross round the
knocker, and leads into a largely 13thC
and Norman interior. Of supreme
interest are the early wall paintings,
among them that of the allegory of the
Three Quick and the Three Dead. Ornate
gabled recesses in the chancel harbour a
medieval knight, heart in hands, and
wimpled lady. **P.** *Open daylight hours
daily.* Tall Berney Arms Mill is a highlight
in the marshland view.

Wilby, All Saints   **15** T10
8½m NW of Diss off A11. A fine,
Decorated church whose furnishings,
renewed after a fire in 1633, give the
interior an impressive Carolean stamp.
Observe the baluster theme occurring in
W gallery, screen and Communion rail.
Benches, on which poppyheads are

exchanged for fleurs-de-lis, and family
pews are addressed by a three-decker
pulpit. Fittingly, Charles I's Royal
Arms reign over all. **P.** *Open daylight
hours daily.*

Wymondham, St Mary and   **15** T10
St Thomas
In a graceful town with a charming
market cross dated 1616. The
magnificent, formerly monastic, medieval
church has two proud towers,
representing a certain discord between
monks and townspeople, who divided
the church in half. Admire especially the
lavishly adorned 15thC N porch, the
hammerbeam roof, gloriously arrayed
with angels and starry bosses, above the
impressive Norman nave, the N aisle
roof, the font on which lions, wild men
and angels figure, Comper's sumptuous
gilt reredos, and the unusual 16thC
turreted terracotta monument with a
Renaissance character. A most rare
treasure is the 13thC Corporas Case. **P.**
*Open Easter–Oct 10.00–18.00 daily, winter
11.00–15.00.*

◁ CAMBRIDGESHIRE ▷

Alconbury, St Peter and St Paul   **10** P9
4m NW of Huntingdon off A1. Old cottages
fringe the village green, where a brook
babbles under a 15thC bridge and the
stately church dominates the scene. The
church is a pure expression of Early
English Gothic, most beautiful in its
graceful tower and broach-spire and the
chancel, which is decorated by rich
arcading. Look up at the angels flying
round the Perpendicular roof. Y-tracery
distinguishes the clerestory and the N
aisle has 14thC windows and a fine
Perpendicular font. *Open 09.00–17.00
Mon–Sat, 07.30–18.45 Sun.*

Barnack, St John Baptist   **14** O10
3m SE of Stamford off B1443. In its lower
stages the superb tower is Saxon,
characterised by long-and-short work,
pilaster strips and windows of
intriguingly different shapes and sizes.
Saxon too is the wondrously fine carving
of Christ seated in Majesty. The 13thC S
porch is magnificently detailed, and the
remarkable font, adorned with leaves and
prominent flowers, is of the same period.
Panelled canopies and a spectacular E
window enrich the 14thC chancel. The

monuments are worth examining. **P.**
Open 09.00–dusk daily. Barnack stone was
quarried extensively in the Middle Ages
and Peterborough and Ely cathedrals are
built of it. The quarry, started by the
Romans, is to the S. The village is
picturesque, and 2m NE is splendid
Elizabethan Burghley House, where
glorious ceilings and silver fireplaces
feature among the treasures.

Buckden, St Mary   **10** P9
4m SW of Huntingdon on A1. The 15thC
church steeple and the brick tower of the
former palace of the bishops of Lincoln
soar in memorable juxtaposition. The
battlemented and pinnacled S porch
displays a rich feast of medieval carving,
including an animal frieze outside and a
star-vault with bosses inside. Angels of
wood and stone decorate the chancel
roof. 16thC Flemish panels of the Passion
may be studied on the readers' desks.
The Jacobean pulpit is handsome and
impressive monuments include an ornate
19thC Gothic triptych. Two uncles of the
nine-day queen, Lady Jane Grey, are
buried in the churchyard. **P.** *Open 09.00–
18.00 Mon–Wed, Fri & Sat, from 07.15*

Thur; 07.30–19.30 Sun. Dashing coaching inns, timber-framed and brick, face one another in the attractive High St.

St Mary the Virgin, Burwell

Holy Sepulchre, Cambridge

Burwell, St Mary the Virgin　　**10** R9
10m NE of Cambridge on B1102. Ely Cathedral inspired the octagonal Perpendicular tower top, which crowns a Norman base. Within all is light and loftiness, arches soaring slenderly to the clerestory and a beautiful rose window sparkling above sumptuous tracery over the chancel arch. Ornate canopied niches enrich the chancel walls and angels the roof. The aisle roofs also harbour angels and the nave roof is carved with bosses and friezes. A palimpsest brass shows a 16thC abbot on one side and parts of a canon and deacon on the other. **P.** *Open 09.00–18.00 Mon–Sat, 07.30–19.00 Sun.* To the W is the site of 12thC Burwell Castle, which was never completed, but whose moat remains. Handsome and interesting buildings compose the village.

Cambridge, Holy Sepulchre　　**10** R9
Bridge St. As one of only four in England, the round church exercises all the magnetism of a rarity. Abbot Reinald of Ramsey Abbey granted land to build a church to 'Randolf with the Beard of Cambridge . . . and others of the Fraternity of the Holy Sepulchre', c1130. Though much restored in 1841, the round nave is impressively Norman in character, with eight powerful pillars surrounded by an ambulatory, where zigzag is prominent on part of the rib-vaulting. The fine N aisle and choir roofs rest on angels. Seats beckon invitingly in the garden, rose-arboured in summer. **P** nearby. *Open 09.00–dusk Mon–Sat, 08.00–18.30 Sun.*

Cambridge , St Bene't　　**10** R9
Bene't St. Amazing to reflect, the church was here before any other building in the city and King Canute reigned when it was built in the 11thC. Saxon fabric is visible in the walls but the tower is the outstanding remaining Saxon structure with long-and-short work ascending the angles. The tower arch inside is also complete, and spectacular monsters usher you through. The body of the church was rebuilt c1300 and enlarged in the 19thC. *Open 07.00–22.00 Mon–Fri, to 21.00 Sat, 07.30–22.30 Sun.* Visitors are welcome to wander around the magnificent colleges and grounds, but there may be restrictions during term time. The willow-decked 'Backs', sloping to the peaceful riverside, make a perfect picnicking spot for a lazy summer's day. Punts and poles are available to the intrepid.

Cambridge, St Mary the Great　　**10** R9
St Mary's St. University degree ceremonies were held in this, the university church, until 1730, and university sermons are preached

regularly. Cambridge men who led the Reformation spread their views from here. Tower and church rise in Perpendicular splendour reminiscent of great Suffolk churches, although the tower-top turret pinnacles are late additions of 1608. Inside, elegant arcades soar up to spandrels decorated with blank tracery and to the beautiful nave roof, enriched with bosses, whose timbers were given by Henry VII. Exquisitely carved stone niches either side of the window and the gilded wooden Christ in Majesty by Alan Durst, 1960, form a fine focus at the E end. Observe the charming ornamentation of the font, the screens leading into the chapels from the aisles, and the alabaster monument to eminent physician, Dr William Butler, d1618, who treated James I when he fell from his horse at Newmarket. *Open 07.15–18.30 Mon–Wed, from 07.45 Thur & Fri, from 09.00 Sat; 07.45–19.30 Sun, to 16.30 Dec & Jan.* The Gothic glory of King's College Chapel rises opposite.

Castor, St Kyneburgha　　　**10** O10
4½m W of Peterborough on A47. In a riverside village built upon the remains of a vast 3rdC Roman mansion, whose reception and dining rooms stood behind the church, it is not surprising that Roman brick appears in the N transept.

St Kyneburgha, Norman tower

The church's dedication to St Kyneburgha is unique. She was a daughter of Penda, King of Mercia, who founded Peterborough Abbey. The central Norman tower is mightily impressive and unforgettable in its lavish ornamentation of arches. Parapet and spire were added in the 14thC. The ancient inscription over the priest's door in the chancel records the consecration of the church in 1124. Inside, take time to scrutinise the capitals of the tower pillars, with intertwining patterns and a variety of subjects, including scenes of vigorous action. A refashioning of the church took place in the 13thC. Look in the chancel for the Saxon carving of a saint and in the N aisle at the 14thC wall paintings depicting the story of St Catherine. **P.** *Open 08.00–18.15 Mon–Sat, 10.00–19.30 Sun.*

Cherry Hinton, St Andrew　　　**10** R9
2m SE of Cambridge off A1307. The Early English chancel is the most glorious part of the church and the nave shares in its grace. Rich details in the chancel include the beautifully arched twin lancet windows with elegant shafts between, the lovely double piscina and the sedilia. The E window is a Tudor insertion into the pure 13thC design. Admire the restored 15thC rood screen. **P.** *Open 07.30–17.45 Mon, Thur & Fri, to 21.00 Tue, Wed & Sun, 09.00–17.45 Sat.*

Godmanchester, St Mary the Virgin　　　**10** P9
Though of the late date of 1623, the fine tower pursues the Perpendicular style successfully. Built of brown cobbles, the 13thC-15thC church has a very remarkable mass dial, in the form of a rose window, on one of the buttresses of the 13thC chancel. Delightful animal carvings figure on the 15thC misericords. The rood screen and the reredos are by Bodley. Details of a murderer's trial and execution are recorded on the gravestone of his 21-year-old virgin victim as a warning. **P.** *Open 09.00–17.00 Mon, Thur & Sat, from 07.00 Tue, from 08.00 Wed & Fri; 07.30–19.30 Sun.* Once a Roman town, Godmanchester has a picturesque core, where Queen Elizabeth's grammar school of 1559 meets the Victorian town hall. Ducks, swans, islands and the captivating Chinese bridge of 1827 ornament the river Ouse, and half-timbered houses the town, including proud Tudor House, declaring its date of 1600–3, which brings it to the brink of Stuart England.

Grantchester, St Andrew **10** P9
and St Mary
2m SW of Cambridge off A603.
Immortalised by First World War poet
Rupert Brooke, whose poem about life at
the Old Vicarage captured the
quintessence of nostalgia in its wistful
musings. Check whether the clock still
stands at ten to three. Above it an 18thC
copper-gilt weathercock revolves jauntily.
Ancient masonry survives from a
predecessor, but the church's chief glory
resides in the Decorated chancel, which
presents itself magnificently through
distinctive flowing window tracery and
niches with nodding ogee arches. Rupert
Brooke is commemorated on the
churchyard War Memorial. **P** nearby.
Open 08.30–dusk daily. Meadow-fringed,
the village is a punt ride from
Cambridge.

Isleham, St Andrew **10** R9
7m N of Newmarket on B1104. Do not be
deterred by the undistinguished 19thC
tower, which is married to a fine and
spacious Decorated church, beautifully
refashioned during Henry VII's reign.
Admire the blank arcading inside the
gabled S porch. The tall clerestory makes
a wonderful flourish, complemented by
the roof, adorned with angels. Shields of
the Peyton family who built both appear
in the spandrels of the nave arches.
Quite a congregation of Peytons can be
met in handsome effigy, including
Thomas, d1484, and his two wives,
whose brasses are elaborately detailed,
one wife wearing a richly patterned dress
and both a haughty demeanour. Be sure
to examine the marvellously inventive
carving of the Jacobean altar rail. **P.** *Open
08.30–17.50 Mon–Sat, from 06.30 Sun.* A
small, simple and rare early Norman
priory church is a close by.

Kimbolton, St Andrew **10** O9
8m SW of Huntingdon on A45. Kimbolton
Castle and the medieval church
command the small, interesting town
from either end. Little heads look out
from the top of the beautiful 14thC
tower. Inside, 13thC arcades stretch up
to a 14thC clerestory and fine stone
corbels support the roof. A wonderful
screen leads into the S chapel, retaining
four paintings of saints, including an
exquisite St Edmund. Carved figures
decorate both the Perpendicular chapel
roofs. The grand marble monument to
the First Earl of Manchester, d1642,
exercises dominance over abundant
memorial tablets to lesser mortals. **P.**

Open 08.00–18.00 daily. Vanbrugh
remodelled Tudor Kimbolton Castle in
1707–10 and Robert Adam added the
gatehouse late in the 18thC. Catherine of
Aragon, Henry VIII's first wife, lived
here and puts in an occasional ghostly
appearance in the Queen's room.

Kirtling, All Saints **10** R9
5m SE of Newmarket off B1063. Tudor
Kirtling Tower and moat are impressive
neighbours to the largely Perpendicular
church. Christ sits in Majesty above the
effervescent zigzag carving round the
Norman doorway. The door retains
Norman ironwork. Examine the
delightful details of the niches either side
of the N aisle E window and the head
corbels supporting the roof. The first
Baron North, d1564, builder of Kirtling
Tower and of the fine brick chapel in
which his marble monument stands,
helped handle the spoils of the
Dissolution and skilfully parried the
political obstacles of serving under Mary
and Elizabeth I. Greater decorative éclat
and less taste characterise the monument
of the second Baron North, d1600. The
North family hatchments are well worth
looking at too. **P.** *Open daylight hours
daily.*

St Wendreda, angel roof

March, St Wendreda **10** P10
Church St. Justly famous for the glorious
hovering hosts of angels in its double
hammerbeam roof, the Decorated and
Perpendicular features of the church form
a beautiful vessel for them. From the
19thC chancel, gaze through tier upon
tier of feathery outspread wings
illuminated by the clerestory, to the tall
tower arch and lovely flowing tracery of
the W window. Notice the fine
decoration of the exterior. **P.** *Open 09.00–
dusk daily.*

Over, St Mary 10 P9
9m NW of Cambridge off B1050. Highly
enjoyable gargoyles command the fine
14thC S side of the church, along which
a delightful ballflower frieze runs and an
exquisite porch projects. A medieval
sanctus bell hangs above the E end of the
nave. The ornately embellished interior
has castellated shafts on the
Perpendicular nave pillars, while niches
with little figures support the roof. Stone
seats extend round much of the walls. A
small man in a big hat and a dragon
devouring a man are among the
engaging carvings on the arms of the
chancel stalls. The Perpendicular rood
screen retains its vault on the E side.
Note the charming ogee canopy which
forms the Jacobean pulpit's sounding
board, and the octagonal font. **P.** *Open
07.30–17.15 Mon–Sat, to 20.00 Sun.* Next
to the church is the handsome 18thC
vicarage.

Ramsey, St Thomas a Becket 10 P9
High St. Built spaciously as the abbey
guest house, or hospitium, in the late
12thC, the conversion to a church confers
great interest on it. The Norman chancel
is rib-vaulted and the nave arcades verge
upon the 13thC in their details. Examine
the lectern, which has openwork tracery
and a rotating top, and the stained glass
by Morris and Co. The tower of 1672
incorporates 13thC fabric, and this,
together with the presence of a 13thC
font pinpoints the century of
transformation from a guest house. **P.**
*Open 08.30–19.30 Mon, Tue & Thur, to
20.00 Wed, to 21.00 Fri, from 09.00 Sat;
07.45–20.00 Sun.* Part of the gatehouse
forms a remarkable relic of the important
medieval abbey.

St Neots, St Mary the Virgin 10 P9
Church St. The tower of this sumptuous
Perpendicular church is glorious and
shares characteristics with Somerset
towers. Its ascent is punctuated by
friezes and decorated buttresses ending
in pinnacles, and culminates in
marvellous corner pinnacles and an
elaborate parapet. Inside, it is hard to
take your eyes off the roofs, which are
carved with an enchanting profusion of
animals, birds and angels. But lower
them to admire the screens, especially
the W screen of the Lady Chapel, carved
with a beautiful trail of vine leaves and
grapes. And be sure to see the
elaborately detailed monument of 1893 by
F. A. Walters, in the chancel. **P.** *Open
summer 09.00–18.30 Mon–Sat, to 19.30*

Sun; winter to 16.45 Mon–Sat. The
riverside market town has a number of
pleasing buildings.

Soham, St Andrew 10 R9
5m SE of Ely on A142. Sumptuously
crowned with battlements and pinnacles
decked with flushwork, the
Perpendicular tower is a stately sight.
Flushwork also decorates the N porch
which is finely panelled inside. The
arches of the former late Norman
crossing tower are an arresting feature of
the interior, but even more so is the
magnificent roof of alternating tie-beams
and hammerbeams with angels.
Rewarding too are the 14thC chancel,
whose E window has gorgeous flowing
tracery, the charmingly crested and
traceried screen that leads into the N
chapel and the poppyheaded and other
bench ends. **P.** *Open 09.00–17.00 Mon–
Sat, 08.00–19.30 Sun.*

Sutton, St Andrew 10 R9
6m W of Ely on A412. The tower of the
ridgetop church has a wonderful late
14thC two-stage octagonal lantern,
inspired by that of Ely Cathedral.
Gargoyles guard the clerestory and S
aisle with its beautiful vaulted porch, in
which prominent bosses figure, as do the
arms of 14thC bishops Barnet and
Arundel of Ely, who built the entire
church opulently. Blank arcading covers
the aisle and chancel walls and niches
flank the lavish E window. Head corbels
look out from the lofty arcades and the
tower vault is decorated with bosses.
Open 08.00–16.00 daily.

St Andrew, Sutton

Swavesey, St Andrew 10 P9
6m NW of Cambridge off A604. The church
presents an impressive 14thC S side, in
which the fine S door heralds a spacious
interior. See the prettily traceried
windows of the aisle, the admirable

roofs, the splendid sedilia and piscina in the chancel, and the grand procession of medieval bench ends, together with Victorian imitations, carved with figures and animals. A further embellishment is the monument to Lady Cutt, d1631, watched over by exquisite life-size angels. *Open 09.00–18.00 daily.*

Thorney, Abbey church of   **14** P10
St Mary and St Botolph
5m NE of Peterborough on A47. Originally founded in the 7thC on what was an island in the fens, the Saxon abbey was rebuilt by the Normans in 1085–1108, on a sumptuous scale. Vandalism followed the Dissolution and what remained was restored as the parish church in 1638. This consists of part of the nave and the magnificent W front, whose impressive octagonal Norman turrets are crowned by Perpendicular battlements and linked by a screen containing statues. The E end is 19thC, with a splendid stained glass window copied from Canterbury. **P.** *Open summer 09.00–18.00 Mon–Sat, from 08.00 Sun; winter to dusk.* Handsome houses neighbour the church and a 19thC water tower in Jacobean style is a rival for visual supremacy.

Tilbrook, All Saints   **10** O9
6m NE of Rushden on A45. Crane your neck to spot the crawling man up among the gargoyles on the fine 14thC tower. The tower is united to a handsome, largely Decorated church, the W part of whose arcade is Norman. Above the S porch entrance a man whips an animal. The glorious 16thC rood screen retains its vault and paintings of saints. Pause too to admire the 15thC N aisle roof adorned with angels. **P.** *Open summer 07.30–20.00 daily, winter to 17.45.*

Trumpington, St Mary   **10** R9
and St Michael
Suburb S of Cambridge on A1301. Beneath a fine ogee arch lies a perfect medieval knight in brass, wearing chain mail, shield and sword. He is probably Sir Roger de Trumpington, d1326, and the brass is one of the oldest in England. A memorial tablet by Eric Gill is also worth examining. Grace characterises the nave arcades. What remains of the rood screen is opulently detailed. Fine fragments of medieval stained glass are in the chancel and the E window tracery is exquisite. Inspect the double piscina, the roof with carved bosses, to which original colouring was restored in 1964, and medieval graffiti on the blocked N doorway. This led to a chapel now demolished, whose piscina can be seen outside. **P.** *Open 08.00–21.00 Mon, Wed, Fri & Sun, to dusk Tue, Thur & Sat.* The village cross commemorating the First World War is by Eric Gill.

Willingham, St Mary and   **10** P9
All Saints
7m NW of Cambridge on B1050. An octagonal spire handsomely crowns the 14thC tower. Relics of a Norman doorway are preserved in the S porch. Embellishing the nave is a marvellous Perpendicular double hammerbeam roof, whose assembly of angels creates a celebratory air. Be sure to pay attention to the fine screens, one of which is patterned and coloured enchantingly, and to the medieval wall paintings, which include the Visitation on the S and a Doom above the chancel arch. N of the chancel is a small and delightfully detailed sacristy. **P.** *Open 08.00–18.00 daily.*

◁ LINCOLNSHIRE ▷

Ancaster, St Martin   **14** O11
6m N of Grantham on A153. On Roman Ermine Street, the village has yielded thousands of coins current in the Camp of Causennae, whose remaining earth ramparts and ditches, near the church, tell the forceful tale of Roman occupation. Coffins reputed to be Roman can be seen in the churchyard and porch. The church has a Norman chancel, arcade and font, an impressive Decorated steeple, and a Perpendicular display of battlements and pinnacles on the S aisle.

P. *Open 08.00–dusk daily.* Finds from Causennae, including pottery and sculptured goddesses, as well as the coins, are housed in Grantham Museum.

Bag Enderby, St Margaret   **14** P12
6m E of Horncastle off A158. Set in a sylvan landscape deep in the Wolds, money was left for building the charming little church of local greenstone by Albinus de Enderby, who died in 1407; an inscription in the nave records the fact. An iron boss, reputedly from a

Saxon shield, decorates the door. On the Perpendicular font are carvings of the pietà, emblems of the Passion and a seated figure with a lute. There are lovely fragments of medieval glass, a rood screen, and monuments that bring to life the ancient inhabitants of the now thinly populated village. **P.** *Open daily.*

Belton, St Peter and St Paul   **14** O11
1m N of Grantham on A607. In the small, much-restored church a great Norman pillar, incised with spectacular diamond decoration, upholds the arches; the font has a delightful assembly of naively carved figures, including a bird, a bishop, a squirrel and a knight; and an imposing congregation of Brownlows, lords of Belton House, await resurrection on magnificent monuments. However Sophia, Lady Brownlow, d1814, by Antonio Canova, is commemorated by a statue of a Grecian woman pointing upwards, presumably to indicate the present whereabouts of the deceased. Sir R. Westmacott sculptured the grieving girl kneeling by a broken column in memory of the first Lord Brownlow, d1807, and J. Bacon made the delightful tablet showing a maiden with a lamb in 1793. **P.** *Open summer 09.00–18.00 daily, winter to early afternoon.* Belton House is a very handsome 17thC neighbour with a splendid interior and the model village of 19thC cottages is in Tudor and Jacobean style.

St Peter and St Paul, Norman font

Boston, St Botolph   **14** P11
The majesty tower, inaptly called the 'Stump', commands the river. Its crowning octagonal lantern makes a glorious exploration of refined forms in dainty openwork parapets and flying buttresses, tall windows and slender pinnacles. The Decorated church is splendid in its entirety. Having entered through one of the extravagantly detailed doors, first step under the tower for a view of the soaring star-vault. Look up at the flower frieze making its way round the top of the nave and chancel. The misericords of the late 14thC stalls provide fascinating reflections of the medieval mind in subjects whimsical, winsome and gruesome, such as an organ-playing bear, a unicorn and virgin, a mermaid and sailors, wolves eating a man, and bear-baiting. Examine the brasses, alabaster effigies, and the Tournai marble slab, incised with a praying wool merchant from Münster, Wissel Smalenburg, d1340. Also, the Victorian Gothic font by Pugin, the fine pulpit and the Victorian stained glass in the E window. *Open 08.45–16.30 Mon–Sat.* Boston was a prestigious port in the Middle Ages and the partly rebuilt 15thC Guildhall is a picturesque relic of its prosperity. Now a museum, exhibits include the iron-gated cells in which the first Lincolnshire Pilgrim Fathers were held after their abortive attempt to leave for America in 1607.

Bourne, St Peter and St Paul   **14** O11
The impressive Norman nave remains from the abbey church founded in 1138. A grand design for twin W towers was initiated in the 13thC, then abandoned until one of the towers was given a Perpendicular crown. A clerestory was also added in the 15thC and the chancel was rebuilt in the 19thC. The chandelier of 1742 is a sumptuous surprise. *Open 07.30–17.30 Tue–Sun.* Reputedly the birthplace of Hereward the Wake, the evidence connecting Hereward with the de Wake family, who held a Norman castle here, is slight. The Catholic Digby family, who were involved in the Gunpowder Plot, once owned Red Hall, a mansion whose dignity is diminished by proximity to the railway.

Caistor, St Peter and St Paul   **14** O13
8m N of Market Rasen on A46. The tower has Saxon, Norman, 13thC and 14thC parts and the 13thC S doorway is spectacularly detailed. Medieval effigies include those of a knight and lady. The

Gad Whip is a fascinating relic of an old custom of obscure origin. **P.** *Open 09.00–17.00 Mon–Sat, 12.15–18.00 Sun.*

**Cherry Willingham, St Peter   14 O12
and St Paul**
2m E of Lincoln off A158. A small Georgian gem built in 1753, with classical columns and pediment round the doorway, and a lantern with a charming ogee top. The unelaborate interior is pleasing and its most prominent feature is the handsome reredos. Equally restrained is the monument to the founder, Thomas Becke, d1757. *Open 08.00–19.30 Mon–Fri, 10.00–19.00 Sat, 08.00–19.00 Sun.*

Corby Glen, St John   14 O11
9m SE of Grantham on A151. In a village which has held an annual Sheep Fair since 1238, it is fitting that the 14thC and 15thC wall paintings in the fine medieval church should include shepherds (wearing Robin Hood style jerkins) on the way to Bethlehem with their sheep, which are painted with enchanting naivety. A giant St Christopher and a Warning to False Swearers, in which devils and debonair youths figure, are among other subjects. Beautiful 15thC stained glass shows St John holding a palm branch. Not far from the porch lies auctioneer Joseph Wright, d1835, with a touchingly apt epitaph:

'At length old Death with visage queer
Assumed Joe's trade of auctioneer,
Made him the lot to practise on –
With Going, Going, and anon
He knock'd him down, so poor Joe's
      gone.'

P. *Open 09.00–dusk daily.* Beside the church are the vicarage built in 1619 and the manor house, which is the present vicarage. The august Stuart grammar school is now the library.

**Crowland, St Mary,   14 P10
St Bartholomew and St Guthlac**
7½m N of Peterborough on A1073. Fenland Croyland Abbey, reputed burial place of Hereward the Wake, was founded in 716. It suffered Danish sackings, during one of which Abbot Theodore was slain while praying at the altar for his assailants' souls, fires, and even an earthquake. (Preserved in the church since the 9thC, the Abbot's skull, in which the deadly sword thrust remained visible, was stolen in 1982). Stability was achieved in the 12thC when the monks enjoyed prosperity and entertained kings and nobles. Work from the period is on the S side of the great W front; the central

portal and statuary are 13thC. The Perpendicular parochial N aisle and the tower remain intact from the abbey's destruction at the Dissolution and Civil War. Especially evocative of former splendour is the tall Norman arch spanning the empty fenland sky. **P.** *Open 09.00–dusk Mon–Sat, 07.30–dusk Sun.* Ascend the tower for a fine view. Be sure to visit ancient, triangular Trinity Bridge, over which a seated figure of Christ presides, probably formerly on the W front of the abbey.

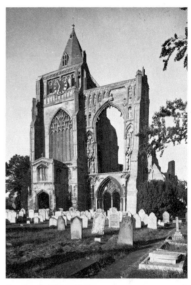

Croyland Abbey, W front

**Donington, St Mary   14 P11
and the Holy Rood**
Church St. Heads and gargoyles congregate outside the church. The base of the stately Decorated tower forms a grand vaulted entrance porch, while its tall spire commands the surrounding fenland. Other fine Decorated features are the ornate W doorway and lovely E window of the S aisle. Perpendicular details include the lofty nave arcades with castellated capitals and the clerestory. A tablet in the chancel commemorates the explorer, Captain Matthew Flinders, d1814, as does a stained glass window of 1980 in the N aisle. What looks like a sentry box is a genteel Georgian invention for the parson's graveside shelter at wet funerals. **P.** *Open 09.00–17.00 daily.*

Edenham, St Michael   **14** O11

1m NW of Bourne on A151. Prominent pinnacles crown the Perpendicular tower and imps feature in the rich decoration of the S porch. A 13thC doorway leads into a medieval interior, much distinguished by the survival of two sculptured Saxon ornaments, or roundels, above the 13thC S arcade. The greatest monumental sculptors of the day, including Cheere, Roubiliac and Nollekens, had a hand in honouring successive members of the Bertie family, Lords Willoughby d'Eresby and Dukes and Earls of Ancaster, whose splendid monuments form a large, patriarchal assembly. Robert Bertie died commanding Charles I's army at the battle of Edgehill in 1642, at the outset of the Civil War. Monuments to Victorian nobles spill out into the cedar-clad churchyard. Angels and little green dragons figure in the restored 15thC nave roof. **P.** *Open daylight hours daily.* Charles Kingsley is popularly supposed to have written *Hereward the Wake* in the Georgian vicarage. 2m W is magnificent Grimsthorpe Castle, whose N front is to Sir John Vanbrugh's design of 1722 and where his Great Hall makes a spectacular show of two-tiered arcading.

Folkingham, St Andrew   **14** O11

8m S of Sleaford on A15. The splendid Perpendicular tower with a fanfare of friezes, battlements and 16 pinnacles on top, crowns the scenic hillside village. The S porch is similarly enriched. In the earlier medieval interior are a beautiful rood screen, an 18thC font and the village stocks. **P.** *Open daylight hours daily.* Remains of a staid 19thC House of Correction, which received those condemned at the Quarter Sessions court once held here, stands where Norman Folkingham Castle towered. As well as punishment, the presence of the Quarter Sessions conferred a gracious air on the Market Square, prominent in which is a 17thC coaching inn.

Friskney, All Saints   **14** R12

7m S of Skegness off A52. The grand Perpendicular marshland church has a Norman base to its tower and an impressive chancel with gargoyles and pinnacles outside and endearing little men carved either side of the E window inside. There are fine screens, a Commonwealth pulpit and sounding board and interesting 14thC wall paintings, unfortunately faded. Animals guard the base of the churchyard cross. **P.** *Open daylight hours daily.*

Gainsborough, All Saints   **13** N13

Church St. The Perpendicular tower is attached to a nave and chancel of 1736–44 in classical Georgian style. Grace and light characterise the interior, which is furnished with galleries, box pews, a sumptuous chandelier of 1723 and a remarkable 19thC pulpit, with a Corinthian capital at the base and a pretty ironwork parapet. **P.** *Open 09.00– 17.00 Mon–Sat.* The Old Hall is a venerable and exceedingly interesting timber-framed and brick neighbour.

Glentworth, St Michael and   **14** O13
All Angels

7½m E of Gainsborough on B1398. The 11thC tower was built before William conquered in 1066. The E window and screen are Tudor and the nave was rebuilt in the 18thC. Sir Christopher Wray, d1592, builder of now derelict Glentworth Hall, and Chief Justice of England under Elizabeth I, appears in effigy with his wife on a magnificent alabaster monument in the chancel. Their son kneels above and daughters wearing ruffs and farthingales, but without hands, below. Also in the chancel is a white marble monument to Elizabeth Saunderson, d1714, in the centre of which three cherubs' heads cluster, while charming, plump putti lament either side. **P.** *Open daylight hours daily.*

Grantham, St Wulfram   **13** O11

Church St. The tower and spire of matchless magnificence enhance the fine townscape. Stop to look at the variety of carved heads and figures assembled outside the church; some are fiendish, others amusing. The Norman core of the church is seen in the central pillars of the nave, but Decorated and Perpendicular styles predominate. Take time to examine the Decorated tracery in the windows of the S side of the Lady Chapel, which displays wonderfully inventive forms, almost capriciously explorative from window to window. The Perpendicular font is sumptuously carved with biblical scenes and has a colourful Victorian Gothic cover which opens to reveal statuettes of saints. The church has an interesting chained library, but lost its Communion plate in 1808, when a reward was offered for the suspects, 'one on a Bay Galloway, blind of one Eye, and the other on a Chestnut Galloway, one Eye of which was quite out'; which disadvantages you might think would have aided their capture, but didn't. And

St Wulfram, Grantham

when G. G. Scott restored the church in the 19thC, all the fittings and furnishings were auctioned. *Open 09.00–18.00 Mon, Thur, Fri & Sat, to 13.00 Tue.* Grantham is a very ancient and rewarding town and has in the Angel and Royal Hotel one of England's finest medieval inns, with a memorable 15thC front. Parts of the building date back to the 12thC, when it is believed to have been a manorial hall. Richard III signed the Duke of Buckingham's death warrant in it.

Greatford, St Thomas a Becket   14 O10
9m NW of Peterborough off A15. A stately 13thC and 14thC tower dominates the church. Notice the fine leaf capitals on the Decorated porch entrance. Especially remarkable inside are the Decorated squint and piscina with six oak leaves delightfully carved round the drain, and the memorial by Nollekens to Francis Willis, d1807, who treated George III's first attack of lunacy. A 4thC Roman stone coffin, excavated from a local field, is in the churchyard. **P** nearby. *Open 08.00–18.00 daily.* 17thC Greatford Hall burnt down in 1922, but was faithfully rebuilt.

Holbeach, All Saints   14 P11
7m E of Spalding on A151. Tulip fields and flower festivals in Apr-May garland the beautiful Decorated church with additional glory. A splendid steeple, an

ornate N porch entrance flanked by two round towers, and a sanctus bellcote distinguish the exterior. Fine flowing tracery in the chancel windows and lofty arcades and clerestory are notable features inside. Pay your respects to the late 14thC stone effigy of Sir Humphrey Littlebury, on a tomb-chest with ogee-arched niches, and two 15thC brasses, one of a headless knight. **P.** *Open 08.00–17.30 daily.*

Lincoln, St Mary-le-Wigford   14 O12
St Mary's St. The outstanding feature of the church is the slender Saxon tower with a Roman tombstone used as a foundation stone. The Saxon builder speaks through an inscription recording that Eirtig built the tower to the glory of Christ and St Mary. An impressive arch opens from the tower into the nave and 13thC work includes a fine S doorway and chancel. The font is Perpendicular. **P.** *Open 10.00–16.00 Mon–Fri, to 12.00 Sat.* Built on a steep hill rising from the surrounding plain, the silhouette of the cathedral, one of the major glories of European religious architecture, reigns supreme over Lincoln. Also to be explored are the remains of William the Conqueror's impregnable castle and a wealth of medieval buildings.

Long Sutton, St Mary   14 P11
12m E of Spalding on A17. Market Pl. This famous fenland church was founded

St Mary, 13thC steeple

c1170 by Nicholas de Haye, a friend of King John. King John, by the way, lost his crown jewels and baggage negotiating the marshes around nearby Sutton Bridge. The substantial 13thC tower, once detached from the church, is a thrilling sight, crowned by the earliest English lead-covered timber spire (restored 1970–3) with spirelets nestling round like offspring. Notice the elaborate N doorway, the two-storey monk's cell in the NE corner, and the pretty stair turret beside the vaulted S porch, 15 yds S of which is an interesting thatcher's tombstone. The Norman nave retains its original clerestory, enclosed by Decorated and Perpendicular additions. In the N aisle are the former reredos and altar rail from the time of William and Mary, a poor box of 1712 and the vaulted monk's cell with a squint through which you can see the altar. **P.** *Open 10.00–17.00 Mon–Sat, 08.00–20.00 Sun.*

Louth, St James   **14** P13
Westgate. The Perpendicular steeple of svelte and exquisite proportions is a late celebration of medieval Gothic. The height of tower and spire is almost equal and the spire was added in 1501–15. Tall windows in the tower, soaring corner pinnacles and delicate flying buttresses joining the crocketed spire create an impression of striking gracefulness. This is continued inside, where the tower arch is amazingly lofty and beneath it is a marvellous star-vault 86ft high. See the sculptured angels brought down to earth from a roof, the stalls and the screens. **P.** *Open 09.00–18.00 Mon–Sat, to 19.30 Sun.* Georgian and Victorian styles mingle happily in the striking market town.

Marton, St Margaret of Antioch   **13** N12
5m S of Gainsborough on A156. Beautiful Saxon herringbone masonry is clearly visible in the wonderfully intact tower, and the 11thC nave roof line can be seen in it. Prominent leaf capitals decorate the 12thC N arcade. In the 11thC chancel are a niche with a pedestal for a statue of the patron saint, and an ancient stone crucifix. Aisles and porch were rebuilt in the 15thC. **P.** *Open daylight hours daily.*

Rippingale, St Andrew   **14** O11
4½m N of Bourne off A15. Gracing a village between fen and forest, the handsome tall-pinnacled Perpendicular tower is attached to an earlier church, with a long S aisle of c1300. Geometrical tracery highlights the windows. Study the curious 'body brush' displayed near the font, whose purpose is uncertain; it is thought to have been used to brush feet of the dying and dates from c1700. Fascinating monuments include a rare effigy of a deacon holding an open book, and effigies of a 14thC lady under an ogee canopy, a 13thC cross-legged knight and a 15thC knight with two wives. Perhaps they helped build the church. A precious part of the rood screen canopy survives and hints at former opulence. **P.** *Open 09.00–18.00 Mon–Sat, 08.00–20.00 Sun.*

Somersby, St Margaret   **14** P12
9m S of Louth off A16. Set deep in the wolds, a quaint rusticity characterises the little 15thC church. 'Time passeth', admonishes the sundial over the door. Inside, the plain font gains distinction by being that in which the poet, Alfred Lord Tennyson, was baptised. (See the replica of Woolner's excellent bust.) His father was rector from 1808 and is buried in the churchyard. Also in the churchyard is a beautiful 15thC cross. **P.** *Open daily.* The old rectory (privately owned) in which Tennyson was born is almost opposite, and nearby is a fine 18thC redbrick grange attributed to Vanbrugh.

Stamford, All Saints   **14** O10
All Saints Pl. In a cardinal position in the beautiful town, the exterior of the church is distinguished by 13thC blank arcading and by its fine Perpendicular steeple. The 13thC S arcade, with opulently carved leaf capitals immediately arrests attention inside. Perpendicular additions were made by two merchants of the Staple of Calais, William Browne, d1489, whom Leland described as 'a marchant of very wonderful richnesse', and his brother John, d1475. Both are commemorated with their wives in fine brasses as is their father John, d1442. Woolpacks at the feet of John senior and William emphasise the source of their wealth. **P** nearby. *Open 07.00–17.00 Mon–Fri, from 09.00 Sat, 07.30–19.30 Sun.*

Stamford, St George with St Paul 14 O10
St George's Sq. The medieval church has the distinction of c200 mottoes of the founder members of the Order of the Garter in stained glass. William de Bruges, first Garter King of Arms, left money in his will of 1449 towards rebuilding the church. Observe the angels and bosses in the nave roof and the impressive monument of 1797 by John Bacon. **P** nearby. *Open 09.00–17.00 Fri–Sun.*

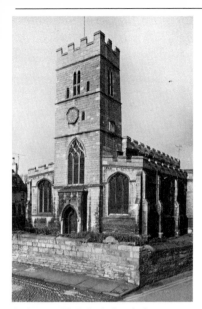

St George with St Paul, Stamford

Stamford, St John the Baptist   **14** O10
Red Lion Sq. Roofs resplendent with
angels greet you in this 15thC church.
The beautiful medieval stained glass
should not be missed and includes in the
N aisle the Virgin of the Mantle,
shielding small souls in her cloak and
interceding for them with God the
Father. Nor should the brass of Nicholas
Byldyson, d1489, who wears a fur-lined
alderman's gown and a capacious purse,
and is accompanied by his wife and nine
children. The ornate screens are also
noteworthy. Sir Malcolm Sargent was a
choirboy here and his father organist. **P.**
*Open 07.15–17.00 Mon–Fri, from 09.30 Sat,
07.30–19.30 Sun.* The town's buildings are
a treasury of taste and charm, among
which the 18thC is particularly graciously
represented. St Martin's church contains
an imposing six-poster monument to
Lord Burghley, d1598, Elizabeth I's
adviser, and St Mary's a lavish medieval
monument and an exquisitely
ornamented chapel ceiling.

Stow in Lindsey, St Mary   **14** O12
the Virgin
6m S of Gainsborough on B1241. This
mighty Saxon and Norman church is
quite awesome. Start at the Saxon core
formed by the crossing arches for a sense
of pre-Conquest power and soaring

invention. The present tower is
Perpendicular. Next explore the Saxon
transepts, branching off from the
crossing, then come back to the early
Norman nave. The W and S doorways
make flamboyant zigzag statements
belonging to the middle of the 12thC, but
the culmination of lavish ornamentation
is in the late Norman chancel, which
makes it worth saving until last. The rib-
vaulting was added by Pearson in the
19thC, according to the original design.
The 13thC font displays small but delightful details, such as a green man's
head and two monsters. **P.** *Open 09.00–
dusk daily.*

Whaplode, St Mary   **14** P11
3m E of Spalding on A151. In a spruce and
tree-bowered churchyard, the 12thC–
14thC tower is very impressive – its
surprising position is at the E end of the
S aisle – and the beautifully detailed
Norman church large. Observe the
difference in the pillars and capitals at
the W end of the nave, built later in the
12thC than those at the E end. The
church recovered its original altar stone
from a dyke. Other remarkable features
include the Jacobean pulpit, the imposing
tomb of Sir Anthony Irby, d1610, on
which he lies in effigy with his wife,
their children kneeling below, and the
fine foliated cross on a stone coffin at the
W end. **P.** *Open 09.00–17.00 Mon, Wed &
Thur, from 09.30 Tue & Fri; 10.00–18.00
Sat, 07.30–18.00 Sun.* Spalding Flower
Parade is a colourful nearby attraction in
May.

St Mary, Whaplode

Wilsford, St Mary   **14** O11
4m SW of Sleaford on A153. The interesting
13thC church has vestigial Saxon work, a
Norman arch and an elegant 15thC
spire. Delightful Decorated tracery
distinguishes the E window and lively
carvings decorate the bench ends. **P.**
*Open summer approx 09.00–21.00 daily,
winter to 17.00.*

CUMBRIA &
— NORTHUMBRIA —

Cumbria   Northumberland   Durham
Tyne and Wear   Cleveland

When we get into Cumbria, place names begin to show a Scandinavian origin, with terminations such as *-thwaite, -thorpe* and *-by*, and with the common prefix Kirkby. *By* comes from the Swedish word for a village and *kirk* of course means church – *churchvillage*. Kirkby in this area means what Minster means in Dorset, and it is in these places that we should look for the most distinguished churches.

The eastern part of the county was protected by the powerful Percy family and the wealthy Prince Bishop of Durham but in the west, border warfare, together with the Black Death, militated against church building; churches tend to be scarce, small and built with an austere simplicity. Many of them were originally whitewashed, like the Hawkshead church known to Wordsworth – 'the snow white church upon her hill'. He also wrote that the architecture of these tiny churches was 'not less appropriate and admirable than that of the dwelling houses . . . A man must be very insensible who would not be touched with pleasure at the sight of the chapel of Buttermere'.

Against a general background of poverty, wealth stands out in clear relief and was frequently responsible for endowing the churches. A notable secular patron of the 17thC was Lady Anne Clifford, Countess of Pembroke, who restored seven places of worship on her estates, and when the Book of Common Prayer was banned by Parliament, she was sufficiently powerful to insist on its use in her churches. Great religious foundations, as at Furness Abbey, Lanercost and Cartmel, have left their mark not only on the churches but on the landscape of Barrow and Ulverstone.

In both Northumberland and Durham ecclesiastical and political factors have been the dominant influences. The vigorous evangelisation of the area towards the end of the 7thC by Cuthbert and his successors at Lindisfarne has left us a number of churches which seem indestructible – like Escomb in Durham, built in the 7thC and appearing likely to outlive its execrable, modern industrial surroundings. The coming of the Normans and the building of the great Cathedral at Durham created a new and obvious impact. It was here that the pointed arch made its first appearance and opened the way for the Gothic style, but the Norman style held sway for longer in Northumbria, which was still using round arches long after they had been abandoned elsewhere. Nurtured during the Restoration by Bishop Cosin, came the belated flowering of Gothic woodcarving. Besides the stalls of Durham Cathedral, perhaps the best example is Brancepeth (Durham), where Cosin had previously been rector.

A great church like Alnwick could exist safely under the protection of the castle, but often the church and vicarage formed a defensive ensemble. This is probably why Corbridge is usually regarded as the typical Northumberland church. The vicarage is fortified and the church itself, with its pre-Conquest tower still embattled, incorporates stonework from a Roman fort which bears impressive witness to the agelong struggle of the border counties to keep the Scots at bay.

Of the two new administrative counties, Tyne and Wear used to belong to Northumberland and is largely industrial, but can still boast the glorious Saxon monastic church at Jarrow, while Cleveland reflects the heritage of Durham and the North Riding of Yorkshire.

◁ CUMBRIA ▷

Ambleside, St Mary　　　　**17** H16
Church Wlk. In the heart of Lakeland, looking out to fells fringing Lake Windermere, the spire is an impressive feature of the Victorian town church, designed by Sir George Gilbert Scott, 1850–4. At the W end is an engagingly lively mural by George Ransom, 1944, of the rushbearing ceremony which takes place on the first Saturday in July. Rushes and reeds from the lakes are woven with flowers and brought to the church, commemorating the early custom of strewing fresh rushes on earth floors.

St Mary, Victorian steeple

Much of the stained glass is vivid and appealing, and includes memorial windows to Wordsworth, Matthew Arnold and W. E. Forster. **P.** *Open 07.00– dusk daily.*

Brampton, St Martin　　　　**20** J18
9m NE of Carlisle on A69. In border country, close to Hadrian's Wall, a sense of adventure adheres to Philip Webb's only church, built in 1874–8. Many details make you blink and look again, such as the distinctive gabled N side, with striking outsize crenellation, and the unusual roofs inside, but all engage interest. Webb was a close associate of the Pre-Raphaelites and marvellous stained glass by Burne-Jones and William Morris sparkles jewel-like from the windows. It forms a fascinating catalogue of Victorian values as distinct from medieval themes: the Crucifixion, Resurrection and Judgement are absent and the Good Shepherd, Childhood and Paradise appear instead. **P.** *Open daylight hours daily.*

Burgh-by-Sands, St Michael　　　　**20** H18
5m NW of Carlisle on line of Hadrian's Wall, off B5307. On the site of a Roman fort that straddled Hadrian's wall, the church is built largely of stones from the fort. The stout 14thC tower was raised with a view to standing no nonsense from raiding Scots. Parts of the church are Norman and Early English. The original iron gate, or yett, leading to the tower from the nave is preserved. **P.** *Open 07.00–21.00 daily.* 1m NW is a tall

monument to Edward I, who died in camp on Burgh Marsh in 1307.

Carlisle, St Cuthbert **20** H18
St Cuthbert's La. The interior of this lovely Georgian church is lined with classical colonnades and has a broad chancel arch framing a handsome Venetian E window. Its most outstanding furnishing is the vast, movable pulpit of 1905, which runs on rails to take up a dominant position before the altar. So prominent a piece would permit no dozers, even in the gallery. Pretty copies of 18thC candelabra hang in the nave. **P.** *Open 09.00–17.30 Mon–Sat, to 19.30 Sun.* The blood-stained history of Carlisle is reflected in the churchyard: here are buried men who died in the siege of 1644–45, and others executed for participating in Bonnie Prince Charlie's rebellion in 1745. In the W wall a little gravestone commemorates a Negro slave who died of pneumonia in 1789. The city is distinguished by many fine buildings, including the cathedral and castle.

St Cuthbert, movable pulpit

Cartmel, Priory church of **17** H15
St Mary and St Michael
4m S of Newby Bridge off A590. In a picturesque valley village, on a peninsula jutting into Morecambe Bay. The beautiful church formed part of a priory founded in 1190. Miraculously, it survived the Dissolution intact, although only the 14thC gatehouse remains of the priory buildings. The tower's top stage is uniquely set diagonally, a most unexpected sight. A sumptuous Norman S doorway leads into a rather short 15thC nave. But grandeur reasserts itself in the richly detailed Transitional chancel. Here too are 15thC stalls with an extensive and inventive series of misericords, surmounted by an opulently carved 17thC screen of elegant columns

entwined by vines. The glorious Perpendicular E window contains 15thC stained glass. Sir John Harrington built the S chapel, or Town Choir, in 1340, and its windows brim with flowing tracery and retain fine 14thC stained glass. The Harrington tomb, with effigies of Sir John, d1347, and his wife, is extremely elaborate and interesting, though damaged. The presence, at the base, of sculptured canons engaged in chanting for the salvation of Sir John's soul immediately illuminates the concept of a chantry chapel. The remains of mourners carved alongside the effigies are extraordinary too. In different vein, notice the nearby Georgian monuments, in which draperies and playful putti create an almost frivolous atmosphere. **P** nearby. *Open summer 08.00–17.30 daily, winter to 15.30.*

Crosby Ravensworth, St Laurence 17 J17
12m SE of Penrith off B6260. A gentle stream trickles by and fells rise up all around. Gargoyles project dramatically from the 15thC tower. In a history marked by vicissitudes, the 12thC Scottish raids stand out, during one of which the Norman church was burnt. A fine dogtooth-decorated 13thC doorway leads into the lovely, spacious interior, which has 13thC nave arcades and a Victorian chancel opening out from a Norman core. Investigate the massive 16thC tomb, lying anonymously beneath the N chapel arch. In the churchyard are part of an ancient cross, old tapering coffin lids and a tombstone unusually carved – with a turnip. **P.** *Open 08.00– dusk daily.*

Gosforth, St Mary **16** G16
10m SE of Whitehaven on A595. In the churchyard is a quite amazing 10thC Viking cross, 14½ft high and very slender, in whose carving Nordic myth and Christian teaching meet. A large number of dragons with gaping mouths, plaited, winged and otherwise, feature on it. Inside what is now largely a 19thC church, in Decorated Gothic style, is the unlikely ornament of a Chinese bell, brought from a fort on the Canton river, and two fascinating hogback tombstones. They covered the graves of Norse chieftains and two armies with round shields stand face to face on one of them. **P.** *Open 09.00–18.00 daily.*

Grasmere, St Oswald **17** H16
2m NW of Ambleside on A591. William Wordsworth is buried beside the river in

the churchyard, under the shade of one of the eight yews he planted. The tower of rough boulders and the medieval interior with rustic two-storeyed arcading and thrilling forest of roof timbers inspired his description in the *Excursion*:

'Not raised in nice proportions was the pile,
But large and massy; for duration built;
With pillars crowded, and the roof upheld
By naked rafters intricately crossed,
Like leafless underboughs in some thick wood,
All withered by the depth of shade above.'

A profile medallion by T. Woolner commemorates the poet. Examine too the 12thC carved stone and alms box dated 1648. A rushbearing procession winds its way through the village to the church each year as at Ambleside. **P.** *Open 08.30–dusk daily.* Crag, lake and quaint hillside Dove Cottage, where the Wordsworths lived and were visited by Coleridge and De Quincey, are among the manifold attractions of Grasmere and surroundings.

Greystoke, St Andrew   **17** H17
4m W of Penrith on B5288. High fells and a 19thC Elizabethan-style castle, peering from the edge of a wooded park, are impressive neighbours of the late Perpendicular church, in origin 13thC. 15thC stained glass of St Andrew in the E window delights with its glow. Alabaster effigies of a 14thC knight and a 15thC noble, brasses, engagingly carved misericords and the delicately traceried rood screen are all of great interest. **P.** *Open daylight hours daily.* Close by are three fortress-like folly farms, whimsically added to the landscape by the 11th Duke of Norfolk in the 18thC.

Hawkshead, St Michael and   **17** H16
All Angels
4m W of Windermere on B5285. Wonderfully situated on a hillock commanding wide views of fells and Esthwaite Water, with stone seats on which Wordsworth liked to sit outside the E wall. The interior of the 16thC church has striking painted decoration round arches and pillars, and its whitewashed walls are bright with 17thC and 18thC biblical inscriptions, set amid delightfully rustic adornments, in which cherub heads abound. Archbishop Sandys – who founded Hawkshead Grammar School, attended by

Wordsworth – rebuilt the N aisle in 1578, and effigies of his parents lie in the chapel at its E end. *Open daylight hours daily.* The enchanting village is sometimes overwhelmed by visitors.

Holme Cultram Abbey Town,   **20** H18
St Mary
6m W of Wigton on B5302. Founded in 1150, the abbey struggled to maintain prosperity in the face of repeated Scottish raids and obligations to entertain visitors, including Edward I, his entourage and troops in 1300 and 1307. At the Dissolution, the parishioners petitioned for the preservation of the church and while the monastic buildings were quarried for local construction, most of the 12thC nave remains. A double bellcote sits prettily in the gable above the fine porch, which is inscribed with the name of the abbot, Robert Chambers, who built it in 1507. Monks kneel before the mitred and croziered abbot on his monument inside the porch. Most splendid of all is the mighty Norman portal beyond, leading into the nave, whose impressive arcades are filled by 18thC walls. **P.** *Open 09.00–20.00 daily.*

Kendal, Holy Trinity   **17** J16
The spectacularly five-aisled church is a magnificent sight. Its history appears to begin in the 13thC, from which time the three E bays of the nave arcades survive, but a fragment of a Saxon cross shaft in the outer S aisle testifies to a more ancient origin. It is a memorable experience to stand in the nave and look through vistas of pillars stretching off in every direction. The corona of 1970 is a striking feature over the high altar. Additions belong largely to the 15thC and 19thC, and include the Flemish Aisle, which originally accommodated Flemish weavers, who settled in Kendal in the Middle Ages, and a glorious array of chapels containing monuments and brasses. Among these, the black marble tomb in

Holy Trinity, Kendal

the Parr Chapel is thought to be that of Sir William Parr, grandfather of Catherine Parr, Henry VIII's sixth wife. **P.** *Open 08.30–19.30 Mon–Sat, 07.30–20.00 Sun.* Kendal is justly proud of the nearby Abbot Hall Art Gallery, a Georgian house whose exhibits include a historical display of Lakeland life. Tower, dungeons and exhilarating views are offered by the 12thC ruined castle, once the home of Katherine Parr, and narrow alleys and yards are part of the town's charm.

Kirkby Lonsdale, St Mary   **17** J15
Market St. You may wish to take a view first from the churchyard gazebo, which features in Turner's painting of the Lune river, and follow the path below to see the sublime confluence of river and fells that sent 19thC sage, John Ruskin, into ecstasy. Continuing in impressive vein are the great W doorway and powerful Norman N arcade pillars, arresting attention immediately on entering the church through the S door. On two of them are boldly incised diamond patterns, imitating work at Durham Cathedral, and together with the massive intervening pillar they stand out from the others in the most extraordinary way. Eyecatching woodwork includes an exuberantly carved cupboard at the W end, and the equally flamboyant Jacobean pulpit. Only slightly more sober are two handsome Stuart chairs sitting in the chancel. The large ladies representing Faith, Hope and Charity in Victorian stained glass in the S aisle also command notice. **P.** *Open 08.00–20.00 daily.*

Kirkby Stephen, dedication   **17** K16
unknown
18m NE of Kendal on A685. A 19thC classical colonnade stands at the churchyard entrance. The fine Perpendicular tower has an impressively lofty arch, matched in stateliness by the 13thC nave arcades. Be sure to scrutinise the ancient and unique 'Loki' stone, near the S door, which features the devil bearded and bound. It is of Scandinavian ancestry. Notice the imposing marble pulpit, the elegantly detailed sedilia and piscina and the monuments, including that of Sir Richard Musgrave, d1409, whose effigy wears jousting armour. Reputed to have killed the last wild boar on Wild Boar Fell, he was found to be buried with his wife and a boar tusk during 19thC restoration. **P.** *Open 07.30–18.00 Mon–Sat, to 20.00 Sun.* Majestic Pennine scenery is round about. 3m S, near Mallerstang, are the remains of

Pendragon Castle, home of the reputed father of King Arthur, Uther Pendragon, and of Sir Hugh de Morville, one of the four knights who murdered Thomas a Becket in 1170.

Kirkoswald, St Oswald   **20** J17
6m NE of Penrith on B6413. The tower stands rather jauntily on the hilltop, while the church nestles against the side of the hill, from which a spring flows under the nave and issues at the W end at St Oswald's well. Here, in the 7thC, King Oswald converted pagan worshippers of the god of the spring to Christianity. Inspect the ancient coffin lids round the church walls, carved with symbols denoting the occupation of the deceased. With the founding of the contiguous College in 1523, the church received its present form and was restored in the 19thC. *Open daylight hours daily.* Remains of a moated castle add further lustre.

Lanercost, Priory of St Mary   **20** J18
Magdalene
2m NE of Brampton off A69. Sequestered beside the river Irthing, serenity emanates from the softly textured stone of the partly-ruined priory, whose W front is framed by the remains of the gatehouse. A magnificent doorway, dainty arcading and gracefully soaring lancets compose the 13thC W front, at the apex of which an eloquent statue of Mary Magdalene miraculously survives, a kneeling monk at her side. Founded c1166, close to Hadrian's Wall, the scene was not always so peaceful. The priory suffered sackings from over the border and was often used as a military base. Edward I and Queen Eleanor stayed in the guest house in 1280; in 1306 the King made a long sojourn with his household and a considerable incursion into the priory's prosperity. After the Dissolution, Sir Thomas Dacre became the proprietor and converted the W range of buildings into a house. His ancestor of the same name, who fought at the Battle of Flodden in 1513, is buried in the S transept. The nave, clerestory and N aisle form the present church and beyond them the roofless tower, transepts and exquisite choir stand gloriously intact up to the eaves. Visit the impressive, vaulted undercroft, formerly surmounted by the canons' refectory. Where food was once stored, Roman altars from Hadrian's Wall and neighbouring camps are gathered, including one to Silvanus, god of the woods. **P.** *Open 08.30–dusk daily.*

Morland, St Laurence　　　**17** J17
7m SE of Penrith off A66. Saxon up to its
top stage and charming, crowning
spirelet, the tower is the most ancient in
Cumbria. Inside it is a venerable ladder
of 1673. Early English transepts with fine
lancet windows branch out from the
nave, and the late Perpendicular chancel
contains the top rails from a 14thC
screen, engagingly carved with heads of
kings, bishops and angels. The font of
1662 has a lovely cover and the pulpit an
elegant Georgian design. A palimpsest
brass commemorates vicar John Blyth,
d1562, on one side and a knight on the
other. **P.** *Open 08.00–dusk daily.*

Newton Arlosh, St John　　**20** H18
the Evangelist
11m W of Carlisle on B5307. The staunchly
defensive border pele tower, with a
diminutive turret, is very impressive.
Built in 1303, it has no outer doorway
and is pierced by only the narrowest of
slits. There are two vaulted chambers on
the ground floor and a priest's room with
fireplace and secret chamber above.
Refuge was taken here at times of attack,
and the castellated parapet provided a
lookout across the Solway. Doubtless oil
was boiled to precipitate onto assailants'
heads. The contemporary nave, which
partly survives, was tiny, its E window
11 inches wide and door 27. The church
was restored and extended in the 19thC.
P. *Open daylight hours daily. No access to
pele tower.*

Patterdale, St Patrick　　**17** H17
11m SW of Penrith on A592. Amid sublime
scenery, the small 19thC church with a
saddleback roofed tower is by Salvin. It
contains vivid tapestries, made by Ann
Macbeth, c1940, in which religious
subjects are set against lyrical Lakeland
dales and fells. **P.** *Open daylight hours
daily.*

Penrith, St Andrew　　**17** J17
The great Norman tower was retained in
the dignified classical rebuilding of the
church in 1721. Two chandeliers of 1745
branch out gleamingly in the nave,
whose unusual colour scheme is of 1972.
Local artist Jacob Thompson painted the
dramatic chancel murals in 1845. Notice
the elegant pulpit and the stained glass
portraits of the parents of Cicely Neville,
mother of Richard III and Edward IV, in
a S aisle window. In a N aisle window
are further medieval fragments, including
a sceptred king. **P.** *Open 07.30–17.00*

*Mon, Fri & Sat, from 09.00 Tue & Thur,
from 07.00 Wed, to 19.00 Sun.* In the
churchyard, the Giant's Grave, consisting
of two Saxon crosses, c11ft high, and
four hogback tombstones, and the
Giant's Thumb, present a scene
astounding enough to make you
gasp.

St Bees, Priory church of　　**16** G16
St Mary and St Bega
3m S of Whitehaven on B5345. A prominent
Scandinavian-style dragon presides over
a gateway facing the spectacular Norman
W doorway. Follow the swirling patterns
on the capitals and the beakhead and
scintillating zigzag decoration of the arch.
Alternating round and octagonal pillars
and pointed arches form the 13thC nave
arcades, to which a Perpendicular
clerestory was added after the 12thC
priory had been dissolved. William
Butterfield rebuilt the crossing tower as
part of his restoration in the 19thC, and
designed the fine ironwork screen. Note
the ornate gabled Gothic tomb of four-
year-old Maria Claudine Lumb, d1865.
The organ of 1899 was built by Father
Willis, most celebrated of Victorian organ
makers. Exquisite Early English lancet
windows fill the former chancel, now
part of St Bees School, which was
founded by Archbishop Grindal in 1583.
P. *Open summer 08.30–approx 21.30 Mon–
Sat, from 07.30 Sun; winter to 18.30 Mon–
Sat, to 20.00 Sun.*

Urswick, St Mary　　**17** H15
and St Michael
6m N of Barrow-in-Furness off A590. The
impressive tower, as broad as the nave,
has a crenellated Tudor top,
incorporating red sandstone, probably
quarried from nearby Furness Abbey.
Inside the church, testifying to the great
antiquity of the site, a large fragment of
an ancient cross asserts that 'Tunwinni
set up this memorial to his son Torhtred.
Pray for his soul. Lyl wrought this'. The
three-decker Georgian pulpit has a
charming scallop shell sounding board of
1912, upheld by two putti. Much fine
wood carving of 1907–11 embellishes the
church, including that of the organ case
and choir stalls. The altar painting of the
Last Supper is by 18thC local artist,
James Cranke, and a second painting, by
his son of the same name, hangs above
the Gale pews. Some medieval stained
glass is preserved. **P.** *Open summer approx
08.00–21.00 Mon–Fri, from 07.30 Sat &
Sun; winter to approx 16.00.*

◁ NORTHUMBERLAND ▷

Alnwick, St Michael   **21** L20
the Archangel
Sequestered on a hilltop, with bosky
banks and river below, the tower and SE
turret are sturdily impressive. Of
Norman origin, the present church is
largely of rich Perpendicular design,
restored in the 19thC. Most sumptuous is
the chancel, where capitals lushly carved
with foliage and surmounted by angels
stand out. Notice in particular the
Hotspur Pillar, bearing the crescents and
lockets of the great Percy dynasty. See
too the interesting array of Victorian
stained glass, the 15thC roundel of a
pelican, the 14thC effigies and the
magnificent 14thC Flemish chest carved
with dragonish monsters, dragons face to
face whose tails burst into foliage, and a
scene of the chase. **P.** *Open 07.30–18.30
Mon–Fri, from 09.30 Sat, to 19.00 Sun.*
When visiting formidable Alnwick Castle,
seat of the Percys, watch out for the
stone warriors commanding the
battlements.

Berwick-upon-Tweed,   **21** K21
Holy Trinity
Wallace Grn. A most rare church, built
1648–52 during the Commonwealth,
when few churches were constructed in
England. Tradition has it that on his way
to the Battle of Dunbar, Oliver Cromwell
forbade the building of a tower, since he
disapproved of towers and bells. Gothic
battlements mingle with classical details
outside, such as the pedimented
doorway that ushers you in to the fine
interior, and to immediate admiration of
the Jacobean-style W gallery. Notice the
medallions of Flemish stained glass in the
W window, the Venetian windows and
the dignified nave, leading to the chancel
of 1855 with a reredos by E. Lutyens. **P.**
*Open 09.30–dusk Mon–Sat, 08.00–19.30
Sun.* Highly picturesque, the town has
the unique distinction of Elizabethan
bastions. Three historic bridges span the
river Tweed, which is populous with
salmon.

Chollerton, St Giles   **21** K18
5m N of Hexham on B6342. The 18thC
tower and chancel, gothicised in 1893,
and unassuming body of the church, give
no hint of the astonishing presence of
Roman pillars inside, forming the S
arcade. They were brought from the
great Roman Fort of Chesters, on the
other side of the river. A further surprise
is the Roman altar, converted into a font.
The church is also distinguished by a
pretty chamber organ. **P.** *Open summer
08.15–18.30 Mon–Sat, to 19.30 Sun; winter
to 17.00 daily.* Hugging Hadrian's wall,
Chesters is the best example of a cavalry
fort in the whole of the uncovered
Roman empire.

Corbridge, St Andrew   **21** K18
17m W of Newcastle upon Tyne on A68.
Although 9th Danish invasions destroyed
an 8thC monastery at Corbridge, the base
of the tower survives from the monastic
church, and a Roman arch from
Corstopitum, ½m W, opens from it into
the nave. Amazing to contemplate, it
dates from the 2ndC. Interesting features
of a later date are the Norman S doorway
and the beautiful restored 13thC chancel,
lit by lancet windows. **P.** *Open daylight
hours daily.* In the SE corner of the
churchyard is the intriguing medieval
Vicar's Pele, a tower built of Roman
stones from Corstopitum, to which the
vicar could retreat from raiders. A
notable 19thC cast iron cross stands in
the Market Pl, and a handsome 17thC
bridge crosses the river Tyne. Nearby
Corstopitum was a supply station for the
Roman army manning Hadrian's Wall
and also housed Greek and Syrian
merchants. An early excavator was

St Andrew, Roman arch

King John, whose men unsuccessfully searched for treasure in 1201.

Hexham, Priory church   **21** K18
of St Andrew
A powerful sense of the Saxon world is conveyed by Wilfrid's 7thC crypt, built of Roman stones, some of which are inscribed or ornamented. The splendours of the church that stood above the crypt were incomparable north of the Alps, according to Wilfrid's biographer. Sacked by the Danes in 876, the church was refounded as part of an Augustinian priory in 1113. The present church is Early English, with Victorian additions and a nave of 1907–9 in Decorated Gothic style by Temple Moore. Enjoy the exquisitely graceful lines of the Early English N transept, and the evocatively worn monks' night staircase in the S transept, down which they must have stumbled sleepily from their dormitory to sing the night offices. Be sure to see the tombstone of the Roman standard-bearer Flavinus, on which he appears with flamboyant plumes on his head, the Saxon Frith Stool, the exuberant Tudor rood screen commemorating Prior Smithson, Prior Leschman's (d1491) Chantry Chapel and effigy, on which his cowl is drawn down over his eyes, the 15thC wooden sedilia, stalls and misericords. *Open 09.30–17.00 daily.* Travellers interested in history find much besides to absorb them in this ancient market town, including the 14thC Moot Hall and prison.

Holy Island, St Mary   **21** L21
the Virgin
5m N of Belford off A1 by causeway. On ground hallowed by 7thC saints Aidan and Cuthbert, whose Christian mission reverberated throughout pagan Northumbria, a sense of awe is still experienced on stepping onto Holy Island. The exquisite Lindisfarne Gospels were penned and illuminated in the monastery c700. Their light shone forth from here until the Danes extinguished it in 793, after which the monks whispered a last benediction and fled. The Gospels are now safely housed in the British Museum. Lindisfarne Priory ruins, stretching out evocatively to sea and sky beside the church, date from an 11thC refoundation of the 7thC monastery by the Bishop of Durham. The little 13thC church is beautiful; massive buttresses meet in an arch surmounted by an 18thC bellcote on the W side and the fine long chancel is lit by lancet windows.

Red and white stone alternates strikingly round the Norman arches of the N arcade. The S arcade is Early English, as is the pointed chancel arch, above which peers its round Norman ancestor. The 18thC font has a delightfully bulbous baluster stem. **P.** *Open summer 07.00–22.00 Mon–Sat, from 07.30 Sun; winter to 19.15.* Sir E. Lutyens converted 16thC Lindisfarne Castle to a romantic house in 1903. Monkish mead is produced on the island.

Kirknewton, St Gregory   **21** K20
the Great
15m S of Berwick-upon-Tweed on B6351. An interesting 19thC exterior conceals a medieval interior whose powerful and primitive nature speaks eloquently of proximity to a strife-torn border. The pointed chancel vault springs from very low walls of tremendous thickness, creating a cavernous effect, and in the S transept the vault begins at floor level. The church has a great treasure in an engaging 12thC stone relief of the Adoration of the Magi, in which the magi appear to be wearing kilts. Moreover, they look as if they might be dancing a jig. **P.** *Open daylight hours daily.* In a hamlet close to the Cheviot hills.

Norham, St Cuthbert   **21** K21
6m SW of Berwick-upon-Tweed on B6470. Norham's place at the hub of borderland history is dramatically emphasised by the jaggedly ruined 12thC castle, built by the prince-bishops of Durham, that towers above the river Tweed and a steep ravine. The church shares in the castle's Norman majesty. Outside, take a close look at the marvellous decoration round the window arches on the S side of the chancel, and, inside, at the immensely impressive S arcade. The remainder of the church is largely of the 19thC. A fine Decorated canopy shields a knight's effigy in the chancel. The Royal Arms of Charles II are notable and so are the ornate 17thC pulpit and vicar's stall from Durham Cathedral. *Open summer 09.00–18.00 daily, winter to dusk.*

Ovingham, St Mary the Virgin   **21** L18
8m W of Newcastle upon Tyne off A69. In a Tyne valley village, close to Hadrian's Wall. Fascinating features of the church are the slender Saxon tower and fragments of Saxon crosses, on one of which a saint in a niche and a hunting scene figure. A composition of beauty and grace is offered by the Early English chancel and transepts, arrayed with tall

St Mary the Virgin, Saxon tower

lancet windows. Thomas Bewick, the famous wood engraver, is buried in the churchyard. **P.** *Open daylight hours daily.*

Rothbury, All Saints   **21** L19
10m SW of Alnwick on B6341. In beautiful Coquetdale, a headstone in the churchyard to an angler, Walter Mavin, is carved in celebratory fashion with its hills and streams. Much of the church was rebuilt in the 19thC, although it preserves its long, 13thC chancel with lovely lancet windows. Conferring a special glory on the church is the font, whose fine bowl of 1664 stands on part of the outstanding Rothbury Saxon cross. Wonderfully viv-acious carvings include that of the Ascension, with Christ disappearing, seated on a cloud lifted by angels, and the apostles craning their necks below. **P** nearby. *Open 08.30–19.00 Mon, from 09.00 Tue, Thur & Sat, to*

All Saints, Rothbury cross

19.30 Wed, to 18.30 Fri; 07.45–19.30 Sun.
Up a leafy hillside, aptly named Cragside Hall was built with theatrical panache by Norman Shaw in 1870.

Simonburn, St Mungo   **21** K18
7m N of Hexham on B6320. The rebuilt medieval church has a handsome Georgian rectory as neighbour and is set in a hillside village looking down to the North Tyne valley and up to exhilarating fells. A charming bellcote sits above the W end and in the porch a fragment of a carved Saxon cross testifies to the antiquity of the site. Other interesting remains are gathered here. Note the sloping nave floor, the 13thC double piscina and the assembled figures from a Jacobean monument. **P.** *Open 09.00–dusk daily.* The ruins of Simonburn Castle, poised between two ravines, are reached by a steep path beyond the confluence of two burns.

Warkworth, St Lawrence   **21** L19
8m SE of Alnwick on A1068. Tower and broach-spire form a stately composition. Once inside the church, attention is immediately drawn to the splendidly detailed Norman chancel arch and chancel beyond, where zigzag decoration leaps up the beautiful rib-vaulting. The 15thC S aisle was built by the Percys, Lords of Warkworth Castle. Particularly noteworthy is the noble effigy of a 14thC knight offering his heart. **P.** *Open 07.30–17.00 Mon–Sat, to 18.30 Sun.* The river Coquet ripples by the churchyard to the medieval bridge and bridge tower. Part of Shakespeare's *Henry IV* is set in mighty and lofty Warkworth Castle, home of Northumbria's champion, Harry Hotspur.

Whittingham, St Bartholomew   **21** L20
7m W of Alnwick off A697. Saxon in its lower parts, the tower was given a Victorian Gothic pinnacled crown in 1840. The base is thought to date from the reign of Ceolwulf, c737, the king to whom the Venerable Bede dedicated his History, and the next stage from the 9thC. The S arcade and transept are 13thC, but the Norman N arcade was replaced in 1840 by one corresponding in style to that opposite. **P.** *Open 09.00–dusk daily.* Nearby classical Callaly Castle has rich Georgian and Victorian refinements, including sumptuous plasterwork in the drawing room of 1750, as well as a 13thC tower.

◁ DURHAM ▷

Aycliffe, St Andrew   **18** L17
5m N of Darlington on A1. In a village
with a lovely green, Saxon, Norman and
13thC fabric composes the fine church,
which was restored in 1882. Two Saxon
cross shafts, with carvings of the
Crucifixion and an interlacing pattern,
are of great interest among the early
sculptural fragments. Notice the
prominent nailhead decoration on the
chancel arch, and the contrasting nave
arcades. Delightful details distinguish the
17thC seating. **P.** *Open summer 14.00–
16.00 Fri & Sat.*

Brancepeth, St Brandon   **21** L17
4m SW of Durham on A690. Set beautifully
in the park of Brancepeth Castle, onetime
stronghold of the Nevilles, earls of
Westmorland, the broadly battlemented
tower is authentically Norman and
13thC, whereas the castle is largely a
19thC rebuilding. The body of the church
dates from the 13thC–15thC, when the
chancel was rebuilt with large,
impressive windows. Luxuriant details in
the N porch hint at the magnificent
carvings which characterise the interior,
and which date from the incumbency of
John Cosin, in 1626–40, who later became

St Brandon, pulpit

Bishop of Durham. Perhaps most
glorious is the chancel screen, a
wondrous expression of Gothic forms,
culminating in openwork canopies. The
pulpit uses exuberant Jacobean motifs
and its sounding board is crowned by a
sumptuous display of pediments,
openwork pinnacles and curly scrolls.
Pews, choir stalls, chancel ceiling and
font cover, all join in this gorgeous
celebration of 17thC wood carving.
Inspect too the panelling above the
chancel arch, the 15thC reredos and arch
between chancel and S chapel, the
traceried 14thC chest with monsters at its
sides, which forms the front of the S
chapel altar, the larger-than-life-size
effigy of Robert Neville, d1319, truculent
'Peacock of the North', and the wooden
effigies of Ralph Neville, d1484, and his
wife. **P.** *Open 09.00–dusk daily.*

Chester-le-Street,   **21** L18
St Mary and St Cuthbert
Church Chare. The medieval church has
an ancient foundation and quaint
features, such as the Anchorage beside
the picturesque W tower, whose tall spire
rises from an octagonal storey. Home of
an anchorite from 1383 until the
Dissolution, a narrow squint opens from
the Anchorage into the church. It now
houses some Saxon sculptural fragments.
A splendid array of Lumley warriors,
from the time of Edward the Confessor
onwards, lines the N aisle in bold effigy.
Three are original and others Elizabethan
reproductions, tellingly illustrating how
early imitation of medieval forms began.
John Lord Lumley, who accomplished
this display of family pride in 1594, is
also present in effigy. **P.** *Open 08.00–
17.00 Mon–Sat, to 11.00 Sun.* Impressive
14thC Lumley Castle, home of the
Lumley warriors, stands in a wooded
setting 1m S.

Darlington, St Cuthbert   **18** L17
Market Sq. Almost entirely 12thC–13thC,
the lofty elegance of the former collegiate
church's design is enhanced by rows of
pointed lancet windows and arcading,
the upward lines culminating in the tall
14thC spire. Don't miss the lavish details
round the windows in the chancel and S
transept, the arched stone rood screen,
or pulpitum, and the misericords on the
15thC choir stalls, among which angels
and monsters figure. The magnificent

Gothic font cover of 1662 is of the type introduced by Bishop Cosin into Durham churches. **P.** *Open 08.30–17.00 Mon–Sat.* North Road Station Railway Museum houses the world's first passenger train, Locomotion No 1, which took to the rails in 1825.

Escomb, St John the Evangelist 18 L17
2m W of Bishop Auckland off B6282. Powerfully moving and eloquent in its antiquity and stark purity, this small church stands in a rebuilt valley village, where the presence of a number of culverted streams suggests the former importance of the site. Probably as a result of its obscurity, it has survived, almost intact, from the 7thC. Outside the N wall, look at the rosette carved on a stone which may have formed part of a Roman altar, and at the stone set upside down inscribed with the legend 'VI', which once read 'LEG VI', referring to the Sixth Roman Legion. To the right of the porch a serpent curls round a Saxon sundial, believed to be the oldest in England in its original position. Look out for the fragments of Saxon coloured glass and stone crosses in the porch. Tall and narrow, the nave, with five tiny, original windows, culminates in the chancel arch, which may have come complete from the Roman cavalry fort 2m away at Binchester, although the long-and-short work is typically Saxon. Much of the stone came from the fort and the quality of the beautifully-squared ashlar blocks is remarkable. **P.** *Key available during daylight hours daily.*

Staindrop, St Mary the Virgin 18 L17
8m SW of Bishop Auckland on A688. The tower climbs up through the centuries from an 11thC–12thC base to a 15thC top, and in the beautiful medieval church original Saxon windows survive above the arcades. The pre-Reformation rood screen and chancel stalls date from the foundation in 1422 of a college for priests and laymen by Ralph Neville, first Earl of Westmorland and lord of Raby Castle. He died in 1425 and lies in serene alabaster effigy between his two wives. See too the oak effigies of Elizabethan Nevilles. Because of their part in the Northern Rising of 1569, the Nevilles were supplanted as lords of Raby Castle by the Vanes, whose effigies sometime thereafter join the noble congregation. **P.** *Open 09.00–dusk Mon–Sat, 08.00–20.00 Sun.* Many 18thC stone houses border the greens sweeping picturesquely through the village. To the N is massively impressive medieval Raby Castle.

Trimdon, St Mary Magdalene 18 M17
9m NW of Hartlepool on B1278. Built on an ancient mound in the middle of the village, the church is quaintly small and simple, with a charming bellcote rising from the softly coloured stone. A Norman horseshoe arch divides the chancel from the nave, whose ancient masonry is pierced by 19thC windows. The N aisle was added in 1874. **P.** *Open 08.15–18.30 Mon, Tue & Fri, to 19.15 Wed, to 19.00 Sat, 09.30–18.00 Thur, 08.45–19.00 Sun.*

◀ TYNE AND WEAR ▶

Cullercoats, St George 21 M18
1½m NW of Tynemouth on A193 on coast. J. L. Pearson's church of 1884, in Early English Gothic style, exerts an ennobling influence on the sea front. Its polygonal apse and unusually placed tall, slender steeple are striking external features, while stone vaulting and big clerestory windows make a magnificent display in the lofty interior. **P** nearby. *Open 09.00–dusk daily.* A popular beach lies below.

Earsdon, St Alban 21 M18
2m W of Whitley Bay on A192. A prominent landmark, the distinctive tower – with halfway as well as crowning pinnacles – and church were built in 1836–7 by J. and B. Green. The chancel is

of 1889. Heraldic Tudor stained glass made for Henry VIII's Hampton Court throws out vividly glowing colours from two windows. It was given to the church in 1874 by Lord Hastings of Delaval Hall. The Hartley monument commemorates the victims of a pit disaster of 1862. **P.** *Open summer 14.00–19.00 daily.* Some Georgian houses distinguish the village.

Houghton-le-Spring, 21 M18
St Michael and All Angels
Broadway. An animatedly carved Norman tympanum pinpoints the fine church's beginnings, although it is largely of the 13thC–15thC. Observe the elegant row of 13thC shafted lancet windows in the chancel, the 14thC E window with its

St Michael and All Angels

gorgeous flowing and flowering tracery, the Tudor brass, and the huge altar tomb of Houghton's most famous rector, Bernard Gilpin, d1583, whose generosity was legendary. He held open house on Sundays, and earned the sobriquet 'Apostle of the North' by making many trips into the wilds of Teesdale. His death came as a result of being knocked over by an ox at Durham market. **P.** *Open 07.30–13.00 Mon–Sat, from 08.00 Sun.* Old almshouses and school are picturesque neighbours.

Jarrow, St Paul　　　　　**21 M18**
Church Bank. Part of a monastery founded in 681, the church possesses a thrilling survival in the Saxon dedicatory stone, inscribed in Latin with the date: 'the 9th of the kalends of May in the 15th year of King Ecgfrid', that is, 23 April 685. The 7thC tower base and chancel are as venerable as Bede, who spent most of his life in the monastery, first as a novice and later as a renowned teacher and

St Paul, Jarrow

scholar. (Sacked twice by the Danes after his death in 735, some walls remain of the monastery refounded in the 11thC, but nothing of the 7thC monastic buildings.) Incredibly tiny windows peep out of the chancel S wall, with unimpeachable Saxon veracity, but the chair claiming to be Bede's is probably a 14thC imposter. The tower was heightened in the 11thC and the nave rebuilt in the 18thC and 19thC. **P.** *Open summer 09.00–17.30 Mon, from 10.00 Tue–Sat, from 11.00 Sun; winter 09.00–16.30 Mon, from 10.00 Tue, from 11.00 Wed–Sun.* Take time afterwards to visit Bede Monastery Museum in nearby Jarrow Hall, where fascinating exhibits from the monastic site illuminate its history, and where coffee is available.

Newcastle upon Tyne, St Andrew 21 L18
Newgate St. Spectacular zigzag ornament highlights the Norman chancel arch, which dominates the nave of the same period. See the double piscina and the squint in the restored 13thC chancel and, in the baptistery, the wonderfully ornate 15thC font cover, the Hanoverian Royal Arms and the painting of the Last Supper by L. Giordano. **P.** *Open 09.00–15.30 Mon–Fri, 09.30–12.00 Sun.*

Newcastle upon Tyne,　　　**21 L18**
St John Baptist
Grainger St. The medieval church has a 15thC tower with prominent pinnacles, and 14thC nave arcades. A cruciform opening in the former chancel once communicated with an anchorite's cell, and a window close by contains fragments of ancient stained glass, including the earliest known representation of the arms of Newcastle. Classical and Jacobean motifs are delightfully combined in the 17thC pulpit, and pinnacles and canopies generously adorn the remarkable medieval font cover. **P.** *Open 08.00–18.30 Mon, Tue & Thur, to 20.00 Wed, from 07.00 Fri, from 09.00 Sat; 08.00–12.30 & 18.00–20.30 Sun.* The castle which gave Newcastle its name is bisected by that much later engineering feat, the railway. On one side is the Norman keep, built by Henry II in 1172–77, with an elaborately detailed chapel in its forebuilding, and on the other the Black Gate of 1247.

◁ CLEVELAND ▷

Hart, St Mary Magdalene 21 M17
3m NW of Hartlepool of A179. The mighty
Norman tower and unadorned church
present themselves with pleasing
simplicity, in a hillocky, tree-shaded
setting with a view of the sea.
Immediately striking looking down the
nave is the top of a Saxon arch peeping
above the 15thC chancel arch and, higher
up, a Saxon doorway. There are other
Saxon remains: part of a blocked window
above the N arcade and, congregated at
the W end, baluster shafts and fragments
of crosses. Look at the large Norman font
and at the delightfully ornate 15thC font,
whose base is decorated by eight male
heads, four of them tonsured. Carved on
the bowl are figures with intricate curly
coiffures, as well as the signs of the
Evangelists and the Resurrection. Three
witches feature in the church registers,
including aptly named Old Mother
Midnight of Elwick. **P.** *Open May–Sep
14.00–16.00 Sun.*

St Mary Magdalene, Hart

Kirkleatham, St Cuthbert 19 N17
7m E of Middlesborough on A1042. This
model of Georgian grace was built in
1763, beside James Gibbs' spectacular
octagonal mausoleum of 1740. The
mausoleum's rusticated base, circular
windows and pyramidal roof crowned by
an urn, form an exciting Baroque
composition, entered from the chancel by
a doorway presided over by cherubs and
garlands. It was built to commemorate
Marwood Turner, who d1739 at 22, while
on the Grand Tour of Europe; his elegant
statue by Scheemakers stands inside,
surrounded by his books. Here too are
the plain monument to Sir William
Turner, d1692, founder of the Hospital,
Kirkleatham's sumptuously designed
almshouses, and a child's coffin of the
9thC. Fine furnishings in the church
include the pulpit, the font and its cover,

seating cut down from 18thC box pews,
the oak altar adorned with cherub heads
and the richly carved 14thC chest. There
are also good brasses and monuments,
mostly to Turners. **P.** *Open 14.00–17.00
Sat.* Mausoleum *open summer 14.00–17.00
Sat.* Visit the museum and the Hospital
chapel (by prior arrangement) for its
magnificent fittings and stained glass.

Norton, St Mary 18 M17
Village on outskirts of Stockton-on-Tees.
Handsome High St houses and modest
cottages fringing the green, stand in
worthy fraternisation with the church,
which is distinguished by a marvellous
Saxon tower. The entire N transept is
Saxon too. Built by monks from Durham,
the then cruciform church soon became
collegiate, with a vicar and eight secular
monks. Much of the present interior is
Transitional including the nave arcades.
Make a close inspection of the knight's
effigy under the tower, in truth a 14thC
Fulthorpe, but victim of a takeover by a
16thC member of the Blakiston family,
who altered the arms on the shield to his
own. Charming details surround the
curly-haired knight, who wears chain
mail and surcoat. **P.** *Open May-Sep 14.00–
16.00 Sat.* In the churchyard is the grave
of John Walker, inventor of matches.

Redmarshall, St Cuthbert 18 M17
4m W of Stockton off A177. Tree-
embowered, the restored Norman church
has a Perpendicular crown to its tower
and Perpendicular sedilia in the chancel.
Box pews and the balustraded altar rail
are distinctive 17thC contributions to the
furnishings. See the armoured effigy of
Thomas de Langton, d1440, and the
horned headdress worn by his wife. **P.**
Open 14.30–16.30 Sat.

Stockton-on-Tees, St Thomas 18 M17
High St. A chaste classicism characterises
the graciously proportioned church of
1710–12. But the chancel, rebuilt in 1904–
6, incorporates Baroque features with a
touch of exuberance, such as the details
round the Venetian E window inside.
Look especially at the fine 20thC
furnishings in the chancel, the impressive
remains of the former three-decker
pulpit, the ornate mayor's pew, and the
beautifully carved 20thC bench ends.
*Open 09.30–15.30 Mon–Fri, to 14.00 Sat;
10.00–12.30 & 17.30–19.00 Sun.*

YORKSHIRE
─── & THE ───
NORTH WEST

Cheshire   Greater Manchester   Lancashire
Merseyside   Humberside   Yorkshire

It is an open question to what extent a church should resemble a house. To those preoccupied with the pursuit of the Holy there are strong reasons why it should not, but if religion is not be pigeon-holed for Sundays, if the 'trivial round, the common task' can really furnish the materials of a living faith, then this likeness is not improper. It is in Cheshire that the greatest resemblance to secular dwellings is likely to be found. The south aisle of Lower Peover might be one of the wings of Little Moreton Hall, the classic 'black and white' house of the north west. Undoubtedly a number of Cheshire churches conformed with this custom, but against it must be set the fact that parishes tended to be very large and churches had to be capable of housing a large congregation; these are built of stone and not in the domestic style. The very remoteness of many parishioners from their parish church encouraged a proliferation of private chapels, some in noblemen's houses, some in modest squires' homes. These buildings more often date from the 17thC or 18thC and are, once again, domestic in style.

Going north from Cheshire, we come to Lancashire – a county which divides into at least four districts. As Sir William Addison noted: 'the churches of south Lancashire have little attraction for tourists in search of local style'. What they do find are some interesting specimens of what has been called 'Commissioners' Gothic'. The name derives from a Commission set up in 1818 to build churches in the new industrial areas. Lancashire received the largest number and the names Pugin, Gilbert Scott, Street or Taylor are to be found among their architects.

What was once the single county of Yorkshire has been divided for administrative reasons into Humberside, North Yorkshire, South Yorkshire and West Yorkshire, and the entries in the gazetteer that follow are shown under their 'new' counties. This brief introduction considers the area as a whole.

It was the Cistercian Order that really colonised Yorkshire, where the wild inhospitality of the land appealed to their ascetic ideals. But they soon cleared the forests, drained the marshes and gave the land the beauty which it largely still possesses, while deriving from it a wealth which was to be their spiritual downfall. They built with a simplicity that was demanded by their puritan standards and much of the 13thC building in Yorkshire reflects this austerity. But one can be austere on the grand scale, as the ruins of Fountains and Rievaulx, only the grandest among a large number of lesser houses, proclaim.

To build on this scale demands a ready supply of stone and in this Yorkshire is well stocked. The beautiful countryside of the Cleveland and Hambleton Hills yields a fine Jurassic limestone – the best of it at Aislaby. When Walpole was building his extravagant mansion at Houghton in Norfolk he imported his stone from here. The other important quarries are at Roche Abbey, where a magnesian limestone of great beauty has been extracted since Roman days. York Minster, Beverley and Ripon are all built of it. Unfortunately it does not tolerate pollution and most buildings in this stone have recently had problems on a massive scale.

The great towers of York and Selby could not fail to have an influence locally and towers are as much a feature of this part of the world as they are of Somerset.

Also included in this section are the sprawling conurbations of Merseyside and Greater Manchester, separated from their former counties by governmental re-organisation, but preserving their distinctive, historic heritage in both churches and municipal buildings.

◀ CHESHIRE ▶

Audlem, St James   **12** J11
10m W of Newcastle under Lyme on A525.
Standing on a mound in the picturesque village centre, the church makes a fine display with its prominent, shining clerestory. Further notable medieval features include the 13thC S doorway, with a head carved on one of its capitals, the lovely roofs, and the E window, whose tracery is poised between Decorated and Perpendicular styles. The brass chandelier is 18thC and the pulpit Jacobean. **P.** *Open 08.00–17.00 Mon–Fri, to 19.30 Sat, to 18.00 Sun.* Adjacent allurements are a number of pubs and the Shropshire Union canal.

Barthomley, St Bertoline   **12** K12
4m SE of Crewe off B5077. The substantial and stately tower rises to a pinnacled crown. A Norman introduction to the otherwise Perpendicular church is given by the N doorway. Notice the foliage unfurling from one of the nave capitals, the beautiful panelled roof above, and the intricately carved parclose screen. In the 16thC Crewe Chapel lie alabaster effigies of a 14thC knight, and a praying rector, d1529. An extravagant Victorian Gothic monument of 1856 commemorates the first Lord Crewe and a white marble

effigy Lady Houghton, d1887. **P.** *Open 09.00–dusk daily.* Black and white houses congregate in the village, and the church has a congenial pub as neighbour.

Birtles, St Catherine   **12** K12
4m W of Macclesfield on A537. Originally the private chapel of a stately home, this octagonal towered church of 1840 is adventurously adorned by richly gleaming 16thC and 17thC continental stained glass, and much Renaissance Dutch woodwork, including a screen and a manorial pew. The ornate pulpit is dated 1686 and the candelabra, copied from Milan Cathedral, add an Italian flourish. **P.** *Open 09.00–dusk daily.*

Gawsworth, St James   **12** K12 ˜
2m SW of Macclesfield on A536. Lakes and embracing parkland, the 15thC timber-framed rectory, and Elizabethan Gawsworth Hall form a romantic, courtly gathering about the 15thC–16thC church. Friezes and pinnacles deck the tower and the ornate S porch shares in its festive air. Fragments of 15thC stained glass glow here and there. Impressive monuments to the Fittons of Gawsworth Hall include that to Dame Alice, d1627, who sits disconsolately, head in hand,

wearing widow's weeds. Her children kneel in front and behind. **P** at Gawsworth Hall. *Open daylight hours daily.* Set apart from the churchyard is the tomb of 'Lord Flame', or Maggotty Johnson, dancing master and jester. Flamboyant even in death, his ghost roams neighbouring lanes on a white charger.

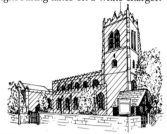

St Mary and All Saints, Great Budworth

Great Budworth, St Mary   **12** J12
and All Saints
8m SE of Warrington off A559. Hilltop centre-piece in a village setting of picturesque perfection, the generously proportioned, beautiful Perpendicular church lifts a crenellated rim on every side. The clerestory illuminates a splendid roof, supported on slender shafts. See the sizeable font, the bench ends, stalls, capacious chest, and the monuments. *Open 08.30–dusk Mon–Sat, 07.45–dusk or after Evensong Sun.* An 18thC baluster sundial stands in the churchyard. Arley Hall, 2m N, is a 19thC Jacobean-style mansion whose gardens are brimful with delights.

Macclesfield, St Michael   **12** K12
and All Angels
Market Pl. Thomas Savage, Archbishop of York, built the Savage Chapel at the start of the 16thC, with an opulent three-storeyed porch, graced by niches and an oriel window. Among interesting effigies in the chapel, those to two John Savages, who died in 1492 and 1527, demonstrate the change in fashionable footwear from pointed to broad. Arresting above all is the Pardon brass, to Robert Legh, d1506, with its consoling assurance that recitation of five paternosters, five aves and the creed brings 26,000 years and 26 days pardon. Archbishop Savage's parents lie holding hands in alabaster effigy in the chancel and here too lies a 15thC knight. The Legh Chapel was rebuilt in 1620 and Sir Arthur Blomfield rebuilt much of the medieval church in 1898–1901. A Jacobean wardens' pew and 18thC font are handsome features. The

church is strikingly positioned. **P.** *Open 09.00–12.00 Mon–Sat.*

Marton, St James and St Paul   **12** K12
4m SW of Macclesfield on A34. This is an enchanting 14thC black and white (half timber, half wattle and daub) church, with an impressive tower, conserving an ancient ladder, and a marvellous forest of timbers inside. Indeed the nave pillars arch up to the roof almost like tree branches. The timber font makes an essentially Victorian statement. The pulpit is Jacobean. Shadows of former wall paintings hover on the W wall. **P.** *Open summer 10.00–19.30 daily, winter 10.00–19.30 Sun.*

Nantwich, St Mary   **12** J12
4m SW of Crewe on A534. Parapets, crocketed ogee gables, and a riot of pinnacles enrich the magnificent Decorated chancel and octagonal tower. Perpendicular features include the E window and the S porch. Inside, the vaulted chancel is sumptuously detailed, as is the stone Perpendicular pulpit. Take time to examine the animatedly carved misericords on the gloriously canopied 14thC stalls. Note the wooden pulpit, dated 1601, and the alabaster effigy of Sir Thomas Smith, damaged but handsome. **P.** *Open 08.30–dusk Mon–Thur, from 07.30 Fri, 09.00–17.00 Sat, 07.30–19.30 Sun.* A former salt town, Nantwich numbers among its fine buildings Elizabethan half-timbered Churche's Mansion.

Shotwick, St Michael and All   **12** H12
Angels
6m NW of Chester off A550. A medieval port, Shotwick is now in rural retirement, 2m from the Dee estuary; it is graced by a 17thC manor house and the ancient church with a prominent Perpendicular tower. Furnishings – a Georgian three-decker pulpit, box pews and a churchwardens' pew – are a cause for delight. 14thC stained glass of the Annunciation in the tracery of the N aisle E window, an 18thC chandelier and the 15thC nail-studded door, also deserve admiration. **P.** *Open summer 10.00–19.00 daily, winter to 16.00.*

Siddington, All Saints   **12** K12
4½m SW of Macclesfield on B5392. In a delightful rustic setting, the church retains its original porch and timber-framed chancel, although the remainder is of brick painted black and white. A pretty rood screen and 17thC pulpit form part of the furnishings. **P.** *Open daylight hours daily.*

◁ GREATER MANCHESTER ▷

Ashton-under-Lyne,   **12** K13
St Michael and All Angels
Stamford St. The stately 15thC church was
rebuilt in the 19thC and has a memorably
lavish Perpendicular-style interior.
Especially eye-catching are the stone
carving in the spandrels of the nave
arcades and chancel arch, stone panelling
in the chancel, the cresting beneath the
clerestory, and the elaborate ceiling. A
puritan ordering of the furnishings is
reflected by the three-decker pulpit,
prominent near the middle of the nave N
arcade, with an angel in attendance, box
pews and galleries. Stained glass of c1500
bejewels the aisles with scenes from the
life of St Helena, kneeling figures of the
Asshetons who built the medieval
church, and kings. **P.** *Open 13.00–16.00
Wed–Sat.*

Eccles, St Mary   **12** K13
Church St. A window of medieval stained
glass and the 15thC nave roof are
particular embellishments of the largely
15thC–16thC church, whose E end was
rebuilt in the 19thC. Part of a Saxon
preaching cross, and the effigies of
Richard Brereton, d1600, and his wife,
with a baby at her side, are also
interesting features. *Open 10.00–17.00
Thur, 10.00–17.00 & 19.00–20.00 Fri,
10.00–12.00 Sat.*

Middleton, St Leonard   **12** K13
St Leonard's Sq. The spacious medieval
church stands on a hill. It has many
fascinating features, such as the gabled,
weatherboarded 17thC top to the tower,
the ornate S porch, the reset Norman
arch making a display of zigzag beneath
the tower, and a window in the chancel,
commemorating the Battle of Flodden
Field in 1513, in which named donors,
including archers, kneel. The Asshetons,
who built the church at Ashton-under-
Lyne, were active at Middleton in the
16thC; their arms are carved at the base
of the rood screen and they put in an
appearance themselves in chancel
brasses. **P.** *Open 10.00–12.00 & 14.00–
16.00 Mon–Sat, 14.00–16.00 most Sun.*

Standish, St Wilfrid   **12** J13
Market Sq. Except for a Victorian tower,
this large, late Gothic church is of 1582–4.
Intriguingly, the nave columns are
classical, although perfect Gothic arches
spring from them. Above is a beautiful
roof. An Elizabethan pulpit, 17thC altar
rail, and accomplished monuments are
further distinguishing features. Especially
remarkable are the alabaster effigy of
Edward Wrightinton, d1658, and the
women attending Richard Watt's
monument, by John Bacon Jr, 1806. **P.**
*Open 07.00–dusk Mon–Fri & Sun, from
09.00 Sat.*

◁ LANCASHIRE ▷

Halsall, St Cuthbert   **12** H13
3m W of Ormskirk on A567. Among
manifold interesting features of this
restored Decorated and Perpendicular
church, fiendish gargoyles clamour for
attention, a bevy of pinnacles, two
turrets and a sanctus bellcote make
appealing Perpendicular statements from
the chancel, and the square tower
finishes in an octagon and spire. Don't
miss the praying man in a boat projecting
from the SE corner of the church. Inside,
look for the wrestlers carved among the
marvellous misericords on the 15thC
chancel stalls, and note the fine traceried
Decorated door, and a 14thC priest's
effigy in an ornate recess. Medieval
stained glass fragments shed a ruby glow
from the S aisle E window. **P.** *Open
summer 08.30–20.00 daily, winter to 16.00.*

Heysham, St Peter   **17** H15
Suburb of Morecambe. Beside the sea and
touched by the wide embrace of
Morecambe, distinctive features of the
former village still stand out, the ancient
church in particular. Curiously carved on
one side of a Saxon cross shaft in the
churchyard is a gabled house with
chimneys, with three busts looking out
of windows and a swathed figure in the
doorway below. The Saxon W doorway
and a hogback tombstone are further
interesting early elements. Note too the
Perpendicular screen. The double bellcote
is 17thC and so is the font cover. **P.** *Open
approx 10.00–dusk daily. Sometimes closed
during winter and spring school holidays.*
Aristocratic Elizabethan Heysham Old
Hall has long gone public as the
Middleton Arms.

Lancaster, St Mary   **17** J15
Castle Hill. Stately neighbour to mighty
Lancaster Castle, which lords it over the
river Lune, the 14thC and 15thC church
has a tower of 1754 and an elaborate
porch of 1903. Roman basilica, Saxon
shrine and Norman priory church have
all stood on the site. 18thC brass
chandeliers branch out beautifully in the
nave and chancel, where canopies carved
with foliage of fabulous luxuriance
embellish the stalls, whose provenance is
possibly Furness Abbey. Saxon cross
fragments carved with a variety of
subjects form an impressive congregation
in the church, and monuments include
one by Roubiliac. **P.** *Open summer 08.00–
21.00 daily, except during Sun services,
winter to 17.30.* Dignified Georgian
houses, the Judge's Lodgings of 1675
and the handsome Music Room are
close by.

Lancaster Priory

Poulton-le-Fylde, St Chad   **17** H14
The confident Georgian classical
rebuilding of 1752–3 is attached to a
17thC tower and asserts itself
prominently in the two S doorways.
Remark too the Fleetwood vault
entrance, dated 1699. Georgian galleries
and box pews, hatchments and
chandelier, form an elegant assembly,
together with the Jacobean screen and
pulpit, flourishing arabesques. **P.** *Open*

*07.45–17.15 Mon–Wed & Sat, to 19.30 Thur
& Fri, 08.00–20.00 Sun.*

Ribchester, St Wilfrid   **17** J14
4m N of Blackburn on B6245. Hills and the
river Ribble, bridged handsomely in 1774,
curve round the attractive village; the
White Bull of 1707 projects a porch on
columns said to come from the Roman
fort of Bremetennacum, on which the
village stands. Beneath the churchyard
lies the fort's treasury, and two of the
columns supporting the W gallery inside
the medieval church are thought to be
Roman. The delightfully elaborate pulpit
is Jacobean and the box pews Georgian.
P. *Open 08.00–dusk daily.* A replica of a
spectacular Roman ceremonial helmet
found on the site of Bremetennacum in
the 18thC is exhibited in the small
museum beside the churchyard.

Tunstall, St John Baptist   **17** J15
11m NE of Lancaster on A683. In a rural
setting, the lovely church, which was
rebuilt in 1415, survives untouched by
restorers. A Roman altar stone from
Burrow Hall, to the N, is built into the
church wall. There is 15thC and 16thC
Dutch stained glass in the E window,
and memorial tablets abound. **P.** *Open
daylight hours daily.* Charlotte and Emily
Brontë came here from the Clergy
Daughters' School they attended from
1824–5 at nearby Cowan Bridge, and
were given food in the room over the
porch after the morning service. Tunstall
is the 'Brocklehurst' of *Jane Eyre.*

Woodplumpton, St Anne   **17** J14
4m NW of Preston on B5411. Delightfully
harmonious union of styles is achieved in
this Perpendicular church with a
Georgian cupola and S aisle and a nave
roof of 1900. In the churchyard witch
Meg Shelton is buried under a boulder
large enough to ensure she does not re-
emerge. **P.** *Open summer some weekdays.*

◀ MERSEYSIDE ▶

Huyton, St Michael   **12** J13
7m E of Liverpool on A5080 or M62. The
medieval church has 17thC and 19thC
additions, but retains its Perpendicular
tower, crowned with Georgian pinnacles,
Perpendicular chancel with a later
hammerbeam roof, and 14thC S arcade.

Remarkable features are the early
Norman font and the delightfully carved
rood screen of c1500, repaired in
Jacobean fashion in the middle of the
17thC. Two stained glass windows in the
S aisle are by Holiday. *Open 14.00–16.00
Thur, 12.30–13.30 Fri.*

Our Lady and St Nicholas, Liverpool

Liverpool, Our Lady　　　　**12** H13
and St Nicholas
Old Churchyard, Pierhead. The parish
church is in the city's dockland heart.
Take the ferry across the Mersey to
Pierhead for a sense of ambitious
Edwardian Liverpool, communicated by a
wide panorama which includes the Royal
Liver, Cunard and Port of Liverpool
buildings. The church has a 14thC
foundation, although no part of the
medieval building remains. It was rebuilt
in 1952 after Second World War
bombing, but the impressive steeple of
1811–15 survives. The spire is a splendid,
soaring structure with pronounced
pinnacles linked to an openwork
octagonal lantern by flying buttresses.
Inside, look for the fine memorial to
Robert Hawkinson, d1829, on which the
three Cardinal Virtues appear. **P.** *Open
08.00–17.00 Mon–Fri, 09.00–10.30 Sat,
08.30–12.00 Sun.*

Woolton, St Peter　　　　**12** H13
Suburb of Liverpool on A562. The red
sandstone Victorian church by G. E.
Grayson and E. Ould is built in imposing
Perpendicular style. See the two stained
glass windows by William Morris in the
baptistery and in the S aisle, the alabaster
font and pulpit and the elaborate timber-
framed lychgate. **P.** *Open 09.00–16.00
Mon–Thur.* This is a place of pilgrimage
for fans of the Beatles. A meeting
between John Lennon and Paul
McCartney at a fête here in the 1950s led
to the formation of the group, whose
music still reverberates round the world.
John Lennon attended the church
spasmodically as a teenager and joined
the youth club for a few weeks.

◁ HUMBERSIDE ▷

Alkborough, St John the Baptist　19 O14
7m N of Scunthorpe off B1430. Fascinating
features include the beautiful cross shaft
in the churchyard, a maze in the porch
floor, and the Saxon tower, which
incorporates Roman masonry in the arch
opening into the nave. The tower summit
is 13thC and so are the finely detailed S
doorway with leafy capitals, and the
nave arcades. The chancel of 1887 is by
J. O. Scott. **P.** *Open 08.00–dusk daily.*
Close by is a large turf maze and a view
of the confluence of the rivers Trent and
Ouse, giving birth to the Humber.

Beverley, Minster of　　　　**19** O14
St John and St Martin
Of cathedral dimensions, the minster
forms an exquisite Early English,
Decorated and Perpendicular symphony
in stone. A panoply of crocketed
pinnacles aspires from the 15thC twin-
towered W front, a composition of
soaring grace. The 18thC W door was
designed by Hawksmoor. From the W
front the minster moves back in time,
along the lavish Decorated nave and
aisles to the 13thC double-aisled
transepts and chancel, which embody the

purity and harmony of the Early English style to perfection. After his victory at Agincourt, Henry V came to give thanks at the shrine of St John of Beverley, which was once supported by the beautiful stone Percy screen. The Decorated Percy Tomb, to an unknown Percy, is encrusted with detail of unrivalled magnificence. Clusters of luscious fruits and foliage, hosts of little angels hovering everywhere, armoured knights squeezed into spandrels, and a serene statue of Christ holding the Virgin's soul in a napkin, invest it with charm and vitality. The splendidly carved sedilia are of the same period. Take time to look at the lively misericords on the 16thC stalls. The Saxon Frith Stool, the monuments and the ebullient font cover of 1713, adorned with scrolls and a dove, are worthy of attention too. **P.** *Open if guides available summer 09.00–20.00 daily, winter to dusk.*

Beverley, St Mary   **19 O14**
North Bar Within. The nave and tower of this glorious, loftily spacious church were rebuilt after the collapse of an earlier tower in 1520. The sumptuous replacement tower rises to a display of panelled parapets and 16 pinnacles. The 15thC W front has two distinctive turrets, whose graceful openwork lantern tops were rebuilt by A. W. N. Pugin, who also designed the stained glass in the W window. See the beautiful vaulting in the 14thC N chancel chapels and the 40 delightful, limber, curly-locked English kings, with scrolls circling behind them, first painted on the chancel ceiling in 1445, though since redone. Donors to the building of the nave pillars, recorded in inscriptions, include the minstrels, five of whom form an endearing assembly at the top of their pillar. Look for the dapper stone pilgrim rabbit, said to be the inspiration for the White Rabbit in Lewis Carroll's *Alice in Wonderland.* Green men, kings, eagles, foxes and monks form part of the congregation carved on the misericords of the 15thC stalls. *Open summer 09.00–19.00 Mon–Sat, 08.00–20.00 Sun, winter to 16.00.*

Bridlington, Priory church   **19 P15**
of St Mary
Church Grn. The magnificent priory church was founded c1120 by Walter de Gant, and the great 12thC Tournai marble tomb slab may be his. Nave, aisle and two towers form the present church, whose choir was pulled down at the Dissolution. A startling contrast is made by the 13thC NW tower and

Perpendicular SW tower, the top stages of which were rebuilt by G. G. Scott in the 19thC. Admire the sumptuous, turreted N porch. Light floods into the 13thC–14thC interior through the beautiful clerestory and triforium. Remains of the priory's cloister have been re-erected in the N aisle. **P.** *Open 10.00–17.00 Mon–Sat.* A museum is housed in the Bayle Gate to the SW; the priory's gatehouse, it is all that remains of the monastic buildings.

Cottingham, St Mary the Virgin   **19 O14**
The large cruciform church has a stately Perpendicular tower with a remarkable stair turret. The W window with lavish flowing tracery faces a Perpendicular window at the other end of the Decorated nave. See the restored brass to Capuchin friar, Nicholas de Luda, d1384, who built the fine chancel. **P.** *Open 09.00–18.00 daily.* Georgian houses lend a gracious air to the village, a suburb of Hull.

Grimsby, St James   **14 P13**
St James' Sq. The majestic, cruciform church has undergone extensive 19thC and 20thC restoration, but retains its 13thC core. The nave pillars and arches are mightily impressive and above them an arcaded passage is unusually combined with the clerestory. Look for the carving of an imp in the N aisle. **P.** *Open approx 12.00–14.00 Mon, 10.30–15.30 Tue, 09.45–15.00 Wed, from 10.30 Thur, from 11.30 Fri; 09.30–11.30 Sat, 08.00–12.00 Sun.*

St Peter and St Paul, W front

Howden, St Peter and St Paul   **19 N14**
The magnificent, tall-windowed tower, and 13thC–14thC church shed lustre on the small market town, and offer a ruined choir and chapter house, built for a college of priests, to fire the romantic

imagination. The choir roof and upper walls collapsed in 1696, and the chapter house roof in 1750. Ornate turrets with crocketed spirelets adorn the W front. Admire the vaulted S porch, decorated by leafy capitals and bosses, the beautiful 15thC reredos and stone screens, knights of brass and stone, and woodwork by the 'Mouse Man', Robert Thompson of Kilburn, which carries his charming signature: a carved mouse. **P.** *Open 08.45–19.00 Mon–Fri, to 18.45 Sat, 08.00–19.30 Sun.*

Kingston-upon-Hull,   **19** O14
Holy Trinity
South Church Side. Rising in Decorated and Perpendicular splendour in the city's heart, the cruciform church is among the largest in England. It displays a very early use of brick in the transepts, tower base and chancel. The Perpendicular windows are so large as to become gorgeous glass screens. Slender pillars and soaring arches make a long, graceful procession up the nave and into the chancel, where Perpendicular window tracery is exchanged for flowing Decorated tracery. See the Perpendicular screens of varying degrees of elaboration, the exuberant Rococo altar and reredos of 1750, the alabaster effigies of Sir William de la Pole, 14thC merchant and first mayor of Hull, and his wife, the lovely 14thC font, decorated with gables and charming details, including a knight and dragon, and angels' wings, and two stained glass windows of 1897 and 1907 by Walter Crane. *Open 09.00–16.30 Mon, Tue, Thur & Fri, to 12.30 Sat.*

Kingston-upon-Hull,   **19** O14
St Mary the Virgin
Lowgate. The tower of the 15thC church was rebuilt in 1697. A Victorian stamp was given to the exterior by 19thC restoration, which included the addition of a second S aisle and the piercing of a passage through the tower. The nave pillars imitate those of Holy Trinity. Look at the memorial to William Dobson, d1666, accompanied by two putti, the Tudor brass, and the screen and rood by Temple Moore. *Open 12.30–16.00 Mon–Fri, 10.30–13.00 Sun.* Explore Wilberforce House, Trinity House, the Town Docks Museum and the Marina.

Lockington, St Mary   **19** O14
5m NW of Beverley off A164. In a picturesque setting, by a 17thC manor house and a moated motte, the Norman S doorway and reordered parts of the chancel arch are the earliest features of the medieval church. The 13thC tower has a later brick summit. Bosses embellish the fine nave and chancel roofs. Note the W screen, composed of 18thC woodwork in 1893, when Temple Moore restored the church, Mary Moyser, d1633, reclining in effigy in the heraldically decorated Estoft Chapel of 1635, and fragments of medieval stained glass in the chancel windows. **P.** *Open daylight hours daily.*

St Mary, Lockington

North Newbald, St Nicholas   **19** O14
9m NW of Kingston-upon-Hull on A1034. The cruciform Norman church is impressively intact. A corbel table on the outside, zigzag in the doorway arches, round-arched windows, and the powerful arches and boldly scalloped capitals of the crossing, all make unimpeachable Norman statements. The Norman font displays delightful leaf decoration. A 13thC belfry was added to the tower and the chancel was rebuilt in the 15thC. **P.** *Open daylight hours daily.*

Patrington, St Patrick   **19** P14
13m SE of Kingston-upon-Hull on A1033. Majesty, beauty and harmony mingle in this 13thC–14thC cruciform church, with double-aisled transepts and a spire soaring from an arcaded, pinnacled crown. Don't miss the lissom 13thC statue of the Virgin below the outside of the E window. Flowing window tracery and foliated capitals on clustered pillars celebrate the Decorated style, as do the ornate font, and crocketed ogee gables of the sedilia and piscina. Be sure to examine the carvings on the Easter Sepulchre opposite, where slumbering soldiers sit under delightful little ogee arches and Christ rises above in an ungainly fashion, as though getting out of bed, while ecstatic angels swing censers either side. The tower staircase

makes a charmingly eccentric appearance above the S arch of the crossing. The small Lady Chapel in the S transept has an apse with a fine stone reredos and a lantern pendant with a carving of the Virgin. **P.** *Open 09.00–18.00 daily.*

Welwick, St Mary   **19** P14
15m SE of Kingston-upon-Hull on B1445. The Decorated church, with lovely flowing tracery in its windows, incorporates earlier work. Notice the window in the chancel S wall, in which a transition from three to four lights was imperfectly made, the effigy of a medieval priest, lying under an ornate rib-vaulted canopy, and the brass commemorating William Wright, brother of two conspirators in the Gunpowder Plot. *Open daylight hours daily.*

◁ SOUTH YORKSHIRE ▷

Aston-cum-Aughton, All Saints   **13** M13
5m SE of Rotherham on A618. Pierced battlements and pinnacles enrich the summit of the Perpendicular tower and busts preside over the Perpendicular porch. The lovely Norman interior has box pews and extends into a restored 14thC chancel. A feature of great curiosity is a small, bearded man with a sword, sitting slumped at the foot of the font, whose significance is unknown. Lord Darcy, d1624, and his three wives kneel in striking effigy, and a Coade stone tablet with a profile portrait commemorates poet William Mason, d1797, who was host to Thomas Gray, author of *Elegy in a Country Churchyard,* in the rectory. *Open daylight hours daily.*

Burghwallis, St Helen   **13** M13
9m N of Doncaster off A1. A Norman tower and early Norman herringbone masonry in the nave and chancel distinguish the little church, whose S door retains its medieval iron hinges. The restored medieval rood screen is a rare treasure in Yorkshire and makes a delightful display. Inspect the brass commemorating Sir Thomas Gascoigne, d1554. **P.** *Open daylight hours daily.*

Conisbrough, St Peter   **13** M13
Church St. Commanding the river Don, Conisbrough Castle imbues the townscape with drama, in which the church is also prominent. Its tower flourishes an elaborate Perpendicular crown and the body of the church displays Saxon work and an impressive Norman core. Vigorously carved capitals stand out in the nave arcades, and an intricately carved Norman tomb-chest rewards close scrutiny. Crowded with movement, a gloriously naive bishop and combative dragon appear in separate scenes on one side and Adam, Eve and serpent on another. Notice the Perpendicular clerestory and font, the 13thC pillar piscina and the modern N chapel. **P.** *Open summer 09.00–17.00 daily, winter to 16.00.* Hameline Plantagenet, half-brother of Henry II, built the formidable 12thC castle keep, remarkable for its circular form and mighty buttresses.

Darfield, All Saints   **13** M13
5m E of Barnsley on A635. Largely a 14thC church, the tower is Norman and has a Perpendicular top. Jacobean pews, balustered altar rails and font cover array the interior handsomely, and ornately carved medieval panels compose a pew in the chancel. Alabaster effigies of a knight and lady of c1400 lie in the S chapel. Dainty 18thC painting adorns the S aisle ceiling. **P.** *Open daylight hours daily.*

Norton, St James the Great   **13** M13
Suburb of Sheffield, on A6102. The church of Norman origin has a 13thC tower and Perpendicular additions. Examine the animal carvings on the 13thC font, and the elaborately detailed tomb with 16thC effigies between the chancel and chapel. Sir Francis Chantrey, d1841, who infused memorial sculpture with life and expression, was born at Norton and is buried in the churchyard. A tablet commemorates him in the church and an obelisk in the centre of the former village. **P.** *Open 12.00–17.00 Mon–Fri, to 18.30 Sat; 08.00–19.30 Sun.*

Owston, All Saints   **13** M13
8m N of Doncaster off A19. Set in the park of an 18thC house, the church tower climbs from a Norman base up to a 13thC belfry and a Perpendicular summit. The body of the church reflects similar stages of growth, and in addition has a Decorated chancel with a fine E window. A pretty Perpendicular rood

screen, a brass to Robert of Hatfield, d1417, and his wife, excellent monuments by Chantrey, and the grave of a Cromwellian captain, are further distinguishing features. **P.** *Open 09.00–12.30 Sun, 12.00–17.00 summer Sat.*

Rotherham, All Saints   **13** M13
All Saints Sq. This is a sumptuous battlemented and pinnacled Perpendicular church with a soaring steeple at its heart. The tower is fan-vaulted and the interior spacious and graceful. Bosses decorate the panelled nave ceiling. In the 14thC chancel are 15thC stalls with delightfully figured poppyheads, and elegant sedilia. A Georgian sounding board consorts with a superlative Jacobean pulpit. The monuments are worth examining. *Open 09.00–16.00 Mon, Tue, Thur & Fri, to 12.00 Sat; 08.00–12.00 Sun.*

All Saints, 15thC stalls

Royston, St John Baptist   **13** M13
3m N of Barnsley on B6428. An oriel window unexpectedly looks out from the substantial Perpendicular tower. Roofs with finely carved bosses embellish the medieval interior. Perpendicular screens lead into the chapels, and Perpendicular and Jacobean meet in the font and its cover. Putti bring zest to two wonderfully imaginative monuments. **P.** *Open approx 07.00–19.00 daily.*

St Mary, Tickhill

Tickhill, St Mary   **13** N13
St Mary's Rd. The majestic, soaring Perpendicular church incorporates the tower base of a 13thC predecessor. The tower top is exquisitely fashioned and below are statues of the donors, a knight and his son and a lady. Flooded with light through the clerestory and large windows everywhere, the spacious interior is heartlifting. Wonderfully fluid lines course round the arches, whose capitals make a modest leafy display. Lovely medieval stained glass remains in the tops of the S aisle windows, a remarkable font cover of 1959 by G. G. Pace surmounts the Perpendicular font, and a grand 16thC monument stands in the N aisle. **P.** *Open daylight hours daily.* Tickhill's Norman castle is a shadow of its former stalwart self.

Wath upon Dearne, All Saints   **13** M13
7m SE of Barnsley on A6023. The Norman tower was heightened in the 15thC and the N arcade, decorated by scalloped capitals, is impressively Norman. 13thC contributions include the S porch, chancel and S arcade. Chandeliers embellish the nave, and the chest carved

with fabulous beasts, animals and lively tracery patterns, rewards close scrutiny. **P.** *Open 09.00–17.00 daily.*

Worsbrough, St Mary   **13** M13
1m S of Barnsley off A61. Of great interest in the medieval church, with a Norman chancel and Perpendicular arcades, are the porch roof and traceried door (whose

inscription commemorates the donors), the 18thC squire's pew, and the painted oak double-decker monument to Sir Roger Rockley, d1534. Sir Roger's effigy lies clad in knightly armour on top, and a ghastly cadaver successfully fills the role of *memento mori* below. **P.** *Open 09.00–18.00 Wed, Fri & Sat, 08.00–20.00 Sun.* There is a working corn mill nearby.

◁ WEST YORKSHIRE ▷

Adel, St John the Baptist   **18** M14
3m N of Leeds off A660. Encrusted with fascinating carvings, the small Norman church is a delight to study. A corbel table of animals and faces extends along the sides of nave and chancel, and along the W gable, below the 19thC bellcote. The gabled S portal, presided over by a worn Christ in Majesty, is spectacular in its lavish detail. The chancel arch shares in its opulence. Among carvings of charm and simplicity on the capitals appear a centaur with a bow and Christ with upstretched arms plunging into baptismal waters, while an angel flies horizontally towards him holding his clothes. There is a rare Norman bronze door ring of a beady-eyed monster about to gulp down a man's head. **P.** *Open 08.00–18.00 Mon–Sat, to 19.30 Sun.*

Horbury, St Peter and   **18** M14
St Leonard
3m SW of Wakefield on A642. Northgate. John Carr, who designed and paid for the building of the handsome church in 1791–3, is buried here. The elegant tower finishing in a rotunda of columns and conical spire, and an imposing Ionic portico are the distinguishing features of the exterior. Inside a gentle vault arches over the nave, which is lined with Corinthian columns and pilasters. The apsidal E end is punctuated by graceful windows. **P** nearby. *Open 07.00–19.00 daily.*

Ledsham, All Saints   **18** M14
3m N of Castleford off A1. The lovely Saxon church stands in a picturesque village. A Norman belfry and a Perpendicular summit and spire complete the Saxon tower base. The ornate frame round the tower doorway is a Victorian renewal, and the Saxon nave and chancel arch are accompanied by a Perpendicular N aisle and chapel. Sir John Lewis, who founded almshouses in the village in

1670, and his granddaughter, Lady Betty Hastings, who founded an orphanage in 1721, each recline on an elbow in fine marble effigy. Lady Betty was universally lauded as a paragon of virtue and intelligence, and continues her education by reading a book. **P.** *Open 09.00–dusk Mon–Sat, to 17.00 Sun.*

All Saints, Ledsham

Leeds, Holy Trinity   **18** M14
Boar La. Designed by Halfpenny in 1721–7, the church lends Georgian grace to its city centre setting. The tower, with an elegant and unusual spire, was added in 1839. Inside, the curved ceiling is supported by colossal Corinthian columns, and Venetian windows light and apse. *Open 09.00–16.00 Mon–Wed & Fri, 09.00–11.00 Sun.*

Leeds, St Peter   **18** M14
Kirkgate. The large, interesting, early Victorian church braves an unappealing setting near the railway. R. D. Chantrell designed it in Decorated and Perpendicular style for Dean Hook, vicar from 1837–59. The imposing tower has pierced battlements and pinnacles. Immediately striking upon entering are canopied galleries stretching along the nave. Observe too the panelling below the clerestory, and the plaster vaulting in the apse, which was decorated in 1876

St Peter, Leeds

with mosaics by Salviati of Venice. The Saxon cross from the preceding medieval church is marvellously carved. Medieval brasses, a knight's effigy, and a multitude of 18thC and 19thC monuments are gathered in the church. **P.** *Open 08.00–18.00 daily.*

Otley, All Saints   **18** L14
Kirkgate. The church is composed of diverse stylistic elements, including a late Norman N door and chancel windows, a 14thC tower, much 15thC work and a Georgian porch. Earlier than all are the wonderfully carved Saxon cross fragments, whose various subjects include a thoroughly admirable dragon and portrait busts under arches. Examine too the reredos by Bromett and Thorman, which bows to Art Nouveau and Gothic. Monuments commemorate Fairfaxes and Fawkes's. In the churchyard a scale model of Bramhope Tunnel commemorates those killed in its construction, 1845–9. *Open 09.00–17.00 daily.*

Tong, St James   **18** L14
3½m SE of Bradford off A650. A 17thC cottage joins in the picturesque ensemble formed by the church of 1727 and brick Tong Hall of 1702. A Norman arch and Perpendicular window tracery in the tower are relics of a medieval predecessor. The handsome interior is furnished in pure Georgian fashion, with W gallery, squire's pew, three-decker pulpit and box pews. *Open 10.00–17.00 daily.*

St James, Tong

◁ NORTH YORKSHIRE ▷

Askrigg, St Oswald   **18** K16
15m SW of Richmond off A684. The church looks W into wonderfully scenic Wensleydale and E into the picturesque village, where immediately striking features are the cross, pump, and ornamented door lintels on the houses opposite. Clarity characterises the late Perpendicular design, in which nave and chancel are continuous. The oak timbers of the ceiling make a glorious display and under the tower four stone ribs, crossing from side to side instead of diagonally, are prominent in the vault. **P.** *Open 09.00–dusk daily.*

Aysgarth, St Andrew   **18** K16
13m SW of Richmond on A684. In Wensleydale, close to exhilarating Aysgarth Falls, the large 19thC church stands in a spacious churchyard. The base of the tower remains from the medieval church and so do some sumptuous furnishings from Jervaulx Abbey. The exquisite screen on the S was taken from the abbey at the Dissolution, and the vicar's stall is made from two poppy-headed bench ends, carved with delightful intricacy. Stained glass in the vestry commemorates a rector's rescue from robbers in 1860. *Open 07.00–dusk daily.*

Bedale, St Gregory　　　　**18** L16
6m SW of Northallerton on A684. Brian
Fitzalan, lord of Bedale and a favourite of
Edward I, added the S aisle to the church
c1300, and Matilda, his second wife,
probably built the powerfully defensive
14thC tower, to which a Perpendicular
belfry was joined. Brian Fitzalan's
impressive alabaster effigy lies near the
tower arch inside, with that of his first
wife Muriel. Strikingly, her effigy is
frozen in vigorous movement, instead of
expressing the perfect composure
common to medieval monumental
sculpture. Two medieval knights and a
priest also appear in effigy, and a
classical memorial by Sir Richard
Westmacott commemorates Henry Peirse,
d1824. Notice the barrel-vaulted S porch
with huge ribs, the vaulted crypt beneath
the 14thC chancel and the N arcade of
c1200, whose details display an
extravagant creative impulse. A 14thC
wall painting of St George and the
dragon also commands attention. **P.** *Open
daylight hours daily.* In a dignified setting
with Georgian Bedale Hall close by.

Bilton-in-Ainsty, St Helen　　　**18** M15
7m W of York off B1224. The Norman
church presents an august W front with a
13thC bellcote. In the Norman S doorway
is a door dated 1633. Bold zigzag
decorates the chancel arch and a little
fleur-de-lis the S arcade. Examine the
fascinating figures carved on the remains
of Saxon crosses. **P.** *Open daylight hours
daily.*

Bolton Abbey, Priory church　　**18** L15
of St Mary and St Cuthbert
5m NE of Skipton on B6160. In a
Wharfedale setting of picturesque
perfection, the nave of the priory church,
founded in the 12thC, forms the parish
church. Beyond it stretch the choir and
transepts in ruins resonant with
romance. Norman work remains in the
14thC chancel. The beautifully detailed
13thC W front is shielded by an ornate
16thC tower base, whose ascent was
halted by the Dissolution. The majestic
13thC nave has an impressive wall
passage on the S, running below tall
windows containing stained glass by A.
W. N. Pugin. *Open daylight hours daily.*

Bolton Percy, All Saints　　　**18** M14
7m S of York off A64. An ancient timber-
framed tithe barn stands picturesquely
nearby. Notice the churchyard sundial
and the fine 15thC cross on the E gable,
with the Virgin on one side and a crucifix

on the other. Built by a rector at the
beginning of the 15thC, the church has a
magnificent chancel. Saints bestow
blessings from medieval stained glass
glowing in the E window, and an angel
ministers at the piscina. Knobs give a
finishing touch to the Jacobean box pews.
The font cover of the same period makes
an elaborately carved ascent above the
Norman font. Among the monuments,
that of 1807 by John Bacon Jr is
charming. Limited **P.** *Open 09.00–19.00
daily.*

Bossall, St Botolph　　　　**19** N15
9m NE of York off A64. Woodland and
handsome Bossall Hall enhance the
setting of the lovely 12thC and 13thC
cruciform church, which retains its
impressive crossing arches intact. An
opulently detailed 13thC S doorway
shelters in a 19thC porch. Fluted lobes
shape the 12thC font unusually. The
Royal Arms of 1710, and the Jacobean
monuments are also remarkable. Kempe
contributed to the stained glass. **P.** *Open
daylight hours daily.*

Brayton, St Wilfrid　　　　**19** N14
1½m S of Selby off A19. The splendid
Norman tower stands in startling
combination with an octagonal
Perpendicular lantern and spire, which
make a wide survey of the countryside.
The Norman work, brimming with
vivacity, was directed by a monk named
Hugh, who later became the second
abbot of Selby Abbey. Canopied saints
and interlacing foliage are among the
carvings on the capitals of the S
doorway, while beak-head, figured
medallions and zigzag curve round the
arch. The zigzag-decorated chancel arch
throws a huge span across the 14thC
chancel and displays heads and dragons
on its capitals. The plainness of the
Perpendicular aisles and clerestory is in
noticeable contrast. In the chancel, which
is longer than the nave, the 16thC Darcy
tomb has interesting details but headless
effigies, and flowing tracery dramatises
the E window. **P.** *Open 09.00–17.00 Mon–
Sat, 08.00–20.00 Sun.*

Burneston, St Lambert　　　**18** M16
6m NW of Thirsk on B6285, just off A1.
Generously Perpendicular, the church is
a worthy receptacle for an entire set of
Jacobean pews of plain but magnanimous
design. Presiding over them is a three-
decker pew bearing caryatids and an
inscription which declares that Thomas
Robinson paid £50 for them in 1627. See

the lavish sedilia in the chancel and canopied niches either side of the E window. **P.** *Open 08.00–dusk Mon–Sat, from 09.00 Sun.*

Catterick, St Anne   **18** L16
4m SE of Richmond on A1. By green and stream, the church was built in 1412–15, according to a contract between Lady Catherine de Burgh and her son and Richard of Cracall, mason. Brasses of members of the de Burgh family are one of the highlights of the church. See too the knightly effigy of Sir Walter de Urswick, Chief Forester to John of Gaunt in the Forest of Swaledale. The handsome black marble font is the proud bearer of the arms of the de Burghs and other great medieval families. **P.** *Open approx 09.00–dusk daily.*

St Michael, Thomas and Henry Belasyse

Coxwold, St Michael   **18** M15
7m SE of Thirsk off A170. Stone houses climb the hill to the prominently positioned Perpendicular church, whose impressive octagonal tower surveys beautiful countryside. Openwork parapets, gargoyles and a pinnacle parade distinguish the exterior. Inside, attention is irresistibly drawn to the ornate Belasyse monuments, expressive of sentiments secular and spiritual, which

dominate the chancel of 1774. The altar rail loops out into the chancel to accommodate them. Most remarkable are the vainglorious figures of Thomas Belasyse, d1700, and his father Henry, who wears a Roman tunic in combination with a curly Stuart wig. Refusing the earl's coronet offered by his son, Henry Belasyse appears to opt for the heavenly crown held aloft by gorgeous, chubby cherubs, and clearly believes it is his for the choosing. Other interesting features are the bosses which stud the nave roof, the 15thC stained glass in the window tops, the Georgian Royal Arms, the W gallery and the box pews. Laurence Sterne, author of *Tristram Shandy*, was rector from 1760–68. Buried in London, he was reburied here in 1969. *Open 08.30–dusk daily.* Shandy Hall, where Sterne lived, is on the edge of the village and Newburgh Priory, home of the Belasyses, is nearby.

Drax, St Peter and St Paul   **19** N14
4m SE of Selby off A63. Outside, gargoyles command the battlemented Perpendicular clerestory of sumptuous design, while inside beautifully carved saints and apostles hold sway. The Norman tower leads up to a Perpendicular belfry and spire, and the N arcade declares its Norman nature in zigzag-decorated arches. Note the fine 16thC bench ends, where Gothic and Renaissance details mingle, and the lovely lancet windows in the 13thC chancel. **P.** *Open 09.00–18.00 daily.*

Easby, St Agatha   **18** L16
1m SE of Richmond off B6271. The crumbling magnificence of Easby Abbey ruins, with Georgian Easby Hall above, the ribboning river Swale, and a panoramic view of Richmond, create a remarkable setting for the lovely, bellcoted Early English church of humble height. The porch with a priest's chamber above and the S aisle were added in the 15thC, and the chancel arch in the 19thC. The replica of the richly sculptured Saxon Easby Cross, whose original is in the Victoria and Albert Museum, is of much interest. Next in antiquity are the Norman font, beautifully decorated with arcading and a frieze, and the S windows in the chancel. 13thC wall paintings in the chancel are a joy to gaze at for their lithe figures, medieval dress and appealing details, such as the crow at the sower's heels. Bishops are frescoed at the back of the sedilia. Medieval stained glass in the E

window shows the habit worn by the canons of the abbey. **P.** *Open 07.00–18.00 daily.*

Hackness, St Peter   **19** O16
4m W of Scarborough off A165. In a sylvan setting near 18thC Hackness Hall. A venerable presence in the church is an exquisitely carved and inscribed 8thC cross, commemorating an abbess of a Saxon nunnery that stood here. Notice the graceful 13thC tower arch, and the magnificent Perpendicular font cover with a bevy of buttresses and crocketed gables. The Norman S arcade and Early English N arcade lead to an impressive Saxon chancel arch. In the chancel are medieval stalls with misericords, beautiful candlesticks and fine memorials, including a poignant sculpture of 1821 by Chantrey. **P.** *Open summer 09.30–19.30 daily, winter to 16.00.*

Helmsley, All Saints   **19** N16
12m E of Thirsk on A170. Splendid Norman features in the church, rebuilt in Early English Gothic style in 1866–9, are the S doorway and the chancel arch. An 18thC chandelier embellishes the nave, and delightful painted decoration by Temple Moore, 1909, the aisle roof. He also designed the altar and reredos. **P.** *Open daylight hours daily.* Helmsley Castle presents a dramatic keep to the market place and surrounding countryside.

Hemingbrough, St Mary the Virgin   **19** N14
1m SE of Selby on A63. The phenomenally tall and slender spire, added in the 15thC to a 13thC tower, defies rules of proportion with spectacular success. Displaying Early English to Perpendicular styles, the light and spacious cruciform church was once collegiate. On one of its stalls is a misericord of twirling leaf design, made c1200, and celebrated for being most probably the oldest misericord in the land. Parclose screens are part of the furnishings, and there is an interesting 15thC stone table in the N transept. A jester and dragons appear among the carvings on the bench ends, of which there is a fine set. **P.** *Open summer approx 10.00–17.00 daily.* 18thC houses form an elegant congregation in the village.

Hornby, St Mary   **18** L16
9m W of Northallerton off A1. Dominating the small village with its size and beauty, the church has a majestic early Norman tower with a Perpendicular top stage, and a 12thC chancel, whose neo-Norman

E wall was built by J. L. Pearson in 1878. The Norman N arcade displays spectacular zigzag in its arches and faces a Perpendicular partner, for which the contract of 1409 survives. Fine effigies of a knight and lady lie in a recess in the N aisle, in the E window of which is some lovely 14thC stained glass. Prayerful alabaster effigies of a knight and lady lie in the S chapel, where there are also interesting brasses. Rich medieval paintings on the chapel screen, of paradisal birds flitting through lush leaves, are such as inspired William Morris's designs in the 19thC. The charming 18thC font makes a Decorated Gothic declaration in its leafy gables. **P.** *Open daylight hours daily.*

Kirkdale, St Gregory   **19** N16
4m E of Helmsley off A170. Thick woods shield the little Saxon church, standing alone beside a stream. Tower and chancel are 19thC. The former conceals a Saxon W doorway, whose tall, thin ascent is marked by long-and-short work. The wonderfully preserved Saxon sundial of c1055, above the S doorway, is the rarest of legacies, with its direct address from the days after Danish devastation and a decade before the Norman invasion: 'Orm Gamal's Son bought St Gregory's Minister when it was all broken down and fallen and he let it be made anew from the ground to Christ and St Gregory, in Edward's days, the King and in Tosti's days, the Earl.' It is even signed, 'And Haworth me wrought and Brand priests.' Examine the two exquisitely patterned Saxon coffin lids as well. **P.** *Open daylight hours daily.*

St Gregory's Minster, Kirkdale

Knaresborough, St John the Baptist   **18** M15
Church La. Prominent above a precipitous cobbled path to the river Nidd, where framed vistas of the castle appear

through the arches of the railway bridge. The handsome 12thC and 14thC pinnacled tower finishes in an appealing lead spirelet. Before entering the spacious and beautiful medieval interior, glance up at the delightful iron fanlight above the S porch entrance. At the W end of the S aisle is a stained glass window by Morris & Co, and the spectacular, scrolly font cover of c1700 with its wrought-iron bracket, should not be missed. Excellent monuments to the Slingsby family include fine effigies of 1602 of Francis Slingsby and Mary his wife, who has an exceedingly long neck; Sir William Slingsby, d1634, cuts a dashing if melancholy figure, standing pensively in a niche. The church has a lovely poor box, dated 1600, agog with knobbly finials. **P.** *Open 07.45–dusk Mon–Fri, from 08.30 Sat, from 08.00 Sun.* Notoriously ugly 16thC witch, Mother Shipton, has a cave named after her, and the famous Dropping Well nearby has a petrifying effect on things thrown into it. The tiny, charming Chapel of Our Lady of the Crag was carved out of the cliff in 1409.

St Mary, Norman crypt

dates the awe-inspiring crypt, redolent of ancient piety. Built as a shrine over St Cedd's burial place, the crypt forms a complete church, in which short columns dominated by colossal capitals lead up the powerfully vaulted nave to an apsidal chancel. The magnificent church above was refashioned in 1228, and fine vaulting was added by J. L. Pearson in 1879. See the early 19thC painting by J. Jackson. *Open summer 09.00–21.00 Mon–Sat, from 08.00 Sun; winter to 18.00.*

Linton-in-Craven, St Michael   18 K15
and All Angels
8m N of Skipton on B6265. Near an enchanting, verdant village, threaded by a boulder-strewn beck, the little church exercises great individual charm. A pyramid-roofed bellcote, a Norman font, Norman and Early English arches, an ornate 14thC recess, and 15thC chapels, combine in delightful harmony. The church possesses an unusual and ancient crucifix. **P.** *Open daylight hours daily.* Take a seat in the churchyard and enjoy matchless views of Wharfdale. An almshouse founded by Richard Fontaine in 1721, possibly designed by Vanbrugh, is a lordly presence overlooking the village green.

St John the Baptist, Sir William Slingsby

Lastingham, St Mary   19 N16
16m W of Scarborough off A170. Moorland stretches skywards around the church, which stands on the site of a monastery founded by St Cedd in the 7thC. Among fascinating Saxon sculptural remnants is a dragon's head which comes from the abbot's throne. Probably destroyed by the Danes in the 9thC, the monastery was refounded in 1078, from which time

Masham, St Mary the Virgin   18 L16
7½m NW of Ripon on A6108. Market Sq. The stately Norman tower, crowned by an octagonal 15thC belfry and spire, presides over the handsome, stone-built market place. Outside the S door is a very striking carved Saxon cross shaft. 14thC arcades frame the wide nave and chancel arch, above which hangs a pallidly attractive 18thC painting of an angel on clouds. Father Time and a frivolous, bubble-blowing cherub appear in the spandrels of the monument to Sir Marmaduke Wyvill and his wife. His eyes are open and hers are closed, to signify the erection of the monument after her death in 1609 but before his in

1617. A dragon glitters in wonderfully fiery stained glass of 1958 in a N aisle window. **P.** *Open 09.00–dusk daily.*

Middleham, St Mary   **18** L16
and St Alkelda
9m S of Richmond on A6108. Bones pronounced in 1878 to be those of the legendary Saxon princess, Alkelda, murdered for her faith by two Danish women c800, are buried in the 14thC–15thC church. Fragments of medieval stained glass in the N aisle W window illustrate the legend. Richard III founded a college of dean and six canons here in 1478. Extraordinarily, it escaped the Dissolution and remained collegiate until 1845. Its last canon was author Charles Kingsley. A remarkable Perpendicular font cover towers above the 14thC font and a tombstone nearby to Robert Thornton, 16thC Abbot of Jervaulx, puns pictorially on his name by representing a tun and thorn-like flowerings emerging from a crozier. **P** nearby. *Open daylight hours daily.* Home of Warwick the Kingmaker and of Richard, Duke of Gloucester, the future Richard III, the ruins of the mighty medieval castle are steeped in the history of the Wars of the Roses. Racing stables add an equine flavour to Middleham's character.

Old Malton, St Mary's Priory   **19** N15
1m N of Malton on A169. Although only a fragment of its former glorious self, this church, which belonged to a 12thC Gilbertine priory, remains impressive. The monastic buildings have all but vanished. One tower instead of the former two graces the W front, which is distinguished by a splendid late Norman doorway and Perpendicular window. The nave, once two bays longer, shows signs of interesting building vicissitudes, partly the result of a fire at the end of the 15thC. The organ case of 1900 is by Temple Moore. **P.** *Open summer 09.00– approx 20.00 Mon–Sat, 08.00–19.30 Sun; winter to 17.00 Mon–Sat.*

Patrick Brompton, St Patrick   **18** L16
7m S of Richmond on A684. Prominent in the small village, the church has a dignified Victorian tower, and a Transitional S doorway with zigzag decoration in its pointed arch. The N arcade is impressively Transitional too. Decorated tracery forms an elegant, netted pattern in the E window and either side of it are niches with nodding ogee canopies. Sculptured heads and

ornate sedilia add to the richness of the chancel. **P.** *Open approx 09.00–dusk daily.*

Ripley, All Saints   **18** L15
3m N of Harrogate on A61. Not always as beautifully serene as now, bullet holes on the outside of the church's E wall were made when Cromwell's soldiers executed Royalist prisoners after the Battle of Marston Moor. As a result of Cromwell stabling his horses in the church, the extremities of Sir William Ingilby, d1618, are missing, and appended to his effusive elegy is the puritan injunction, 'No pompe nor pride, let God be honoured'. On a fine monument in the S aisle Sir Thomas de Ingilby, d1369, wears the armour of the day and his wife a veil and crimped wimple. Charming little sculptures of their children, some of whose names can be read, stand along the sides of the tomb-chest. The medieval screen close by is unusually substantial. **P.** *Open 09.00–18.00 daily.* Eight niches in the venerable 'Weeping Cross' base in the churchyard invite sinners to kneel and repent, a proceeding made suitably painful by their narrowness. The village of Ripley was remodelled in 1827 by the eccentric Sir William Ingilby, of Ripley Castle, to resemble a French village of the Alsace.

Scarborough, St Martin   **19** O16
St Martin-on-the-Hill. The large, stately church, built by Bodley in 1861–2 in 13thC Gothic style, is a treasury of Pre-Raphaelite art. Morris, Burne-Jones, Rossetti, Madox Brown and Webb contributed to the stained glass, which sheds such wonderful lustre in the church. Subjects include the Annunciation in the rose window at the W end, attended by nine angels engaged in striking bells, playing psalteries, harp and other instruments; the parable of the vineyard and the Crucifixion in the E window; and a multitude of saints and prophets. You will want to linger over the pulpit, the most glorious of the church's furnishings, apart from the stained glass. Two panels of the Annunciation by Rossetti are inspired with great lyricism; the evangelists and doctors of the church standing under canopies against a gold background along the front of the pulpit, were painted by Campfield to designs by Morris and Madox Brown. There is much else to admire, including the chancel ceiling by Morris and Webb. **P** nearby. *Open 08.00– dusk Mon & Wed–Sat, from 07.45 Tue, 07.40–19.30 Sun.*

Scarborough, St Mary　　19 O16
Castle Rd. Near the castle, which commands the summit of the rocky escarpment on which the town centres, the church was built in the 12thC–13thC, and restored in the 19thC. The W front presents graceful lancet windows and a fine 15thC doorway, but the upper parts of the two towers were shed at an indeterminate date. The shafted clerestory and great round pillars give a majestic character to the nave, although the S arcade incorporates three pillars of totally different designs. Chancel and N transept were destroyed during the Civil War, when Parliamentarians bombarded the contiguous Norman castle from the church, demolishing half the keep, and Royalists returned the fire. The crossing tower, which now forms the E end of the church fell in 1659 and was rebuilt in 1669. Its E window is by G. G. Pace, 1957. Four S chapels founded as chantries in the 14thC, have impressively ribbed barrel-vaults. Heads and humorously grotesque medieval carvings surprise you from arch and capital around the church, including animals and the jolliest of monsters on the capitals of the St Nicholas Aisle. A large assembly of memorial tablets includes one by Roubiliac to Elizabeth Craven, d1728. **P.** *Open summer 10.00–16.30 Mon–Fri.* Leaving by the S porch, a vista of the bay opens up and a signpost directs you to Anne Brontë's grave.

Selby, Abbey church　　18 N14
of St Mary and St Germain
A miraculously intact survival of the Dissolution; a delinquent French monk, Benedict, who had stolen the sacred relic of St Germain's finger, was granted land for its foundation in 1069 by William the Conqueror. Building was begun c1100 by Abbot Hugh and his splendid, incised pillar stands out on the S side of the nave. The distorted arches opposite, in which the zigzag carving concertinas, also arrest attention. But as they assumed their disconcerting lopsided stance c1150, when the tower foundations settled, they may be depended upon to maintain it. Powerful Norman and 13thC columns, gallery and clerestory sweep magnificently along the nave. The choir, with thickly carved foliage capitals, and glorious swirling tracery in the E window, forms an exquisite Decorated composition. Outside, the choir presents a festive panoply of crocketed pinnacles and the W front is a contrasting study in splendour in its flamboyantly patterned Norman portal and beautiful array of Early English lancets above. The W towers had top stages inserted in 1935. The church was skilfully restored after fire damage in 1906, and the crossing tower was rebuilt in 1908 by Oldrid Scott. Don't fail to see the wonderfully ornate 15thC font cover, a survivor of the fire. **P** in Market Pl. *Open summer 09.00–19.00 Mon–Sat, 08.00–19.30 Sun; winter to 17.00 Mon–Sat.*

Sheriff Hutton, St Helen　　19 N15
and the Holy Cross
9m N of York on A19. The church looks out to moorland, in a village dramatised by craggy 14thC castle ruins and mounds S of the churchyard which formed part of the castle's predecessor. The fine Norman tower received a belfry in the 15thC, the chancel is 13thC, and the S arcade, with delightful leafy capitals, is 14thC. Note the Jacobean and Victorian box pews, considerable fragments of 14thC stained glass, and interesting monuments. Most famous is the effigy of Richard III's son, Edward Prince of Wales, who died at Middleham Castle in 1484, when he was 11. A 14thC knight, Sir Edmund Thweng, also lies in effigy in St Nicholas' Chapel, and a touching little brass of two babies in swaddling clothes, who died in 1491, is near the lectern. **P.** *Open 08.00–dusk Mon–Fri, from 09.00 Sat, 09.00–20.00 Sun.*

St Giles, S doorway

Skelton, St Giles   **18** M15
3m N of York on A19. A perfect 13thC
church in miniature: compact yet stately.
Enjoy the celebration of the mason's art
in the beautiful nail-head and dogtooth
decoration rioting round the lancet
windows, and in the clusters of curly leaf
capitals and elaborate mouldings round
the marvellous S doorway, which was
faithfully renewed in the 19thC. Note the
little gables on the buttresses and the
delightful double bellcote. The interior
also displays rich decorative elements.
Because of close similarities of detail and
the high quality of the work, it is thought
that the masons who built the transepts
of York Minster built the church c1240. **P.**
Open 08.30–dusk daily.

Tadcaster, St Mary   **18** M14
12m NE of Leeds on A64. Kirkgate. The
stately, mostly Perpendicular, church was
taken down and rebuilt in 1875–7 to
protect it from flooding, and remains of
Norman work were incorporated into the
fabric. Beautiful stained glass by William
Morris fills the E window, and other
Victorian glass in the church is of
interest. Gothic and Art Nouveau meet in
striking screens, panelling and the pulpit,
made by Bromett and Thorman early this
century. **P.** *Open 09.00–dusk Mon–Sat,
07.00–19.00 Sun.* Malty odours emanate
from the town's three breweries. A
gracious 18thC bridge crosses the river
Wharfe.

Thirsk, St Mary   **18** M16
10m NE of Ripon on A61. The delicate
pierced parapet confers grace on the
large, majestic Perpendicular church,
built c1430–80, and the clerestory bestows
loftiness. The ground falls away at the E
end, allowing the building of a crypt
underneath. Examine the tracery
distinguishing the S door, the remains of
a brass commemorating Robert Thirsk,
d1419, in the chantry he founded, the
chantry screens, the font cover and the
legs of the altar, which are carved in the
form of bold upright lions leaning on
scrolls. Look up at the fine, carved roofs
and the quaint scene of domestic strife
on one of the chancel bosses, where a
woman hits her husband with a ladle.
Open daylight hours daily.

Whitby, St Mary   **19** O16
East Cliff. 199 steps wind up to the most
enchanting and quaintly endearing of
churches, impossible to view without
delight in the preservation of its 18thC

St Mary, Georgian interior

interior. The squat tower and much of
the church are Norman. Incongruously
dainty, domestic-style Georgian windows
peer out, while white wooden staircases
lead up to galleries and the Cholmley
Pew. Inside, an unruly yet charming
crowd of box pews clusters round the
three-decker pulpit of 1778. Attached to
its back are an exuberant sounding board
and a pair of ear trumpets, used by
Minister Andrews' deaf wife in the
19thC. Irreverently stretching across the
chancel arch instead of a rood screen, is
the 17thC manorial Cholmley Pew,
carved with winged cherubs' heads and
standing on barley-sugar columns.
Galleries with an appealingly wayward
disposition look down from above. There
is no electric lighting in the church, and
the fine Georgian chandelier contributes
to its illumination by candles when
necessary. **P** nearby. *Open Easter–Oct
10.00–18.00 Mon–Sat, from 13.00 Sun;
winter 10.00–12.00.* Views over harbour
and sea open out from the windswept,
clifftop churchyard. The ruins of 13thC
Whitby Abbey are poised in a similarly
spectacular position.

York, St Michael   **19** N15
Spurriergate. The Perpendicular exterior
was rebuilt in the 19thC, and the
magnificent late Norman arcades within
come as a revelation. Interestingly, the

15thC tower arches and pillars imitate the Norman work. Restored medieval stained glass makes a radiant display. Finely carved balusters in the altar rail and a handsome reredos, surmounted by a cherubic St Michael, are early 18thC contributions to the furnishings. The memorial tablets repay close scrutiny. *Open Mar–Oct 09.30–18.00 daily.* York has been the stage for emperors, kings and princes and its streets are steeped in history. A walk round the medieval city walls, the circuit of which stretches about three miles, is rewarded by magnificent views.

York, St Michael-le-Belfrey　　　**19** N15
Deangate. Splendidly sited in the lee of the Minster, the church was rebuilt in 1525–36 to the design of John Forman, Master Mason to the Minster. The W front is largely a Victorian rebuilding, but the interior is intact and impressive. Poppyheaded medieval benches and Victorian Gothic box pews form the seating; the fine reredos and the altar rail are of 1712. Most glorious is the stained glass, much of it contemporary with the 16thC rebuilding, in which saints and kneeling donors congregate. 18thC and 19thC memorial tablets abound. Ill-fated

Guy Fawkes was baptised in the church in 1570. *Open Easter–Aug 10.00–16.00 daily.* Devote a generous allowance of time to absorbing the marvels of the Minster, which contains England's greatest concentration of medieval stained glass.

York, St Olave　　　**19** N15
Marygate. The church's ancient foundation is recorded in the *Anglo Saxon Chronicle*, where reference is made to the burial in the church built by him of Siward, Earl of Northumbria, in 1055. Nothing remains of Siward's church, which formed the nucleus of a monastery until St Mary's Abbey was built beside it in 1089. The 15thC rebuilding of the church was damaged in the Civil War, and the arcades date from 1721–2. The chancel was extended and the richly arcaded S chapel built by J. F. Doyle in 1908. Look at the fine Gothic font cover of 1963, by G. G. Pace, the beautiful medieval stained glass in the top of the E window, the Baroque memorial to William Thornton, d1721, and the churchyard memorial to painter William Etty. **P.** *Open 07.00–19.00 daily.* The ruins of St Mary's Abbey stand in the Yorkshire Museum gardens.

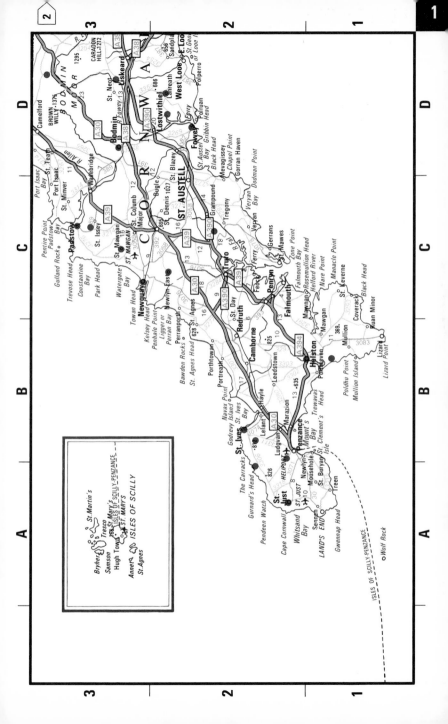

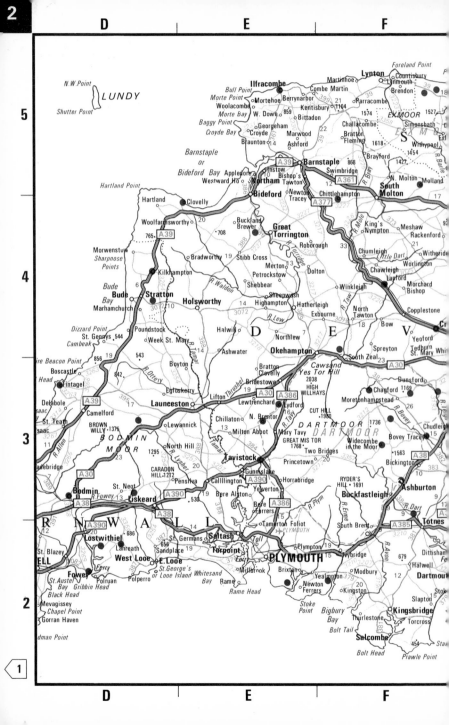

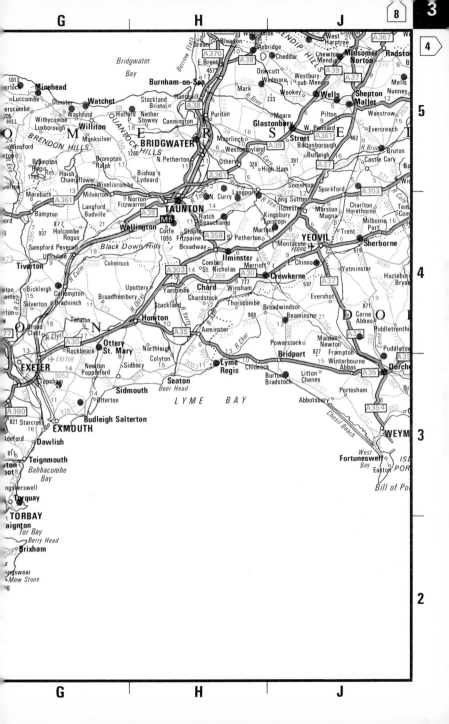

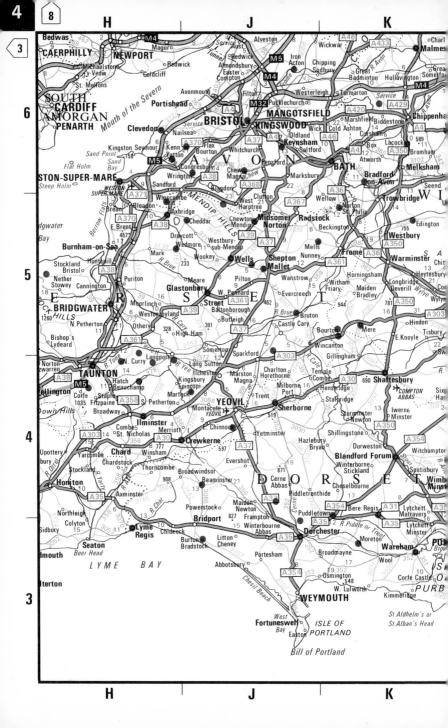

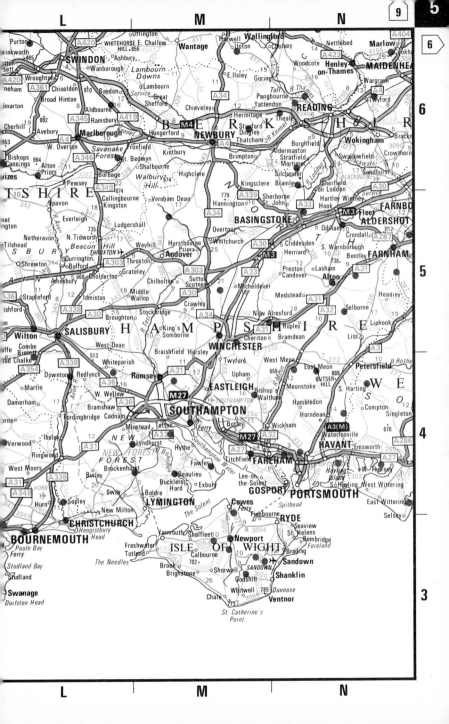

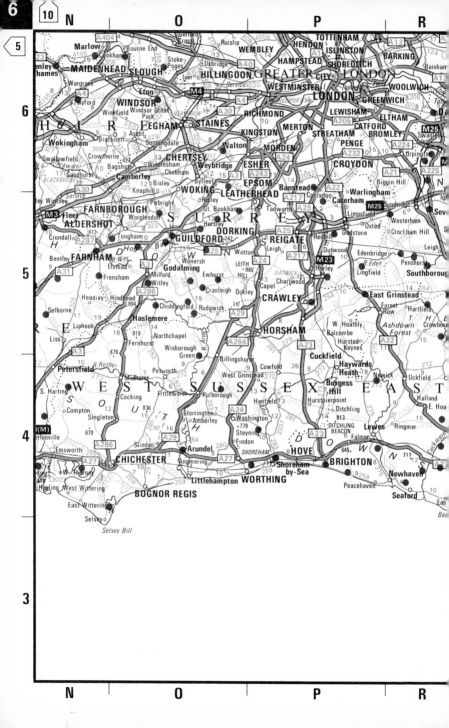

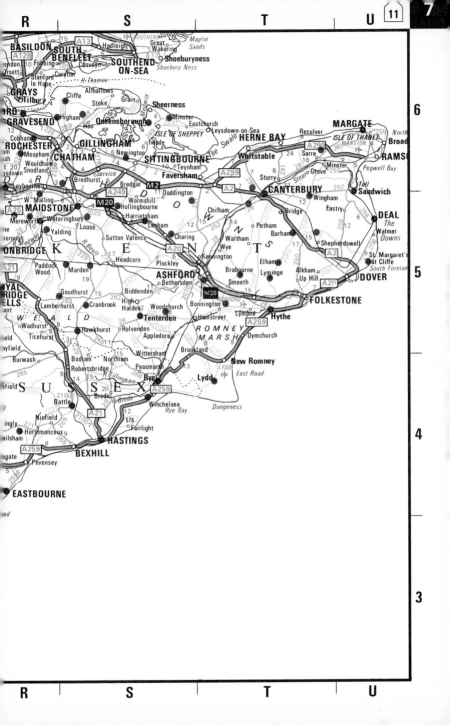

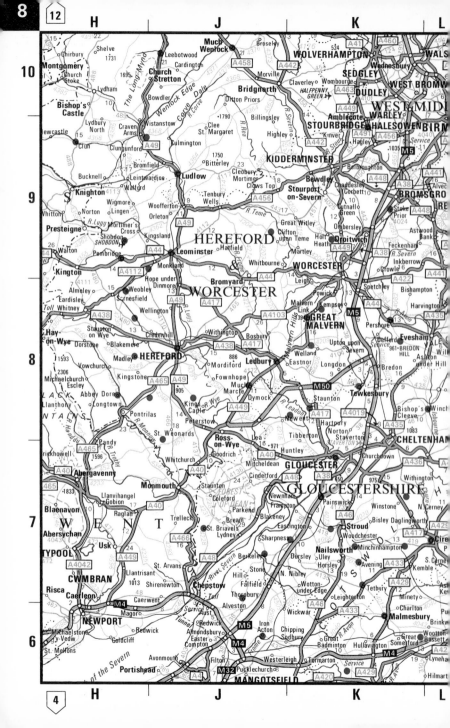

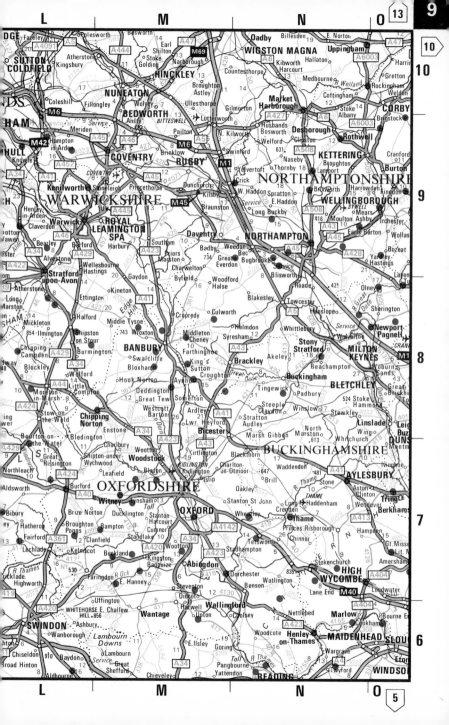

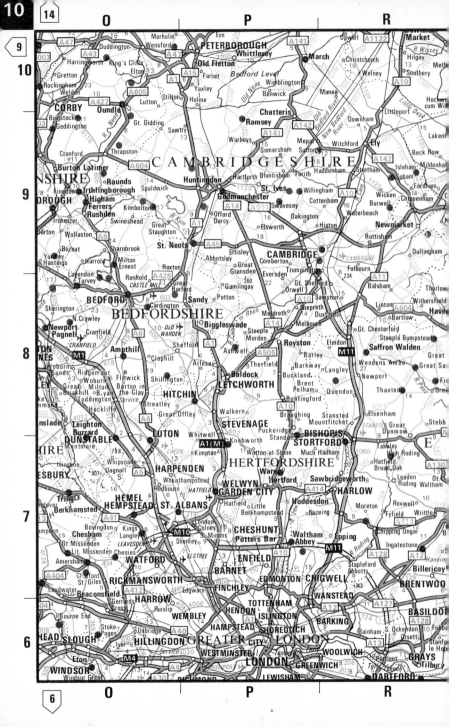

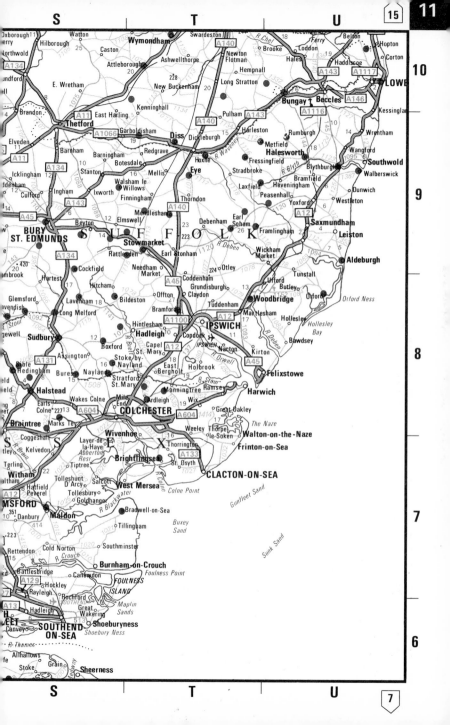

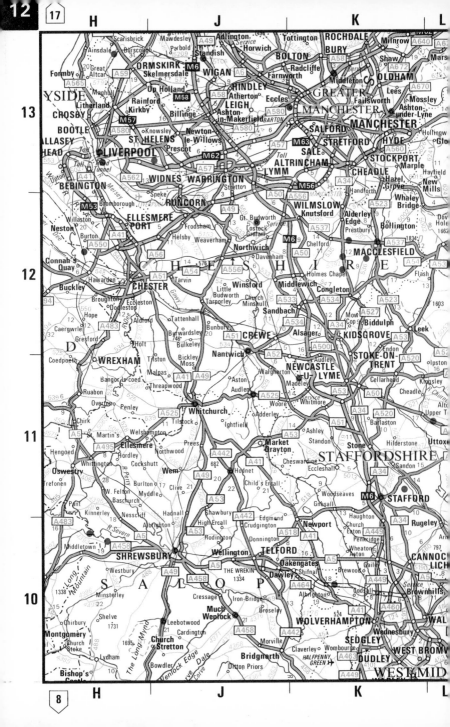

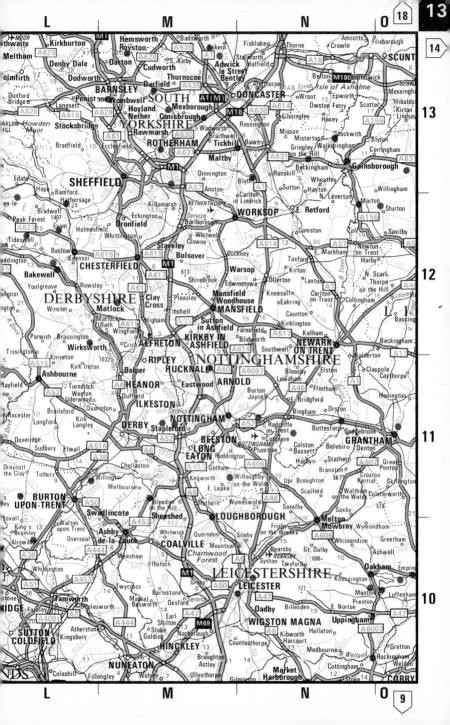

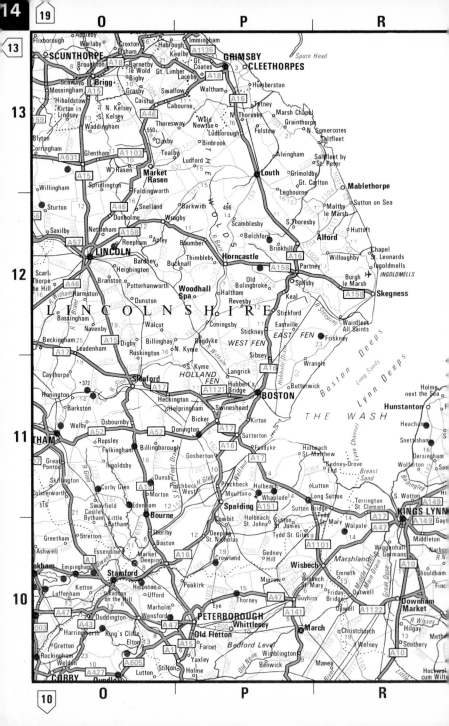

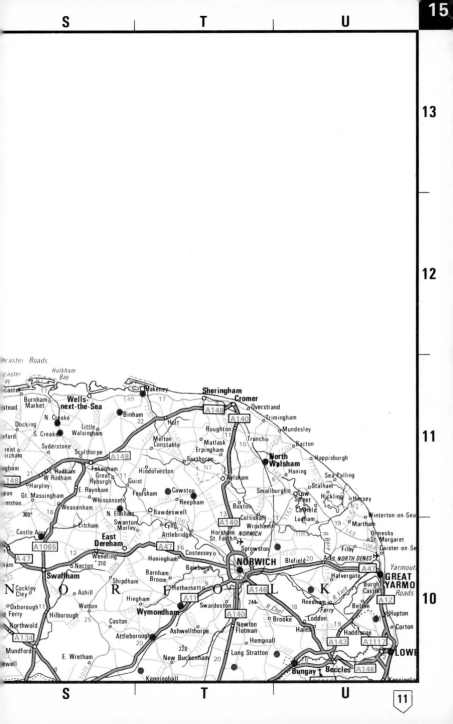

S T U

caster Roads

caster ay

Holkham Bay

caster

17

Burnham Market

Wells-next-the-Sea

Blakeney

Sheringham
Cromer

A148

A140

Overstrand

stead

Docking

N. Creake

Little
Walsinham

Binham

149

17

Holt

Roughton

Trimingham

Mundesley

reford

S. Creake

Syderstone

Sculthorpe

A148

Melton
Constable

Saxthorpe

Matlask
Erpingham

11

Trunch

Bacton

ingham

gton

21

E. Rudham
W Rudham

Fakenham
Ryburgh

Great

Guist

11

Hindolveston

NT

**North
Walsham**

Honing

Happisburgh

Sea Palling

148

Harpley

E. Raynham

Foulsham

Cawston

Reepham

Aylsham

Smallburgh

Low
Street

Stalham

Hickling

Horsey

mston

Gt. Massingham

Weasenham

Whissonsett

1149

Buxton

Catfield
Ludham

146

300'

16

N. Elmham

Bawdeswell

13

A140

Coltishall

3

A151

Winterton-on-Sea

Castle Acre

Litcham

Swanton
Morley

Lyng

14

1062

Wroxham

Martham

Ormesby

NT

**East
Dereham**

A1065

A47

12

Wendling

Attlebridge

1067

Horsham
St. Faith

NORWICH

1062

Filby

St. Margaret
Caister-on-Se

ham

A47

Necton

310

1075

Honingham

Costessey

Sprowston

NORWICH

Acle *NORTH DENES*

Yarmout

Swaffham

Barnham
Broom

Bawburgh

Blofield

20

Halvergate

A47

**GREAT
YARMO**

N

Cockley
Cley

Ashill

Shipdham

Hethersett

A146

Burgh
Castle

Roads

Oxborough

Watton

Hingham

Swardeston

244

Reedham

A12

e Ferry

Hilborough

Caston

Wymondham

A11

A140

R. Chet

Brooke

Ferry

Belton

Hopton

Northwold

A134

Ashwellthorpe

Newton
Flotman

Loddon

Hales

Haddiscoe

Corton

Mundford

E. Wretham

228

New Buckenham

Hempnall

Long Stratton

20

1332

A143

A1117

LOWE

rwell

8

1075

Kenninghall

6

Bungay

Beccles

A146

Kessinglan

S T U

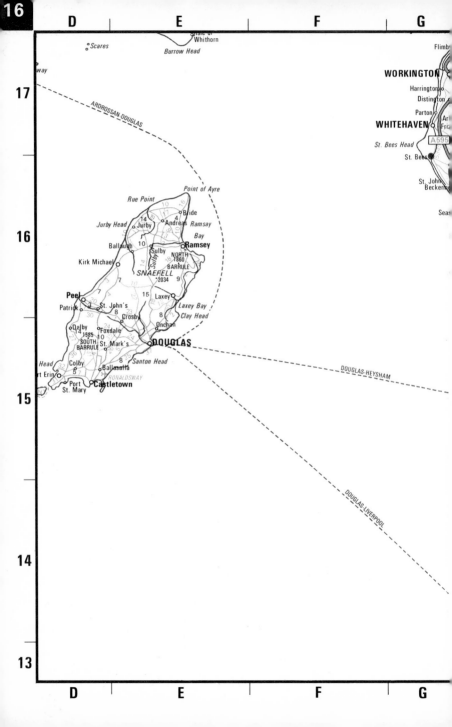

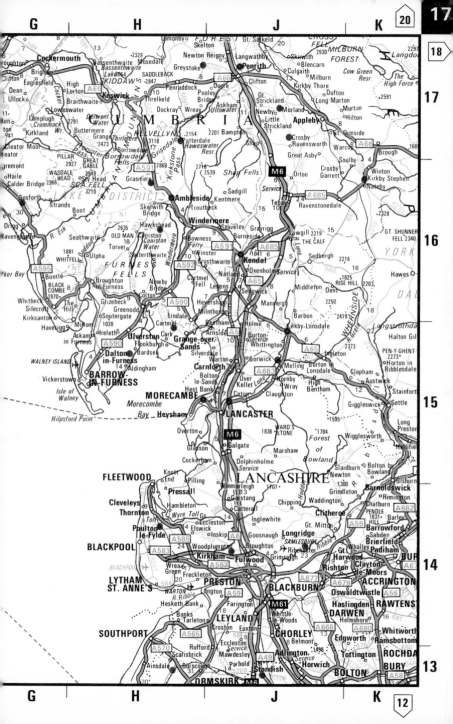

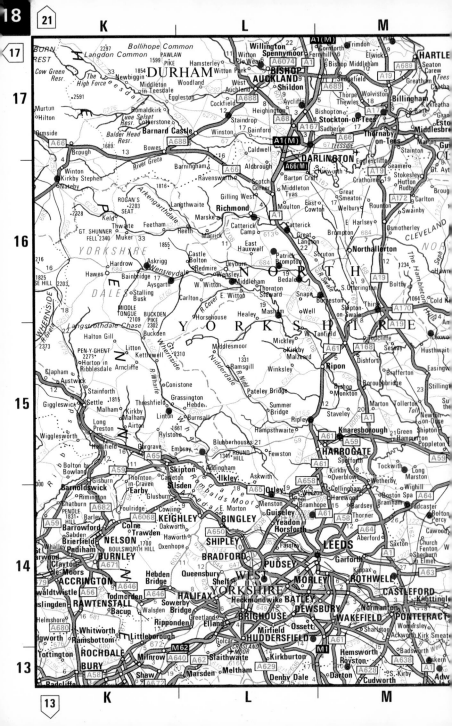

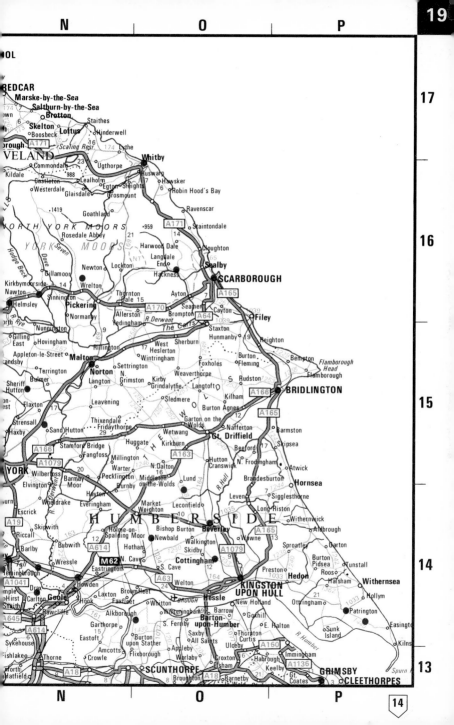

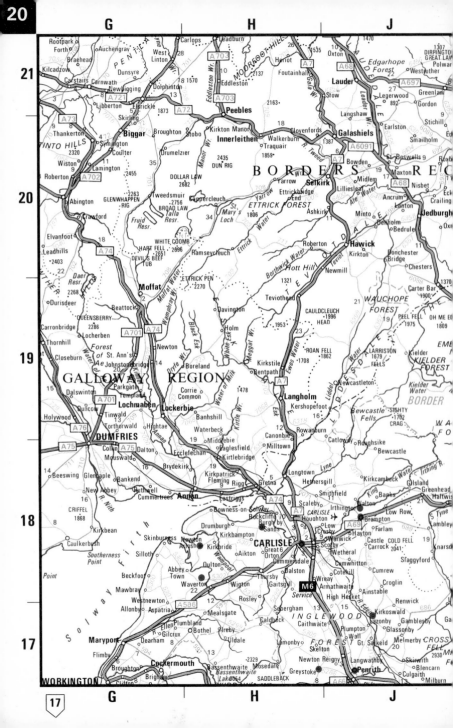

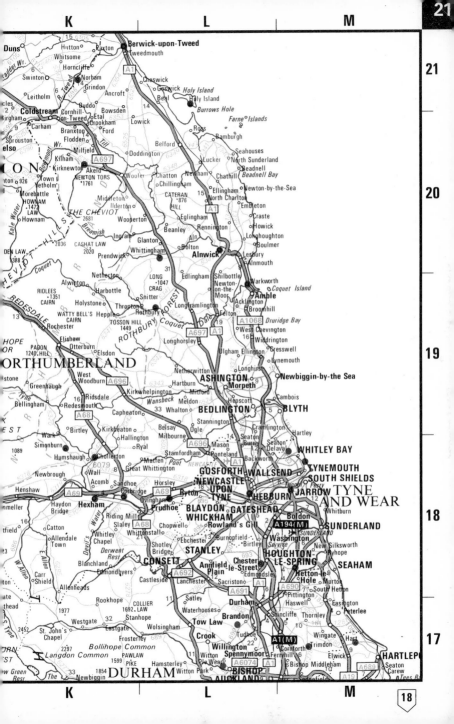

INDEX